Cases and Study Guide

The American Polity
Fifth Edition

Everett Carll Ladd

Cases and Study Guide

The American Polity
Fifth Edition

Everett Carll Ladd

by Ann G. Serow
Kingswood-Oxford School
Central Connecticut State University

W. W. Norton & Company
New York   London

midwood

Printed in the United States of America.

Composition by Roberta Flechner Graphics.

ISBN 0-393-96352-7

W. W. Norton & Company, Inc., 500 Fifth Avenue, New York, N.Y. 10110
W. W. Norton & Company Ltd., 10 Coptic Street, London WC1A 1PU

2 3 4 5 6 7 8 9 0

12/1/9

Contents

The Cases

individuals. "I'm not homeless," Bird said, "I live on the planet" (1989).]

[Government programs to protect Americans from economic disaster don't help everyone (1985).]

[The new class society (1992).]

Loch Johnson, "Now That the Cold War Is Over, Do We Need the CIA?"   198
[The answer is yes, but the CIA will have to learn new skills and develop new talents in the post – cold war era (1992).]

[Environmental photo opportunity, American style (1992).]

The Study Guide

Acknowledgments

Many years (decades) ago, in a then-not-so-large state university, I arrived at freshman registration, a Latin major. Able only to get four courses scheduled because of bureaucratic chaos, I heard someone yell, "They're opening a section of intro. poli. sci. Monday, Wednesday, and Friday at 4:00." I grabbed a place in the class. I was desperate and no longer cared about the odd time of day.

The poli. sci. class was taught by a new professor who had just completed his doctorate at Cornell: Everett C. Ladd. After a few weeks, I decided to abandon the Latin and go all-out for political science. Through the late-afternoon cold and dark of that rugged, hilly campus, I trudged to every class, emerging in December with a cherished A minus. [With a study guide to go with the text, it could have been an "A" maybe.]

Three political-science degrees later, with decades of my own students sprinkled throughout business, education and politics, the lesson emerges: Study hard; find your niche in what you enjoy and do well; stay with each project until it is completed and then tackle the next; be self-reliant, but always leave room for a little help from a guide.

Thanks go to Kingswood-Oxford School. Their support through the Lazear Chair has helped enormously with the *Study Guide* project. Don Fusting at Norton encouraged me, as always, especially when the *Study Guide, Reader* galleys, and *Quizbook* proofs were all moving back and forth in the mail simultaneously. It has been years since anyone has scrutinized my words with red pencil as my manuscript editor, Jane Carter, did. As a teacher, I do this to my students' work daily; I had forgotten how scary but rewarding it is to have your work critiqued carefully and well. The 1991–92 political scientists at Kingswood-Oxford and Central Connecticut State University were eager participants in trying out many of the ideas in the *Study Guide*. Extra thanks go to Rayshida Taylor and Lenore Zavalick: Your judgments were excellent in every case. "Tested on real live students," this guide can claim.

Much gratitude goes to my loyal army of proofreaders: Paul-Anthony Leto, Katherine Godbout, Phuong-Linh Dang, Brian Morrison, Jessica Rutenberg, Melissa Melo, Ryan D'Agostino, Maria Spinella, Brian Federman, Jamie Frank, Valerie Leone, Andrew Weinstein, Seth Levine, and Melissa Sterrett.

Between poli sci term papers and a Tocqueville test, you managed to get the job done—quickly, accurately, and enthusiastically.

Mel Bigley, my good friend and Rough Justice's lead singer, deserves special appreciation for providing me with all the time I needed, but did not have in my teaching schedule, to write the *Study Guide*. The hours I traveled with the band were like a loud but strict study hall. In fact, I can no longer write except in dark, seedy nightclubs at 1 A.M. Not only, Mel, did you keep me working when I pleaded to play golf (which we did manage to do frequently, Brian), but your comments on the *Study Guide* also helped immeasurably.

Ann G. Serow

The Course, the Text, the *Study Guide*, and You

You are about to embark on a course the content of which is interesting and important: American government. Your professor has chosen a sophisticated textbook to provide you with an understanding of the material you will discuss in class. You have invested well in the *Study Guide,* which will assist you with the tough parts of the book. This guide can give you a competitive edge on tests. It can give you confidence when you walk into class. It can keep you company in the late night hours when you are the only one awake, reading, reading, reading.

There are lots of different kinds of students in every American government class, with many and varied reasons for taking the course. Some are satisfying a distribution requirement; others have related majors; a few are hard-core "political junkies" for whom American government is just the start of a long association with the Political Science Department. Regardless of your degree of involvement in politics, or your reasons for taking this course, understanding how the U.S. government functions is important. As a citizen, you can vote; you may belong to an interest group; you may someday run for office —the board of education, perhaps, state representative, or even a higher post.

The American Polity and the *Study Guide* will help you acquire the basic knowledge of how the U.S. government works, as well as equip you to analyze for yourself how America is governed. The course will last you a lifetime.

At the Start of the Course

STRATEGIES FOR SUCCESS

To begin, a few reminders on study techniques are appropriate:
1. Go to class faithfully, equipped with your book and American government notebook, without any loose pages hanging out. If you can sit where you choose, move toward the front of the class.

2. Make a note-sharing arrangement with a classmate who takes good notes and is reliable, so that if you should have to miss class, you can get the lecture notes. Fill in the gap in your notes as soon as possible. No one will lend out a notebook right before an exam, and besides, time before a test is too precious to spend copying old notes. Lend your notebook only to a person who will reciprocate, not to "some kid who said he'd return it the next day but never came back to class and lives somewhere off-campus."

3. Scrutinize the syllabus that your professor has distributed. On it are the assignments, exam announcements, and paper dates. Often these events are not discussed in class; they are merely on the syllabus. Others may show up the day of the midterm not knowing about the exam—not you.

4. After a few classes have met, go to see your professor during his or her office hours. Introduce yourself. Bring a few questions and an observation you would like to voice about the first lecture topics. College is expensive, so try to get the most for your money. Most professors like to meet students. But few students take advantage of the access, because of, well, human nature. You must make an effort to go to see the professor, preferably early in the course; no one will invite you. Do *not* wait until you get your midterm exam back.

5. If you have a graduate assistant assigned to your class, visit her or him. These young (at least in spirit) scholars will usually take the time to talk with you and generally enjoy talking with interested undergraduates about American government. They know the subject thoroughly; ask them all the questions that remain after you have gone through the relevant *Study Guide* chapter. Grad students help make up and grade exams. They correct papers. They are often an unseen presence on the campus, providing a wonderful human resource for students beginning a new subject. Let them practice their craft on you. It is good for them and for you.

6. As the weeks roll by, continue to keep up with the reading. That is a key to success in a course like American government. If you get behind, you will become so buried by work that you will not know how to dig yourself out. Without reading, lecture notes will mean less. You will be unable to contribute. Professors intensely dislike students who are unprepared. (Some strategies for effective reading are discussed a bit later in the *Study Guide*'s introduction.)

Read during the usual hours you devote to out-of-class work—evenings, weekends—but also bring *The American Polity* with you when you are waiting in the Registrar's Office, going to a doctor's appointment, or meeting a friend in the student center who is always late. Certain chapters and certain topics in *The American Polity* are appropriate for reading in short snatches. You will find that you can get a lot of work done this way, relieving the pressure during sustained study periods that can better be devoted to reading that requires full and uninterrupted attention.

7. With the course well under way, prepare to speak out in class if your class provides the opportunity and you have not already done so. Do not answer every question every day. Rather, wait until a topic arises about which you feel informed and confident. Include some specific American government data (a specific term or concept) in your answer, but do not hesitate to include your view (briefly) also. If your class is a huge lecture with no chance for anyone to speak, use eye contact and office hours to communicate your interest to the professor.

8. Prepare for the midterm exam, if one is to be given. A good grade on the midterm will motivate you when you need it most, as the term grinds toward its end. It will lift you out of the crowd in the professor's mind. A good midterm exam will take some of the pressure off you on the final. It is always more satisfying to continue excellence than to try desperately to recover from a disaster, with mediocrity your only hope. (The *Study Guide* will provide tips on exam study in the following pages.)

If you did not do well on the midterm after studying adequately, go see your professor or the graduate assistant. Find out where you went wrong so you can avoid repeating the same mistakes on the final. Often a few words from the person who grades the tests can clarify what that person is looking for in the answers. Before you go in, however, read and think about the comments the professor has written on your exam and ask specific questions about your shortcomings. Do not just toss the mess on her desk and say, "I don't see why you gave me a D."

Bring your copy of *The American Polity* and your notebook with you, since your professor may wish to see where your gaps in understanding originate. Do not expect sympathy with an unread *Polity*, a still-packaged *Study Guide*, and an incomplete, messy, loose-paged, ratty notebook.

9. If a paper (or several short papers) is assigned in the course, select a topic quickly and make an initial search for materials in the library. An early start will ensure less last-minute panic. (This *Study Guide* will give you more help with research and writing papers in pages that follow.)

10. If a term paper has been assigned, submit it on time. A later paper loses points, makes a poor impression, and cuts into precious study time for the final exam.

11. Give the final your best effort. This entails fighting the tendency to let up as the end of the semester nears. All students "just want to get it over with"—professors do too. But professors take a deep breath and dig in till the end as do the good students. At the end of a semester of work you know a great deal, you are well-acquainted with the professor's methods, and you stand to benefit tremendously from a strong final exam. All you need is that bit of extra discipline to keep your energy high until the exam is over. The long-term rewards are well worth the short-term effort.

12. After the course is completed, file your American government notebook away for future reference. Naturally, the authors of *The American Polity* and the *Study Guide* would like you to place those books on the shelf as part of your permanent collection. If you must sell your used books back to the bookstore, resist accepting $5 for a $35 book that you end up needing to look up a Supreme Court case no one else in next semester's class knows how to locate.

SKILLS FOR SUCCESS

The *Study Guide* will now sketch out basic skills useful to any introductory college course. Many books and classes exist to help you develop the skills you may not have perfected in high school. This *Study Guide* will not try to "reinvent the wheel," but only to remind you of what you have been taught in the past and where you might need to brush up.

Reading the text. Your goal in reading should be to arrive in class familiar with the basic information (key terms) and important themes (key concepts). Reading is preparation for class; it is not supposed to take the place of your professor who will choose to stress certain points and omit others. You are not expected to have a complete grasp of terms and concepts when you walk into class. So do not worry about the items in the reading that slip by. Try to be knowledgeable about as many key ideas as you can comfortably assimilate.

You should read the assigned chapters in *The American Polity* once through thoroughly, using the *Study Guide*'s plan to help you attack each chapter. When you read, you should underline or highlight key terms and key concepts. You might wish to write a few notes in the margins. You might want to take a few notes on the reading. The goal is not to have to go back to the text page by page before an exam. Time is valuable then, and rereading the whole text is an inefficient use of time.

Keep up with the reading, underline key terms and key concepts, and use the *Study Guide*. The extra time spent each week reading carefully will pay off in the end.

Taking notes in class. Keep a separate notebook for American government. Put a date at the top of each day's notes. Strike a balance between sketchy notes that lose meaning later and taking down the professor's lecture word for word. Word-for-word note taking is not a good idea because it makes listening to the lecture impossible. It also leaves you with so many notes that you cannot study effectively. if you have done the reading, you should be able to differentiate the key ideas from the tangential material. However, you should take down more than one or two key words per class lest your notes prove only that you were there.

Notes can be neat or not-so-neat, in full sentences or in fragments, in proper outline form or artistically scattered on the notebook page. But write only on one side of each page so that if you underline in your notes later, the marks will not come through onto other notes. When you select a classmate with whom to share notes, try to find someone whose notes resemble yours in their style and the amount of detail recorded.

Analyzing tables and figures. Professor Everett C. Ladd, author of *The American Polity,* is director of the Roper Center for Public Opinion Research, as you will discover in chapter 10 of the *Study Guide.* He has included many excellent tables and figures in the book. Some of you may have no problem with them, but many students hated the charts in high school and continue to despise them in college. Statistics courses will teach you how to read tables and figures proficiently. For now, this *Study Guide* will give a little nontechnical guidance.

Do not try to memorize all the data contained in figures and tables. You need not even examine in depth every figure and chart presented. Professor Ladd includes in his discussion the significant findings shown in each chart. The charts serve to elaborate fully on the point he is making with the data. Still, to be able to make use of the figures and tables in the text, follow along with the *Study Guide* in analyzing three kinds of charts that appear frequently in *The American Polity.*

Figure 2.5 (next page) is one of the graphs you will come upon in *The American Polity.* It uses bars to show relationships. Start by looking at the title of the figure: "Expenditures on Education in the United States, 1960–1990." The title tells you that the graph will measure (1) the amount spent on education and (2) the amount spent over time. Now look at the two axes of the graph. The vertical axis marks off amounts of money spent, in millions of dollars, moving from smaller amounts (a mere $50,000,000) to larger amounts ($400,000,000). The horizontal axis delineates time by decade. Many charts and figures you encounter in a political science course measure these two variables, money and time. In particular, measurement over time is common because it shows important trends and changes. Monetary expenditure is a useful variable because amounts of money are easy to measure. Now look at the actual data. For each year there are three bars: white, shaded, and dark. The color key tells you what each color represents. By looking at the graph you can find the spending for all educational levels, for all public (as opposed to private) education, and for all higher education (beyond high school) for each year.

After analyzing Figure 2.5, you can draw many conclusions. The simplest and most important conclusion you can draw is that from 1960 to 1990 spending for all levels of education in America rose dramatically—from $103,000,000 to $358,000,000. (Professor Ladd has written in these amounts above each bar, but you could determine them roughly by holding a ruler across

FIGURE 2.5   EXPENDITURES ON EDUCATION IN THE UNITED STATES, 1960–1990 (IN CONSTANT 1989–1990 DOLLARS)

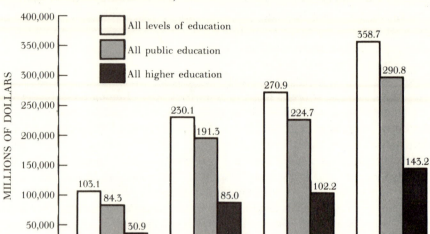

Source: U.S. Bureau of the Census, *Statistical Abstract of the United States*, 1991, p. 134.

the top of each bar till it touched the amount on the vertical axis.) You could choose to carry your analysis much further from the same figure. For example, by some subtraction you could compare public with private expenditures (subtract public from the total to get private). You could compare all spending to spending for higher education in 1960 and in 1990 to see when spending for higher education was highest. To do so for 1960, find out what percent of total spending, spending on higher education represents. The equation would look like:

$30.9 = X \times $103.1
Divide both sides by 103.1 to get X:

$$\frac{30.9}{103.1} = \frac{X \times 103.1}{103.1} = \frac{30.9}{103.1} = X$$

X = .299 = 29.9 percent

For 1990 the equation would look like:
$143.2 = X \times $358.7

$$\frac{143.2}{358.7} = \frac{X \times 358.7}{358.7} = \frac{143.2}{358.7} = X$$

X = .399 = 39.9 percent

Thus, from this figure's data you can find out that higher education takes up a significantly larger percentage of educational expenditures in 1990 than it did in 1960. You could calculate many other relationships from this one figure that are not immediately apparent from the bars. Clearly you would not do these extra calculations for every figure and table in *The American Polity,* but should your professor ask about a particular figure or should data from the book fit perfectly into your term paper, you might do so. (A bit later the *Study Guide* will show you how to document material, such as a figure you borrow from *The American Polity* for your research paper.)

Table 8.1 presents data in a different way, but you really follow the same procedure in reading it. First, read the title. Then, look at each category. If this table were a graph, the time periods (decades) would be shown on the vertical axis. The number of federal government employees are then listed for each year. Just by scanning down, you get the picture! Government has grown. It got a little smaller in number of employees twice (1951 to 1961 and 1971 to 1981). These statistics are interesting when combined with your knowledge of political

TABLE 8.1 CIVILIAN EMPLOYEES OF THE FEDERAL GOVERNMENT, 1816–1991

Year	Total number of employees	Number employed in the Washington, D.C. area
1816	4,837	535
1821	6,914	603
1831	11,491	666
1841	18,038	1,014
1851	26,274	1,533
1861	36,672	2,199
1871	51,020	6,222
1881	100,020	13,124
1891	157,442	20,834
1901	239,476	28,044
1911	395,905	39,782
1921	561,142	82,416
1931	609,746	76,303
1941	1,437,682	190,588
1951	2,482,666	265,980
1961	2,435,804	246,266
1971	2,874,166	322,969
1981	2,858,742	350,516
1991	3,108,899	374,187

Source: United States Bureau of the Census, *Historical Statistics of the United States, Colonial Times to 1970,* Part 2; pp. 1102–03; U.S. Office of Personnel Management, *Federal Civilian Workforce Statistics: Employment and Trends as of July 1989;* idem, *Employment and Trends as of January 1992.*

science. Who were the presidents during these eras? Are you surprised about the growth in federal employees from 1981 to 1991? Here is an example of how data can be used to substantiate or invalidate a theory in politics. For example, it is often believed that the federal government got smaller under President Reagan, yet in terms of number of employees, that is not true. The second column of data is interesting, but not crucial for our purposes here. Perhaps the number of federal employees working in Washington ("inside the beltway") relative to those in the rest of the nation (where most people live) might be an important statistic for your own research. You could figure out from Table 8.1 the relative percentages of those who work in and out of D.C. over time simply by using subtraction and simple equations. Remember, you do not have to do this for every figure and table in *The American Polity,* but when you need a statistic, you can probably find it or derive it.

The visual impact of Figure 12.4 is important: The line of the graph says it all. Professor Ladd is tracing the "percent of voting-age population voting for president since 1920." Along the horizontal axis you can see the election years, while along the vertical axis are the percentages. Observe the relatively low percentage voting in 1924, followed by the steady increase. An analysis of the graph would include the historical events that produced the rise. Note the dip in 1948, and the crest in 1952. Most important, what has happened to voter turnout from 1960 to 1988? You can see the slow, steady erosion of turnout without worrying about numbers at all. You can glean more from the figure by holding a ruler across the graph to the vertical percent axis. In this way you can see when voter turnout fell below 60 percent, for example, or below 55 percent, or even lower.

FIGURE 12.4   PERCENT OF VOTING-AGE POPULATION VOTING FOR PRESIDENT SINCE 1920

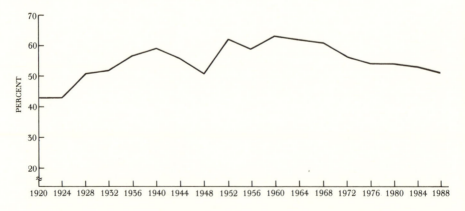

Source: 1932–88: U.S. Bureau of the Census, *Statistical Abstract of the United States, 1979,* p. 513; 1990, p. 264; 1920–28: Idem, *Historical Statistics of the United States: Colonial Times to 1970,* p. 1073.

There are other types of figures and tables in *The American Polity* that you can manage on your own: pie charts, line graphs with several trends compared on the same graph. Remember: you do not have to analyze every piece of data, and just because there are numbers involved does not mean the relationships shown are complicated; figures and tables show relationships that can easily be put into words. Unlike the data on standardized college entrance tests that do not relate to anything you know about, the data in *The American Polity* is on familiar topics that are discussed in the text close to the figure or table.

Studying for exams. It is foolish to deny the importance of doing well on exams. Sad is the student who studies conscientiously, gets all the material down cold, likes the course — but earns a C. While it is true that there are some people in the class who can do the minimum all semester and pull it out at the end with a great exam, for the most part "what goes around comes around." Do the work, know when to take short cuts and when not to, and you will do well. Here are some tips that may help.

Underline *The American Polity* as you read each week. Doing so will mean that you will have much less to go back to in the text before an exam. What you want to avoid is reading for the first time, or rereading completely, before an exam. It is a poor use of time. Also, underline the key points in your class notes in advance. During a lecture it is not possible to write down only the main ideas. The professor goes fast, a lot of material runs together, and, besides, you cannot always tell until she or he has finished a topic what the key points are. Every week or so, go back through your class notes and underline the important parts. When the exam approaches, you will not be facing a sheaf of uncombed pages. Some students make an outline or a key-term sheet from the underlinings in their notebook. Writing key terms on the left hand blank page of your notebook opposite your more complete notes works for some people by keeping all the study materials together. You decide what is right for you.

The timing of exam study is important. Study a bit as you go along if you can discipline yourself to do so. Review a little each week. Start your intensive study about a week before the exam. It is probably better to do this early studying alone. The idea at this point is to pick up as many key terms and concepts as you can. You can employ the *Study Guide* extensively in this stage to review key ideas and to reanswer multiple choice, true/false, identification, and even essay questions. There are students who take the time to write out some of the essays before the exam. Realistically, that is a strategy determined by how much time you can devote to your American government exam prep.

A day or two before the exam is a good time to sit down with a few classmates in a study group to go over the material. You can organize it formally, with individuals being responsible for presenting a brief review of an assigned topic. Or you can just scan through notes and *The American Polity* together. (A humorous version of group study is presented in the film *The Paper Chase* about young law-school students. Rent it, especially if you are considering law school.) Study groups are good because another person may pick up a key point you have missed completely. Sometimes when someone other than the professor explains a dense topic it suddenly becomes understandable. However, some students find study groups make them nervous about what they know relative to others. You decide if study groups are good for you.

In the days and hours before an exam, most advisors would tell you that there is little more you can do to prepare. This is true if you have not prepared over the past semester and over the past week. But if you are well-prepared, a small amount of last-minute cramming can help a lot. At the eleventh hour, you are not trying to learn basics; they are all there, loaded into your immediately-accessible data banks. But you can pick up some stray facts at the last minute that might appear on a multiple-choice question.

Leave yourself some time to relax right before the exam. Try to have had enough sleep and food to be comfortable. Remember that no student is expected to get every answer correct on the exam. Your professor has devoted a lifetime to the subject; the graduate assistant is planning to have a career in political science; Professor Ladd has written edition after edition of *The American Polity*. You have only studied the subject for a semester, along with taking several other courses. Your goal should be to know as many specific terms and concepts as you can so that you will do respectably on the short answer section, while leaving no potential essay topic unstudied.

Answering multiple-choice questions on exams. Some of you may have an understandable hostility toward multiple-choice questions. Yet they are a fact of academic life at almost all colleges, no matter what size your class. This *Study Guide* will get you into the swing of multiple-choice questions by having you face them at the end of every chapter. Take heart with the following realization: The multiple-choice questions you faced on standardized college admissions tests (the place where you may first have learned that you did not like them) are on topics you probably knew nothing more about than what you had read in the disembodied selection before the questions. On your American government exam, the multiple-choice questions will cover material you have studied: read in the text, checked in the *Study Guide*, heard in class. It will be familiar material. You will be able to answer many of the multiple-choice questions with ease, spotting the one correct answer right away. Some questions will be more tricky. Here are some pointers.

Professionals who make up multiple-choice questions develop certain patterns in the answers they supply. Often, there will be an answer that seems right, so you go for it quickly and overlook the piece of wrong information it contains. You get the question wrong needlessly. Take the multiple-choice question below as an example:

1. A cloture vote ends a filibuster when:
   a. sixty members of the House vote to end debate.

  b. a majority of senators vote to end debate.
  c. three-fifths of the Senate votes to end debate.
  d. those filibustering realize that they cannot win on the bill.

Answer "a" is like some people you see walking past you at a party at midnight: looks good at a quick glance, but not upon closer examination. As you will learn in the course, there are no filibusters in the House, only in the Senate, so "a" is wrong. If you know that a cloture vote of three-fifths, which is sixty senators, ends a filibuster ("c"), it is a shame to get the question wrong. Work quickly but not too quickly. Usually the professor will include an obviously wrong or silly answer ("d") as one choice. They are easy to spot.

Difficulty arises when multiple-choice answers are long, require a lot of reading, and contain concepts that you have to think over rather than simple terms that you can identify immediately. Look at the question below.

  2. The most dramatic change in a demographic group's party loyalty during the 1980s came from:
      a. Catholic voters' move toward the Democrats after years of Republican affiliation.
      b. wealthy Americans' new allegiance to the Republican party despite their previous ties to the Democrats.
      c. young people's shift away from the Republican party and toward the Democrats, in contrast to the age cohort that began to vote in the 1930s.
      d. white Southerners' shift away from the Democrats and toward the Republicans.

To arrive at the right answer, "d," you have to read and think about each possibility. For some people, that takes a long time. If your exam contains many of those questions and you are spending a lot of time on each, go on to other, simpler multiple-choice questions and return to the long ones later. But carefully keep the correct place when filling in answers on the answer sheet.

One approach to answering multiple-choice questions that ask you to select the one wrong answer with an *"except"* is to mark each possible answer with a true or false. The one answer that is false is the *"except"*—and the correct answer. For example:

  3. All of the following are protected by the Miranda Rules *except*:
      a. the right to consult a lawyer. [True, it is protected.]
      b. the right to make a plea bargain. [False, it is not protected.]
      c. the right to have an attorney appointed if a person cannot pay for one. [True, it is protected.]
      d. the right to remain silent. [True, it is protected.]

Thus, the *exception* is "b."

In the final analysis, there is no substitute for knowing the basic material when facing multiple-choice questions. Unless your professor is really an awful person (doubtful), she or he is not out to trick you, but to find out how much specific information you know. It is true that not all of the data you study for an exam will stay with you forever, but that is not necessarily bad. You will recall main ideas when events jog your memory. A year after you have taken the course, for example, news footage of a new Supreme Court nominee will bring back the knowledge of the advice and consent procedure. If you need to re-member specific material later, you will know approximately where in *The American Polity* you can look it up.

Answering essay questions on exams. The kind of material you need to know to do well on the essay portion of exams will stay with you much longer than the particulars contained in the multiple-choice questions. However, a crucial in-gredient of every good essay is *specifics*. So while you are studying basic terms and concepts for the multiple-choice section, you are also arming yourself with the data you need to support your essays. There is no more common weakness in students' essays than a polished, sophisticated interpretation, elegantly stated, with *no specifics* to back it up. Professors get more frustrated with those essays than with the crude, ill-written ones that present no evidence.

If you can forgive the brief reprise of your middle-school training, here is how an essay should be structured.

I. The *thesis*, theme, or main point of the essay

This is presented first, using language other than "In this essay I will show that. . . . " Instead try something like: "Interest groups were thought by the framers of the Constitution to be a way to protect against the power of any sin-gle group controlling American politics. Two hundred years later, however, the very success of interest groups has led to their near-total dominance of govern-ment in the United States." You can use the wording of the essay question to help you form your thesis. For example, your professor's question may have asked: "How has the role of interest groups in American government changed from the framers' hope that many groups would protect against tyranny, to to-day's powerful interest-group politics?" From this question, you could nicely formulate the thesis stated above. The thesis must go at the start not at the end, or you will have an essay with no focus, no direction.

A. Offer one main argument to support the thesis, using three or four specific pieces of evidence as support, like names, dates, laws, events.
B. Offer a second point concerning the thesis, again adding three or four pieces of evidence as support.
C. Next, offer an argument that seems to oppose the thesis. Illustrate,

then counter this point, again offering some more substantiating detail.

II. Finally, draw your conclusion: restate your thesis, now proven.

There is no need, and no time, to summarize all you have said. The essay has stated its theme, argued for it, offered supporting data. End with a short, snappy conclusion, and stop.

The reader of the essay should remain unaware of this structure because the essay flows together naturally. Do not worry that a simple structure will mean that your essays will be simple in content. A clear, basic structure will allow you to write rich, elaborate, complex ideas in a clear way.

To prepare for essay questions, write practice essays from the *Study Guide* if you have the time and if it gives you extra confidence before the exam. Try to anticipate what essay questions the professor might ask. Ask others in the class what they think might be coming. Be ready for essays that ask you to bring together two or more topics you have studied separately in the class. Because the exam covers many chapters, the essays may well be designed to have you integrate themes.

Once you are in the exam, be extremely careful to manage your time wisely. Note how much time you can devote to the essay. The professor is not interested in reading an essay that ends with the brilliant conclusion *"no time to finish."* Everyone in the class is under the same time pressure, and the professor knows that everyone could use another hour. You need to get to each part of the essay question, even if there are parts you could have added to. In fact, you can leave a few lines blank at the end of a paragraph when you know you must push on but might be able to get back to add more later.

Professors like to read essays, but reading them is also torture: That is, they like to see what you have to say, but plowing through one-hundred blue books of inscrutable scribble is not enjoyable. While writing briskly, try to make your essays readable so that you get maximum credit for your ideas.

An exam is always designed to test the students' grasp of the subject they have been studying. More than other sections of an exam, the essay lets you tell the professor what you know, not reveal what you do not know. Yet there are basic pieces of information that an essay must include. Do not try to rely on good writing skills to help you "bull" your way through. This will yield an essay that is well-written but has no substance. Image versus substance is a big issue in politics, as you will see in the elections chapter. Your instructor is unlikely to be duped. The optimum result in an essay is a well-written piece, rich in analysis, filled with substantiating specifics. Settle for no less.

Researching and writing a term paper. Not all of you will be assigned a term paper in your introductory American government class. Instead, you might be assigned a series of short papers — position papers that require views but no actual research, class journals, essays on practical politics, book reviews, participation in debates. For these, the instructions of your professor will provide you with an understanding of exactly what is sought. Be sure that you understand what is expected on these kinds of assignments, as the professor often has a specific format in mind that you may not be familiar with from past papers.

But when researching and writing a term paper, an assignment that you will eventually have to face, be aware that your school offers many resources to help you with both the writing and the researching of papers. The library employs professionals who can assist you. The school's writing center is available for help with format, grammar, and documentation style. The computer center gives you a place to work on writing the paper if you do not have your own word processor. Graduate assistants, if assigned to your class, can critique a first draft. Some students make no use of any of these resources, while others know them well. You pay for such support services, and they can be a great help.

Choose a topic early in the semester, even if the paper is due at the end of the course. That way you can make an initial search for materials to see whether sources will be available. Many students have a very hard time selecting a topic. One strategy to overcome this might be to thumb through the *Study Guide* to see what topics lie ahead. Like Congress? Do something on Congress. Hate Congress? Likewise. Topics can be either very specific—an event, a law, a court case, a person—or more abstract, focusing on a principle, a political theory. You decide what fits your tastes.

Once you have a topic, you must establish your thesis. This is done *before* you launch into the research full force, although you may have done some research by, for example, reading *The American Polity*'s treatment of the topic. Do not think about the thesis as you may have in the past. Coming up with a thesis is not just "narrowing the topic," but rather focusing the topic. A research paper of ten to fifteen pages in an introductory course cannot include all that has ever been written, for example, on the weakening of political parties. Professor Ladd and others have written books on that subject. You need to find your corner of the topic to focus on. This corner is called variously:

the thesis
the theme
the "angle"
the focus
the hypothesis
the guiding premise

It is a slice of the bigger topic that you are going to lift out to examine in depth. The key to a good paper is depth, not breadth.

The thesis is your own. It is an original part of the paper in the sense that you have identified it. But do not feel that you must develop an utterly unique thesis, one that has never been thought of before. You are just starting out in political science, and the thesis of your paper will be based on ideas that have been explored by scholars in the field. Still, you are stating the thesis in your own way, in your own words. You may find that you have to adjust the thesis once you get started on the actual research and writing. This is not a problem. But if you do not have a thesis to begin with, you will have no way to focus the research; you will find the project becoming bigger and bigger, wider and wider, longer and longer. At this point in a poorly planned project many writers bog down. If you have a thesis to focus your work from the very start, you will *not* find yourself so swamped by material that you end up with the calamity of a late or unfinished paper.

When assigned a research paper, keep these considerations in mind:

1. Find a topic that interests you by looking through the text and the *Study Guide.*

2. Select a thesis that seems to reflect a valid point of view based on your reading thus far. Write it down in a few sentences, in your own way and your own words. Then formulate an outline of the arguments you will have to include to prove the thesis. Doing so will help you make sure the thesis is woven throughout the paper. Again, you will have to make revisions in the outline as you go. Some arguments will prove to be dead ends; some tangential; new ones will arise.

3. Start the library research. Locate books by looking at the end of the chapter in *The American Polity.* Find a reader in American government and see what important sources are excerpted there. Use the library's card catalog. If you do not know how to use the library's search system, make the time, regardless of how you have to rearrange your life, to take the frequent, library-sponsored sessions on basic research tools. It could be the best two hours you spend in college. For a short paper you do not need hundreds of sources. Locate a few classic books. Include books that are up to date. Make sure you have a few articles from scholarly journals or special-interest political magazines. Interviews, videos, and government documents are the kinds of unusual sources that can add a lot to a paper if appropriate.

4. Research the paper a little at a time if you can possibly exercise the discipline to do this. Take notes, always indicating what you have quoted word for word and what the exact source is. You will need all of this later. Very organized students use note cards. (At any rate please avoid sitting in front of three open books, with copyright dates from the early 1900s, at three A.M. on the morning the paper is due.) By the time you have taken most of your notes, you should have the thesis stated just the way you want it to open the paper. The outline (which no one will ever see) should have all the arguments organized in the order in which you are going to present them. The specific data will all be in your research notes.

5. Write a first draft. Students get writer's block because they feel that every word that goes on paper is there forever. Untrue. Just get something

down in writing by following your outline and sticking in all the pieces of evidence you have uncovered. The best way to do this is on the computer, using a word-processing program. Write for a while. Save what you have written. Make a backup disk. Get back to it days later to insert new information where it fits. Take out whole paragraphs that are going nowhere. Move others to where they fit. Print a draft. Read it for grammar. Send the whole paper through the spell check. Reprint it. Bring the draft to someone else to read, maybe a friend or the graduate assistant. Assess what you have written for: a clear thesis, stated at the start and woven throughout; supporting arguments; detailed, relevant evidence from your research to back up your arguments; clear, polished writing that sounds scholarly but unpretentious.

6. Put all the necessary documentation —footnotes and bibliography —into the paper. You need to footnote (1) all quotes (which need quotation marks as well as a footnote), (2) all facts and statistics that are not common knowledge (i.e., material found in several sources in the same form and therefore so well known that they need no documentation); and (3) all ideas that you have borrowed but put into your own words.

Your writing should neither be all footnoted nor completely unfootnoted. Too many footnotes mean that you have done nothing more than borrowed others' research, that you have written a documented report. Through the thesis, supporting arguments, and comments on what others have found, you can put a lot of original material into your paper. Too few footnotes probably mean that you have not done enough research to locate the studies and findings that will back up your point of view. You may have a good thesis, but you have not proven it sufficiently. You cannot substitute your own generalizations and opinions for evidence from sources. At worst, too few footnotes means that you have taken others' words and ideas without giving them credit —this is *plagiarism.* Plagiarism is a serious academic crime that will bring dire consequences upon you, whether you intended to plagiarize or not. Therefore, you must be very careful to attribute all quotes, opinions you have read, and facts that are not common knowledge to their proper sources.

Any of a variety of documentation methods is fine as long as you are consistent. Two often-used handbooks that cover documentation are Kate Turabian's *A Manual for Writers of Term Papers, Theses, and Dissertations,* and the *MLA Handbook for Writers of Research Papers.* Turabian and the Modern Language Association (MLA) both offer a format for footnotes and bibliographies. As a college student, you should own a copy of a style book and be familiar with its use. Be sure to ask your professor if he or she prefers one style over another. In a pinch, follow the footnote format that Professor Ladd uses for books, journal articles, newspaper articles, and government documents. You will find almost any sample footnote you need at the bottom of a page in *The American Polity.* Use his bibliography form at the end of each chapter. In fact, to become more comfortable with the kinds of information that need documentation, observing where Professor Ladd places footnotes helps quite a lot.

You should approach the documentation of research papers, not as a horror of meaningless conformity to a standardized formal style, but rather as a skill that will make your papers more scholarly and more professional. You can take pride in the research you did, and each footnote advertises your long hours of careful digging.

7. Print the final copy using a printer whose ribbon has some ink left. Make sure that your professor or the department secretary checks off your name as handing in the paper. And make sure you keep a printed copy of the final draft. Leave nothing to chance after all that work.

It is now time to stop preparing and start doing. I wish you well in your American government course. You are headed for a wonderful semester.

To The Instructor

The *Cases and Study Guide* is really two books in one. First, the "Cases" section is a collection of brief readings, each of them selected to accompany a chapter in Everett C. Ladd's *The American Polity,* Fifth Edition. These readings, or cases, offer students an "inside" look at America's political institutions and people. The cases range from glimpses into the young lives of leaders like Thomas Jefferson, Bill Clinton, and Jesse Jackson to the behind-the-scenes politicking of Lyndon Johnson, Ann Richards, and Dianne Feinstein. Other cases highlight downwardly mobile American families, the homeless in New York City, and Washington, D.C., janitors fighting for better pay. Students will discover what it's like to be a "Hill rat" for the Congress and how Alaska's teleconferencing network brings democracy to its citizens. Throughout the Cases, the cartoons in the Critic's Corners focus attention on enduring political issues through humor. All the readings are followed by questions for class discussion so that students can be ready to share their ideas on what they've read. [For instructors who want their students to read supplementary material beyond that included in the *Cases and Study Guide, The American Polity Reader,* Second Edition (Norton, 1993) offers 106 classic and contemporary excerpts covering all topics in American government.] Students are referred to the chapter's case readings in the second part of the book, the "Study Guide," at just the moment when they need a break in their regular work.

The "Study Guide" portion of the *Cases and Study Guide* is for use by students who seek a firm grasp of Professor Ladd's textbook. *The American Polity* is a wide-ranging book, offering a complete look at America's government in the 1990s. It is the kind of text an instructor hopes his or her students will handle with ease by the end of the course. Accomplishing this goal takes time and practice, however. Many of those who take American government are first-year students, so another benefit of the course is that it helps them develop the skills to master college-level material. Toward this end, the "Study Guide" provides students with chapter by chapter assistance in learning to read with understanding, to differentiate main points from supporting evidence, and to integrate basic facts with overall themes. In effect, the "Study Guide" does what an instructor would do if she or he could spend an hour with each student, each day. Without allowing students to by-pass the text, each chapter of the "Study Guide" takes students through the book, pointing out key ideas, explaining difficult concepts, and clarifying broad themes. No two chapters use the same format in presenting the material so students do not get bored by a repetitive approach. At the end of each chapter, students can test their command of the material with multiple-choice, true-false, and essay questions. A small percentage of the multiple-choice and true-false questions are included in the *Test-Item File,* rewarding students who quiz themselves. The instructor can include selected essay questions from the "Study Guide" on exams or modify essay questions for the midterm and final. The "Study Guide" is particularly valuable to students as they review for comprehensive tests on many chapters and, I hope, gives clear yet lively guidance for a first excursion into American government and politics.

Cases and Study Guide

The American Polity
Fifth Edition

Everett Carll Ladd

The Cases

1 | Social Change and Political Response

Individualism, equality, democracy – these were the features of American life which the young Frenchman Alexis de Tocqueville saw when he visited here in 1831. Have these ideas continued? How have they changed? In 1979, almost 150 years later, journalist Richard Reeves retraced the journey of Tocqueville and his friend Gustave de Beaumont.

Months into their journeys, Tocqueville and Reeves headed west to Detroit. Both observers were seeking an American frontier, and each found it in very different forms 150 years apart. Tocqueville and Reeves both saw a paradox in the equality of America: a tyranny of the majority. If all people are basically equal, it is only fair that the majority dominates. The majority can legitimately trample over minorities, especially those groups that seem to oppose the majority's values and that may stand in the way of its goals. Tocqueville wrote about the Indians he saw on the way to Detroit, Reeves about the black residents of inner-city Detroit.

Individualism, equality, and democracy have survived over many decades and through many crises in American life. For most citizens, they are the ideas that motivate and guide their lives. But for others, individualism, equality, and democracy send messages of paradox and confusion.

Alexis de Tocqueville
From *Journey to America*

One of the things that pricked our most lively curiosity in going to America, was the chance of visiting the utmost limits of European civilisation, and even, if time allowed, visiting some of those Indian tribes who have chosen to retreat into the wildest open spaces rather than adapt themselves to what the whites call the delights of social life. But it is harder than one would have thought to get to the wilds nowadays. Leaving New York, the farther we got to the north-west, the farther did the end of our journey seem to flee before us. We passed through places celebrated in the history of the Indians, we found valleys that they had named, we crossed rivers still bearing the names of their tribes, but everywhere the savage's hut had given way to the civilised man's house. The forest was felled; solitude turned to life.

But still we seemed to be following the tracks of the natives. Ten years ago, we were told, they were here; there, five years; there, two years. In the place where you see the prettiest village church, a man would tell us, 'I cut down the first tree of the forest.' 'Here,' another told us, 'the grand council of the Con-federation of the Iroquois used to be held.' – 'And what has become of the In-dians,' said I? – 'The Indians,' our host replied, 'are I do not quite know where, beyond the Great Lakes. It is a race that is dying out; they are not made for civilisation; it kills them.'

Man gets accustomed to everything. To death on the field of battle, to death in hospital, to kill and to suffer. He gets used to every sight. An ancient people, the first and legitimate master of the American continent, is vanishing daily like the snow in sunshine, and disappearing from view over the land. In the same spots and in its place another race is increasing at a rate that is even more astonishing. It fells the forests and drains the marshes; lakes as large as seas and huge rivers resist its triumphant march in vain. The wilds become vil-lages, and the villages towns. The American, the daily witness of such wonders, does not see anything astonishing in all this. This incredible destruction, this even more surprising growth, seem to him the usual progress of things in this world. He gets accustomed to it as to the unalterable order of nature.

In this way, always looking for the savages and the wilds, we covered the 360 miles between New York and Buffalo.

The first sight that struck us was a great number of Indians, who had as-sembled that day in Buffalo to collect the rent for the lands they had handed over to the United States.

I do not think I have ever suffered a more complete disappointment than the sight of those Indians. I was full of memories of M. de Chateaubriand and of Cooper, and I had expected to find in the natives of America savages in whose features nature had left the trace of some of those proud virtues that are born of liberty. I expected to find them men whose bodies had been developed by hunting and war, and who would lose nothing by being seen nude. You can guess my astonishment as I got close to the sight described here:

The Indians that I saw that evening were small in stature; their limbs, as far as could be seen under their clothes, were thin and far from muscular; their skin, instead of being of the copper-red colour that is generally supposed, was dark bronze, so that at first sight it seemed very like that of mulattoes. Their shiny, black hair fell with a peculiar stiffness over neck and shoulders. Their mouths were generally disproportionately large, and the expression of their faces ignoble and vicious. Their physiognomy told of that profound degradation that can only be reached by a long abuse of the benefits of civilisation. One would have said they were men from the lowest mob of our great European cities. And yet they were still savages. Mixed up with the vices they got from us was something barbarous and uncivilised that made them a hundred times more repulsive still. These Indians carried no arms; they wore European clothes; but they did not use them in the same way as we do. One could see that they were not at all made for their use, and they found themselves imprisoned in their folds. To European ornaments they added articles of barbarian luxury, feathers, enormous ear-rings and necklaces of shells. These men's movements were quick and jerky, their voices shrill and discordant, their glances restless and savage. At first sight one was tempted to think that each of them was but a beast from the forest, to whom education had given the appearance of a man but who had nonetheless remained an animal. These weak, depraved beings belonged however to one of the most renowned tribes of the ancient American world. We had before us, it is sad to say it, the last remnants of that famous Confederation of the Iroquois, who were no less well-known for manly wisdom than for courage, and who long held the balance between the two greatest European nations.

But one would be wrong to try and judge the Indian race by this shapeless sample, this straying sucker from a savage tree that has grown up in the mud of our cities. That would be to repeat the mistake that we ourselves commit and of which I shall have occasion to speak later.

We went out from the town that evening, and, not far from the last houses, we saw an Indian lying at the edge of the road. He was a young man. He made no movement and we thought him dead. Some stifled sighs that hardly forced their way from his breast made us realise that he was still alive and struggling against one of those dangerous forms of drunkenness that are brought on by brandy. The sun had already gone down and the ground was getting more and more damp. There was every indication that the wretched man would breathe out his last sigh there, at least unless he was helped. It was the time at which the Indians were leaving Buffalo to return to their village; from time to time a group of them came and passed close by us. They came up, roughly turned their compatriot's body over to see who he was, and then went on their way without deigning to answer our questions. Most of these men were themselves drunk. Finally a young Indian woman arrived, who at first seemed to come up with some interest. I thought that it was the wife or sister of the dying man. She looked at him attentively, called him aloud by his name, felt his heart and, being sure that he was alive, tried to rouse him from his lethargy. But when her efforts were in vain, we saw her burst out in fury against his inanimate body lying in front of her. She struck his head, twisted his face with her hands, and trampled on him. While she applied herself to these ferocious acts, she uttered such inarticulate and savage cries that, at this moment, they still seem to vibrate in my ears. Finally we felt we must intervene and peremptorily ordered her to draw back. She obeyed, but as she went off, we heard her burst into a barbarous laugh.

When we got back to the town, we told several people about the young Indian. We spoke of the imminent danger to which he was exposed; we even offered to pay his expenses at an inn. All that was useless. We could not persuade anyone to bother about it. Some told us: these men are accustomed to drink to excess and sleep on the ground. They certainly will not die from such accidents. Others admitted that the Indian probably would die, but one could read on their lips this half expressed thought: 'What is the life of an Indian?' That indeed was the basis of the general feeling. In the midst of this society, so well-policed, so prudish, and so pedantic about morality and virtue, one comes across a complete insensibility, a sort of cold and implacable egotism where the natives of America are concerned. The inhabitants of the United States do not hunt the Indians with hue and cry as did the Spaniards of Mexico. But it is the same pitiless feeling that animates the whole European race here as everywhere else.

How many times during our travels have we not met honest citizens who said to us of an evening, sitting peacefully by their fire: the number of the Indians is decreasing daily. However it is not that we often make war on them but the brandy that we sell them cheap every year carries off more than our arms could kill. This world here belongs to us, they add. God, in refusing the first inhabitants the capacity to become civilised, has destined them in advance to inevitable destruction. The true owners of this continent are those who know how to take advantage of its riches.

Richard Reeves
From *American Journey*

After their excursions to the wilds of Saginaw Bay and the American and Canadian settlements across the tops of Lake Michigan and Lake Huron, Tocqueville and Beaumont left Green Bay by steamboat on August 10, 1831, for their third stop at Detroit. They had come first, three weeks before, still shocked from their first good look at the natives of America, the Indians. . . .

Tocqueville wrote in his notebook,

". . . a striking emblem of American society. Everything is in violent contrast, unforeseen. Everywhere extreme civilization and nature abandoned to herself find themselves together and as it were face to face."

In Detroit, I stayed in Grosse Pointe Park, a shining suburb of expensive homes, almost small estates, on the city's northern border. The main route from there into downtown Detroit ran along the shore of Lake St. Clair and, then, the Detroit River. The name of the street changed at the border, from Lakeshore Drive to Jefferson Avenue. A few hundred yards, a quarter of a mile or so, and the civilization of Grosse Pointe came face to face, as it were, with a city abandoned.

I drove a block on either side of Jefferson, along streets named Chalmers, Marlborough, Philip, Manistique, Ashland, and Alter. Devastated blocks. There were twenty-nine boarded-up houses and twenty vacant lots where houses had been not long ago on those six streets. They had once been tree-lined blocks of solid two-story brick homes. Now small, dirty children played among the ruins, picking up bits of stone among the glass on the street and flinging them at my car. Black children. . . .

By the time I was on Jefferson Avenue, more than 11 percent of Detroit's housing stock had been destroyed, leveled to vacant lots, and more houses – including the twenty-nine I saw that morning, some of which had to be worth $75,000 in most cities – were boarded up hulks waiting for the wreckers. They were stripped by bands of vandals searching for anything that could be sold, particularly copper plumbing, and serving as homes – "flophouses" was the local term – for drug addicts and dangerous playpens for children, tinder for fires that plagued the city. . . .

Five miles more toward the center of Detroit, the sign marking the intersection of Superior and Orleans streets stands in a weedy plain, almost in the shadow of the Renaissance Center, the gleaming cluster of office and hotel towers built as a symbol of the city's proclaimed rebirth after the 1967 riots. The streets around Superior and Orleans had been leveled at about the same time to make way for public housing that was never built. The empty fields were punctuated with fire hydrants marking what had been the curbs of the erased streets.

The fields of hydrants were bordered by railroad tracks. On the inhabited side of those tracks, the landscape was littered with rusting and rotting cars and refrigerators and smaller junk, with sagging wooden houses that were little more than shacks when they were built 50 or 100 years ago, with charred wood from the fires that seemed to have blackened parts of every standing structure. It was littered with people, too–black Americans lived there, beaten and strangely hopeful that some higher authority cared. Of the 410 households in a 36-square block area along those tracks, from East Forest to Mack Street along Chene Street, 382 were receiving some form of government assistance, some kind of welfare. In the winter, I was told, these streets were sometimes closed for weeks by snow and ice. There were 109 vacant lots in the area, and 15 store-front churches. In three blocks along St. Aubin Street, I passed the Life Tabernacle of Detroit, the True Vine Temple of Christ, the Ephesian Church of God in Christ, the Life and Light Temple, and the Temple of New Life Thru Awakened Vision. . . .

"How do people get by here?" I asked Jason Lovett, Jr., a thirty-seven-year-old black photographer and writer, who showed me around . . . [the] neighborhood. "There's an underground economy," he said. "Gambling, narcotics. Almost everything that goes on here is against the law. But nobody bothers." Paul Thomas, a black patrolman from the Seventh Precinct, which covered the area, confirmed that, after kidding for a few minutes with a prostitute working Mack Avenue: "On the streets she can make a couple of hundred a night. She doesn't hurt no one and we watch out for her . . . I could be running them all in. But why? We're here to protect all the community, not terrorize it."

The prostitutes, the numbers runners, the guards in front of the "casino" on Chene Street, small-time drug dealers and users were usually left alone there, as long as they didn't kill each other or bother people on the outside. It seemed to be a separate country receiving aid from the United States–in the form of the welfare and assistance checks that reached almost every house–and spending and circulating that money by local custom. One "party store" on St. Joseph's Street with a "blind pig" (an illegal tavern) in the back–these things were not secret in the neighborhood–took in $45,000 in food stamps in 1980, almost all of that to pay for liquor.

Live and let live. Lovett and I were driving along Woodward Avenue, Detroit's main street, looking for a public telephone. They were few and far between, but we found one with two men standing nearby. Lovett got out of the car, walked up to the booth, exchanged a few words, and came back to the car. "They're going to be awhile," he said. "They're trying to rob the coin box." . . .

At 3:45 on a Sunday morning, July 23, 1967, Detroit vice officers raided a "blind pig" and began arresting the 82 patrons. The club was on the corner of Twelfth and Clairmount streets and it was called, rather grandly, the United Community and Civic League. A crowd gathered there as a hot dawn began showing to the east. There were curses, then a few rocks were thrown. The police began moving in reinforcements. Someone set fire to a store. In the next four days, 43 people were killed – 33 black and ten white – and there was more than $40 million in property damage as blacks wrecked their own neighborhoods, battling police and federal troops.

Twelfth Street is called a boulevard now – Rosa Parks Boulevard, named after the black woman who refused to go to the back of the bus in Montgomery – and it is lined with neat, two-story units of public housing. "You have to imagine a crowded street of bars and nightclubs, candy stores, barbershops, wig stores," said Jason Lovett. "It was a cultural center. They always find a way to destroy the black centers – a new highway, urban renewal, they keep moving us out."

"What happened after the riots?" I asked.

"They did things like this, built some housing. There were programs and jobs for a while. And the scag came."

"Scag?"

"Pinkish-red capsules," Lovett said. "They were everywhere. I'd never seen them before, but suddenly everybody had scag for 25 cents a cap. Weed and everything else dried up, but you could get all the scag you wanted. It gave you this mellow high. You didn't want no trouble with nobody. . . .

"It was, I think, low grade Mexican heroin. Mixed with milk sugar or quinine or something. Whatever it was, it took you away from here. People needed to go somewhere, but you can't go anywhere if you don't have money. Scag took you away . . . and that was the beginning of heroin in Detroit.

"It was no accident," he said. "I don't know how it happened, but I think it was part of somebody's pacification program."

"You think drugs are a control agent here?"

"Yeah, I do."

"How many other black people think that?"

"Most of them. They don't talk about it that much and white people wouldn't believe them. . . . But we've seen it all. There was no outcry about heroin or any other kind of drugs until it hit white neighborhoods. When it was in Grosse Pointe messing up white kids, then someone cared."

Lovett was a sophisticated man. Among other things, he had earned a degree in political science from Michigan State University. And his calculating view of American race relations was one I heard again and again in Detroit and other places. "Handing out heroin on the streets is easier and cheaper than giving the police machine guns," said Kenneth Cockrell, a black Detroit city councilman, a successful lawyer and a self-proclaimed Marxist. "That's the way it is in this society."

"No one ever gave a damn about drugs in the black community," said Roy Levy Williams, executive director of the Detroit Urban League and former executive assistant to the governor of Michigan. "I'm one of those Americans who is convinced that America can do anything it wants to. If you can get to the moon, you can. . . . So, I'm not sure that America ever wanted to control drugs in the black community." . . .

That view from black America, that black view of America, was not new to me. After months of traveling the United States asking the questions Tocqueville had asked, I was not surprised anymore by the cold and fearful words of black Americans. Some of it, I thought, was exaggerated – a bit of posing to shake the white man and lobby the government for a little more. But the pattern of conversations was too consistent, too clear to be ignored. Black Americans were afraid; all Americans should be. In New York City, Lloyd Williams, a forty-year-old black businessman and a vice chairman of the Harlem Chamber of Commerce, had sat in a luncheonette with me, ticking off the names of his junior-high classmates – "a junkie" . . . "dead, shot in the bar" . . . "jail" . . . "dead, overdosed." He thought half the boys might be dead or drugged or had disappeared – after a while, he said, you stopped thinking of it as accident or coincidence. That is what happens to young black male Americans.

On the other side of the country, the Pacific Coast that Tocqueville never reached, a black member of the Los Angeles Board of Education, Diane Watson, said, "If we really wanted to crack down on drugs, we could make a real dent. But we're not trying. In my moments of paranoia – and they are many – I think there must be a master plan, a conspiracy to keep the poor spaced-out, oppressed, suppressed. I just see it flowing too freely in this city and in our schools." . . .

"If the whites of North America remain united," [Tocqueville] wrote, "it is difficult to believe that the Negroes will escape the destruction threatening them; the sword of misery will bring them down."

The Frenchman linked Indians and blacks in that misery, and it was obvious to him that the Indians were being exterminated. . . .

"The Indians," he continued, "die as they have lived, in isolation; but the fate of the Negroes is in a sense linked with that of the Europeans. The two races are bound one to the other without mingling; it is equally difficult for them to separate completely or to unite."

It was the American anguish and hypocrisy, and Tocqueville sensed it everywhere he went. . . .

It is hard for me to conceive that people 150 years from now will not judge us harshly for life on Chene Street. . . . The payments from the government and the drugs come into the neighborhood; people rarely get out. And for the ones who do come outside the walls, the first doors waiting for them are government doors – to more payments, to military service and discipline. If democracy moves forward by millions of individual decisions, then Americans, silently, democratically, by unspoken consensus, made the decision that this is the way it would be in our time. . . .

In one way or another, the blacks on the bottom – and, to a lesser extent, other poor Americans – will always pose a constant threat to the larger society. Constant trouble, but certainly manageable, either using the essentially benevolent responses of the late 1960s, or using repressive measures and, perhaps, creating zones, large or small, urban or isolated, with perimeters maintained by police power. Whatever such zones, official or unofficial, were called, they would be home to hundreds of thousands of Americans, most of them black, "pacified" in contained communities governed by laws and mores different from the political and social rules of the majority.

Modern equivalents of Indian reservations . . . When Tocqueville, in 1831, saw his first Indians, saw them beaten under the blows of Western civilization, he wrote notes in his diary that have a sad but strong ring in neighborhoods of Detroit still scorched by the fires of 1967:

"One would say that the European is to other races of men what man in general is to all animated nature. When he cannot bend them to his use or make them indirectly serve his well-being, he destroys them and makes them little by little disappear before him . . . Every ten years, about, the Indian tribes which have been pushed back into the wilderness of the west perceive that they have not gained by recoiling, and that the white race advances even faster than they withdraw. Irritated by the very feeling of powerlessness, or inflamed by some new injustice, they gather together and pour impetuously into the regions which they formerly inhabited and where now rise the dwellings of the Europeans, the rustic cabins of the pioneers and further back the first villages. They overrun the country, burn the houses, kill the cattle, lift a few scalps."

Then, after each raid or little war, the tide of white men and their ideas flowed on, around, past, and over incidents and obstacles. With the savages, it took soldiers. Now, ideas may be enough.

QUESTIONS TO THINK ABOUT

1. What do you think the young French aristocrats Tocqueville and Beaumont expected to find in the American wilderness in 1831? What actual observations did Tocqueville make about nature, civilization, and people during the fifteen-day excursion?
2. Why did Tocqueville experience "complete disappointment" when he saw the Indians? Do you think he had a romanticized view of them as "noble savages"? What motivated Tocqueville and Beaumont to try to help the drunken young Indian who lay unconscious at the roadside? Why didn't any Americans express concern for the Indian?
3. Could the nineteenth-century American development westward have been accomplished without the destruction of the native American population? If that had been possible, might later American history, especially the tension between white and black Americans have been different?
4. What picture does Reeves draw of inner-city Detroit in 1979? According to his guide Lovett, was the city always this way? Do you think that government actions actually contributed to the decline of the inner cities?
5. Do you believe that there could be a conspiracy, either conscious or un-

conscious, by white America to subdue and control the black population through the spread of drugs? Would most white people believe such a theory? Would black citizens believe it?

6. Think of different ways a majority can tyrannize a minority: physically, psychologically, economically, and politically. Is a minority with different norms, values, and customs a danger to the majority? Is there really such a group in America as "the majority," or are we all members of minorities? How significant is race in dividing people? How significant is socioeconomic status?

7. What changes do you think Reeves anticipates in inner-city Detroit 150 years from now? What do you predict?

2 | Postindustrial Society

Throughout America's history as an industrializing nation and as a mature industrial state, individuals have enjoyed a great deal of social and economic mobility. Mobility has meant an increasing level of social status for many people, as family members have moved from working-class immigrants to upper-middle-class professionals in one or two generations. Along with social and career status have come material benefits: homes, cars, designer clothes, VCRs, vacations. These things are considered luxuries for the few in most societies, but in the United States they are possessed by many. Indeed, "upward mobility" has been thought of as almost one word.

Now, as America enters the postindustrial era, mobility for some people is no longer upward. Postindustrialism causes major changes in the economy. The effect on individuals' jobs and lives will be enormous. "Downward mobility" is a phrase which Americans may hear more often in the future – *their* futures.

Here are two stories of mobility. Jesse Jackson's boyhood is described by Elizabeth Colton, his press aide during the 1988 campaign for the Democratic presidential nomination. Jackson's upward mobility goes far beyond measures of SES (socioeconomic status). His success lies in his ability to transcend racism in his climb out of childhood poverty in rural South Carolina to prominence in national politics. Unlike Jesse Jackson, John Steinberg is not famous. When Katherine Newman interviewed him, Steinberg was a young man in a downwardly-mobile family whose main income earner had lost his job. Steinberg's dad was an upper-middle-class manager whose career was disrupted in the late 1980s by the economic changes which are occurring with the growth of our postindustrial society.

The Horatio Alger story of success and hard work is not just a myth from America's past. However, the path of mobility is more complicated than it once was. And it's a two-way path, with Americans traveling both upward and downward.

Elizabeth O. Colton
From *The Jackson Phenomenon*

[On March 12, 1988] Jackson's mind didn't linger on Michigan, for he was eager to get back to South Carolina that evening to eat his mother's delicious home-cooked food and to savor the taste of the victory he expected. Later that night we were scheduled to fly back to Chicago to be ready early Sunday morning for another grueling day of campaigning.

Going home to Greenville was always nostalgic for Jesse. It was nestled in the foothills of the Blue Ridge Mountains and had once been the textile capital of the world, but by the time Jesse was growing up there, it had declined and the 15 percent black population of the small city was just a poorer version of the poor whites.

As we flew in and as he walked around there, Jesse was often preoccupied and spoke of his memories. He liked to talk about all the mixed blood he'd inherited – from ancestors who were black slaves, white slave owners and Cherokee Indians – all American. His birth and growing up had taken on a mythical quality for him and also for analysts trying to explain what drove this remarkable man. The core issue, not only for the armchair analysts but for Jackson himself, was his being born out of wedlock – an illegitimate child, a bastard.

In 1941, Helen Burns, Jackson's mother, was a pretty high school student, living at home with her mother, Matilda Burns. Helen had grown up, like many blacks, as an "outside child," never knowing a father. His grandmother was illiterate and worked as a maid for a white family and spent the little money she earned on her daughter, who had a beautiful singing voice. Then, as Jackson would say, "the cycle of pain" was repeated, and his sixteen-year-old mother got pregnant by a married man, their next-door neighbor, Noah Robinson, a relatively wealthy black man.

Jesse's mother had to give up her singing ambitions and the scholarships to music colleges she'd just won. She first went to work as a maid, like her mother, and later went to beauty school and became a hairdresser. With her mother's help and later with the man she married, Charles Jackson, a janitor, she raised little Jesse, who was born in October 1941. Years later, in 1987, Jesse dedicated a collection of his speeches and writings, entitled *Straight from the Heart,* to his stepfather, whom he always called "Charlie Henry." Jackson wrote of his late stepfather that he "adopted me and gave me his name, his love, his encouragement, discipline and a high sense of self-respect."

But Jesse's birth was always remembered as a scandal in their church and their neighborhood, and for years people would remember and taunt young Jesse. In the neighborhood play area, Happy Hearts Park, the little boys would tease Jesse with "Your daddy ain't none of your daddy. You ain't nothing but a nobody, nothing but a nobody." Years later the preacher-politician would cite his illegitimacy in his inspirational speeches to young blacks and then to

America in general: "You are God's child. When I was in my mother's belly, I had no father to give me a name. . . . They called me a bastard and rejected me. You are somebody! You are God's child!"

But it was his real father whose attention Jesse always seemed to want to win. Jackson's early biographer, Barbara Reynolds, in her 1975 book, described a poignant and oft-repeated scene from Jackson's childhood – the young illegitimate son standing for hours in the back yard of his blood father and looking in the window until Noah Robinson would appear, at which point Jesse would flee back home. The father, for his part, used to watch his illegitimate son play in the schoolyard, and he would sometimes give him little presents, but his wife never tolerated the development of a relationship between the father and his son or between her own boys and her husband's illegitimate son, little Jesse.

There was always a contrast in wealth between Jackson's family and the Robinsons, and as a child he was envious of his stepbrothers' advantages. One of them, Noah Robinson, Jr., seemed to have everything, including much lighter skin and enrollment in a private school. Years later, when it was Jesse who had the power as head of Operation Breadbasket, he tried to help his stepbrother, but Noah's business shenanigans always brought some embarrassment to Jesse. However, when the media tried to tie them together by implication, they never succeeded, and Jesse's response was often: "This guilt by association business isn't fair. Nobody gives Jimmy Carter or Billy the burden of each other's brotherhood. That's not fair."

Jesse always talked about how he had never spent the night in the house of his real father. But when he was older, he would phone Robinson on Father's Day. And in 1987, when CBS's Mike Wallace was doing a special about Jackson for *60 Minutes*, Jackson included a visit with Robinson as part of the guided tour of his hometown that he gave the TV crew.

Noah Robinson, Sr., has recalled how little Jesse, at the age of five, boasted that he already knew what his calling was to be. He quoted Jesse as saying to him: "Didi, one of these days I'm going to preach." Robinson then said: "You talking about preaching, you don't even know your ABCs." But Jesse insisted: "My granddaddy Jesse's a preacher, ain't he?" Robinson's father and several ancestors had all been preachers.

"Just you watch, I'm going to be more than you think I can be." Then, as a teenager, he began to talk about his dream that he would lead his people across a river, and he boasted confidently: "I'm a born leader."

On March 12, 1988, that young man was a candidate for President of the United States, and he was flying back home to savor victory in his native state. It was getting toward dusk when we landed in Greenville. At the airport, Jesse told the welcoming party of local campaign officials to drop whatever other plans they'd had, because he wanted to go straight to his old home community for the benefit of the reporters and television cameras before it got dark. He wanted America to see where he'd come from, and maybe then they would see why he was running for the White House. Certainly, they would marvel that a black man from a slum could get so far. It was more striking than Lincoln's log cabin.

The city directories of the 1950s called the area Fieldcrest Village, "a housing project for colored located at the end of Greenacre Road." Jesse's mother and stepfather had managed to obtain a place in the village in the 1950s when Jesse was entering adolescence. It was a step up for them. Jesse would say: "Federally funded housing gave me the chance to have a proper house and helped me get where I am today."

Every time Jackson went back to Greenville during his 1988 campaign, he would return to this place, where he would see again the poor, bare yards and the plain, box-shaped two-story brick buildings, the clusters of row houses with no artistic grace. The poor still lived there, and each time Jesse returned, they would come out to greet their "favorite son."

That night, as the sun was setting and the caucuses were about to close across South Carolina, Jesse gathered the band of local and national newsmen to listen to his story. He spoke nostalgically of the community feeling of the place; it wasn't an anonymous neighborhood. He would always tell the same story: "We didn't have a neighborhood, we had a community. There's a difference between a bunch of neighbors and a community that's made up of common unity where there's a foundation."

He would explain: "There were two or three people in the neighborhood who just kept big pots of vegetable soup on. When folks didn't have any food, they couldn't go to the Salvation Army because they were black. They couldn't get social security; they couldn't get welfare. But folks had a tradition of being kind to one another, because that was our roots."

Katherine S. Newman
From *Falling from Grace*

It took a number of years before John Steinberg's family sank under the weight of prolonged income loss. In the good old days, John had enjoyed summers at the local country club, winter vacations in the Caribbean, and family outings to fancy restaurants. The Steinbergs lived in a magnificent three-story house atop a hill, a stately place fronted by a circular drive. Five years into the disaster, and with no maintenance budget to speak of, it was becoming visibly run down.

John remembers that by the time he was a college sophomore, the paint was peeling badly on the outside. The massive garden, long since bereft of a professional landscaper, was so overgrown he could no longer walk to the back of it. The inside of the house was a study in contrasts. Appliances that were standard issue for the managerial middle class – dishwashers, washing machines, dryers, televisions – stood broken and unrepaired. The wallpaper grew dingy, and the carpet on the stairs became threadworn. The antique chairs in the dining room were stained, the silk seat cushions torn. Chandeliers looked vaguely out of place in the midst of this declining splendor. The whole household had the look of a Southern mansion in the aftermath of the Civil War – its structure reflected a glorious past, but its condition told of years of neglect.

The family car was a regulation station wagon, the kind designed to haul a mob of kids. It aged well, but as John neared the end of high school the car developed signs of terminal mechanical failure. By this time, John's mother had taken a factory job in a nearby town and was dependent on the old wagon to travel to work. The starter motor went out at a particularly bad moment and, for nearly six months, the car could only function by being pushed out of the driveway and rolled down the hill until it picked up enough speed to jump-start in second gear. John remembers being grateful they lived on such a steep incline.

The Steinberg children had, in years past, accompanied their mother on her weekly shopping trips, for the fun of the outing and to make sure special treats found their way home. They would walk up and down the main street of their Connecticut town, stopping at the various specialty stores lining the prosperous commercial strip. Meat came from a butcher shop, bread from a fancy bakery, treats from the handmade candy shop, and staples from an independent, small grocery store. By the time John was in his late teens, the specialty stores were a thing of the past:

> I remember the first time I went with my mother to a big supermarket, a chain store we hadn't been to much before. She went to the meat counter and there were these precut packages of meat in plastic wrap. I had never seen meat set out that way before. We had always gone to the butcher and he cut the meat to order for us and wrapped it in small white packages.

There are many people in the United States and around the world who would be more than satisfied to eat at the table of the downwardly mobile managerial family. None of these people were hungry or malnourished. But food has greater significance than the vitamins it provides. That middle-class families can open the refrigerator and eat their fill is a demonstration of their freedom from want. The recent proliferation of "designer" foods and fancy delicatessens reveals the additional role of food as fashion and of gastronomy as tourism. And not least, food is a symbol of social status.

For affluent adolescents wolfing down pizza, the connection between diet and fortune is obscure. They devote little energy to thinking about how the food they see on their own tables compares to the fare consumed by other, less fortunate families. Downwardly mobile children *do* learn about how high income underwrites a refrigerator stocked with goodies – when these items disappear. John Steinberg again:

> My family was the real meat and potatoes type. We used to have roast beef and steak all the time. After a few years we couldn't afford it and it was just hamburger and more hamburger. That didn't bother me or my sisters. We were teenagers and we were perfectly happy with it. But I can remember one time my mother went out and splurged on what must have been a fairly cheap roast. It wouldn't hold up under my Dad's carving knife. It just fell apart. He was so disgusted he just walked out of the dining room, leaving my mother to face the kids. He was mad about having to eat that way. . . .

It took nearly eight years from the time John Steinberg's father lost his job to the time they lost the house. But when it finally happened, the family was grief-stricken:

> Letting go of that house was one of the hardest things we ever had to do. We felt like we were pushed out of the place we had grown up in. None of the rental houses my family lived in after that ever felt like home. You know, we had a roof over our heads, but losing that house made us feel a little like gypsies. . . .

John Steinberg regularly emptied his small savings account and sent it home to help clothe his younger sisters. He took a year out of college to work on construction sites and sent much of that money to his parents for their support as well. In his own mind, it was the only thing to do. But that did not make it an easy task:

> I was working at this lousy job trying to make enough money to support myself and send money home. Having a construction job in the summer is no big deal, but once fall rolled around and everyone else went back to the classroom, I really started to worry whether I would ever get back on track. I knew I didn't want to be a construction worker all my life, but it was beginning to look like the money would be needed for a long time. It was a very scary experience, because I felt my future was slipping through my fingers. . . .

Suddenly and without warning, the wives of downwardly mobile men found themselves on center stage in the family's battle for economic survival. The imperative for them to go out to work was clear, despite years in the home and in many cases with little in the way of professional or vocational credentials.

But what kinds of jobs could older women, who were either new to the labor market or returning to it after a long hiatus, hope to find? John Steinberg's

mother discovered the unfortunate truth while her husband stood on the unemployment lines. The first job she landed, after fifteen years as a full-time
housewife, was as a bank teller. It didn't last long: Three months later the bank
cut its white-collar staff and because she was "last hired" she was also "first
fired." Next she found a position as a cashier in a high-volume chain store, but
this too came to an end. Customer lines had to be kept moving at a fast pace,
and lacking any experience with a cash register, she made too many mistakes.
It was a traumatic experience:

> My mother lacked confidence in herself when it came to the work
> world. She had spent almost all her time with [her children] for
> nearly fifteen years and suddenly she had to get out there and hus-
> tle. She would get stomachaches from anxiety attacks and she had
> trouble sleeping.

After six months, she caught management's critical eye and was fired, a bitter
blow particularly because Mrs. Steinberg was the only breadwinner in the family.

She next landed a job in a factory in a nearby industrial area. Each morning
she drove from her house in the hills to work alongside working class women
and illegal aliens, molding hot plastic amid conditions riddled with health and
safety hazards – hardly the kind of experience women from the country club set
were accustomed to.

After five years of poorly paid positions, Mrs. Steinberg finally landed a job
in a large store where she could make a respectable living. At $20,000 per year,
she still cannot restore the family to its former glory, but she can provide
steady support. In the end, her success has been a small but significant compensation for the losses her husband endured. . . .

[The adult children of the downwardly mobile] have seen the consequences
of failure close at hand; they know all too well what is destroyed when people
lose their toehold in the class structure. The experience undermines their sense
of security, or more properly, their ability to judge how stable or vulnerable
their occupational positions really are. For when, in the midst of a comfortable,
easy going life, everything falls apart, children never quite recapture that feeling of safety again. Even if, in their own adult lives, all outward indications are
that things are going well and success is just around the corner, they worry that
it is all a mirage. After all, everything appeared to be fine years ago, and yet
everything collapsed before their eyes.

Suzanne Keller, a distinguished sociologist at Princeton University, once described how she felt when as a child she watched the social order in Austria
disintegrate under the Nazi invasion. Her privileged grammar school was
mainly populated by Roman Catholics, but there were a few Jewish children as
well. All were united in their dislike for one boy known as an obnoxious bully.
As the German invasion gripped Austria and the "new order" of Nazism swept
through Keller's school, the bully appeared with a swaztika emblazoned on his

arm. He began to order Jewish children around and taunt his schoolteachers. Keller watched in stunned amazement as authority figures cowered in his presence. All around her, Keller saw adults, who were supposed to be the bedrock of life, the people in charge of the world, waver indecisively or fall apart.

These memories have colored Keller's life ever since. Like other victims of trauma, she cannot forget what upheaval meant, and deep down she does not feel safe even though she has been a senior professor in a prestigious university for twenty years. She always keeps a possible refuge in another country to which she could flee. Permanence and stability remain doubtful concepts in her mind, the legacy of having observed the social order collapse before her eyes.

Downwardly mobile children are internal refugees. Like Keller, they never feel totally safe. They cannot trust the appearance of success, since they suspect that they harbor a slow virus for downward mobility. Like Sisyphus, the higher they climb, the more urgently they sense they are about to fall.

QUESTIONS TO THINK ABOUT

1. What positive forces motivated the young Jesse Jackson toward success in life? How did negative forces, such as racism, affect his future?
2. Why did Jackson feel strongly about returning to Greenville, South Carolina, whenever he could during the primary campaign?
3. Beyond the obvious comforts, why was John Steinberg's family so reluctant to give up the lifestyle they could no longer afford after Mr. Steinberg lost his job?
4. How did Jesse Jackson and John Steinberg each react to having fathers who did not fulfill the traditional role of the American male parent? How did each one's mother contribute to the family's survival?
5. Consider the differences in the ways outsiders – the community – reacted to the difficulties faced by the Burns-Jackson and the Steinberg families.
6. If Reverend Jackson's position of status and influence were to decline suddenly, do you think his children (who are in late adolescence and early adulthood) would be vulnerable to the insecurities described by Professor Keller and felt by John Steinberg?

3 | The American Ideology

America's political ideology originally came from Europe where classical liberalism had its start in the 1600s and 1700s. Liberal individualism, as the ideology is termed today, stresses individuality, freedom, equality, private property, and a popularly chosen government with limited powers. The citizens of the United States borrowed these European ideas, applying them even more enthusiastically than their European counterparts. America has practiced its liberal individualist ideas in a vast, diverse, pluralistic nation made up of people with different cultural, racial, and ethnic backgrounds. As liberal individualists, Americans "out-liberal-individualized" their European mentors.

In the past decades, however, the United States has discovered that it is Japan, not Europe, which is providing the new yardstick for national competition. The competition is economic but it goes deeper. It is also philosophic. Japan is not a liberal individualist society, but rather one with a strong sense of the collective good. Japan's ideology exists in marked contrast to America's. Journalist James Fallows describes why Japan is not like the United States and why the United States should not try to be more like Japan. The rivalry between the two nations goes beyond an economic competition for technology, production, and sales, into a clash of basic ideas and values. It is a rivalry which is forcing Americans to reexamine their cherished creed. Fallows hopes that the citizens of the United States will commit themselves anew to the true meaning of liberal individualism and will decide to become "more like us."

James Fallows
From *More Like Us*

As almost every outsider has pointed out, Japanese culture is far more uniform than that of any other major country. Schools from north to south teach the same subjects during the same weeks every year. Most swimming pools open and close for summer use on the same date across the country, even though the northern island of Hokkaido is subarctic and southern Kyushu is like the tropics. As Jared Taylor wrote, Japan *looks* the same from top to bottom, as if it had taken great care to present people with familiar, uniform surroundings at all times. . . .

All this reinforces the idea that the Japanese are One and non-Japanese are something else – and the One-ness, in turn, convinces each Japanese that all other Japanese deserve basically decent treatment. . . . The standard Japanese slogan during World War II was *ichi-oku isshin* (one hundred million with one heart). Police officials routinely say that "our homogeneous race" is the explanation for Japan's low incidence of crime. When I asked the manager of a semiconductor plant in Kyushu why his chips had fewer defects than those made in California or Texas, he said, "We are all Japanese working here, one race." His company was planning to open a plant in rural Wisconsin. "The people are all Swedish," he said. "They will understand each other without many words. Like us." In fairness, part of the problem is linguistic. The manager and others were speaking in English and may not have understood the weight the word "race" conveys to native speakers. The word they would have used in Japanese, *minzoku,* is closer to "tribe." Still, beyond semantic subtleties the sense of bonding is intense and gives most Japanese an instinctive reason to cooperate with each other.

Most of the Japanese I interviewed have stressed how easy it is to manage a nation when nearly everyone shares the same values. The American group that most resembles the Japanese is the Mormons. Same orthodox family patterns, same virtues of work and thrift, same emphasis on consensus and conventional wisdom, same abundance of steady, high-average performers as opposed to flamboyant superstars. Just as Utah is easier to govern (yet duller) than New York or California, Japan is easier to manage than the United States. And Utah is only 70 percent Mormon; Japan is nearly pure. . . .

In addition to its more obvious conveniences, Japan's racial unity permits its style of meritocracy to work as well as it does. It is a system both more open and more closed than America's. Everyone is given a more or less equal chance in the beginning. Although schools are becoming stratified along family-income lines, as in America, within each school there is no tracking or grouping during the elementary years. All students move along at the same pace; no one skips or fails a grade, including many who would be classified in the United States as retarded. Then, in junior high and high school, a rigorously "fair" system divides students according to examination scores until, in the end, some make the grade into the right universities and others do not. Everyone knows which university is best (University of Tokyo), which is second best, and so on. The best jobs go to graduates of the best university, second best to second best, and on, quite precisely, down the line. The second chance is not a cherished Japanese ideal.

This kind of merit system, based on one or two big dividing points in the teen years, leaves Japan with many people who are, objectively, losers: the men who drive the miniature dump trucks through Tokyo alleys, collecting trash while wearing white cotton gloves, the day laborers on construction gangs in their medieval-looking cloven-toed work booties, the subway-ticket punchers who stand in little underground cubicles and work like robots for hours on end. A more modern tribe of losers is made up of the *madogiwazoko,* or window-side people, those passed over for promotion at big firms but still guaranteed their jobs as part of the social contract. Every society has its losers, but Japan's seem less scorned – and therefore less resentful and more willing to try hard – than losers anywhere else. The Japanese ethic of doing every job well is part of the explanation, but the idea of racial and cultural unity is also important. Certain people have failed, but they're still brothers and cousins – not the Other, as lower-class blacks often are to whites in the United States. In Japan, failures and successes alike are all part of the family, the tribe. . . .

Obviously the United States cannot match the tribal consciousness that provides part of Japan's strength. But Japan and some neighboring cultures get tremendous effort out of ordinary people in a second, less obvious way. People in every culture do their best when they think there is a reward, but in Japan much of the reward is in the effort itself.

This difference is so simple-sounding that Americans may be tempted not to give it the attention it deserves. It is a fundamental difference between Japanese and American culture, because it takes us back to the first principles of what economic life is for.

The starting point of Western economics, especially in America, is that the world is full of "economic men," who go through life making rational cost-benefit decisions. Their appetites and preferences may vary. If wages go up, some people will work more because the payoff is greater, and others will work less because they can earn what they need in a shorter time. But everyone will respond to market signals to get the most satisfying deal for himself. This is the basic force that makes economies run. People choose different specialties; they invent new devices and invest in more productive plants; they buy from lower-cost suppliers in other locations, because every time they do so they have more goods available at a lower cost. This is how two hundred-plus years of capitalism have raised material living standards around the world.

But this picture of economic man rests on an even more basic assumption about the purpose of life – at least the economic part of it. Efficient production and foreign trade are good because they lead to lower prices, and lower prices are good because they let people have more: more food, more clothes, more leisure, more variety, more of everything that money can buy. This is the principal justification for the turmoil of capitalism. Under a competitive, capitalistic system, people suffer indignities as *producers* – companies fail, products don't sell, workers are laid off, competitors force down the price – in order to enjoy benefits as *consumers*. And as long as societies around the world all have the same goal – more – then trade among cities, regions, and nations will steadily increase. Everyone wants a bargain; the best bargains are by definition available from the world's lowest-cost producers; and the constant shift of exchange rates and technical advantages will attract people to bargains in new sites.

For most of its history, the United States has behaved more or less in accordance with the proconsumer capitalist model. Japan has not. The welfare of its consumers has consistently taken second place to a different goal: preserving every person's place in the productive system. The reward of working hard in Japan is to continue to be able to work.

Of course, some people in every part of the world work for the joy of work itself, and some Japanese work only for the pay. Taken one by one, the economic goals of most Japanese are like those of people anywhere else in the world. I've seen housewives in suburban Yokohama poring over prices in the *kutto puraiso* (cut price) corner of the grocery store just as their counterparts in America would. But Japanese society as a whole has goals quite different from America's. American culture and politics usually promote the consumer's interest; Japanese culture and politics are usually biased the other way. Japan has consistently protected its producers – farmers, unions, small shops, big corporations – at the expense of all the Japanese consumers, who must pay exorbitant prices for everything they buy. . . .

Most Japanese now above the age of forty-five attach great weight to the word *mottai-nai*. This is practically untranslatable; it is related to the idea that it is haughty, selfish, and above one's station to live too well. It has some resemblance to the Puritan saying "Use it up, wear it out, make it do, or do without." According to the concept of *mottai-nai*, it is shameful to complain about material hardship, especially when conditions are improving. Year by year since the late 1940s, life has been easier and goods more plentiful than the year before. Naturally many Japanese feel fortunate, even though their standard of living remains well below the West's.

Still, a basic cultural predisposition lies behind Japan's reluctance to consume. Almost as much as its racial harmony, the hard-life ethic that has helped pull Japan's industry ahead reflects cultural values that are not only deeply rooted but also very difficult for America to duplicate.

"The Japanese have never really caught up with Adam Smith," wrote the sociologist Ronald Dore. "They don't *believe* in the invisible hand. They believe – like all good Confucianists – that you cannot get a decent, moral society, not even an efficient society, simply out of the mechanisms of the market powered by the motivational fuel of self-interest . . . The morality has got to come from the hearts, the wills and motives, of the individuals in it."

In countless ways many East Asian cultures, but most of all Japan, show that they value the effort that goes into an activity about as much as the reward that comes out. For example, by American standards Japanese junior highs and high schools are needlessly onerous. Yes, Japan makes nearly all its people literate; yes, sheer memory work is the only way for students to master the written Japanese language. Nonetheless, the schools often seem to be harassing the students for the sake of building character. In her book about the Japanese school system, Merry White, of the Harvard School of Education, quoted this statement of purpose for Japanese public schools: "It is desirable that, in the lower grades, one should learn to bear hardship, and in the middle grades to persist to the end with patience, and in the upper grades, to be steadfast and accomplish goals undaunted by obstacles or failure." It is hard to imagine an American public school that could issue such a document. When my older son was in sixth grade in a Japanese public school, his teacher would make the class of usually squirming boys and girls sit perfectly still for five or ten minutes during "concentration" exercises every few days. The teacher would prowl between the desks with a cane in his hands, rapping the knuckles or necks of students who let their attention wander.

The standardized tests that are so famous a part of Japanese education also reflect the emphasis on duty for its own sake. The Japanese tests differ from American IQ-style tests in their consequences: the major companies hire strictly according to where job applicants went to college, and the colleges admit students mainly on the basis of test scores. But they also differ in their content. Few people in Japan contend that the tests are primarily measures of "ability" or "intelligence." Instead, the tests are straightforward measures of memorized information. No one seems interested in discussing whether the knowledge measured on the tests is related to skills that will later prove valuable on the job. That's not what the tests are about: they are measures of determination and effort, pure and simple, so the pointlessness of their content actually enhances their value as tests of will. The most common encouragement for students in "exam hell," cramming for the tests, is *Gambatte!* In context it means, Keep trying! Never give up! It reflects something deep in the Japanese scheme of values.

Even Japanese sports illustrate the importance of effort for its own sake. Japanese baseball, as described in Robert Whiting's comic masterpiece, *The Chrysanthemum and the Bat,* is a running cultural war between the Japanese baseball team and the few *gaijin* (foreign) players each team is allowed to bring from America each year. The *gaijin* stars are, irritatingly, much more talented than most of the Japanese players. Typically, they are aging sluggers or second-tier journeymen who would have had trouble making the team in the American big leagues but can easily win the batting championships in Japan. The talent gap seems to inspire the Japanese to even greater efforts in an attempt to beat the *gaijin* on guts alone. Japanese coaches and sportswriters criticize the American players for being talented but lazy – like the country as a whole.

Of course there are areas in which American culture encourages pure effort. Political campaigns, athletic teams, fledgling businesses, summer theater troupes – in such groups and others, Americans can be team-spirited, self-sacrificing, proud of the effort itself and not just the payoff. But for the foreseeable future, cooperation, self-discipline, and self-denial will come much more naturally to the Japanese than to Americans. Once in Shanghai, I rounded a corner in a cavernous "Friendship Store" and saw a mass of identically dressed people heading toward me. They had the same white beanie caps, the same white I-am-on-vacation slacks, the same white shoes and turquoise socks, the same matching turquoise sweaters thrown across their shoulders. They were Japanese, members of a group sea cruise who had all bought the matching outfits the tour operators offered. It is hard to imagine any other people on earth voluntarily behaving this way. . . .

Since the publication, in 1979, of Ezra Vogel's *Japan as Number One,* the idea that America should be more like Japan has been a constant theme in American political and intellectual life. American industrial planning should be more like MITI's. American schools should be more rigorous, like Japan's. American labor relations should be more consensual. American companies should treat their employees more like family and take the long, strategic view. Since the American work ethic and American management values have let us down, we should emulate those of the Japanese.

Any attempt to understand another culture is laudable, and some specific Japanese practices might work well in the United States. To respond to Japanese export-promotion or market-shielding policies, the United States may sometimes be forced to resort to similar tactics. But the underlying idea, that America should imitate Japan, is flawed. America is not like Japan and can never be. From the American perspective, some of Japan's most distinctive traits look praiseworthy and others do not. The emphasis on duty is admirable; the anticonsumer bias seems foolish (what's the point of success if it feels like failure?); and the racial-purity fetish is the ugliest thing about Japan. "Let's be like Japan!" an American diplomat who used to serve in Tokyo likes to say. "First we rig politics so that one party is always in power and big-city votes basically don't count. Then we double the cost of everything else but hold incomes the same. Then we close the borders and start celebrating racial purity. Then we reduce the number of jobs for women by 70 or 80 percent. Then we set up a school system that teaches people not to ask questions. After a while we can have a trade surplus too!"

Whether these Japanese traits are "good" or "bad" is not really the point. They are different from those elsewhere in the world, especially America. They give Japan certain advantages America cannot match. For Japan, they are the right traits. They allow the voluntary efforts of ordinary people to serve the whole nation's needs. But for America, they are wrong.

Can the United States ever harness individual efforts as fruitfully as Japan has? Yes, if it understands the traits that make it unique.

QUESTIONS TO THINK ABOUT

1. How do Japan's approach to meritocracy, the producer-over-consumer emphasis, and the nation's inherent unity work together to create Japan's dominance in international trade?
2. Is *mottai-nai* a part of your personal value system? Are there any groups in the United States who choose to live modestly, deliberately depriving themselves of excess material items? Will younger generations of Japanese continue to follow *mottai-nai*?
3. Compare the Japanese sense of societal unity – Oneness – with the American tendency to identify with groups such as political interest groups, ethnic associations, social and sports clubs, fraternities and sororities. How do these differing approaches to interpersonal relationships reflect basic national differences between Japanese and Americans?
4. Can the United States and Japan arrive at a cooperative economic arrangement satisfactory to both nations in view of their cultural differences?
5. How well have Americans held to the principles of liberal individualism? What do you think are some of the specific traits that Fallows believes are uniquely American?

CRITIC'S CORNER

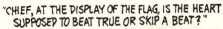

Keeping in mind Professor Ladd's discussion of American ideology in chapter 3, what type of Americanism does this cartoon criticize? How does it show the dangers of intolerant Americanism? In your own experience, in what instances have you seen an intolerant American creed?

4 | The Constitution and American Democracy

How is America governed? Easy question. The United States has a written constitution, rooted in the past but open to change through interpretation by the Supreme Court and by constitutional amendment. Citizens of the United States elect leaders democratically, through "one person, one vote" and majority rule. There are protections for individuals and minorities, insured by the judiciary. American democracy is republican: voters select representatives to run the government. A system of separation of powers and checks-and-balances divides leadership among three branches – legislative, executive, judicial – and distributes responsibility between the federal government and the states. The detailed answer to *how* America is governed is a big part of this course.

The other part of this course examines *who* governs America. Tough question. Maybe the people do, all equal, with an equal say. Or it could be a tiny elite, conspiring together to make complex decisions in late-night secret phone calls. Perhaps all the debating, struggling, and compromising among the many diverse points of view in America substantiates a pluralist power structure based on active interest groups. Every citizen must answer the question of "who governs?" for herself or himself. It's an opinion, not a simple fact. Each student's own answer is probably the most important "final exam" of this course.

Robert Christopher has bad news and good news. There *are* powerful elites in the United States. One of his examples is the influential private not-for-profit association, the Council on Foreign Relations. But new groups of Americans representing many ethnic and minority interests are now "crashing the gates" of the elite, Establishment CFR. They have ended the dominance of white Anglo-Saxon Protestant men who once controlled the Council along with almost all other positions of power in America. "Who governs?" asked the preeminent political scientist Robert Dahl in 1961. De-WASPed elites, answers Robert Christopher in 1989.

Robert C. Christopher
From *Crashing the Gates*

In 1980 when George Bush resigned from New York's Council on Foreign Relations amid a well-orchestrated flurry of publicity, his motivation was painfully transparent. In an effort to dispel the aura of elitism that clouded his presidential ambitions, he had decided to pander to a common populist obsession: the belief that there is a nexus of power in the United States that is even less responsive to the public will than big government or big business. As devotees of this theory see things, vast and unhealthy influence over the nation's affairs is exercised by a network of institutions that like to describe themselves as "not for profit" – which, among other things, means that they are not, in fact, directly answerable either to stockholders or any general electorate.

In its more extreme form, this populist notion is simply another conspiracy theory of history and reflects nothing more than the political paranoia of its proponents . . . .

Nonetheless, it is not just paranoids who ascribe undue influence to the not-for-profit sector. More nuanced and moderate versions of that view enjoy the support of perfectly reputable intellectuals and academics. In a revision of his book *Who Rules America?* published in 1985, Prof. G. William Domhoff of the University of California at Santa Cruz declared: "Corporations and corporate leaders finance and direct a network of tax-free foundations, policy-discussion groups, think tanks, and other organizations that formulate policy alternatives and attempt to shape the social and political climate. The leaders of these groups, along with men and women active in high-level positions in the corporate community, are the core of the power elite that is the leadership group for the upper class as a whole."

Along with many like-minded observers, Domhoff to my way of thinking overemphasizes – at least by implication – the manipulative nature of this country's not-for-profit institutions. From the start of our history, successful Americans have shown a stronger inclination than most national elites to see in their personal good fortune an obligation to contribute in some manner to the general welfare. To ignore or minimize the role that disinterested altruism has played in the extraordinary proliferation of American institutions avowedly dedicated to advancing the public interest in one way or another seems to me not only unduly cynical but misleading as well. To argue, for example, that the Rockefeller Foundation was primarily concerned with the welfare of privileged Americans when it promoted the "green revolution" in Third World agriculture involves more than misreading a particular situation; it requires the employment of logic and semantics so fundamentally distorted as to rule out rational analysis of public affairs in general.

Yet it would be equally foolish to pretend that altruism is the sole or even the decisive motivation of many movers and shakers in America's not-for-profit sector. As often as not, I am convinced, there is also a substantial measure of calculation at work – not so much in terms of class interests as of purely personal ones. For anyone who wishes to win full acceptance as a member of the American Establishment, financial success is not enough; it must be reinforced by demonstrations of public spirit and the achievement of leadership positions in what are generally considered worthy public enterprises. In one of its more transparent manifestations, this reality is embodied in the persistence of lavish charity balls; the management of such affairs is a time-honored device through which the wives of the nouveaux riches improve their social status. On a more substantial level, the search for status also helps to explain why busy men and women of affairs are prepared to devote so much time and energy to service on the boards of hospitals, universities, museums, foundations, public policy groups, and the like.

But it is more than a yearning for caste marks that underlies the attraction for the titans and would-be titans of corporate America of what are sometimes rather pompously described as *pro bono* activities; such activities have a very practical utility as well. Specifically, they open the way to a degree of influence over political and social affairs that financial power alone can never ensure. . . .

Because the American Establishment essentially consists of a self-perpetuating set of interlocking directorates, it is virtually certain that anyone who serves on the board of a major foundation will also turn out to be a luminary of another key sector of the not-for-profit universe: the one made up of what are sometimes referred to as policy discussion groups.

In reality, the phrase "discussion group" considerably understates the role of these bodies: a number of them conduct ambitious research and study programs, publish or sponsor the publication of periodicals and books, engage in a variety of educational activities, and provide public figures with platforms from which to launch trial balloons. And all of them, in greater or lesser degree, help to shape whatever social, political, and economic consensus prevails in the Establishment at any given time.

At least in theory, however, the central function of these organizations is to furnish a neutral ground for informed discussion of policy alternatives by their members. And whatever special interest anyone may have, there is bound to be at least one policy discussion group that focuses on it. If you are particularly concerned with Japanese-American relations, the Japan Society is clearly the place for you, but if your concern is with the Far East in general, the Asia Society is the ticket – and for the Eurocentric there's the Atlantic Council. To cover the full range of international affairs, of course, one can turn to the Council on Foreign Relations or the Foreign Policy Association. Economic policy and other issues of special concern to the corporate community are the particular province of the Conference Board and the Committee for Economic Development. And so it goes down a list that is so long and composed of organizations so varied in the networking opportunities they afford that those who enjoy elite status or are in the process of acquiring it frequently feel compelled to participate in several of them. . . .

[But] as Leonard Silk proclaimed in *The American Establishment*, if one wishes to hobnob with that potent confraternity "in its purest form," then "the Council on Foreign Relations is the place."

Simply in physical terms, in fact, the CFR bears the unmistakable stamp of the Establishment. Housed in a stately old mansion at the corner of Park Avenue and East 68th Street in Manhattan, the Council boasts huge, high-ceilinged public rooms decorated in the solidly opulent style of a good men's club and hung with portraits of past leaders bearing names such as Hamilton Fish Armstrong, Bayless Manning, and Winston Lord. From the ground floor a broad, semicircular marble staircase leads impressively to what was once obviously a ballroom and now serves as a meeting room in which statesmen from all over the world make their pitch to blue ribbon audiences.

That the audience will on any occasion be an impressive and challenging one is assured by the makeup of the Council's 1,800 members. In a study he made of the CFR membership list for 1978-79, sociologist G. William Domhoff found that 70 percent of the one hundred biggest U.S. industrial enterprises had at least one officer or director who was a Council member, as did twenty-one of the nation's twenty-five biggest banks and sixteen of its twenty-five largest insurance companies. And to reinforce the potent delegation from the business and financial communities, the Council's roster abounds with leading figures from journalism, academia, the law, and government.

To the Council's credit, its general membership, although restricted to American citizens, includes a substantial number of women and has long been thoroughly diverse ethnically. Until the early 1970s, however, its leadership was in fact though not in theory essentially chosen by a controlling oligarchy composed almost exclusively of male WASPs. And when a committee (on which I served) was charged with democratizing the institution's electoral process, the changes that it managed to agree upon were so modest that I concluded they would have little real effect. But that proved an excessively pessimistic forecast. By early 1986, in fact, people of "minority" background–three women, five Jews, two blacks, two Greek Americans, and one Italian American–made up half of the Council's Board of Directors.

Even more notable has been a development to which I referred at the very beginning of this book–the ethnic change that occurred in 1985 in what might be called the CFR's public face. To be sure, the election of Greek-American Peter Peterson to the chairmanship of the Council and of Jewish-American Peter Tarnoff to its presidency in no way marked any departure from the traditional elitism of the CFR. Peterson, after all, had been successively the CEO of a major corporation (Bell & Howell), a cabinet member in a Republican administration, and chairman of one of the country's most prestigious investment banking houses. As for Tarnoff, he is a personable, incisive ex-Foreign Service officer whose choice to head the Council's sizable permanent staff was obviously at least partly inspired by the fact that he had served as special assistant to longtime CFR power Cyrus Vance when the latter was secretary of state.

All that being conceded, however, the fact remains that two of the most conspicuous positions in what is sometimes rather grandly described as "the foreign policy community" are now occupied by men whom that community would have regarded as rank outsiders only a generation ago. And that marks a change that cannot be shrugged off as insignificant. For unlike . . . [some other groups], the Council on Foreign Relations does have real impact upon the conduct of the nation's affairs. Articles in its weighty periodical *Foreign Affairs* frequently help to establish the terms of debate in Washington, and the findings of the numerous CFR study groups have on more than one occasion contributed to the launching of major new initiatives in American foreign policy. But perhaps most important of all, the Council is less prone than . . . a number of other policy discussion groups to concentrate primarily upon the recruitment of people already at the peak of their careers. Both in its selection of members and its staff appointments, the CFR also seeks out people who are still on the way up, and by so doing it influences the mindset of America's leadership of the future.

For all its preeminence, however, the CFR is by no means unique among policy discussion groups in having become markedly less WASP-dominated in the 1970s and 1980s. Where once they were content simply to be accepted as rank-and-file members, "ethnics" increasingly began to move into leadership roles in these institutions. Thus, over the years since 1970, Isaac Shapiro, a partner in the lofty New York law firm of Milbank Tweed & Hadley, has served as president of the Japan Society, Polish-born Zbigniew Brzezinski as director of the Trilateral Commission, and Greek-American Stephen Stamas as president of The American Assembly, a group established by Dwight Eisenhower while he was president of Columbia.

Quite obviously the widespread admission of non-WASPs to positions of influence in the major policy discussion groups coincided, broadly speaking, with a trend toward greater questioning of traditional assumptions on the part of such institutions. This, in turn, makes it tempting to conclude that the first of these developments was responsible for the second. But while it is possible that such a cause-and-effect pattern may actually emerge in the years ahead, it is difficult to establish that it has done so yet. Just as in the case of the big foundations, the transformations that have occurred in the policy discussion groups so far, both in terms of ethnic diversity and receptivity to new ideas appear to be consequences rather than causes – the result of the changed social, economic, and intellectual circumstances that the turbulent events of the 1960s created in the United States.

Staff, *People*
"The Man Who Would Not Quit"

No law, varying the compensation for the services of the Senators and Representatives, shall take effect, until an election of Representatives shall have intervened.

It only took 202 years, but last week United States Archivist Don Wilson officially certified that the U.S. Constitution has a new amendment. Given the current hostility to Congress, the new measure captured the mood of a fed-up electorate. It prevents Congress from giving itself pay raises retroactively or in mid-term, which it has done from time to time. Despite the new amendment's popularity, it would probably never have become law if thirty-year-old Gregory Watson, an obscure administrative assistant to a Texas state legislator, had been a less persistent man. Ten years ago, while a student at the University of Texas—Austin, he began a one-man campaign to enact the Twenty-seventh Amendment. His reason? He got a C on a term paper.

The paper, for a government class, argued that the amendment could–and should–be passed. At the time, the proposal, originally drafted by James Madison in 1789, had been ratified by only eight states, six of them during the eighteenth century. Watson says his professor felt the amendment was a legal dead letter, even though it had no time limit, and gave him the low mark. "I was very disgusted," he says, "but undaunted."

He ran his campaign the old-fashioned way–by mail, writing to legislators in states that had yet to pass the amendment. He spent $6,000–all of it his own money. He refused all outside help. "I wanted to do it by myself," he says. "I wanted to prove that one person could do it alone."

Prove it, he did. On May 7, Michigan became the thirty-eighth–and deciding–state to okay the amendment, which had to be ratified by three-quarters of the states in order to take effect. Later that same day New Jersey voted its approval, and on May 12, Illinois joined in. Watson, who is single, was jubilant. "I wanted to show the American people what can be done if they just put forth a little elbow grease," he says. "You can wield a great deal of power, and one person can still make a difference in this country."

QUESTIONS TO THINK ABOUT

1. What kind of people join the Council on Foreign Relations, and what reasons do they have for belonging to a not-for-profit policy association?
2. How could CFR membership both help and hurt an individual in public life? Why did George Bush resign from the group in 1980?
3. Locate a recent issue of the CFR's journal, *Foreign Affairs,* in the library's periodical collection. First, look at the short biographies of each author.

Who gets articles published in this prestigious journal? Look also at the names on the editorial board of *Foreign Affairs*. Then, read at least part of one article. Does the article seem to express an "Establishment" point of view? Consider: How strongly are history and continuity stressed? Is emphasis placed on the leaders or on the masses in the nation(s) discussed? Does the author suggest radically new solutions, or does he or she view foreign policy as an ongoing, gradual process of adjustment to maintain stability? Finally, speculate on who reads *Foreign Affairs*.

4. Does racial and ethnic diversity guarantee diversity of viewpoint in the CFR or in any organization such as a university or a corporation? Is "de-WASPing America's power elite" important symbolically, in actual policy making, or in both ways?

5. Is Christopher's description of today's CFR evidence of an egalitarian, elitist, or pluralist power structure in America?

6. What were the "turbulent events of the 1960s" that Christopher credits with changing the composition and the views of policy associations like the Council on Foreign Relations?

7. What motivated George Watson to push for the passage of the twenty-seventh amendment more than two hundred years after it had been proposed?

8. Why did Madison want to defer legislative pay raises until after the subsequent congressional election? Why was 1992 a perfect time for his amendment to be ratified?

5 | The American System of Divided Government

Divide and conquer: that describes the founding fathers' basic strategy in designing a government structure for the American nation. To prevent the government from assuming powers that rightly belong to the people, the Constitution separates and overlaps governmental authority. In the next chapters on governmental institutions you will read about many examples of checks and balances among the legislative, executive, and judicial branches.

Another feature of America's divided government is federalism, which separates power between national and state governments. Students of American politics sometimes neglect state government because the problems and personalities in each state are less well-known than national issues and national political figures. Yet much of the action in American government occurs at the state and local levels where there are exciting campaigns, active citizen involvement, and important decisions made. Texan Ann Richards has been a prominent political leader at the state level. She gave the keynote address at the 1988 Democratic national convention. Her 1990 candidacy for governor of Texas raised some interesting and controversial issues related to her personal life (a past problem with alcohol dependence) and her Republican opponent's views on women's rights. Here Richards remembers back two decades to her early years in Texas state politics, first working on another woman's campaign, then serving as a public official herself, and finally traveling to a small Texas border town to visit her grassroots constituents. She was inaugurated as governor of Texas on January 14, 1991.

Ann Richards with Peter Knobler
From *Straight from the Heart*

When I left Dallas, I promised myself I would never have anything to do with politics again. It was like when I went to high school and was going to be the new me. Women, it was painfully clear, weren't going to be allowed to use their brains and I certainly wanted to use mine. I didn't see politics as producing anything fruitful for me. My kids were school age, which meant I could get out of the house more often, and I saw this as an opportunity to go back to the university and take some courses, learn some new things. . . .

I got involved with our neighborhood, serving on the local zoning and planning commission. I learned that people take their property very seriously, and that it was a real tightrope walk trying to keep property owners' interests in balance with the overall good of the community. It was next to impossible to keep people satisfied.

One day in late 1971, two years after we had arrived in Austin, I got a call from a woman named Carol Yontz. She wanted me to have lunch with a young woman who wanted to run for the Texas legislature. I carefully explained to her that I was not involved in politics, I wasn't going to do that anymore, that I had other interests that I wanted to pursue. Carol said, "Just come and talk with her. Just visit with her. We really do need advice. Her name is Sarah Weddington."

I had seen Sarah Weddington's name in the newspaper; she was the woman who argued *Roe* v. *Wade* before the Supreme Court. Somehow I had the impression that she was an older woman, in her late fifties or sixties. I thought I was dealing with some old-guard progressive whom I simply had never run across.

I went to lunch and was stunned to meet a very attractive young woman, twenty-five years old, with lots of curly blond hair, who was all business. She wanted to run for the Texas legislature but had been unable to find any man with practical experience in politics who would agree to help her. Her husband was all for it; they practiced law together, but professional politics was run by men and there were no men willing to take her on.

She said to me, "I really want to serve in the Texas legislature; there are a number of laws that need correction." She wanted legislation giving a woman the right to credit in her own name and not her husband's. She wanted laws that would stop the practice of putting the woman rape victim on trial for her character rather than the assailant on trial for his assault. She wanted to make it illegal to fire a teacher because of pregnancy.

But the main issue of the campaign seemed to boil down to the fact that Sarah was a woman. Government, to that point, hadn't been women's work. She had to convince Travis County that she was up to it, and she was running against two men.

What impressed me about Sarah Weddington was that she was pretty and feminine, and yet she talked about really tough issues involving women – and she made sense. She was not threatening to the men we interviewed. I don't think I had been around any women who I would call out-and-out feminist activists until I met Sarah. She had absolutely no concrete political experience, didn't know how to organize a campaign, project an image, or get voters to the polls. All she knew was that she wanted to get to the legislature and fight for good laws. I listened to her talk and I was really taken by the fact that she, at that age, was willing to carry on this kind of pursuit.

I agreed I would help her. I was about ten years older than Sarah and the group of aides and helpers in her campaign, and Sarah in essence agreed that she would listen to what I had to say and then do what I told her to do.

I don't mean to suggest that I ran the whole campaign, because it really was a cooperative effort. Sarah's husband, Ron Weddington, and Carol Yontz had a big part in directing the effort. But all the same, this was the first time I had had a candidate come to me and willingly listen seriously to anything I had to say about what to do.

I don't want you to think I was down there pointing my finger and cracking a whip, because it wasn't that way. We encouraged cooperation in that organization, and, being women, we were more apt to give and get than the people in other Democratic campaigns in which I had worked. Our problem, if anything was volunteers: how to find enough things for all of them to do.

Women were coming out of kitchens all over Austin to get involved; the fact that Sarah was making this race was a very dramatic step.

Sarah's campaign was run out of her law office. I still had the kids to handle and the house to run, but I would go into town every day and we would review what was to be done. My role largely involved coaching Sarah on how to act, how to carry herself, how to respond to questions. Once, when we went to a Rotary Club luncheon, Sarah was asked, "What do you think about flat-track betting?" She thought he was talking about mattresses and sheets; I had to explain to her quietly that he was talking about horse race gambling.

Most people, when they think of political campaigns, have a romantic notion that the candidate and his or her advisers sit and wrestle with issues. What they usually sit and wrestle with is how to save money, how to get something done for cheap. Sarah's campaign was that in spades.

At one point we literally ran out of money. We didn't start with much and not a whole lot ever came our way, and during one of our lowest moments a big Democratic rally was about to be held where each of the candidates could set up a booth, hand out literature, make their biggest impact. We didn't have enough money for the booth, and if they gave us the booth we didn't have anything to give away.

Somehow we scrounged up the dollars to reserve the space, but the fixings were beyond us. I thought long and hard about how we could get Sarah's name around. Finally it dawned on me that all of these people who were going around picking up pencils and emery boards and brochures with all the other candidates' names on them would need something to put the stuff in.

We called a friend, Vic Ravel. Vic and his wife Myra were good Democrats, and he ran a paper company. We asked Vic if he would donate some shopping bags to the cause. Paper sacks. We had a bunch of bumper stickers, so we took the bumper stickers and stuck them onto our free sacks, and when people struggled by laden down with other candidates' freebies we handed them a Sarah Sack to put it all in.

There was such a clamor for these Sarah Sacks that we ran out of bumper stickers. We still had a good supply of sacks, though, so some of the campaign workers and I sat in the back of the booth and wrote "Sarah Weddington" in longhand across the face of the bags and started handing them out. When word got out that we had "autographed Sarah Sacks," people just came in droves. . . .

Crafting a campaign, I found, was like accomplishing any other project; you have to determine who can give you what you need to win. And the key to success is finding your allies. In Sarah's race we had to seek out those people who would naturally be our friends, among them environmentalists, women, blacks, Hispanics, students.

I felt then and feel now that minorities and women are natural allies. Not only minorities but schoolteachers, farmers, young people . . . anyone outside the power structure. What has held us back has not been the lack of talent or brains, it has been the lack of education and opportunity. We can't win if we can't play. The main thing that has held us all back is ignorance and prejudice, and they stem from the same source. Anyone who will make disparaging remarks about blacks or Hispanics or Asians, will make disparaging remarks about women too. If it happens to be a woman, then she's a fool.

Anti-Vietnam War activism was becoming strong at the time and the University of Texas campus was alive with political awareness. This was part of Sarah's natural constituency. . . .

We looked inside these voting groups for issues where Sarah felt comfortable and those she could do something about once she got elected. Historic preservation was important to Austinites; clean air and water cut across all lines; carefully planned highways served everyone. All of these issues affect neighborhood groups in the present and the future.

But elections are won by more than issues. In fact, issues are often not at the top of the list. People will very definitely align themselves along issue lines, but by and large I firmly believe that they vote for people they trust.

Most of us don't expect candidates or elected officials to think exactly as we think on every issue. It would be impossible. What we do want is someone who has balance, someone we believe has judgment, and someone who seriously cares about us. Sarah was all of that. She was warm and compassionate. Plus, in the field she was a high-quality performer, she thought well on her feet, and she looked good on television.

I was truly excited to take on this challenge, with the issue very clearly being whether a woman could do this job or not. I was stimulated by the opportunities to go places and have a forum and speak in a way that seemed productive. I had participated in marches before, protests, demonstrations. But this time we went and, whether they wanted you there or not, they heard you once you came. Or, they heard Sarah. . . .

No one could have been more surprised than I that we won.

The nice thing for me was that Sarah went to the Texas House of Representatives to serve and I went home. That's what I liked best. I loved the crafting and figuring out how to put it all together, how to get it done on election day. And then I got to go home to the real world.

My retirement didn't last long. After one session of the legislature, Carol Yontz, Sarah's original administrative assistant, left to take a job in Washington and in 1974 Sarah asked me to take her place. Well, by then the kids were in school and there didn't seem any reason for me not to do it. I made one stipulation: I had to set my own hours. I would certainly give Sarah Weddington her money's worth, but I had to have some flexibility. If I needed to leave work to come home or to deal with one of the kids in school, she must understand that I was going to do that; my family came first. Sarah was agreeable, so I came on board.

I worked for Sarah for one legislative session. At one time I was managing five interns from the LBJ School, plus a secretary and a receptionist, and we were all in two very small rooms. I got to know firsthand how the Texas House of Representatives works, I got a deeper and more realistic understanding than I'd ever had of real-world politics: how bills become law, how to deal with constituents' problems. I drafted all of Sarah's correspondence, helped lay out a legislative package, planned with her what she was going to do in the session, and hired staff to help track those bills through. . . .

But running Sarah's office was my job, not my life. My life was with my family. I was really involved with my kids' PTA, school board meetings, gardens, and pets. . . . [But later Richards ran for county commissioner.]

The figures didn't lie. My grass-roots organization worked like a dream, and I won. I beat the Republican candidate easily, and I was the new county commissioner of Precinct Three.

I got voter feedback almost immediately. The phone rang one afternoon and when I answered, a woman said, "Mrs. Richards, I have your cat."

I was perplexed. "Yes," I told her, "I have cats. Did one run away?"

"No, Mrs. Richards. You wrote me on that postcard and said if my calico cat ever had kittens, that you wanted one? I have her for you."

[My husband] David wanted to know what else I had written on those cards that might be coming across our path, and I told him it could be anything. But I went over to the woman's house and got that cat; she turned out to be a darling kitten, and I still have her.

Johnny Voudouris was not pleased about getting beat. When I got to the county commissioner's office he had cleaned it out. I mean, there was not a file in the place. We were starting with nothing. . . .

If I was active during the campaign, I topped it when I took office. How many times have you heard about a politician who forgot about the people? I wasn't about to be one of them.

When you're an officeholder your work day does not end at a specified time. There are always neighborhood club meetings, environmental group meetings, Salvation Army suppers, or Rotary Club dinners after work hours. At least David had the good sense to know that he was not expected to go to all of them with me. If there was something involving labor or unions, people he knew, he would come with me. Otherwise, it was my deal.

Another vital part of being an officeholder is being on good terms with your workers. People will do their jobs much better and more happily if they feel they are being recognized for their work.

Very shortly after I was elected I had lunch with James Weir, the foreman of the Precinct Three road crew. James really had no interest in working for me; he was close friends with the man I had just defeated. I found him to be a reasonable and nice person, and by the end of lunch I told him that I would like him to stay on. He agreed to try it.

The next step was to meet the men.

The road office is the base for the men who actually maintain the roads, the road crew. Each precinct has its own road office, and they were run like little kingdoms where the commissioner reigns. Johnny Voudouris had ruled this one for twelve years and the men were his. Some of them were highly skilled, others were not. They had worked very hard for his reelection; they knew how to get along.

These men had been told that they were all going to be fired and replaced by minorities and women, neither of whom they had much use for. Particularly women. They just did not want to go down to the beer hall on the weekend and have to say that their boss was a woman.

The road office was in a community called Oak Hill. It makes sense to put your road office near the roads – that way you don't have to move your equipment far. It was a grim and rainy day when we drove out, the kind where you really have to drag yourself out of bed. We pulled into the yard, and as I was about to climb the stairs to the heated loft where the meeting room and coffee pot were, I passed a dog. It was a real ugly coarse-haired animal with big liver spots, and it was lying in the doorway all wet.

"My," I remarked as I started up the steps, "isn't that the ugliest old dog you've ever seen in your life?"

Upstairs there were about thirty men sitting on folding chairs and they had been gathered especially to hear me. I was their boss now and not only didn't they like it, there was nothing they could do about it. There was a real chasm between us.

But I needed these men. They knew where the roads were. I had some vague notion of the road system, but that was about it. If these men lay down on the job I was in big trouble.

I had prepared a speech about us all working together, and how important they were to me and to Precinct Three, and when I was finished I asked if they had any questions. Well, they all just sat there and stared at me and didn't say a word. This was not working out.

Finally, just to break the ice and get them talking, I asked them about their dog. Texas men will always talk about their dogs.

Nothing. No one said a word. There was some shuffling of feet.

I thought, "There must be something unseemly about the dog's name, it's the only answer." I looked around the room and they were ducking my gaze. "Let me tell you," I said, "that I am the only child of a very rough-talking father. So don't be embarrassed about your language. I've either heard it or I can top it.

"So, what's the dog's name?"

An old hand in the back row with a big wide belt and a big wide belt buckle sat up and said in a gravel bass, "Well, you're gonna find out sooner or later." He looked right at me. "Her name is Ann Richards."

I laughed. And when I laughed they roared. And a little guy in the front row who was a lot younger and a lot smarter than most, said in a wonderfully hopeful tenor, "But we call her Miss Ann!"

From then on those guys and I were good friends.

James Weir and I spent hours in his pickup and I quickly found out where the roads were. They really were little fiefdoms out there, each precinct with its own budget, its own equipment, its own suppliers. It was not the most efficient operation. Road and bridge money got tougher to come by each year, and at one point I tried to get the court to agree to a unitary road system, which would have benefited the county but altered the commissioners' power.

Under the system in place when I was elected, there were four separate road offices. Under a unitary road system we would pool our resources We could run individual crews if we wanted, but rather than duplicating very expensive equipment we could cut the machinery budget and share the savings. Some machines were sitting idle half the time, and if we scheduled them through a central office we could put them all to use and save a ton of money.

I didn't have the staff or near enough money to commission the kind of technical study that would be necessary in order to sell this idea to the court, and I didn't feel right about asking the court to hire an engineering consultant. But I knew that we had to have some concrete data before I could bring the idea to the court's attention. So I called over to the University of Texas School of Business and found a young man named Tom Granger who agreed to do the study as a course project. I used his data to go before the court.

I was not successful in convincing the other commissioners to give up some of their power. But several years later thy did institute a unitary road system and I believe there are substantial economies and savings being made there now.

There was a big loop being built around the western part of Travis county, and there was going to be a bridge built over the Colorado River. One of the issues in my campaign had been the rocks and boulders cascading down into the river at the bridge site, and the blight it caused on the landscape. My campaign literature had shown a photograph of the demolition, with earth and rubble spilling into the water.

I didn't want them to slap up one of those shortest-distance-between-two-points bridge monstrosities; this was one of the prettiest parts to the river and it shouldn't be despoiled. But, of course, when I went out to the Highway Department to review the design, it was everything I had feared it would be. Just a straight, flat bridge with metal railings and stanchions plunging down into the water, anchored in huge cement protectors. Awkward industrial lights. It was just awful.

I contacted two architects, Hal Box and Chartier Newton. We were fools rushing in where angels fear to tread. They put together a slide show of beautiful bridges and accompanied me to a meeting with the Highway Department engineers.

So we were making our presentation and the engineers were sitting there, rolling their eyes, thinking, "Oh, Lord, deliver us from this," when one of them pulled me aside and said, "Ann, don't bring those architects back out here again; architects and engineers don't mix." I said, "I don't know any other way to get you all to take this bridge seriously. This is an opportunity for the Highway Department to really look good. I know if you put your heads to it you will come up with something that will make us proud."

They agreed that they would see what they could do. I said, "I'll keep in touch with you to see how you are doing."

They came up with a beautiful bridge. It is an arched span and the roadbed itself is supported by the structure. There are no stanchions into the water, and it's made of rusty Cor-Tin steel that blends in nicely with the hill country. I am really proud of that bridge. . . .

The Travis County Commissioner's Court worked to make it easier for people to register to vote. We set up substations at various places in the county where people could sign up, and lobbied to keep people from being purged from the voter rolls.

What a refreshing change! I used to sell poll tax. In Texas up until 1966, you had to buy the right to vote. We would set up card tables at grocery stores and try to get people to buy a poll tax. It's amazing to think how we got people to the polls at all in those days, when not only did they have to get there, they had to pay for the privilege.

With all these issues and answers, you might forget that government is really run by human beings, and the human comedy is very much at work. Strange things, goofy stuff, seemed to happen almost daily. . . .

On my forty-ninth birthday Claire Korioth put together a fund-raiser/costume party. Everyone was dressed in my old costumes, Wonder Woman, Santa Claus, the Wicked Witch of the West. And they all had masks with my face on them. It was pretty cute.

By the end of my first Treasury campaign we had run out of every piece of printed material we had; the signs, the brochures, the bumper stickers – everything was gone. We were in the little town of LaJoya, in South Texas, where my good friend Billy Leo, and his father before him, Leo J. Leo, ran the general store. These tiny Texas towns are built right on the highway, and Billy Leo's store was next to a dirt patch that served as a parking lot. Next to that was the one-story building that served as the city hall and the senior citizens' center.

In all of these small South Texas towns there is a center called the Amigos del Valle, the "Friends of the Valley." These centers are where the elderly gather for a hot meal. But the Amigos del Valle are more than just places to get something to eat, they are the connection that the old people have with the community.

The man who runs the Amigos of the Valley is Amancio Chapa, and he really does run a fantastic program. Each year they crown a king and queen, and it is a big event. Each center sends a man and woman as its representatives, and the competition is stiff. I came for the crowning one time and it was fabulous; they were all so dressed up and having such a good time. The entertainment was Tito Guizar, who was a Mexican movie star years ago. He is in his late seventies and still tall and imposing, and the people were all very excited and thrilled that he was there.

Going into centers like the Amigos, where they are doing handicrafts and playing dominoes, you want to stop and say, "What I ought to be doing the rest of my life is working here." They are so appreciative that you have come, and it makes you realize how little most people ask of life.

These people have worked hard all their lives, raised families, and now they are really poor and getting old. They don't want a lot of money, they don't want to go a lot of places, they don't want a lot of things; they just want human warmth and affection.

We had gone to the Amigos del Valle center in LaJoya and I had talked with the people there. I think Hobby was on that trip, and maybe Hightower. The old folks were so pleased if you gave them something that had your picture on it, and I was out of material; we had given away everything we had. Cecile was with me, and she remembered the masks. They were in the back of the van, so she went and got them and we gave them away.

It was late afternoon by the time we were going to leave, kind of dusky on the highway. And as we were pulling away I saw a little woman, she couldn't have been over four and a half feet tall, probably in her early eighties, standing by the highway waiting for her ride. She was a frail woman in a cotton print dress that hung straight to her ankles.

I really thought, looking out that window, that that little woman is what our business of public service is all about. She has faith in us to do right by her and by the place where she lives. She will never know the intricacies, the machinations, the pull and tug and harshness of politics, and it doesn't matter. What she does need to know is that there are people serving in public office who care about her and her community. That's all she needs to know.

And it's important that we be true to her. Because, in the big fights and big issues over how money is spent, if we lose sight of these people we have really lost sight of our goal.

She had a mask. She was standing in front of Billy Leo's store wearing my face. I waved at her. She waved back.

QUESTIONS TO THINK ABOUT

1. What strategy did Ann Richards design to get Sarah Weddington elected in a political environment largely hostile to women candidates?
2. Describe Richards's view of her own role in Weddington's campaign. What limitations did she place on herself as a staffer after the election? How did Richards's degree of involvement in politics later change?
3. How did Richards win over the Precinct Three road crew? How well did she handle the engineering and architectural problems on the county bridge construction project?
4. Do you feel that Richards's concern for the old people in LaJoya was genuine? What characteristics of a successful state politician does Richards display?
5. Richards won the 1990 election for governor of Texas. In the anecdotes you have just read, can you identify reasons for her victory?

6 | Congress

The American people judge Congress harshly as a lawmaking body. Congress is usually perceived as slow, ineffective, unresponsive, concerned with special interests and reelection. However, as a representative body, Americans like Congress, the same Congress they criticize as lawmaker. The public, it seems, approves of the people it elects more than it approves of what those people do in office.

Does this sound a little like high school student government? Popularity, personality, and visibility are important ingredients in success. There is no one single formula for a winning political personality – representatives and senators are as varied as their constituents. A few examples demonstrate the range of personalities and attitudes in Congress.

Christopher Matthews describes a young Lyndon Johnson on his first job in Washington as staff aide to a Texas congressman. Note the use of techniques that Johnson later refined as he climbed to leadership in the Senate and then to the presidency. Next, former South Dakota Democratic Senator James Abourezk gives some insight into another powerful legislator, the extremely conservative southern senator James Eastland (Democrat of Mississippi). A thirty-four-year veteran of the Senate, Eastland headed the powerful Judiciary Committee until he retired in 1977. His was an old-style brand of politics but probably one that still works well today.

Two former congressional staffers have recently written inside accounts of their experiences on Capitol Hill. Mark Bisnow's time in Washington began during his college years and ended up decades later with an important position in Republican leader Robert Dole's office. Bisnow's memories are good. John Jackley was a "Hill rat," whose critical look at the Congress and its staffers reveals people with bloated egos, amoral attitudes, and power-hungry ambitions. Jackley looks back at his time in Washington with disgust. Americans who live "outside the beltway" have two versions of life "inside the beltway" to chose from.

Christopher Matthews
From *Hardball*

When I arrived in Washington, Capitol Hill was one of the most dangerous places in town. There was a dirty old map hanging in the Capitol police station marked with little *x*'s for all the corners, sidewalks and alleys where people had been murdered recently.

Life on the Hill had become so precarious that a fleabag hotel near Union Station offered a special cafeteria price to all local policemen: all they could eat for a dollar. With the constant threat of holdups, the management of the Dodge Hotel liked having the view from its cash register blotted with blue uniforms.

By the spring of 1971, the Dodge had already been targeted by the wrecking ball. It was ending its days as a cheap place for buses to stop, an affordable overnight for the senior-class trip. In the tourist guide, its one remaining star was for location.

As I would come to learn, the Dodge deserved at least one more star for history. What happened there one winter more than half a century ago belongs in the first lesson of any political education.

In the Depression days of 1931, the Dodge had become a boarding hotel, accommodating several U.S. senators and at least one Supreme Court justice. It also housed a less glittering tenantry. Two floors below the lobby level, there stretched a long corridor of cubicles, all sharing a common bath. At night this dank underworld came alive, percolating with the dreams of young bright-eyed men lucky to be working for the Congress of the United States.

One of the subterranean residents was a gawky twenty-two-year-old giant with elephantine ears who had just become secretary to Congressman Richard M. Kleberg, Democrat of Texas. Just two weeks earlier he had been teaching high school in Houston. Now, his first night at the Dodge, he did something strange, something he would admit to biographer and intimate Doris Kearns in the months just before he died. That night, Lyndon Baines Johnson took four showers. Four times he walked towel-draped to the communal bathroom down along the hall. Four times he turned on the water and lathered up. The next morning he got up early to brush his teeth five times, with five-minute intervals in between.

The young man from Texas had a mission. There were seventy-five other congressional secretaries living in the building. He wanted to meet as many of them as possible as fast as possible.

The strategy worked. Within three months of arriving in Washington, the newcomer got himself elected Speaker of the "Little Congress," the organization of all House staff assistants.

In this, his Washington debut, Johnson was displaying his basic political method. He was proving that getting ahead is just a matter of getting to know people. In fact, it is the exact same thing.

Before I came to understand the workings of Capitol Hill, I had a hard time comprehending how someone like Lyndon Johnson could rise to such heights. The man was hopeless on TV, sweating and squinting at the TelePrompTer with those ridiculous granddaddy glasses. His notorious personal behavior – flashing his appendectomy scar, picking his beagles up by their ears, conducting business enthroned on the john – did nothing to improve the image. Yet there he was in the turbulent 1960s telling us, his "fellow Americans," of the grand plans he had for us. Like many a college student of the era, I was stymied by the riddle: How in a functioning democracy could this figure have climbed over dozens of appealing, able and engaging men to make war and shape peace?

In the years ahead I would come to appreciate how Johnson's mastery of person-to-person dealings, what professionals refer to as *retail* politics, worked so well . . . .

James Abourezk
From *Advise and Dissent*

Senator James O. Eastland was the last of his kind. When he retired from the Senate I felt a certain sadness, even though he had voted against civil rights legislation, in favor of corporate interests, against every issue I was for, and in favor of every issue I was against. He was a classic racist, who once commented to a colleague after Egyptian President Anwar Sadat spoke to a joint session of Congress, "Ah believe that fella's a nigger."

When Chilean dictator Augusto Pinochet visited Washington, Eastland told me, as we sat in the cloakroom one day, that he had hosted the general at a luncheon. "Ah told Pee-no-shet that I thought he ought to jail all the leftists and hang all the Communists. And he said that was exactly what he was doing."

But Eastland had one quality that very few in politics possess – at least today. He never tried to fool anyone about himself or his positions. He knew where he stood, and so did everyone else. Eastland was able to get along with liberals such as Ted Kennedy, mostly, I think, because he recognized that each member of the Senate ultimately had to answer to his or her constituency. As long as others recognized that he, too, was responsible to his constituency, they would get along just fine.

As chairman of the Judiciary Committee, Eastland had one rule – every senator in the Democratic majority could chair a subcommittee, even if this meant creating a new one. Thus, John Tunney chaired one called Constitutional Rights. I chaired a couple of different subcommittees, moving from Separation of Powers to Administrative Practices and Procedures. The important thing about subcommittee chairmanships was that a substantial amount of money for hiring staff came with them.

When I was first appointed to the Judiciary Commmittee in 1975, I went to Eastland's office to talk about appointments to various subcommittees. Some of my liberal colleagues had advised me with respect to "Eastland protocol," so when Eastland offered me a drink, I accepted. We talked and drank, and several toddies later I was appointed chairman of one subcommittee and a member of several others.

One of Eastland's staff had interrupted a time or two during our drinking bout to tell him that the chief executive officer of TransAmerica Corporation was in the waiting room. "Let him wait," Eastland growled, "We'ah talkin'." Eventually we ended our conversation, and as I lurched out of his office, I stopped in front of a photograph of Eastland standing beside an old man wearing bibbed overalls, a pointed hat, and a beard cut straight across at the bottom, a perfect stereotype of a Southern mountain man.

Admiring the photo, I asked who it was.

"That's old E.C. Clark of Clark County, Mississippi," Eastland replied. "In Clark County, you either get all the votes, or none, depending on what E.C. says." Then he said with a grin, "Ah get all the votes."

"When that picture was being taken," he went on, "E.C. was telling me how he had just got done fixin' a jury."

Eastland used the English language sparingly. He rarely made a speech on the Senate floor, and when he did, it was only to read a short, written statement. He generally limited his conversation to asking his guests what they wanted to drink, and he avoided issue discussions at all costs.

On the third floor of the Capitol just above the Senate floor there is a small office occupied by the secretary of the Senate. It must seem to anyone in the corridors that a great deal of important business is conducted there because of the steady flow of U.S. senators in and out of the office. The core of the office is an inner room that holds a sofa, a few chairs, and, of course, a portable bar. It was one of the better watering holes around, a preferred meeting place where Jim Eastland used to preside in characteristic silence.

Whenever I showed up at the office, the conversation would inevitably turn to the subject of Indians. Because few people in the Senate had ever bothered with American Indians – except to try to take away their land and water – I was looked upon as an eccentric because I was an advocate for Indian rights.

One day in the third floor office I was sitting with several other senators when Senator John Pastore of Rhode Island began talking about Indians. Everyone took their turn telling what they knew about Indians, when suddenly, in a burst of loquacity Jim Eastland sat forward, lifted his glass, and in his best back country Mississippian accent announced, "Ah nevah saw an Indian woman who wasn't virtuous."

Then he settled back into his corner of the sofa, reverting to total silence once again. It was a silence broken only when he would order his car to be brought around, or when he would direct the Cotton Council, the cotton industry's lobbying group, to deliver another case of Chivas Regal to the Senate secretary's office.

Mark Bisnow
From *In the Shadow of the Dome*

A . . . legislative internship beckoned the following summer, and there was no resisting. It would be in Washington, D.C., the mother capital itself and pure ether to a burgeoning political junkie. I would be working for a congressman, and of course I knew that, like my Sacramento experience, it would consist in large measure of mundane office-boy chores. But I was equally confident that any workaday regimen would again be flexible enough to permit the celebrity watching and reception hopping necessary to satisfy the social drive of a college sophomore. I concluded that calloused fingertips from excessive use of a letter opener would be a small price to pay for replenishing my store of political gossip to relate when I returned to school the following September.

The trip to Washington was my first east of the Mississippi, and the long flight from Los Angeles evoked the sense of an exotic foreign journey. On that day in June 1971 nothing could have seemed as exciting as touching down at Dulles Airport with the prospect that I would soon be working in the halls of Congress. I had been engrossed during the plane ride in the best-seller of the time, *Future Shock,* and on the bus drive along the scenic edge of the Potomac River into town, I mused upon the importance of Washington in guiding modern economic and social change. Already the city had begun to take on mythological proportions in my mind, so it was inevitable that realities would prove at once tantalizing and disappointing.

Each morning I rode the bus in from Chevy Chase, transferring twice and peering through the windows at the massive subway construction that was tearing the downtown area asunder. The seats were jammed with white-collar bureaucrats who commuted from outlying areas in Maryland and were serially deposited at the departments of Commerce, Agriculture, Justice, and other federal agencies. Their professional lives were oriented to the details of national policy, interests that spilled into their personal realms. I regularly over-heard animated conversations concerning stories from the morning newspaper that few other Americans would have debated; I was delighted to find an entire city absorbed in interests like my own. Still, these were not politicians but ca-reer government workers. Only when I arrived at the Capitol Building did au-thentic political life begin.

I had come for the summer to work in the office of freshman Democrat George Danielson of Los Angeles. Fortuitously, I had made his acquaintance at cocktail receptions the summer before when he had been serving as a state senator in Sacramento. I teamed up with an old friend whose father had been a prominent Danielson supporter, and we presented ourselves as a unit. The of-fice generously accommodated us, dipping into its clerk-hire allowance when the special internship kitty proved insufficient to pay our combined subsistence wages. In return for my friend's political clout, I arranged Spartan quarters in the home of a college classmate. More than once my folding cot collapsed in the middle of the night, and our lack of kitchen privileges made sustenance continually uncertain. But all of this was part of the hand-to-mouth existence that interns have romanticized to be an integral part of their summer experi-ence.

In these and other respects we typified the army of collegians who descend each year upon Washington. Today over five thousand students serve short pe-riods on Capitol Hill in the course of a year, mostly during the summer. (Interns are not to be confused with pages, who are in their early teens and spend much of their day fetching water glasses on the House and Senate floors; nor with "patronage" appointees, who are older, on the permanent payroll, and perhaps best exemplified as the superfluous operators of the Capitol's auto-matic elevators – although even these positions can launch political careers. Jimmy Carter's top aide, Hamilton Jordan, came to Washington the first time to run not the White House but an elevator assigned him by Georgia senator Richard Russell.) Interns find their positions through persistent letter writing, the intervention of school placement offices, or the timely use of political con-tacts. Arriving in Washington, their creative abilities are tested again as they scramble to find shelter in dormitories, group houses, or spare rooms. For this they are paid modestly, if at all, but their assignments are expected to be com-mensurately lenient. It is for many a first job, and the emphasis resides in the experience rather than the work product.

Summer interns of my era spent twelve weeks at it, but today's students are often ushered in and out of offices by the month, like patients in the waiting room of an efficient dentist. No matter. The point of the experience in part is to be able to say "I was there," an objective not dissimilar to the Hill tradition of raising and lowering American flags every few seconds so that they can be distributed to constituent groups with the legitimate claim that they have flown over the U.S. Capitol. Students come, as the internship supposes, to gain in-sight into the legislative process and, even within such a short time, do indeed make a bowing acquaintance with much of the jargon and ritual of Congress. But the keen competition for positions suggests other purposes as well. The opportunity to gild one's resume does not escape the calculation of students anticipating application to graduate schools; a summer sojourn in government is regarded in yuppie quarters as the hallmark of an educated gentleman. Others see an internship as the equivalent of free admission, and a ticketbook of rides, to a political Disneyland. But in the end the effect is anything but frivolous: Most students feel they have touched the political process, leaving Washington acutely more aware of their own democratic system and, I think, renewed in their sense of civic responsibility.

Danielson enjoyed the usual congressional experience; compared with his life as a state legislator, he must have felt he had reached the big time. His higher office was, for one thing, larger. Instead of two secretaries and an administrative aide, he now had a battery of staff assistants, including those who, for example, possessed specialized legislative expertise or dealt exclusively in press relations. He may not actually have represented so many more constituents than before (nearly half a million in both cases), but he did so with heightened influence and recognition. He had greater resources at his disposal, contended with larger and more newsworthy topics, was addressed by a more illustrious title, and received a bigger salary. Flying back across the continent frequently, while physically tiring, gave him a jet-set élan. All of this went beyond mere social status; as someone dedicated to public service, Danielson was excited by the opportunity to deal in broader national policy, an attitude that infected even the lowliest summer intern. The state and local issues I had encountered the previous summer receded quickly from focus and began to seem less important.

My Sacramento experience did qualify me for slightly more substantive duties in Washington. One of my first assignments was to tally a survey of constituents, whose opinion on issues congressmen regularly solicit. Typically households are queried by means of mass-mailed newsletters and simply asked to mark their answers and send them back. In part, of course, this provides guidance on voting, and the results may be treated very seriously. But other motives lurk. Voters tend to be flattered by the idea that someone cares to know their opinion, and they credit their representative with fidelity to his electorate. ("I want to know what *you* think," the congressman will write, "so I may serve you more effectively.") And unscientific polling techniques permit questions to be tailored that elicit desired replies and can be used to justify controversial votes. (Of course only a small percentage of recipients respond, and those who do so may be motivated precisely because they hold opinions that depart from the norm.) At first I assumed that our tabulation required the utmost accuracy and was daunted to see a growing mountain of returns. "There's a lot of work here," I said with a sigh. One of the congressman's aides graciously reassured me. "Don't worry," he said, "you can count every tenth one. Just so the numbers look realistic."

The episode taught me a first lesson about Congress. Much of its work is geared to public relations and in particular to the imperatives of perpetually impending reelection contests. There is nothing intrinsically wrong with such an orientation of course; Congress is *supposed* to be responsive to voters. Devotion to constituents is one thing, however, creating illusions is another. Yet Congress is quite capable of engaging in make-believe. The *Congressional Record,* a daily "transcript" of floor proceedings, sometimes bears little resemblance to what is actually uttered in live debate given the latitude members enjoy to "revise and extend" their remarks. Congressmen employ computerized typewriters and "autopens" (machines that carefully replicate their ink signatures) in an effort to convey the impression that their letters are personal. Members praise each other as "honorable" and "distinguished" when, like Shakespeare's Marc Antony, they mean precisely the opposite.

These values were made clear to me when I had my official picture taken one day with Congressman Danielson, an essential souvenir of any summer experience. I followed him through the mazelike corridors of the behemoth Rayburn House Office Building to a small room tucked away in a corner of the basement. There our picture was snapped in what might as well have been a Hollywood sound stage: a set consisting of an impressive mahogany desk, formal bookcases, and, instead of a window, a blown-up photograph of the Capitol dome and western facade, set off by elegant drapes to convince the casual observer that it was the real thing. Few in Congress had offices looking out on such spectacular views, so for promotional purposes there was no choice but to create the setting artificially.

It was hard to reconcile these superficial preoccupations and occasional deceptions with the underlying integrity of congressmen and the nobility of their activities. The representatives I observed that summer seemed, for the most part, deeply interested in issues and determined to pursue their respective views of the public interest. Indeed it was a particularly inspiring time to see Congress in action as it tangled increasingly with President Nixon's overreaching assertions of executive power. Why, then, the crass electioneering? Partly because it was an embedded tradition of the institution, lending it the weight of social acceptability. Partly, perhaps, because it seemed to involve only "white lies." Why shouldn't constituents get official-looking replies if they had taken the trouble to write? Why shouldn't statements be published on behalf of their good causes even if congressmen didn't have the time to deliver them personally? What was wrong with calling an enemy "honorable" if it helped preserve a tone of civility? Admittedly these purposes coincided with congressional self-interest. But that may have produced the most compelling justification, as crystallized by the politician who once explained, "We have to save our seats before we can save the world." . . .

Of course neither a congressman nor his senior staff can spend much time with their student help, and the impressions one takes back from a summer experience come, in large part, from imbibing atmosphere. To an intern Wash-

ington is above all a place of political glamour. Famous figures pass constantly
in the halls; the hearings that one observes are reported in headlines the next
morning; and, as functional as they are fashionable to someone always on the
prowl for his next meal, any of a dozen elaborately catered congressional buf-
fets are available each evening for the enterprising intern to infiltrate and for-
age. . . .

When opportunities to experience the Washington political scene did not
present themselves, I did my best to create them. One morning I learned that
President Nixon would be visiting the Capitol later in the day to assist in un-
veiling the portraits of former Appropriations Committee chairmen under
whom he had served many years before as a congressman. He wasn't my favorite politician, but he *was* the president. For a couple of hours another intern
and I raced among strategic Hill offices, armed with letters from Danielson
and motivated by an insatiable desire to attend the event. Evidently security
measures were not so tight then as now, for at the appointed time we found
ourselves part of a small, private gathering in Statuary Hall seated behind Defense Secretary Melvin Laird and Speaker of the House John McCormack.
(The moment was also remarkable because it was the first time I realized that
renowned public figures could be afflicted by ordinary dandruff.) Nixon entered, smiling grandly at his adulatory reception, and for the next thirty minutes stood behind a solitary microphone like a variety show emcee, delivering
extemporaneous recollections of his years in Congress. Even so, my principal
memory of the event is of the repeatedly whispered exclamation during Nixon's
remarks by a senior Republican congressman seated nearby: "Isn't he great?
No notes!"

I might have considered this the high point of my summer's sightseeing had
it not been for another event concerning the presidential entourage. One day I
paid my first visit to the Old Executive Office Building, an imposing granite
edifice adjoining the White House that quartered the president's staff. Lee
Huebner, an acquaintance who had once served as my summer debate coach,
was now prestigiously installed there as a speechwriter. An excursion through
these important executive halls would have been interesting enough, but my
visit took a more dramatic turn as I left the building. Thirty feet ahead I saw
Henry Kissinger and a small group of associates walking briskly away. The national security adviser had become recognizable to the general public only recently on the revelation of his clandestine mission to China. "Dr. Kissinger, Dr.
Kissinger," I shouted, running to catch up and hoping only to say hello and
take the measure of this mythic Washingtonian. I came within two feet of him,
my arm outstretched to shake his hand, and suddenly the men I had taken to
be his aides pulled me violently aside. This was my first encounter with the
U.S. Secret Service, and indeed my most eventful to date. Wholesomeness
must have been written all over my face, for no one asked to see identification
before Kissinger apologized. I congratulated him on the opening to China,
marveled to myself at his unexpected accent, and reconsidered the juvenile

thought of requesting an autograph. Instead, I walked away contented that the mere telling of the story would epitomize the thrill of a first summer on the Potomac. . . .

My return to Capitol Hill occurred abruptly. One day in the spring of 1986, I found myself sitting in a windowless room at the Communications Satellite Corporation in Germantown, Maryland, performing what in the legal business is euphemistically known as document discovery. It is for good reason that this exercise is considered the bane of litigators, itself a specialty in the law that I had never wanted to practice, which my firm had assured me I would not have to practice, but which, alas, I was now practicing. For purposes of a large and complex lawsuit on behalf of a client, we desired to examine all internal correspondence over many years that might bear on certain issues. Many thousands of documents fit this description. Carton by carton they were brought in to our small conference room, where half a dozen of us pored over each page, eyes glazed over, looking for key words and names. After stoic effort we would complete each carton and feel a momentary sense of satisfaction, only to see another carton wheeled in shortly. The process looked endless, and after several days the same thoughts started obsessing me: What have I done with my life? Is this what I left the Hill for? How am I ever going to get out of this room?

Jarringly the phone rang; I was barely aware that the room had a phone. It was passed to me, and the voice at the other end identified herself as the secretary to Senator Robert Dole of Kansas. "The Leader," she intoned, "wants to see you." Dole had succeeded Baker as Senate majority leader, and the term "Leader," I knew enough to realize, was the title by which the occupant of the position is widely, if somewhat pretentiously, known. "Why would he want to see *me*?" I asked. I did not know him, and the call had been completely unexpected. The secretary did not know but was sure she had the right person. I asked what might be a good day. "Today," she said. I explained that this was impossible, since I was many miles on the outskirts of the city, without my own transportation, and working on this assignment in blue jeans. "The Leader wants to see you *today*," she repeated with a finality that ended debate. I agreed, hung up the phone, and turned to my colleagues, smiling as the beauty of the thought began to register: "I'm afraid I will have to be leaving you," I announced. I opened the door, stepped over several waiting cartons, and was on my way.

By now I realized what might be afoot. I had in fact spoken many months before with Dole's former chief of staff, Rod DeArment, about an interest in volunteering – or conceivably working – for Dole if he pursued his widely reported ambition of running for president; I greatly admired Dole's intelligence and political skill. Perhaps Rod, a very gracious sort, had remembered and raised the possibility. I charged home, changed, and miraculously arrived at the appointed hour. Dole greeted me in the reception room of his Capitol suite and took me around a corner onto a secluded outdoor ledge just a few feet from the Senate chamber. Two patio chairs were set up as though this was an accustomed habitat. From such a vantage point a visitor could gaze clearly down the Washington Mall on this crisp spring day and feel almost like the majority leader himself to see so much of Washington spread out before him.

We talked for over an hour largely about his prospective presidential campaign: who his rivals would be, ideas for potential themes, strategies for the primaries. I had expected him to be coy about his plans, the usual etiquette for this stage, but he was not, and I was impressed by his directness. I suggested a Harry Truman "plain speaking" campaign motif, which seemed well suited to Dole's laconic style and the nostalgia of American voters for the haberdasher from Missouri. Dole nodded, less because he agreed, I realize now, than because he had probably heard the suggestion a hundred times before.

He seemed reluctant to broach the obvious question of what I could do for him. At first I assumed that this was because he was wisely reserved about making any offers until I had passed his oral examination; but later I was to learn that, like many politicians, he was simply uncomfortable discussing personnel matters. The problem was compounded because no one else was present either to stimulate needed discussion or follow it up; I could, at a moment like this, see the value of staff. In fact Dole only elliptically reported our conversation to his chief of staff, Sheila Burke, who was responsible in this matter, as in others, for translating his broad sentiments into concrete action. Immensely competent though she was, even Sheila could not always puzzle out her boss's intentions.

Dole mentioned to me his possible need of advice on international trade; important legislation on that topic was wending its way through the Congress. Now that I had gone to the trouble of becoming a lawyer and had acquired specialized knowledge in trade law, advising him on that subject was of greater professional interest to me than becoming a political operative again. This turned out to be the key: Soon Dole offered me a position in his office as adviser on trade, with an understanding that I might also be asked to render campaign advice. It required little deliberation to accept. I had not planned to reenlist on the Hill, but neither had I bargained for the tedium I encountered in a law firm; I could return to law practice later. For someone so eager to sample Hill experiences, the opportunity to work in the Leader's office was irresistible. . . .

For the next year and a half I worked in the office of the Senate majority leader, although it was euphemistically renamed the office of the "Republican Leader" when election reverses returned the Senate GOP to minority status at the beginning of 1987. It was located just a few feet down the hall from the Senate chamber and functioned as Dole's legislative nerve center, housing the handful of aides who advised him on the politics, procedures, and substance of daily floor action. (This was in addition to Dole's "personal" office, which was dedicated to home state matters and tucked away in the elephantine Hart Office Building half a mile away; although Dole epitomized the "national" senator oriented to the largest and most visible issues, he did not neglect the local concerns and voters that kept sending him back.)

Bob Dole cut an imposing figure in the Congress. He was tall and athletic and looked younger than his sixty-four years. He had been a senator since 1969 and risen to national prominence when Gerald Ford selected him as his running mate in 1976, only to attain equal notoriety when some blamed Dole's "hatchet man" manner for the ticket's defeat. His badly organized 1980 campaign for president folded after the first primary, and Dole would joke in 1988 that fortunately, because of this, no one remembered it. In 1981 he became Finance Committee chairman and seized the opportunity to rebuild his reputation. Focusing on the deficit issue, he achieved new statesmanlike stature by shepherding through the Congress a bill that closed tax loopholes and gave lobbyists fits, this at a time when neither the Reagan White House nor the Democrats wanted anything to do with raising taxes. In 1984 he became majority leader and continued to enhance his image of strong leadership.

It was Dole's style, as much as his institutional position, that explained his power. In an era when Jimmy Carter, George Bush, and so many others were derided (often unfairly) as "wimps," Dole was seen as "tough." When he made a decision, he stuck with it. He spoke his mind, but always plainly and to the point; his upright mien and hardened gaze caused few to doubt his single-minded determination to win. Even his famous lighthearted quips were delivered with a straight face. One weekend he came to the office in a cardigan sweater; normally he dressed as formally as Richard Nixon, who was known for walking the beach in a suit coat. Someone complimented Dole on his new attire as he strode near my desk. "It's worth ten points in New Hampshire," he said, walking on without cracking a smile. So devoted was he to work that a friend of mine, Roger Sandler, a photographer on assignment to take pictures of VIPs *at play,* found himself stumped. He had snapped cabinet secretaries weightlifting, other senators jogging. A session was arranged with Dole in the hot summer months. At the appointed time Roger was brought to Dole's outdoor ledge. What, Roger wondered, could his extracurricular activity be? Sitting on a chaise in the summer sun, soaking up the sun's rays, it turned out, in a starched French-cuffed shirt. . . .

Dole also had a reputation for a hot temper, confirmed in the public mind after tart-tongued comments to rival George Bush during the 1988 presidential primaries. I can only say that during my tenure I never once saw him raise his voice or utter a profanity. To the contrary, the usual manifestation of his anger was a silence toward people or things that displeased him. One day a key aide said, shrugging, "I've been trying to figure out why he hasn't spoken to me in two weeks." Dole was highly controlled and had an aloofness rare in politicians; as much as he saw of his staff, his personal relationships were distant. He was not one for chitchat and rarely said "good morning"; Jo-Anne Coe, a twenty-year staff veteran, was quoted as saying that she had never heard him say "thank you." Once when he wrote "good" above someone's memo, more than one colleague in the office suggested framing it. He was a strong, silent type and seemed to assume that everyone else was too. Early on, Dole invited me to join him one evening at an event downtown, so naturally I asked if I could ride with him; the majority leader was, after all, supplied with a car and driver. He nodded, and the ride – he sat in the front and I shared the back with his pet schnauzer "Leader" – was quite pleasant, although unaccompanied by elaborate dialogue. But when I recounted the incident later, other staff members were startled to learn of my audacity. Asking for personal accommodation of this nature was just not done.

Perhaps it was this very sense of discipline and occasional sternness that gave him such an impressive presence; one staffer said she felt such respect for him that her instinct was to stand when he entered the room. Indeed we all held our boss in awe, and I found myself admiring him immensely. His succinctness and candor were refreshing, his acerbic tongue a source of constant amusement, and his quick, intuitive grasp of issues and process a strength that inspired confidence in his ability to govern and lead. Even his humor was not to be underestimated. Once I made the mistake of thinking I could write jokes for him. He was giving a speech at a dinner at the Brookings Institution, and I imagined that for such an occasion they would need to be particularly subtle and sophisticated. I wrote out several possibilities, each a paragraph or two long. Dole did me the honor of sitting down and reading them. "Good try," he said charitably, but handing them back. "People won't follow them." Of course I was sure he was wrong, and feared he would turn to his ordinary repertoire. We went to the dinner that evening, and he used the standbys he had relied on in every speech that month. For example, a major highway bill had just passed, and he began by saying, "Elizabeth would have been here but she was busy changing fifty-five-mile-per-hour signs." I braced for silence, but instead heard a roar. . . .

For my part I had charge of international trade and occasional economic issues and, like everyone, pinch-hit when gaps in coverage arose. Dole's work habits dictated our own. I would arrive usually by 7:30, by which time others might already have started the coffee percolating, and Dole might well have convened a breakfast meeting with visitors in an adjoining conference room. Our full forces would be in position by 8:30, entrenched for the rest of the day in the middle of the Senate legislative maelstrom. I made up for my virtuous arrival time by trying to leave "early," at 6:30 or 7:00 in the evening, a necessity if I were to see my small children before they went to bed. Others on the staff remained until late into the evening, sometimes ordering in pizza and almost literally ensuring that the lights of the Senate were turned out, which on occasion did not occur until midnight or later.

Our quarters were cramped in the classic manner of Congress, perhaps even more than usual because we occupied the most prime real estate of Capitol Hill. Many visitors imagine that congressmen and their staffs maintain offices in the main Capitol building, near the Rotunda under the lofty granite dome. Only the leadership staffs do so; they need to be in constant proximity to their bosses, who spend much of their day on the chamber floors. (To be precise, senior senators are granted small, unmarked "hideaways" in the back halls where they can take refuge from the sometimes oppressive demands of their own staffs.) Our offices were far more ornamental than the buildings other senators inhabited on the outskirts of the Capitol. Those who came to see us would get a taste of our status at the appointments desk on the ground floor; while ordinary tourists had relatively unrestricted freedom of movement at that level, only visitors whose names we had cleared in advance were allowed to proceed to our second-floor suite. This had a necessary security purpose – a small bomb had exploded some years before in a hall outside the Senate chamber (no one was injured) – but it also lent our office neighborhood an aura of prestigious exclusivity.

Appearing at the front door of the Leader's enclave, guests would be greeted by attentive receptionists, who seated them in Dole's own elegant reception room while they waited to see us. There they could peruse photo albums of his recent overseas trips, page through large and glossy picture books on Kansas, New Hampshire, and Iowa, which just happened to grace the coffee table, or wonder about the identity and function of an official-looking young man often seated at a rococco desk in the back of the room. (It was Dean Burridge, an aide who accompanied Dole much of the day, holding loose papers, reminding him of impending appointments, coordinating the movements of car and driver, nudging away unwanted visitors, and otherwise providing the aura of a mini-entourage.) The prized moment would be catching a sudden glimpse of Dole himself entering or leaving his adjoining inner office, a reminder that despite the ceremonial appearance of this ornate space, it actually served real-life functions. (In fact the line sometimes blurred: Dole often played host in this room to illustrious visitors, such as baseball greats of yesteryear in town for an old-timers' game, and in the halls nearby I had seen special tours accorded Brooke Shields, Ginger Rogers, and Woody Allen. Was this "real life"?)

Meanwhile our visitors, having beheld such splendor, were in store for disappointment when escorted back into our cozy legislative den. There we would need to find empty chairs to pull up alongside us, making sure to move the wastebaskets so as not to block the well-traveled paths among our desks. The incommodiousness of these circumstances was partially redeemed by vaulted ceilings and imposing chandeliers; at least we could claim our offices had character. . . .

Life in the Leader's office gave old experiences a new twist. Years before, as an ordinary LA, I was free at most times to walk onto the Senate floor, but I needed first to sign in opposite the Senate reception room and then clip a large badge onto the breast pocket of my suit coat. For all the status of mingling in the company of senators, displaying such a thing made me feel like a prisoner wearing striped clothes in polite society. Of leadership staff, however, no badges were required; we could use the entrance nearest our office, where the plainclothed officers who guarded it would recognize and wave us through.

I missed another peculiar ritual. When bells rang for a vote, LAs often rushed to position themselves near the bank of elevators on the second story of the Capitol, opposite the Senate floor. As the door of the "Senators Only" elevator opened, their bosses would pour out, having come up from the tram in the basement that carried them from their offices. If they did not know what they were voting on (votes occurred frequently throughout the day, and it was hard to keep track), and if an aide had not already intercepted them en route, they would glance to the side to see if someone were waiting. A staffer might wave and run up for a huddled conference behind a pillar; or if the senator were in a hurry to make the fifteen-minute deadline for voting, he might simply expect a quick thumbs-up or thumbs-down gesture.

In compressing their advice so crudely, of course, aides were not merely expressing their own arbitrary notions as to a "correct" vote; more often they were translating what they knew to be their bosses' positions. A senator might know, for example, that an impending vote concerned Social Security cost-of-living increases; but he might not know that it was phrased as a Hollings motion to table a Mitchell substitute to an Inouye amendment. In addition an aide might be able to provide critical last-minute information, such as the fact that an important constituency group had just phoned pleading for support or that Senator So-and-so (whom the aide's boss particularly respected on the issue) was recommending a particular position. In the aide's absence other cues were available. A senator could expect to be greeted on the floor by colleagues proselytizing pro and con; he could walk to the well of the chamber and examine the tally sheets to see how other senators had already voted; or he could find Howard Green, or one of the other Republican or Democratic cloakroom attendants, to ask for either basic factual information or candid political advice. Now that I worked for the Leader, I didn't have to run over to the Capitol anymore and idle next to the elevators. I was already in the area, and I knew exactly where my boss would be: on the floor himself and supremely knowledgeable about the vote taking place.

The hallowed custom of editing transcripts of floor debate was also greatly simplified. Many Senate LAs routinely go into the clerk's office minutes after their bosses speak to emend their remarks. Stenographers walk the Senate floor taking shorthand on quaint machines that they carry strapped from their necks like ice-cream vendors at the ballpark; afterward, their notes are quickly transcribed for inspection by aides before going to the Government Printing Office to be incorporated into the *Congressional Record,* which will appear on every office's doorstep the next morning. In theory aides are supposed to review the transcripts only for grammatical or factual errors, but the fact that in practice even wholesale changes can be made is suggested by the presence of scissors and tape on the table in the middle of the clerk's room where the aides do their work.

Indeed it is not uncommon simply for a senator to say what he wants, hand in a prepared text that he does not actually use, and expect the aide to go in and reconcile everything afterward. The *Record* is so notoriously inaccurate that, in one macabre instance, a speech by the late House majority leader Hale Boggs appeared as part of a debate that was stated to have taken place two days after he had perished in an airplane accident over Alaska. . . .

Some years back, one of Senator Dole's aides had occasion to deliver remarks before a group while the senator sat nearby on the dais. After the aide had spoken a few minutes, the senator passed him a note in his rather illegible handwriting, which the aide, glancing quickly, had trouble reading. Looking again, he decided that it said, "More detail." With his boss just a few feet away, he had no choice but to comply. He reached back into his memory and began to recall anecdote after anecdote about the issues under discussion. Much later he concluded his presentation and returned to his seat, passing a frowning Senator Dole. The aide sat down and pulled the note from his pocket to examine it again. He stared and stared, trying to make it out. Finally it dawned on him: The note said not "more detail" but "move faster."

Rod DeArment, a former Dole aide and now deputy secretary of labor, swears this happened, and I don't doubt it. It is precisely the job of aides to guess what their bosses want, but it would be surprising if they always got it right. Senators are busy people and give them only quick and skeletal direction; yet their aides' actions have consequences all the same. It has become commonplace to question whether congressional aides have become too powerful. I am not sure that is the real issue. It implies an abuse of authority, as if their bosses have not delegated them the power they exercise. Yet I think their bosses know well their power and generally *want* them to use it, even if they don't control it very closely. The real question that large staffs raise is how powerful Congress itself should be.

A modest example of the issue? Of all the lobbyists who plied Capitol Hill, my favorite were the chocolate manufacturers, who sought help in reducing excessive Japanese tariffs that inhibited the export of their candies. It was a virtuous and easy position to support, especially since they sent Hill offices unending supplies of one-pound bags of M & M's to sweeten our consideration. I personally wrote letter after letter in my boss's name making polite demands of the Japanese; Dole would hardly have taken the initiative himself, but he had no problem approving mine. One day Prime Minister Nakasone, on a state visit to Washington, arrived on Capitol Hill for a private meeting with the two Senate leaders; around a small table with him sat Senators Byrd and Dole and U.S. ambassador to Japan Mike Mansfield; a couple of staff aides sat discreetly on the side. Trade relations with Japan were tense, and we nervously awaited Nakasone's words. What momentous issues would he address: Steel? Autos? Electronics? The yen–dollar exchange rate? After diplomatic pleasantries he came to his point; he had an olive branch to offer. We leaned forward to hear more. What could it be? Knowing both senators' acute interest in the issue, he said, he had ordered a reduction in the . . . chocolate tariff.

John Jackley
From *Hill Rat*

We are, after all, professionals.
This is the story of a breed, and these are my people.

Go ahead, ask anyone in town. There is something about this special species of Washington political operative that makes them instantly detectable on the subway, at parties, anywhere. They are smug. They are arrogant. They believe they work on a political Mount Olympus from which they survey the rest of the planet. It shows, and they do not seem to care. The god of this town is power and its currency is power, defined a thousand ways.

Power: the twenty-three-year-old legislative assistant on the down elevator in the Cannon House Office Building at 6:20 P.M., flush with success from jerking around some GS-12 in the Department of Agriculture. "I told that sonofabitch that if he didn't have that letter *on my desk* by ten tomorrow morning, I'd have my boss slap the assistant secretary in Thursday's hearing in front of the press. . . . you could hear his asshole pucker all the way over here."

Power: veteran lobbyists called hall sharpies prowl the corridors of the office buildings, darting in and out of the legions of out-of-towners (the dreaded Constituents) with their nametags and slick briefing materials produced by their trade or professional association. In contrast, hall sharpies travel light. Very few briefcases, mostly a few shards of paper folded into a jacket pocket of a dark suit. They smoke a lot, too, and their eyes seem to be permanently narrowed into the flitting, searching look of the professional hunter. They don't amble and they don't second-guess. They know who and what they're looking for and they know where to find them. They're either waiting for someone or they're on their way somewhere – the hushed meeting, the whispers under the stairwell, the furtive trading of confidential paper and gossip – this is the stuff of the House.

Power: the lunchtime talk drifting from the Longworth Building cafeteria, the Being In The Know clatter from the gaggle of staff, members, lobbyists, constituents, and visitors milling around the *Washington Post* vending machines by the front door: ". . . got to make sure the *key* staffers are on board before we go to the committee. . . . And I said, can you believe the balls on that guy? We ought to leak a totally wrong story and fuck him good. . . . Just between you and me, there's no way she can get away with it without . . . And then the computer went down and we lost every targeted letter. . . ."

Power: once you're in, you're in. You're here. You're happening. You're part of the biggest, baddest, greatest show on earth and you damn well know it.

Most true Hill rats work in the members' personal offices, the political equivalent of a big city emergency room on a hot Saturday night. It is showtime the minute the Hill rats walk in the door to plug the wounds and perform meatball surgery on the body politic.

The members? Many Hill rats consider them bothersome necessities that come and go; Hill rats endure and prevail. I once joked in a 1983 staff meeting about a newsletter and said it "usually took me a member or two to get this thing right." Freshman Congressman Ron Coleman was not amused.

The play's the thing on the Hill. And the true Hill rat's credo is: "Ask not what your member can do for the issue, but rather what the issue can do for your member."

The message is clear: get the job done and do whatever you can get away with. If you crash and burn, if the sin is not too egregious, maybe you can turn the situation to your advantage. If not, you might have to resign or go through a ceremonial firing so that the member can go through the obligatory cleansing process in the press and the public consciousness.

Employment is granted and withdrawn with equal suddenness. When Rep. Tony Hall (D-OH) was appointed to succeed the late Rep. Mickey Leland as chairman of the House Select Committee on Hunger, the staff director of the committee found she had been replaced by reading a newspaper article; twenty-four hours after Hall's appointment, Miranda Katsoyannis was gone. *Roll Call,* Capitol Hill's house organ, pointed out that "the abrupt firing of important Hill aides is business as usual in the rough-and-tumble self-styled macho culture of Congress. This sort of commonplace brutality hurts the institution; it encourages cynicism and discourages long-term commitment." Those with their ears to the ground, however, discovered that Katsoyannis had supported a rival member's attempt to be appointed chairman by the Speaker. And so the game goes . . .

Once in, it is not all easy going; pitfalls lurk for the unwary or those blinded by hubris. Elwood Broad, a former Hill rat who worked for U.S Rep. Gus Yatron (D-PA), sued Yatron in May 1991 for restitution for alleged forcible kickback payments to the congressman. Broad claimed he was required to pay Yatron's wife $700 a month from his congressional salary. Yatron, in turn, called Broad a disgruntled employee who had some questions of his own to answer about missing campaign funds. The Federal Bureau of Investigation has taken up the matter.

Another case had an even stranger twist. In 1984, the *Washington Times* reported that documents seized during the 1983 U.S. invasion of Grenada revealed that Carlottia A. Scott, an aide to Rep. Ron Dellums (D-CA), had developed a personal relationship with Grenada's late Marxist prime minister,

Maurice Bishop. Scott, in her letters to Prime Minister Bishop, addressed him as "My Sweet," "My Dearest," and "My Darling Comrade Leader." Following a "fact-finding" trip to Grenada by Rep. Dellums, Scott, and Dellums's administrative assistant Barbara Lee, Ms. Lee hand-carried Dellums' official report on the trip to Grenada to clear it with the prime minister. Scott wrote on House of Representatives letterhead, "I still love you madly."

Hill rats are a special breed, all right.

Where else can $18,000-a-year legislative assistants in their early twenties make life miserable for civil servants at the peak of their careers, some of them confirmed by the United States Senate?

Where else can young press secretaries twist Cabinet secretaries in knots, or gleefully and shamelessly spearhead rumor campaigns against the highest officials in the land?

Where else can a Hill rat like R. Spencer Oliver, chief counsel to the House Foreign Affairs Committee, get profiled in a national newspaper for his skill at political "war-by-investigation" and be criticized in the Republican minority report in the Iran-contra affair for conducting a "wide-ranging fishing expedition into irrelevant political issues"? Oliver probably uses that line to buff his resume.

This is the place. The Twilight Zone. Powertown personified. Derivative power, of course, but the incredible time demands on the members stretch them so thin that each staff member has become the deputy congressman for Press, deputy congressman for Defense and Foreign Policy, and so on. As one of my friends put it, "Lord Acton was only half right. Power might corrupt, but absolute power is a blast."

Jonathan Yates, a former Hill rat writing in *Newsweek* about his experiences, observed, "Just 23 and fresh out of college, I was dealing daily with generals, ambassadors and business executives." This kind of power disturbs some people. In the 1989 *Blanchard v. Bergeron* decision, Supreme Court Justice Antonin Scalia wrote in a concurrence, "What a heady feeling it must be for a young staffer to know that his or her citation can transform into the law of the land, thereafter dutifully to be observed by the Supreme Court." Scalia took a narrow view of so-called legislative intent, by which the judiciary attempts to divine the meaning of many of the laws passed by Congress, and criticized current practice: "As anyone familiar with modern-day drafting of congressional committee reports is well aware, [the references] were inserted, at best by a committee staff member on his or her own initiative, and at worse by a committee staff member at the suggestion of a lawyer-lobbyist, and the purpose of those references was not primarily to inform the members of Congress what the bill meant . . . but rather to influence judicial construction." Scalia went on to state that the judiciary should only consider language in the actual law, language that was voted on and passed, and not the parenthetical comments in committee reports that were not voted on by the whole Congress.

I called a friend of mine, a former Hill rat and now one of those lawyer-lobbyists excoriated by Justice Scalia. He scoffed. "Great. I'm all for doing it by the statute. Who do you think writes those bills anyway? We write the bills, not the members. Screw 'em. That's what I'm doing right now, trying to get something into the Science and Tech report. You wait and see. What would Washington do without lawyer-lobbyists?"

"It would work," I suggested with a laugh. He chuckled in return and said, "We'll talk about it over lunch."

Hill rats are also important because of a procedure called a "staff mark," another one of Congress's secrets. Before a major piece of legislation is "marked up," or changed and then voted on in committee, Hill rats who work for the committee members commonly divide up the spoils. Each Hill rat is trained, of course, to represent the member's best political interests. And since the staff knows what the member needs – probably better than the member himself – it saves the elected official from any unduly burdensome thinking.

Several years ago, when the nation's patent and copyright laws were being overhauled, the House received from the Senate a huge comprehensive bill that had taken three years of painstaking legislative craftsmanship to complete. But the Senate had not bothered to consult the House while writing the bill, and the bill was sent over with only five weeks left in the session in the expectation that the House would comply meekly with the Senate's wishes.

The size, complexity, and late arrival of the bill meant that it was headed for a staff mark. The legislative assistants assembled at the office of the committee staff director, who asked, "Okay, who really wants to do this shit?"

Everyone groaned. The various staffers were up to their ears in their bosses' end-of-the-session political fights. No one wanted to spend an inordinate amount of time, probably weekends and nights, learning the arcana of copyright and patent law, no matter how much money was at stake.

"Well, how much do we really have to do?" one staffer finally asked.

The staff director replied that a bare-bones version would only involve two or three items, and he could take care of it in a day or so.

Heads began to nod. U.S. copyright and patent law had fallen into the hands of overworked Hill rats, and the deal was done. . . .

. . . The town pays homage to the power of Hill rats. People fork over fees upwards of hundreds of dollars to attend seminars that teach how to deal with us. "What do Members expect of these staffers that you should know about that help the staffer, and in turn yourself, to succeed?" an advertisement for one such seminar read. "Where do you fit into competition for Members' attention? The KEY: Learning the right touch. . . . And doing it quickly without wasting their time." Remember: Hill rats are the currency of power. One of the bitterest complaints of House Republicans against the Democratic leadership, in fact, is that they do not receive a fair allocation of staffers on the various committees. In March 1990, the problem became so acute that Republicans threatened to vote against administrative funds for all committees if more Republican Hill rats would not work for them. As one of the many Congressional Research Service analyses of this issue pointed out, "Although the number of employees allocated to each committee has grown . . . the allocation of staff [to Republicans] has not necessarily kept pace."

Perquisites follow closely behind power. Pay for Hill rats increases each time the members vote themselves a raise (and they never vote pay cuts). In 1991, the House voted 275 to 139 to delete a proposed $50,000 increase in congressional staff pay, but the House Administration Committee issued a letter stating that, the vote notwithstanding, it would fund the raise. As of July 1991, at least 130 House staffers were making from $100,000 to a maximum of $115,092 in salary.

Power offers the perquisite of genuflection, which in one form or another is pervasive. Theodore Mathison, administrator of the Baltimore/Washington International Airport, sent a letter on February 24, 1987, to every congressional office offering free valet parking to members and Hill rats: "We guarantee the availability of spaces for you . . . [and] we will make every effort to have your car started and warmed up by the time you arrive to pick it up." Washington associations also treat them well; every year the American League of Anglers and Boaters holds a champagne breakfast exclusively for Hill rats, and the Eastern Professional River Outfitters invites selected staffers to spend a day white-water rafting in West Virginia to "talk issues."

The Hill rat also enjoys countless lavish receptions. If you could freeze-frame your standard Capitol Hill reception, you would have a poster of a pond, complete with scum at the top. Let's say the event is sponsored by the National Association of Manufactured Widgets. Young people crowd the room, which means someone in Restaurant Supply passed the word that the NAMW bought the "A" menu. Forget cheese and crackers. We're talking two open bars, a live jazz band, and a long table in the middle of the room piled high with fruit, vegetables, and fine food. Across from the band sits another long table covered with ice on which are stacked fresh stone crab claws, shrimp, raw shucked oysters, and clams.

The NAMW's Washington representatives are slick. Whenever a member enters the room, the band pauses while he or she is escorted by the NAMW's president to a stirring round of applause. All eyes in the room rivet on the demigod who deigns to step down from Olympus to shake hands with mortals from Memphis and Tacoma and Dubuque. The rich food, of course, is only a loss leader. Buying, selling, trading, copying, and borrowing influence – all these are the universal spice at the banquet of politics.

The emphasis, moreover, placed on staff by the reception circuit and favor-seeking lobbyist is not misplaced. I once had breakfast with some Appropriations buddies, and the morning's topic was the book *Liar's Poker*. "The name comes from an incident in which a Wall Street bigwig bets one million dollars on a single hand of liar's poker," I explained.

One staffer hunched over his sausage and eggs and peered at me. "A mil? One lousy mil?" He grinned. "I can do *ten* mil with report language and not even have to ask the chairman." That may or may not have been true, but his disdain was palpable.

"But you don't get to keep it," I protested.

"Keep what?" he countered. "The money? Who cares about keeping the money? I'd rather be the one with the stones to power it through. They can keep their lousy one mil. It's a lot more fun to shove a *hundred* mil up someone's ass and then knock off for the rest of the day for a cold one."

Even the Internal Revenue Service pays tribute to the power of the Hill Rat. Every tax season, it opens an office in the Cannon House Office Building to personally assist members and staff to prepare their income taxes. It can get complicated; one newspaper survey in 1989 found that at least eighty-five members, including Democratic Majority Leader Richard Gephardt and Republican Minority Whip Newt Gingrich, dramatically raised the pay of their key Hill rats just before or just after they had gone on leave to work on the members' reelection campaigns.

Foreign governments get in the act, too. Philip Mosely, the Republican staff director of the House Ways and Means Committee, accepted trips from both the Taiwanese and the People's Republic of China in 1988. His wife Norah was, and is, his $41,624-a-year assistant. Expecting sympathy instead of raised eyebrows, Mosely described his overseas schedule to the *Austin American-Statesman* as "brutal."

Like their members, many Hill rats actively sought out speaking fees, or honoraria. In April 1989, Richard Sullivan, chief counsel of the House Public Works Committee, was paid $2,000 by a toxic waste disposal company to visit a plant. In 1989, Kevin Gottlieb, staff director of the Senate Banking Committee, made approximately thirty speeches at $600 apiece for an organization called Washington Campus. Gottlieb, in fact, earned more money in speaking fees in 1989 than U.S. senators were allowed to make. "I'm not shortchanging the committee," he told the *Washington Post*. "I'm good at what I do."

They are all good at what they do. Check out Capitol Hill at a quarter to nine on any given morning. The dark blue K cars are already appearing, each one chock-full of supplicants from the executive branch. Corporate lobbyists are popping out of their limos and taxicabs, $400 briefcases in hand. Concerned and earnest citizens wander about aimlessly as the subway disgorges its human cargo in waves.

In the midst of this great flotsam of democracy, the Hill rats truck in . They come in all shapes, sizes, races, sexes, and income brackets. But they have one thing in common. They all sport that "Christ-please-no-constituents-today" sneer, and they have that knowing walk, that here-I-come, ready-or-not, three-piece-suited swagger that says here be Hill rats, and they be bad.

But sometimes their Hill rat persona drops, and I see haunted, driven eyes as they scurry through the halls. We are the apprentice shamans of America's civic religion, hurling lightning bolts of fear and authority that bear the names of Founding Fathers, constitutional doctrines, and national saints. We legitimize the fundamentally irrational behavior of politicians by manipulating hallowed symbols and stories. So I wonder: Do they think inside? Are they like me? Do they think about these things as I do?

We pass looking, never seeing. I never ask, either, because Hill rats do not exist in a vacuum. Our behavior and attitudes take place within Capitol Hill's political culture in which, despite protestations, all of this is considered perfectly normal. . . .

I had this haunting dream.

Suddenly I am all the people who exist on America's margin – forty-year-old parking lot attendants, the elderly couple down the block who sweep lint out of apartment laundry rooms, people who write their congressmen about lost government checks without which they cannot eat. It is very cold and I have a baby in my arms. I have no blankets. Desperately, I tear through the closets, but they are empty. The baby shivers. Its cries weaken. I am helpless, overwhelmed by frustration, clawing against unseen enemies and cursing a God who could let this happen. . . .

I know from where the dream comes but I do not know why I only seem to remember it when I go down the Hill to the Democratic Club to find out what has happened to our heroes after the battles of the day.

The Democratic Club is three-and-a-half blocks away from the Capitol, adjacent to the Democratic National Committee complex and across the street from the power plant that provides electricity exclusively to Congress. There is steady foot-traffic up and down the Hill's slope between the club, congressional office buildings, and the Capitol itself.

The Democratic Club is private. But it opens its door to the greater Democratic community – members of Congress, Hill rats, lobbyists, political consultants, campaign officials, and similar species. Journalists are prohibited from joining or entering. No photographs can be taken, ever.

It is a place where the bar talk – if remembered or recorded – could be called the exercise of power by history. You can drop in for a hamburger and see people the public believes are leaders, or get from the lobbyists what Ernest Hemingway called the "true gen" – the inside skinny, the real score – on everything from the prospects of legislation to the latest rumors of leadership maneuverings. Later in the day, you can rub shoulders (from a respectful distance) with the floor managers of the day's legislation. If you strain to listen, you can hear their frontline reports of the debate and the voting: who stood with them, who betrayed the cause, who knuckled under to whom and for how much, how the powerful performed. Names like Gephardt and Panetta, Fazio and Murtha, Bonior, Obey, Wilson, and other temporary deities dominate the conversation. On one typical day, former Speaker of the House Thomas P.

"Tip" O'Neill held court at the table in front of the wine rack. To his right, a man complained to a woman about "the goddam commies giving up and sending all the defense contracts to hell." Two tables away, a black-suited short man stuck a large, equally black cigar between his teeth and smiled.

At the Club you sense that for all their sophistication, these hardened political operatives have a superstitious fear that something beyond the walls and out of their control might be "playing in Peoria" – that an issue or idea might be making an impact Out There. I have seen grown men – tough, no nonsense fixers who deal regularly with the highest officials in the nation – become despondent over newspaper headlines or reports from congressional sources about a flood of "real mail" on some issue. In Washington parlance, "real mail" comes from "real" people, those without a Washington-based political stake in the issue. Outside the Beltway, it is called public opinion.

You can tell the Democratic Club is an insider's place as soon as you walk in past the coat-check and manager's office: soft lighting, the coarse laughter of cronies, ironed dinner napkins and good silverware, darting eyes scanning the entranceway from every angle. Experienced Washington hands can eat an entire meal without looking each other in the eye, one person covering the front entrance and the other the dining area as they hold lengthy conversations, speaking past each other yet remembering it all. The seating is arranged expressly for this purpose. Photographs of all current Democratic committee chairmen are on the walls. Across from the entrance to the dining room and in front of the elevator are signs telling political action committee representatives and lobbyists which members are holding fundraising receptions in which rooms. The signs are changed daily.

The usual crowd of lobbyists will be at the bar, hidden from immediate view while they watch the House floor proceedings on C-SPAN, news on CNN, or a ball game. If the House is in session, members will take up positions at the bar or at tables in the dining room. Outside, their cars and drivers wait to take them to the floor if a vote is called. For those who cannot see the television behind the bar, a voice breaks onto the intercom, "Two bells recorded votes, two bells recorded vote, members have fifteen minutes to vote on . . ." The regulars' table, full at lunchtime, thins out later; stragglers head for the bar around 2:00 P.M. to play liar's poker. Years ago, at this bar I learned from an accomplished lobbyist the Hill's ancient admonition: "Money talks and bullshit walks."

Three-and-a-half blocks away, House Speaker Thomas Foley presides, a modern monarch unruffled by the intrigue of the restless lords below. More than geography separates us. The Speaker is praised, and rightly so, for restoring stability and ethics to an office badly tarnished by the Jim Wright scandal. But no one asks the Speaker what he had to do to earn $555,140 in political action committee contributions for election year 1988 alone. When Speaker Foley responded to President Bush's 1990 State of the Union message by proclaiming, "Let's be blunt about it: don't we all know there's too much money being raised and spent in American politics?" no eyebrows were raised. This is a town, after all, where you still have to hit all the right notes even when they give you an easy melody to sing for your supper.

But the Speaker has to understand, as I do, that at the end of any journey into the heart of politics lurks a Captain Kurtz–the emotive, irrational beast one rides at one's peril, but also, for those of us who have chosen the political path, general and foot soldier alike, because one must. This is one of the Hill's secrets: that all the fine latticework of policy elevated to the public spotlight is somehow hostage to one of the dark, eyeless, pulsating beasts of politics in the shadows below. Policy is interest, interest is politics, and politics is appetite in its rawest form imaginable.

I have always been struck by political scientists who search for statistical clues in voting patterns and computer-generated correlations of interest group support. They yearn to dehumanize politics, to pretend it is bloodless and has nothing to do with deals and anguish. But the political world in which I lived was a world of shadows and uncertainty, a place where right and wrong became genuinely as well as deliberately confused; it was a constant walk along a precipice where you were buffeted by fate as well as favor. . . .

And yet . . . and yet, despite it all, part of me loved this town and this Hill. Part of me sensed that the 1980s was our time for that luckiest sliver of the most affluent generation in history that found itself in the middle, to paraphrase a popular bank commercial of the time, of working for the most important people on the most important Hill in the most important city in the most important country in the world. We laughed at our vaunted insider's status, joked about it, dismissed it when necessary, but deep down, deep down we *knew* that for better or worse, this is where it was happening–and we were part of it.

And perhaps that is why I only remembered dreams of dying babies when I was at the Democratic Club. We were insiders to the point of losing touch with the outside and all the people in the "provinces," as one congressman termed it. Political battles are bloody only in an abstract sense. Those who wield the sword and shield of press release and fax machine never see the human consequences of their exertions. The Hill insulates and protects. There is no room in this inn for real flesh and blood, and certainly no stomach. The soul of Washington's political culture may well reside in places like the Democratic Club and countless other hideouts in this town–a soul slick and darting, and truly without mercy. . . .

A Democratic Club joke:

An explorer was heading upriver in the heart of the jungle. After a day of paddling his canoe, with the sun low on the horizon and the shadows lengthening, he spied a settlement and, before long, he tied up at the dock and sat down at the restaurant, surrounded by the usual mix of other explorers, smugglers, mercenaries, and the like. But one glance at the menu told him he was in cannibal country. The menu read:

Explorers	$ 5.25
Missionaries	$ 6.00
Doctors	$ 5.75
Members of Congress	$ 49.95

Puzzled at the extraordinarily high price for members of Congress, the explorer motioned to the maitre d' and said, "The prices for the first three seem reasonable, but why in the world are congressmen so incredibly expensive?"

The maitre d', taken aback, replied, "Ever tried cleaning one of them things?" . . .

. . . The real low of 1986 was reached on September 30, when a Scripps-Howard reporter arrived at the office to interview the congressman for the news service's "Take 10" project, designed to promote literacy by urging people to spend at least ten minutes a day reading. Reporters also interviewed members of Congress on their favorite books, and on their recent recreational reading.

"So what's [Texas Congressman Ron] Coleman been reading?" I jokingly asked Paul Rogers a couple of days before the interview. "Danielle Steele? Scotch bottle labels?"

He frowned. "Hell, I don't know," he said. "I'll call him."

He returned a little while later to tell me that Coleman liked history and biography.

"*Liked* history and biography?" I asked. "What good does that do? What has he *read*?"

"Well, he thinks he likes Churchill."

"Look, I know he likes the sound of history, biography, and Churchill, but what's he read – as in the names of the books?"

"Shit, I don't know."

"Okay, okay, I get the picture." This deal could turn real ugly if we did not get a handle on it quickly; we couldn't back out because we'd already committed to the interview.

The only one in the office with a liberal arts degree, I read and collect books on history, literature, classics, and politics, and I had a fairly extensive library at home. I returned the next day with a stack of volumes from which Rogers could choose Coleman's recent readings.

"Solzhenitsyn," I recommended strongly. "Gotta have *The Gulag Archipelago*. Big book, looks impressive, plus it's anticommunist in a big-time way. It'll look great for the conservatives."

"What if he's asked about it?"

"Don't worry. Reporters never read either. Plus I'll do cards."

"Okay. *Gulag's* okay."

"And Churchill. He likes Churchill, right? What about William Manchester's biography? Surely he knows enough about Churchill's life to talk his way out of any problems."

"Yeah, great. What else you got?"

We sifted through six or seven more volumes of history and biography and Paul picked out a couple more.

"Uh-oh," I said when we had finished. "The Bible."

"What about the Bible?"

"Should we include the Bible too?"

Paul hesitated for a moment, then shook his head. "No," he said. "They know him better than that."

I returned to my desk to type up little index card-sized book reports on each volume. *I'm going to burn in hell for this one,* I thought. Dirty deeds, as the song goes, and they're done dirt cheap.

The reporter arrived the next morning. My books were stacked just so on the congressman's desk. She asked him a general question about reading.

"My love of reading began at an early age . . ." he started to say—or read, more precisely, because he had placed a set of general talking points I had written on the desk blotter in front of him. "You know, I can't remember a time when I *wasn't* reading . . ."

I cringed. Then I looked up. The reporter was busily writing down everything the congressman was saying.

"As the father of an infant son, I hope to pass on my own love of reading to him someday . . ."

Atta boy, atta boy, I silently cheered. *Use that devotion to family and children.* Now wrap it up . . .

"Reading and literacy are the keys to everything else in life." He smiled, leaned forward, and casually but expertly shuffled the talking points into another stack of papers. "Any questions?"

QUESTIONS TO THINK ABOUT

1. What is "retail politics," as practiced by Lyndon Johnson in his earliest years in Washington? Do politicians still use this approach successfully today?

2. What does Abourezk admire about Senator Eastland? What variety of attitudes toward Eastland do you think existed among his Senate colleagues? Do you see a relationship between Eastland's political views and his relaxed personal manner?

3. Mention the aspects of congressional life that young staffer Bisnow admired? What did he dislike about a representative's job?

4. How effective is Senate Republican leader Robert Dole in establishing rapport with other politicians, with staff, and with important interest groups? What techniques does he use to relate to people?

5. Overall, how does Jackley feel about his years working as a "Hill rat" in Washington? Does he admire politicians? How does he compare the "inside-the-beltway" world of places like the Democratic Club with the real world of average Americans outside the beltway?
6. How much responsibility is given to staffers for actual policy making, according to Jackley?
7. How might you account for the drastically different assessments of life as a young congressional staffer provided by Bisnow and by Jackley? Whose view do you believe is closer to the truth?

CRITIC'S CORNER

" THE GOOD NEWS, CONGRESSMAN, IS YOU RANK AHEAD OF LAWYERS IN THE LATEST POLL — THE BAD NEWS IS YOU RANK BELOW COCKROACHES."

What reasons does this cartoon suggest for the lowly standing of members of Congress in the public's mind? How are "pork," bounced checks, red ink, and taxes related to congressional incumbency? Do you feel that "Rep. N. Cumbent" is a typical legislator in his attitude toward public service?

7 | The Presidency

The American president and the staff around him are serious people engaged in serious business. The official statements, speeches, press conferences, and meetings all transmit a sense of weightiness. More tangible evidence of the pressure on the president is in pictures before and after his term: grayed hair, lined face, and aged posture testify to the burdens that the office places on its holder. Each senator and member of Congress is one among 535. Black robes and life tenure give Supreme Court justices protection from the public eye. The president stands alone, constantly in the spotlight of public attention.

Although sometimes it's easy to forget they exist, certain vice presidents grab the spotlight, too, and not always in the best way. From the time of his selection to run for vice president, President Bush's choice of young Indiana senator Dan Quayle provoked much controversy as well as praise. Garry Wills highlights the problems that haunted Quayle as a holder of high national office. W. Lance Bennett uncovers the collegian Quayle going to see *The Candidate*, a movie that had a deep and lasting impact on the young political science major.

The spouses of presidents provide moments of levity and of gravity. Do you remember the stories about Nancy Reagan's consultations with an astrologer? Peter Hay's fascinating collection of anecdotes about "presidents' ladies" seems terribly sexist – it is about "their childhood, education, romance, marriage, family life, political and charitable activities, and their role as hostesses to the leaders of the world." Maybe, though, it's not Hay's book that is sexist. "Presidential ladies" have often accepted stereotypical traditional female roles. Eleanor Roosevelt, wife of President Franklin Roosevelt, was certainly an exception, Hay discovers.

Who answers the phone when Americans dial (202) 456-1414? The White House is manned by many volunteers who take phone calls from citizens in distress, channel mail to the right offices, answer letters, and catalog gifts. The people who show up for work each day at the White House are the subject of Bradley Patterson's research.

Finally, back to the serious men in the serious office: Fawn Brodie explores Thomas Jefferson's college years; Fitzhugh Green describes George Bush's youth; and Charles Allen and Jonathan Portis discuss the young Bill Clinton. Almost two hundred years apart, the portraits of Jefferson, Bush, and Clinton show three very different personalities who attained the pinnacle of power in America.

Garry Wills
"Late Bloomer"

Can one, at this point, disentangle Dan Quayle from Dan Quayle jokes? He seems to induce a short attention span in others, leaving them stunned with a serene vacancy. The *New Republic* has penalized with mock awards people who are foolhardy enough to speak well of him. Can anyone be taken seriously who takes Quayle seriously?

As the polls show, Quayle has not recovered from the way he was shoved into the public arena under a rain of blows. Gallup reported last month that 54% of the public – including 43% of Republicans – said he is not qualified to be President; 49% thought Bush should pick a new running mate for '92. . . .

If he seemed for much of his life unaffected by the world around him, that may have been an advantage, considering the world he lived in. He avoided the Viet Nam War, but he also ignored much that led to Viet Nam. Inattentiveness is sometimes a survival skill. . . .

One of Quayle's college professors has an indelible memory of trying to make a point with Quayle, and talking into air. "I looked into those blue eyes, and I might as well have been looking out the window," says William Cavanaugh. . . .

Is Quayle serene merely because he is vacuous, preferring drift to ideology? That view obliges one to explain how, in politics, he drifted often and early to the top. Even his friends admit that his success was not by any blaze of intellect. Says M. Stanton Evans, the ex-editor of the Indianapolis *News,* who helped Quayle get his first political appointment: "There is a cycle in all of his offices. When he comes in, he is underestimated – too young, too inexperienced – and then he surpasses people's expectations." In other words, Quayle first gets the job and then gets qualified for it. But for a politician, getting the job is the primal qualification. How did he succeed at that? The only answer his critics have been able to come up with is a false one – family influence.

Influence should have counted at DePauw University, an old Methodist school in northern Indiana with loyal alumni and great institutional pride. Quayle was a third-generation Pulliam at the school, a member of the same fraternity (Delta Kappa Epsilon) to which his grandfather [publisher Eugene Pulliam], father and uncle had belonged. His grandfather founded the national journalism fraternity Sigma Delta Chi at DePauw, gave the school many bequests and served on its board. There was a Pulliam Chair in History until just before Dan's arrival on campus. "If I had known he was a Pulliam," says Ted Katula, the athletic director who was Quayle's golf coach, "that would have impressed me. Pulliams are big here. I didn't learn he was one till he was running for Congress." Yet Katula was the member of the university staff Quayle saw the most. Little was made of Quayle's being a Pulliam because few people knew it. He did not bring the subject up. In his experience, family ties were as much a source of division as advantage.

Quayle got special treatment at DePauw in one provable case: he graduated with a major in politics without taking the required course in political theory. When he flunked the theoretical parts of the final exam, he was given a special exam without those parts. He was one of two students for whom this was done that year, and the common denominator in their case is not family (the other man was not a Pulliam) but a quarrel between the department head and the teacher of political theory over the size and kind of assignments given in the course. The two students had dropped the class when there were protests that the teacher, newly arrived from Harvard, had too long a reading list, protests the department head energetically backed. If other teachers went easy on Quayle, it was because he is the kind of person for whom people like to do favors. They were just doing what George Bush would later do on a colossal scale.

Quayle, who has refused to release his college and law school transcripts, was certainly no student at DePauw. The teachers who disliked him did so because he was good at getting by on charm. He was serious only about golf, a family passion instilled in him during the long Arizona days of his adolescence. . . .

There had not been much war protest on the DePauw campus by the time Quayle graduated in 1969. Quayle's father was writing editorials backing the war in Viet Nam, but his son was not paying attention. As graduation approached, Quayle had to do some shopping around to find an opening in the National Guard. . . .

During his service in the Guard through much of the academic year 1969-70, Quayle decided he did indeed want to study the law. Admission would not be easy after his admittedly poor academic performance at DePauw, but here a personal contact *was* helpful. He knew the admissions director of the Indiana University law school in Indianapolis – through his family, as he knew most older people. This admissions director, Kent Frandsen, was a judge in the little town of Lebanon, outside Indianapolis. Another prominent citizen there was

Quayle's grandmother, Martha Pulliam, who was given the Lebanon paper as her own in the divorce. (She was the one Quayle would live with.) Frandsen gave Quayle a break, something he was doing for many others at the time. The night school was expanding its enrollment – it would move into a new and larger building in 1970 – and Frandsen had a summer program to try out marginal cases. Quayle, out of school for a year, went into that program. . . .

Structurally, Quayle's position with Bush, a man never quite accepted by the right as "one of our own," is that of Nixon with Eisenhower – bridge to the right, voice of the right, pacifier of the right. In the latter role he has already been criticized by the *National Review* and conservative columnist Eric Breindel. It is a high-risk position, since reflex anticommunism is not the right-wing glue it was before Mikhail Gorbachev. Quayle has treated changes in the Soviet Union as suspect, while saying he does not differ from the President (the refrain against which all Vice Presidents must play their own tunes). Quayle is loyal to individuals, as he showed in the Senate in 1986 by his frantic efforts to win a judgeship for Daniel Manion (whose written opinions were more embarrassing than Quayle's spur-of-the-moment inanities); but he does not play to lose. If Bush wants to get rid of Quayle, he may get as little cooperation as Eisenhower got from Nixon. . . .

During the 1988 campaign, people wondered about Quayle's actions (and even his whereabouts) in the Viet Nam War. But the startling thing is that, if he inherited the Oval Office tomorrow, Quayle would be the first President since World War II who did not serve in the military during *that* war. Even Jimmy Carter, the U.S. President of most recent birth (1924), was a Navy cadet during the war. Not only was Quayle born after the war – the first baby boomer so near the top – he is also the first man to have grown up entirely within the confines of the modern conservative movement. He was surprisingly unscarred by that (or any) experience when Bush chose him. Quayle claimed John Kennedy was just as young in 1960; but Kennedy had known prewar Europe as well as the wartime Pacific.

Stan Evans traces an arc in Quayle's career of rising (if belatedly) to expectations. The angle of the arc must now go up, dramatically. Quayle was born not only roughly a quarter-century after any preceding President; he spent another quarter-century blissfully AWOL from history. His press secretary, David Beckwith, calls the Vice President a "classic late bloomer" – which means that the first three decades or so of his life do not matter, just the last decade. That is starting late even for a faster learner than Quayle has given evidence of being. How can he "rise to expectations" when the U.S. can expect all the troubles of a world coming out of the cold war, and when the person doing the rising came in with the cold war himself? That is why, for all the jokes, we must take Dan Quayle seriously. We must do so, because Bush did not.

W. Lance Bennett
From *The Governing Crisis*

Given the present course [of electoral politics], it is not too farfetched to imagine the ideal candidate of the future being selected precisely for a lack of ideas, the absence of strong personal character, and a corresponding willingness to be scripted, directed, and marketed down to the last detail. This is a frightening possibility, but it is not absurd. In this connection, Dan Quayle, the man the polls have repeatedly featured as America's worst nightmare in the presidency, comes immediately to mind. Larry Sabato, a political scientist concerned about the growing impact of media control and candidate marketing on the democratic process, reports a story attributed to Quayle's best friend in college. Quayle and his friend had gone to see Robert Redford in *The Candidate,* which is a film about an attractive but directionless politician who is packaged and marketed all the way to the presidency. In Sabato's account, "The friend reported that Quayle said it was the greatest film he had ever seen, and Quayle was so exited about it that they talked for eleven hours straight after the movie. Of course, this movie became in some respects the story of Dan Quayle's life. Upon hearing of Quayle's fascination with *The Candidate,* the film's screenwriter, Jeremy Larner, tried to point out that real-life candidate Quayle had failed to grasp the whole point of the movie. In Larner's words, "I am amazed to have inspired Dan Quayle. Inspiring such candidates was not our intention and I don't think [he] understood our movie. . . . [He] missed the irony. Unless, in a way we never could have foreseen, [he *is*] the irony."

Whether or not The Candidate of the future turns out to be Dan Quayle, the moral of the story remains the same. Failing to grasp the point of a simple movie may not be a liability in the candidate of the future. To the contrary, it may represent a great advantage, rendering the candidate wholly malleable and uncompromisingly marketable. Indeed, this sort of Frankenstein fantasy may have crossed the minds of political consultants who may be tempted to test the limits of their art. Sabato suggests, for example, that George Bush's surprising choice of Quayle as a running mate came largely at the urging of Bush's managers: "It's pretty well known that George Bush did not have a close and continuing relationship with Dan Quayle; they didn't know each other very well. So how did the Quayle pick happen? Well, Bob Teeter, Bush's pollster, and Roger Ailes, his media consultant, had both handled Dan Quayle's previous congressional campaigns in Indiana. And they knew just how attractive and malleable Dan Quayle was. . . . It's clear that not only did they put his name on the list, but at least in the case of Roger Ailes, they became advocates for the candidate." In this view, the only trouble with such perfect media candidates is that "they may be better at running for office than governing." This only appears to be a problem, I suppose, if one insists on some nostalgic link between elections and the idea of government.

Peter Hay
From *All the Presidents' Ladies*

Eleanor Roosevelt . . . took immediate steps to broaden the social spectrum of her [White House] invitees list. Some functions remained exclusive, such as the movie-stars luncheons or the one organized by Cabinet wives for the Senate ladies. But she also gave enormous tea parties, instituting what the staff called "the double-header tea." Whereas her predecessors were content with having on a few occasions a few hundred people for the whole afternoon, Mrs. Roosevelt thought nothing of inviting four or five hundred people for 4:00 P.M. and another group of the same size for 5:00 P.M. She also invited people from many different walks of life, something that did not entirely please the Washington social elite. Chief Butler Fields repeats a story circulating during the early days of the Roosevelt era about a lady who had been invited to a White House reception and consequently had let her maid have the afternoon off. In the receiving line just ahead of her she was astonished to see her maid, who had received a separate invitation. The society matron suddenly was seized with malaise and left in a hurry. . . .

In 1946 Eleanor Roosevelt took her friend, the attorney Fanny Holtzmann, across the Hudson from Hyde Park to the Wiltwyck School for Boys. The school at Esopus was an interracial center for troubled youngsters that was one of Mrs. Roosevelt's favorite causes. As Edward Berkman narrates in his biography of Fanny Holtzmann, Mrs. Roosevelt believed in getting her hands dirty:

Arriving at the school, Mrs. Roosevelt was instantly surrounded by a dozen small residents, mostly black. Every one of them was clamoring for her attention – and, Fanny noticed, every one of them got it. The former First Lady addressed each boy by name, bestowing a word of praise here, a smile of recognition there.

Then she led Fanny through rickety halls into the main dormitory. Bedding was in wild disarray. One corner was a jumble of old baseball gloves, leftover bicycle parts, and discarded clothes. From the lavatory beyond came a powerful stench of small boys in their most casual manifestations.

Mrs. Roosevelt noticed Fanny's dismay. "We have a hard time getting help from Harlem. Nobody wants to look after deprived problem children; it's pleasanter to work in the sunny kitchens of the wealthy. Actually, this doesn't smell any different from a dormitory at an exclusive boarding school. Little boys are all alike."

She went to a closet and took out cleaning equipment: pail, mop, scrub brush. Fanny, at her elbow, inquired if she could help.

"My dear, it looks to me as if you're about to throw up. But you can give me a hand changing these sheets. I'll take care of the rest."

Together they replaced several soiled bed sheets. Then the President's widow moved on into the lavatory, where, dropping to her hands and knees, she methodically scrubbed the floor.

It was a scene Fanny would never forget, "an act of humility, responsibility, love. There, in that washroom for forgotten little boys, I felt in the presence of greatness."

Bradley Patterson
From *The Ring of Power*

The White House Telephone Operators

In 1878 it was "the Executive Mansion" and its newly installed telephone number was 1. More than a century later, the famous number, 202-456-1414, is receiving 48,000 calls a day, with peaks as high as 136,000 (when U.S. aircraft bombed Libya). Some twenty operators, including an all-night shift, staff the main switchboard in the Executive Office Building. They are professionals in their high-tension work; one chief operator retired in 1978 after twenty-nine years of service. At their fingertips is a file (going back to the Roosevelt administration) of ten thousand VIP names; any person who is in the news is a candidate for inclusion.

The White House operators are accorded the special privilege of being able to interrupt a connection anywhere, and they are famous for locating the sought-after recipient of a VIP phone call wherever he or she is in the world. The first position operator handles the president's calls, one of her first concerns being the authentication of people who call in to speak to the chief executive. The caller is put on hold while offices or spouses are checked for verification; the call is then logged for name and time.

Smaller switchboards are usually set up at presidential retreats, such as Johnson's ranch in Texas, and operators flown out to staff them. "I always kept a change of clothes in a bag" remembered one veteran of eighteen years of duty.

Caroline Kennedy (at age five) called and asked to speak to Santa Claus. With the help of a gruff-voiced gent in the Transportation Office, the call was completed, and she told him of her Christmas wish list. "John-John wants a helicopter," she is reported to have added; "he sees his daddy using one all the time."

Crank calls, children's calls, president's calls, all part of the working day.

One night after midnight, the president's light went on; Kennedy had one question: "Where can I find a can opener?"

The Volunteer and Comment Office

As chief of state, the president is "president of all the people," say the textbooks, and it appears that more and more of the people themselves are discovering this axiom. By the 1970s, the White House switchboard operators were becoming swamped with calls from the general public. The Nixon staff designed a supplementary answering system; volunteers were invited to come to the White House to help answer the thousands of public queries. The idea worked; like other White House staff innovations, the successful initiative of the seventies has now become a standard service. The White House staff today finds itself augmented by five hundred men and women who, as regular volunteers, help the president, with little other reward than their own pride of service.

The volunteers are typically supporters of the president; a new group – equally indispensable – would join up after a turnover inauguration. They are organized in the Volunteer and Comment Office, where a director and two assistants mobilize the principal volunteer activities: answering public calls and addressing and mailing presidential cards.

Twenty cubicles have been built into a ground-floor room of the Executive Office Building. Several of them are staffed daily by volunteers who donate their time one or two days a week. On the nights of presidential speeches or press conferences, all twenty phones are covered to handle the flood of calls. A separate telephone number, 202-456-7639, has been listed to lead directly to this office; during Reagan's time, some evangelical television stations displayed it during their broadcasts, urging viewers to "call to say you love the president!" They did. In fact on any typical day, five hundred calls are received by the Volunteer and Comment Office. 252,000 came in during 1986.

But love is not their only sentiment. Most of the callers comment on current issues, supporting or disagreeing with the president. "We are delighted to have your opinion," they are told, and the numbers of calls are carefully tallied: from what state, what issue, pro or con. Monthly totals are shown to the president. Many ask questions: "Why is the flag at half-staff today?"; "Has the White House always been white?" – and the volunteers consult their reference sources. A few threaten the president (the Secret Service handles these).

On some issues, hundreds will use identical wording – evidence that a campaign is being mounted. Most of the callers ask to speak to the president; he is the White House, he is their president. "I gave my dollar to his campaign; surely he can talk with me!"

Some sixty a day call with personal problems. They may be elderly or lonely, confused in what they perceive as a complicated and impersonal society. They telephone the White House and, fortunately, find themselves talking to a friendly voice.

The toughest of all to handle are the people in urgent need, men and women who are sick, jobless, homeless, with no money, no food – they call the White House as the nation's parsonage of last resort. The volunteers try to suggest federal, state, or local resources that are available – such as churches and charities. They are always sympathetic, sometimes motherly. "I have four kids myself," one will say. If, in spite of sympathy or referrals, the caller's problem seems insoluble and if the emergency can be identified as legitimate (a few are recognized as repeaters), the volunteers make up a "hardship case" note that is passed to a special desk at the White House (see below). In each day, typically, six such cases are recorded.

The volunteers will give out their first names but never their last (they don't want such calls at home). They don't say they are volunteers, with the result that some citizens upbraid them: "Why are they paying you if you can't help me?"

There is warm satisfaction when a hardship case is solved. One night a grandfather called from an Appalachian state; his daughter's baby had diarrhea, was dehydrating, had been refused admission at the local hospital. The Volunteer and Comment Office telephoned the hospital manager ("What? The White House?") and arranged for the baby's admission. They then called the grandfather and told him to have his grandchild taken to the hospital. When they called the hospital the next morning, the baby had improved.

The second principal volunteer contribution is arranging for presidential greeting cards – Birthdays over eighty (especially centennials), golden wedding anniversaries, graduations, marriages, Gold and Eagle Scout awards – to citizens young and old; the president is the nation's pastor. In a tradition going back decades, he greets, encourages, and congratulates his flock. In 1986 he and the first lady reached out, in this pastoral role, 604,000 times. . . .

The Correspondence Office

Write the president! . . .

Some letters come in foreign languages (they are sent to State), a few in Braille (with help from the Department of Health and Human Services they are answered in Braille); visitors, especially children, leave notes behind after their White House tours.

A staff of ninety-one White House and twenty-eight Postal Service employees, helped each day by volunteers, refer some of this deluge to departments and agencies; the White House itself, however, responds in a volume that also spirals up each year. In some cases, acknowledgment cards are used (219,000 in 1985), and in response to children a special booklet is sent (189,000). In 1985 the director of correspondence signed 119,842 letters; 53,091 bore the president's signature.

About thirty letters a week – representative of the variety – are pulled from the enormous intake and sent to the president. Reagan, a softy for warm human stories, on occasion took up yellow paper and pen and scrawled personal answers; after they were typed, he would often add a written postscript, might even include a personal check in a hardship situation.

Much of the White House mail is exuberant – the folks want the president to know of their happiness as well as their problems. On the wall of the Correspondence Office are five bulletin boards, every square inch of them jammed with snapshots of weddings, new babies, and anniversaries. The thousands of smiling little pictures are a daily reminder to the beleaguered correspondence staffers: the president is National Friend, sharer of joys as well as of tribulations.

Can any White House staff do justice to such a numbing volume? The Correspondence Office is confident it can, and proud of doing so – even 8 million times a year.

Presidential Letters and Messages

If events or personages deserve greater recognition than the printed card of presidential greetings, robotyped letters or even specially drafted messages are furnished – these, too, being part of the pastoral role of the American presidency. Many of the 19,000 nonprofit organizations in the nation sent in requests; they arrive at the rate of 750 a month. The more attention the letter or message will attract, however, the greater is the need for careful staff checking before the presidential signature is added. There are rules and limits; none are sent to judges, for example, or to fund-raisers; commercial events are taboo. The counsel or the national security assistant often must review both the request and the message itself. Unfortunately, there are individuals or groups who try to manipulate the message tradition for selfish purposes. They are foiled only by meticulous and mature review; the two most recent staff members who have had the message-preparation responsibility served eighteen and twenty-two years respectively. Even the best of screening can fail; on one occasion a message of greeting to a testimonial dinner for a mafioso was caught only by President Johnson personally just before he signed it.

The rules, of course, can be bent. A codification of the proprieties for messages was set forth in the Eisenhower administration, which had this paragraph near its end:

> Because the White House is located on the growing fringe of precedent, and because the President is a human being – with a heart much bigger than protocol or policy – he can make exceptions to all the above rules and regulations. He can write a little girl who has lost her cat. He can write a golfer who can't control his slice. He can write anyone, anywhere, for any purpose – and the addressee is always delighted.

On perhaps six hundred occasions each month, the specially drafted greetings are dispatched to organizations or events that meet the criteria. A staff of eight supports this contemporary extension of a long-observed presidential tradition.

The gracious presidential favor of yesterday, however, may have become the mere routine of today. A veteran of the message business asks the recurring question: do messages that issue at a six-hundred-a-month clip signal "the ticky-tacky presidency?" Has the pastoral tradition become too "canned," too manufactured? An even more troubling question is raised at the same time: has the auto pen to too great an extent replaced the president's hand?

The "Agency Liaison Office"

Masked under this prosaic label, five staff members in an Executive Office Building room personify the latest and most elaborate extension of the pastoral presidency. To them are given the hardship cases – those requests scrawled in letters, those taken down from the telephone calls. *In extremis,* hundreds of desperate people write or call the president; for them he is the ultimate ombudsman.

The agency liaison staffers' first recourse is to refer such a hardship case to one of the Cabinet departments, or to state agencies, or to local organizations in the needy person's hometown. Each referral is registered in a computer, as is every departmental or White House action taken. The White House aides will often locate and telephone the individual citizens, get more of their stories firsthand, find out what efforts they have already made to help themselves. Repeated writers and those "milking the system" are easily identified, but the cases of real need are kept current until some answer is provided.

A twelve-year-old Indian boy wrote that his father, a veteran, was out of work; the White House discovered that a Labor Department contractor was looking for just the kind of skill his father had. A street-cleaner called; someone had stolen his broom. The agency liaison staffers found a local charity to get him a new one. On Christmas Eve, a family called from Denver; they were living in an automobile. The White House called the Salvation Army, who aided the family and helped the father find work. They later came to Washington to thank the White House staffers personally. A woman whose power was cut off was found to be owed thirty thousand dollars by a state disability office that was slow in processing her papers; a call from the White House pushed the state officials into action. A woman in Mississippi had her power cut off; the White House found a local minister who ran an extension cord from a neighbor's house. When the police objected, asking who authorized the plug-in, the answer was "the White House."

"Case work" of this sort has long been a staple of congressional offices. Now those offices themselves are referring their most intractable emergencies to the White House, which helped to push the total number of cases handled by the "Agency Liaison Office" in 1986 to 49,039, 27,000 more than in 1985.

The Gifts Unit

There was a "black hole of Calcutta" once, and it was in the White House itself. It was the joking term for the storage area underneath the Cabinet Room where gifts to President Truman had piled up – "so many we didn't know what to do with them," one aide remembered.

Today the facilities are different, but the tradition of sending gifts to the president continues. To the same president who is "pastor," his "flock" is generous. Some nine thousand gifts flood into the White House each year. What can be accepted, however, is limited by the laws, and by the Constitution itself.

It is the Gifts Unit that receives every incoming gift, registers it, judges its acceptability, arranges for the note of thanks, and sends the donation to its next destination. Eight staff members handle this delicate assignment; one alumna of this office served for twenty years; another was on the White House staff from Coolidge to Kennedy.

Gifts from foreign governments are considered as being presented not personally to the president but to the nation. If they are of more than "minimal value" (currently defined as $165) they may be displayed temporarily in the White House but then are sent to the National Archives to be part of a presidential museum or for disposal. The president and first lady received 121 such gifts in 1985, 67 in 1986; the list is made public annually by the Department of State.

Gifts from private citizens arrive from everywhere in the world, principally of course from American admirers. Exactly 9,491 came to the White House in 1986. If a president has a hobby, he is deluged with gifts suitable to it. The Reagans were sent horses and boots, the Fords skis and ski clothing; Johnson was given dozens of pairs of cowboy boots, Vice President Bush got boxes of jogging shoes. Most private gifts are redonated or returned; if they are kept and are worth more than a hundred dollars, they are reported to the Office of Government Ethics, which makes the list public.

If there are children or grandchildren in the president's immediate family, toys come in by the hundreds. In 1954 toymaker Louis Marx sent over eight hundred to Eisenhower for his grandchildren; they were donated to charities in Washington and to Secret Service agents with kids.

Whoever he is, without regard to politics, thousands of Americans regard their president with benevolence and affection. An elderly gentleman wills the president his cherished grandfather clock; an excited fisherman puts his prize catch on ice and sends it to the White House. (Unfortunately, all food is destroyed unless it comes from close friends.)

Less benevolent are gifts with a selfish purpose, for business promotion or advertising, or that could give even the appearance of exploitation. The Gifts Unit calls on the counsel to help spot donations that might cause embarrassment.

For the Gifts Unit, interwoven with their never-ending judgments about laws, regulations, and proprieties, are threads of warmth and humor. Staff members come back from foreign or domestic trips loaded down with presents pressed into their hands. "Glad you visited our school today," said one donor, "Love from Andy." Which school? Who was Andy? The Gifts Unit would be sleuths so that the proper thank-you could be sent.

A retired nun knitted President Ford a ski cap, which he kept. Seeing him wearing it, on a television news clip, the donor was worried that it looked too tight. A letter came in with her further instructions: he should wet it and let it set on his head until dry.

Among the hundreds of pets sent in (they are never destroyed, always donated elsewhere), one admirer sent Nixon a fancy, live rabbit. The Gifts Unit called the zoo; yes, they would take the bunny, but please let them know ahead of time when the White House van would come; if the rabbit got mixed up with their other small animals, it would get fed to the pythons! . . .

The Executive Residence

"The White House" of pictures and tourists, the famous mansion has a problem: It may be famous for too much. It is a home, for husband and wife, children, grandparents, grandchildren, guests, and pets (including ponies). It is also a museum of American history and culture, an exhibition gallery, a collection of presidential furnishings, a magnet for tourists, and a secure redoubt. The Residence has seen service as a wartime map and command post, a wedding chapel, a funeral parlor, a nursery, and a church. Today it is simultaneously a backdrop for TV productions, a press-conference auditorium, a concert hall, and a banquet center (75,000 were served there in 1980). The mansion or parts of it serve as a flower stall, performing-arts center, physical fitness emporium, Easter-egg-rolling yard, movie theater, heliport, parade ground, carpentry shop, art gallery, library, arboretum, clinic, office building, conference center, and sophisticated communications hub. (Some reports allege that it is a missile base as well, though officials there deny it.)

Can the same place meet all these demands? Its staff do their damnedest.

The chief usher is the manager of the Executive Residence. While all who work there serve at the pleasure of the president, the entire staff is proud of its tradition of being career professionals. There have been only five chief ushers since 1891; the staff average has been twenty years of service on the job, and two recent employees served forty-four years apiece.

The staff inside the Residence numbers ninety-three; in addition, thirty-six National Park Service experts take care of the grounds and manage the outlying greenhouse and storage warehouse. Volunteers help arrange cut flowers and decorate the Residence at Christmas.

The food-service group, led by world-class chefs, is augmented by contract help to serve a state dinner's thirteen tables of ten (the thirteenth table is called Number 14), or, as has happened at least twice, a South Lawn outdoor sit-down dinner for thirteen hundred (they were under tents and each of those dinners required setting out thirty-seven thousand pieces of tableware.) Twelve work-years of overtime are included in the mansion's $5.4 million budget, but many thousands of hours beyond that are gifts to the United States from a staff whose dedication is legendary. "When I hired them," commented one former supervisor, "I said, 'Don't plan on celebrating any anniversaries or birthdays with your family.' " They have no job descriptions; the unpredictable is routine. Are the cut rosebuds not sufficiently unfolded? Some warm whiffs from a hair dryer will get them ready for the party. Does orange pollen from the lilies stain white uniforms? Fetch towels and shake out each bloom before the guests arrive.

Some presidents have brought personal servants, but no staff now live in the mansion, nor are they responsible for any of the president's out-of-town residences. Presidential overnight guests at the White House are personal; visiting chiefs of state usually stay at Blair House across the street.

Close to the north foyer, the usher's small office is crammed with noiseless reminders of both the present and the past. A digital screen flashes the location of each member of the first family; computer terminals blink out the details of the fine-art collections, menus, supplies, and the budget. But above them on the wall hangs a piece of charred wood from the British fire of 1814.

"The growing fringe of precedent" is everywhere in the White House, and the old mansion almost trembles under its new uses. The East Room floor, new in 1950, was nearly worn through by 37 million tourists when it was relaid in 1978. In a recent musicale, heretofore the occasion for decorum and calm, the usher counted 27 two-person Minicam news teams.

Events started by one president become "traditions," hard if not impossible to change. The Easter egg roll is now a "tradition" (30,000 tots and parents scramble in), so are the spring and fall garden tours (15,000 inspect the blooms), as well as the three nights of candlelight tours each Christmas (20,000 view the decorations).

For each press conference, the technical crews monopolize the East Room, jamming the stately ballroom with mikes and lights. The hosting of a huge outdoor dinner means resodding the lawn. The helicopter blades whoosh the petals off the spring flowers.

Can the new presidency preserve the old graciousness? The mansion staff's loyalties run in two directions: to serve the house's masters who are there, and at the same time to stand in trust for a revered place that belongs to all the American generations.

Fawn M. Brodie
From *Thomas Jefferson: An Intimate History*

As it turned out, the holiday season of 1759 was a significant time for decisions. After consulting on New Year's Day with his mother's cousin, Peter
Randolph, he [Jefferson] decided to go to William and Mary College. . . .

Once installed in Williamsburg, where he matriculated surprisingly late in
the spring, March 25, 1760, he was quickly caught up in a circle of young people, where pairing off and passionate exchanges of confidence were commonplace. It was not only the young men and women who delighted in the company
of this tall, sandy-haired youth, with an imperturbable temper, evident kind-
ness, and slight shyness with its hint of vulnerability. Older men too were captivated.

William Small, professor of mathematics and natural philosophy, one of the
seven men who made up the faculty, was a Scot with an instinct for smelling
out greatness. Later, in England, where he went to study medicine after a bureaucratic dispute with the college authorities, he would number among his
friends Erasmus Darwin, James Watt, Joseph Priestley, and Josiah Wedgwood.
During Jefferson's first year at William and Mary, Small taught him rhetoric,
belles-lettres, and ethics as well as mathematics and natural philosophy. Almost
at once he discovered or generated in the young student a fervor for learning.
Nor was the attraction one-sided, as Jefferson recorded with pleasure at sev-
enty-seven in his *Autobiography:* "It was my great good fortune, and what
probably fixed the destinies of my life, that Dr. William Small of Scotland, was
the Professor of Mathematic, a man profound in most of the useful branches of
science, with a happy talent of communication, correct and gentlemanly man-
ners, and an enlarged and liberal mind. He, most happily for me, became soon
attached to me, and made me his daily companion when not engaged in the
school; and from his conversation I got my first views of the expansion of science, and of the system of things in which we are placed."

Jefferson wrote to one friend that Small was "as a father" to him. And in a
graceful and grateful phrase he pointed out that Small "filled up the measure
of his goodness to me" by introducing him to two good friends, George Wythe,
who became his law teacher, and Francis Fauquier, British governor of Virginia colony – in Jefferson's words, "the ablest man who ever filled that office."
There developed an extraordinary friendship. Fauquier, "Dr. Small and Mr.
Wythe, his *amici omnium horarum* [friends of all hours] and myself," Jefferson
wrote, "formed a *partie quarée,* and to the habitual conversations on these occasions I owed much instruction." . . .

Fauquier was happy to have the gifted young fiddler play in his weekly con-
certs, and he soon found Jefferson rewarding also in other respects. At their
frequent dinners together with Small and Wythe, Jefferson wrote, "I have

heard more good sense, more rational and philosophical conversation than in all my life besides."

Small returned to England in 1764; Jefferson never saw him again, and it is not certain if Small wrote to him. But when the Revolution broke out, Jefferson felt compelled to explain his own position, and this letter has come down to us. Writing to Small on May 7, 1775, he deplored the Battle of Lexington, fought by "our brethren of Boston," against the King's troops, noting that a "phrenzy of revenge seems to have seized all ranks of people." Like a good patriot, however, he deplored King George's "incendiary" declarations and "haughty deportment." Then to make clear that for him their cherished friendship was in no way impaired by the political dissensions, he sent six dozen bottles of Madeira – on two different boats to insure their arrival – Madeira he had kept aging in his cellar for eight years. Thus he expressed his gratitude, and demonstrated what would be a lifelong habit for keeping his friendships in repair.

Fauquier died after a lingering illness in March 1768, before the Revolution could strain his friendship with Jefferson. Scientifically curious to the end, uncertain of the cause of his own "tedious" illness, he provided in his will that his body might be dissected for the benefit of medicine. It was not done. Of the uncommon trio comprising Jefferson's mentors in college, only Wythe was left. By every standard he was the most important. Jefferson described Wythe in his *Autobiography* as "my faithful and beloved mentor in youth, and my most affectionate friend through life." In letters to friends he was more explicit, calling Wythe "my second father," "my antient master, my earliest & best friend" to whom "I am indebted for first impressions which have had the most salutary influence on the course of my life."

Wythe was a fine Greek and Latin scholar, and when at thirty-five he accepted the nineteen-year-old Jefferson as a law student, he was one of the most respected lawyers in Virginia. Jefferson biographers express astonishment that the apprenticeship with Wythe lasted five full years, 1762-67, at a time when almost no one studied law for more than two. Patrick Henry studied "not more than six weeks," or so at least he told Jefferson, and Wythe for one was so convinced of the inadequacy of Henry's training he refused to sign his license. Jefferson's years under Wythe, years of virtually uninterrupted reading, not only in the law but also in ancient classics, English literature, and general political philosophy, were not so much an apprenticeship for law as an apprenticeship for greatness.

In the beginning Jefferson disliked the study of law. To his friend John Page he wrote on December 25, 1762, of Edward Coke, author of the standard text on property and tenure: "I do wish the Devil had old Cooke, for I am sure I never was so tired of an old dull scoundrel in my life." And after seven years of practicing law he cheerfully abandoned the profession for politics. But reading became a necessity for Jefferson, like music and gardening, a special nutrient without which he withered. . . .

Jefferson had many passions in his youth, and obvious among them was the passion to make all knowledge his province. His delight in mastering everything, which only a young man can experience, led to an astonishing regimen of self-discipline which came close to being obsessive. When another young friend, Benjamin Moore, shortly after entering law practice, asked him to prescribe a proper reading list for him, Jefferson replied with a letter – now famous among law students in America – which mirrored his own past. Jefferson rose always at dawn, or sunrise, and he began by telling young Moore what he should read *before* 8 A.M. "Employ yourself in physical studies, Ethics, Religion, natural and sectarian, and natural law," he wrote, and suggested a list of books to be consulted before breakfast. From hours eight to twelve he prescribed reading in law, from twelve to one in politics. The afternoon, he said, should be occupied by history, and "From Dark to Bed-time," *belles-lettres,* criticism, rhetoric, and oratory.

One of Jefferson's friends stated that "when young he adopted a system, perhaps an entire plan of life from which neither the exigencies of business nor the allurements of pleasure could drive or seduce him. Much of his success is to be ascribed to methodical industry." Jefferson's five years of "methodical industry" can best be described in Erik Erikson's happy phrase as an "adolescent moratorium," a deferring of decision-making in preparation for possible future greatness. . . . With Jefferson, between nineteen and twenty-four, when most of his friends were hunting, gambling, cockfighting, speculating, marrying young, or wenching among slaves, he seems to have been largely buried in books, and in the kind of books most of his friends avoided as difficult or esoteric. Patrick Henry, who often moved in with Jefferson when he came to Williamsburg to court, once looked over his library and said, "Mr. J., I will take two volumes of Hume's Essays, and try to read them this winter." When Henry returned them, Jefferson remembered later with some contempt, he said, "he had not been able to get half way into one of them."

Jefferson's abnormally prolonged postponement of entering the profession of law suggests in part a reluctance to accept maturity, to abandon the role of son and student which he was enjoying under Wythe. But with the postponement came a consciousness of inner worth, a consciousness common to great men. What it was that Jefferson was preparing for he could not know, but he did it with such industry and conscientious zeal that one must believe he had serious fantasies about one day becoming great. Such fantasies must surely have been stimulated by the trio of extraordinary men in Williamsburg, Small, Fauquier, and Wythe, who accepted him as one of them with affectionate admiration when he was only nineteen.

Charles F. Allen and Jonathan Portis
From *The Comeback Kid*

There is a dignified old building in downtown Little Rock known as the Old State House. It was Arkansas's first capitol, remaining in use from 1836 to 1914, when a larger one was built.

The Old State House sits on a rise above the Arkansas River and faces the financial district of downtown Little Rock. Primarily a museum now, it is sometimes used for ceremonial functions. With its gleaming white columns, crowning oak trees and iron fence, it looks more like an old Southern mansion than a government building. In fact, it vaguely resembles the White House.

At noon on October 3, 1991, Governor Bill Clinton of Arkansas would announce his candidacy for president while standing on the steps of the Old State House.

Shortly before 9 A.M. on that day, a bright, warm Thursday, Bill Clinton jogged alone down the sidewalk in front of the Old State House. A few reporters and photographers were standing nearby when Clinton came running down Markham Street and turned up Spring Street. The reporters approached him, but he waved them away, shouting on the run that he wanted to finish his three-mile jaunt.

"I don't know how many more mornings I'll have like this, and I wanted to spend this one like I normally do," he said. The photographers snapped pictures of Clinton in his T-shirt ("The Jacksons Tour," it said) and ill-fitting gym shorts as he chugged by. A well-wisher who had reached out to shake the governor's hand suddenly lost his balance and fell backward. The governor stopped, helped the man to his feet and made sure the man was not hurt. Clinton then headed further downtown, dodging the cars and eventually vanishing. Few people took notice. It was a common sight to see the governor running alone on the sidewalks and streets of downtown Little Rock.

A three-miler was quite a distance for an overweight forty-five-year-old governor; but it was nothing for Bill Clinton. He had been running after one thing or another all of his life. . . .

The family bought its first television set in 1956, when Bill Clinton was nine years old. The glowing machine was to have an immeasurable effect on the impressionable boy. He immediately became fascinated while watching the 1956 political conventions.

"I think it sort of came home to me in a way on television that it wouldn't have otherwise," Clinton has said. Already an avid reader, he had been poring over the newspapers for years. But television was different. It brought a sense of immediacy and participation to Bill Clinton. He watched in awe as John F. Kennedy and Estes Kefauver fought for the vice presidential nomination during the Democratic convention.

In 1963, the summer that Bill Clinton turned seventeen, he again was exposed to politics, this time at Boys State, a camp where high school boys and girls learned the electoral process by joining fictitious parties and running for office. It was the perfect laboratory for Bill Clinton. His old friend, Mack McLarty, was elected governor of the fictitious state. But Bill Clinton was shooting higher. He wanted to be elected a delegate to Boys Nation, which meant a trip to Washington and a chance to participate in the real thing. He won the election.

The delegates to Boys Nation made the rounds of Washington, D.C., visiting politicians' offices and the historic sites. Clinton dined in the Senate dining room with Senator J. William Fulbright, a Democrat from Arkansas who was chairman of the powerful Senate Foreign Relations Committee.

The boys also went to the White House. When President John F. Kennedy walked outside to greet the boys, Bill Clinton was ecstatic. Here was his idol, standing only a few feet away. Clinton walked up to the president and shook hands with him. That hot July day in 1963 was a turning point for Bill Clinton. He had entertained thoughts of becoming a Baptist minister, or possibly a musician or teacher. Now he knew he would become a politician.

Four months later, President John F. Kennedy was assassinated in Dallas.

"Shaking hands with John Kennedy and sitting in the Senate dining room with Senator Fulbright, whom he admired, that touched him," said Patty Howe Criner, a Little Rock real estate agent who grew up in Hot Springs with Clinton and later worked on his staff in the governor's office.

Clinton's mother said her son told her when he returned from Washington that he was determined to enter politics.

"When he came back from Washington, holding this picture of himself with Jack Kennedy, and the expression on his face, I knew right then that politics was the answer for him," [Clinton's mother, Virginia] Kelley said.

Clinton believes the experience of Boys State and Boys Nation changed his life. Just being elected a delegate was an accomplishment, he said.

"I didn't know if I could win a race like that," Clinton said, "because when I was a student politician [in high school], I was about as controversial as I have been in my later life. I was not one of these guys who won all of his races. And I wasn't always universally popular."

Though he had been president of his junior class, Clinton got an early taste of political defeat when he became a senior at Hot Springs High School. He was running for senior class secretary against his good friend Carolyn Staley. Staley recalls that the future governor said to her outside the auditorium where the balloting was going on, "If you beat me, I'll never forgive you." She did beat him, but the two remain friends today.

Staley remembers that Clinton was always competitive in high school. "He had to be the class leader. He had to be the best in the band. He had to be the best in his class, in grades. And he wanted to be in the top in anything that put him at the forefront of any course."

One example of his aggressiveness concerns an incident Staley says Clinton's mother related to her. "He ran in and he was holding his paper and he was just screaming, 'I beat Jim McDougal on a math test!'" McDougal, Staley said, was "a math-science genius in our class. And we were blessed with a lot of those, so that the competition in our high school was fierce."

Bill had another major interest in his early life – music. He was a leader in the Hot Springs High School Band. In his high school senior yearbook, Bill Clinton is pictured blowing his saxophone in a jazz combo with two classmates, Joe Newman and Randy Goodrum, all wearing dark glasses. Classmates later remembered the group, Three Blind Mice, as "not bad." Of the three, only Goodrum went on to a music career, becoming a highly regarded songwriter in Nashville and Los Angeles.

Criner said Clinton had a fine tenor voice and that he loved to cruise around town doing Elvis Presley imitations. His rendition of "Love Me Tender" was especially good, she recalled. "Bill wanted to be a musician long before he wanted to be a politician," Criner added. . . .

Though it was a tough call for a teenager in the rock 'n' roll sixties, Clinton chose politics over music. Upon graduation from high school, Clinton had a few opportunities for college scholarships to study music. Instead he chose to attend Georgetown University and pursue an undergraduate degree in international studies.

In later years, Arkansas political columnist John Brummett commented on Clinton's career choice: "One can only wonder what might have happened if young Billy had not been elected at Arkansas Boys State to represent the state at Boys Nation, and if, just suppose, he had met Elvis Presley instead of JFK that summer."

Clinton's high school music teacher, Virgil Spurlin of Hot Springs, remembers him as "a very talented person." Clinton took band classes in elementary school, junior high and high school. "He made All-State, of course, in high school on tenor sax. And even in grade school he was just outstanding," Spurlin said. "As he went along he not only developed his musical talents but all the other talents that he has as well. He was one of my top officers . . . I couldn't furnish him with enough sight-reading music to satisfy him. He just took all the classics and everything and just played them as if that saxophone were a violin, and it didn't matter what key or anything. And as far as his leadership ability . . . fantastic. He was a leader from the word go, and he set an example for others. He didn't just say 'Go to it,' but he said, 'Follow me.'"

Spurlin said he believed Clinton made his choice for public service over music because "I don't think the opportunities were as real for him in that field [music] as they are in politics – and education especially." Spurlin emphasized Clinton's high intellectual ability. " I just haven't seen anything quite like him in my teaching experience," he said. "There have been other bright people for sure, but Bill Clinton just has it easily head and shoulders above anybody in leadership ability." . . .

Spurlin said that it didn't surprise him at all when Clinton played the saxophone "as well as he did" later in life as Johnny Carson's guest on *The Tonight Show.*

Today, Clinton considers his experiences in the Hot Springs band some of the most important of his youth. "All my musical competitions were great because it was so competitive, but, in a way, you were fighting against yourself. And music, to me, was – is – kind of representative of everything I like most in life. It's beautiful and fun but very rigorous. If you wanted to be good, you had to work like crazy. And it was a real relationship between effort and reward. My musical life experiences were just as important to me, in terms of forming my development, as my political experiences or my academic life." . . .

Clinton attended public schools in Hot Springs, experiencing firsthand the Arkansas educational system. This was a system that had progressed dramatically since its beginnings but still had many shortcomings. . . .

Clinton particularly liked teachers who not only were good disciplinarians, but who made learning fun, who "had a good sense of humor."

One teacher he remembers is Doyle Cole. "I was in his class when John Kennedy was assassinated. It was the first year we [were] taught trigonometry. We had seven people in the class. So I was able to take algebra one and two, geometry, calculus and trigonometry. And it was just an exhilarating experience. All the other students were real smart, and I loved that."

An English teacher whom Clinton still holds in high regard is Ruth Sweeney, "who had lived in Chicago and a lot of other places in the country, and I thought she was a sophisticated, neat person." For Sweeney, Clinton memorized one hundred lines of *Macbeth*. In 1990 he would recall those lines and recite them to a high school class in the small town of Vilonia, Arkansas.

"I hadn't [recited] it in twenty-something years," Clinton said, "and I started reeling it off, and these kids, their eyes got as big as dollars. I quoted this whole soliloquy. And it was all because of Ruth Sweeney."

Another teacher whom Clinton remembers fondly and communicated with until her death at age ninety was Kathleen Schaer, "a remarkable women." She told him the day he was graduated from elementary school that he would end up either in jail or as governor. "She actually said that," Clinton recalled.

On graduation from Hot Springs High School in 1964, Clinton embarked on an ambitious higher education program. Dr. Paul Root describes the seventeen-year-old Clinton fresh out of high school: "I could see then that he was becoming . . . I don't know if we'd call it a visionary or not, but he was really thinking long-range, and he knew where he was going, or knew where he wanted to go, and was finding ways to get there."

From Hot Springs High School, Clinton entered Georgetown University in September 1964, shortly after he turned eighteen. Georgetown, a Jesuit-founded school in Washington, D.C., was the only college to which Clinton had applied. He had asked his high school counselor which was the best school if one wanted to be a diplomat and she had answered, "Georgetown University."

"It was late in the year when he was accepted," Kelley said. "I went up with him for orientation, and we went into this Jesuit's office and he started questioning Bill, and he asked Bill about his foreign language, and Bill said, 'I haven't had any [modern] foreign language; I've had four years of Latin' . . . asked him about his religion, and Bill said he was Southern Baptist. All the wrong answers."

When the two walked out of that office, Clinton told his mother not to worry. "By the time I leave here, they'll know why they accepted me."

Today, Clinton says he selected Georgetown for three reasons. One, when he went to Boys Nation, he "fell in love with Washington" and wanted to go back there to college. Two, he wanted to "go to the place that was the most rigorous academically." And three, he wanted to attend a school "where I could get a good background in foreign affairs." His interest in foreign affairs, he says, was because "I thought America would become more involved in the rest of the world in my adult lifetime."

If he had not been accepted by Georgetown, he would have gone to the University of Arkansas at Fayetteville. "They had the open admission policy if you were a good student," Clinton recalled.

Clinton said Georgetown was an opportunity for him "to try to get exposed to the rest of the world." But at the same time, he already knew that he "wanted to come back home to Arkansas and be in public life. And I knew that politically it would be advantageous for me to stay here [Arkansas] to go to school. But I felt that if I went away to school and exposed myself to the rest of the country and learned something about the rest of the world, then if I ever could get elected down here, I'd do a better job."

There was a magnetic pull in Washington, and Clinton could not resist it. . . .

Bill Clinton enrolled in Georgetown in 1964, interested in international studies as preparation for a career in politics. His family could barely afford to pay for such an expensive school. Clinton had to work at part-time jobs to bring in extra money. During the summer he returned to Arkansas to work in the campaign of Frank Holt, a candidate for governor.

David Pryor, now a U.S. senator from Arkansas, also campaigned that summer as a candidate for Congress. Pryor was walking down Main Street in a south Arkansas town, carrying a bucketful of thimbles promoting his campaign, when he encountered Clinton.

The two men introduced themselves to each other and began talking politics.

"I was very impressed," Pryor said, "even though it was just a sidewalk chat."

While campaigning for Frank Holt, Clinton came to know Arkansas Supreme Court Justice Jack Holt, who was Frank Holt's nephew. Although Frank Holt was defeated for governor, the campaign paid off for Bill Clinton. When it was time for Clinton to return to Georgetown in the fall, he was desperately in need of money to continue his studies. He had always admired Senator J. William Fulbright, so he decided to seek a job in Fulbright's office. He asked Chief Justice Jack Holt for a recommendation.

Clinton won the job on Holt's recommendation to Lee Williams, Fulbright's administrative assistant. "Jack [Holt] and I had worked for his uncle Frank, in his campaign for governor, and I needed a job to go back to Georgetown," Clinton said. "I couldn't afford to pay for it anymore."

Clinton remembers the night Williams called him in Hot Springs to offer him the Washington job. "He said, 'Well, you can have a part-time job for $3,500 a year or a full-time job for $5,000.' And I said, 'How about two part-time jobs?' And this is a verbatim conversation – he said, 'You're just the guy I'm looking for.' He said, 'Be here Monday.' And that's a true story. It was Friday morning. I'd had no sleep. I got up, got all my bags packed and everything, and I was there Monday for work."

Pryor saw the student again in 1968 when Clinton came by the congressman's office in Washington and brought Pryor up to date on his educational career. "I saw in that meeting an intensity in this young man that truly impressed me," Pryor said. "I felt he was someone who not only was very gifted but, in addition, he has a tremendous commitment to causes and to ideals along that line."

Clinton majored in international government studies at Georgetown, pursuing a bachelor of arts degree, which he obtained in 1968. He was voted class president in both his freshman and sophomore years.

Clinton today considers Georgetown "an incredible experience" and describes his years there as "like a feast . . . I'd never been out of Arkansas really very much, and there I was with people from all over the country and all over the world . . . teachers from all over the world.". . .

High school friend Carolyn Staley visited Clinton at Georgetown and remembers that he had a clear sense of vision and the determination to right injustice even as a college student. One visit that stands out in her memory occurred at the time of Martin Luther King's assassination in 1968. America's major cities were engulfed in race riots.

"I remember flying in and seeing the city [Washington] on fire," she said. Clinton and Staley served as volunteers in the riot zones, driving Red Cross emergency vehicles that weekend. Staley said they pulled hats and scarves over their faces, as they had been instructed, to hide the color of their skin.

"We got out and walked throughout the city and saw the burning, the looting . . . and were very much brought into face-to-face significance with what was going on," Staley said. . . .

Old friend Patty Criner was in Arkansas when Clinton attended Georgetown. He wrote to her on a regular basis and told her school was "really hard."

He also told Criner, "You won't believe this, but the professors want me to apply for a Rhodes Scholarship." Although he told Criner he felt he didn't have "a chance in the world" to get the scholarship, he was "really studying and really working hard."

Criner remembers the day Clinton won the scholarship. She was with his mother in Hot Springs, awaiting the news. "It was the most exciting thing in the world for him," Criner said.

Kelley remembered sitting by the phone all day until her son called with the outcome of the interview. "I never refused to do an anesthetic [procedure] before in my life. But this was on a Saturday . . . and the doctor called me, and I said, 'I'm sorry. You'll just have to call somebody else.' I did not leave the phone all day long. I gave him a London Fog raincoat for good luck for him to take to New Orleans [where the Rhodes Scholarship interviews were conducted]. And it was around five o'clock in the afternoon, and he called and he said, 'Well, Mother, how do you think I'll look in English tweed?'"

Clinton's final interview followed a competitive selection process. Clinton told his mother that he had picked up a *Time* magazine at the airport and read an article about the first heart transplant. It turned out that one of his interview questions was on that subject. The excited Clinton told his mother that picking up the magazine had been "the luckiest thing in the world."

Fitzhugh Green
From *George Bush: An Intimate Portrait*

From early youth July and August was one endless party for the Bush children. Their parents would pile them into the family station wagon along with baggage and dogs and trundle them to Walker's Point in Kennebunkport, Maine.

Washed clean by sun, wind and sea, Kennebunkport gleams like a jewel on Maine's coast. In the pre-spring days before the tourist hordes begin their trek to the area, the tiny town of less than a thousand differs little from when it was discovered by summer colonists, except for the cars, paved streets, power yachts and modern fishing trawlers. Kennebunkport and nearby Cape Porpoise form a kind of social unit.

One veteran year-round inhabitant laughed to me that if Bush were running for sainthood in this area he'd make it unopposed. They've known the man since boyhood. As I walked in and out of stores and talked to people of all levels and professions in the spring of 1988, that rather extreme opinion went unchallenged.

Some sage has observed that for a growing boy home is where you spend the summer. Home is where you catch your frogs, swim, canoe, fish, camp, hike, go bicycling, play tennis, have your picnics, play parlor games, see movies, first become aware of girls as a different breed.

For George Bush all this meant Kennebunkport. More specifically it meant Walker's Point, a ten-acre spit of rocks and soil reaching into the Atlantic Ocean. There, on the edge of the sea, sits a large, ten-bedroom house. Bush's maternal grandfather, George Herbert Walker, and his father, David, had bought that house together for summer vacations.

For his daughter, Dorothy, and her husband, Prescott Bush, George Walker added a simple, unpainted wood bungalow a hundred yards shoreward. At first their stays were peaceful and private. They grew increasingly hectic as the children started coming, one after the other, until there were five.

But there was respite for all seven: During the week, the kids' father would return to his New York office and their mother would eat supper with her parents in the great house. This arrangement afforded the five youngsters welcome freedom from parental discipline for at least part of every day. It also helped to weld sibling bonds that remain close even today. George Bush is the quintessential family man, one who enjoys spending time with his family above all else. His summers at Kennebunkport did much to make him that way.

Like some of the better-known East Coast watering spas, Kennebunkport began attracting city dwellers from the south around the turn of the century. Escaping the summer heat, those who could afford the costs of travel came mostly by train, since neither good roads nor automobiles were available in those early years.

The year-round residents welcomed these "economic royalists," as FDR later would call them. They spent money on food and services and domestic helpers from the town. The different cultural strata of those days tended to separate people along income lines, so the summer visitors and the "natives" didn't mingle much.

Still, Kennebunkport was more democratic than other more elaborate resorts like Bar Harbor, Marblehead, Nahant, Newport and Southampton. It also drew more of the intelligentsia. Nationally known sea and landscape artists, for example, Abbot Graves, Louis Norton and Prosper Senat, came to absorb and recreate its natural beauties. Famous authors like Booth Tarkington and Kenneth Roberts rested and wrote there. Summer theatre in the Kennebunkport Playhouse attracted popular actors like the late Edward Everett Horton. Russell Nype comes there currently, but the Playhouse, adjacent to the town's Cape Arundel Golf Club, burned down many years ago.

By the 1930s, when the young Bushes were reveling in their Kennebunkport vacations, the natives and the well-to-do summer colonists got on tolerably, although they kept their distance during mealtimes. In other words, they didn't go to each others' houses to dine.

Unaware of these socio-economic inequities, the growing Bush offspring would spend idyllic summers fishing, learning tennis, swimming and running free with their friends. . . .

Nancy [the president's sister] (now Mrs. Alexander Ellis) reminisces about their youth together, as she and I lunch on the porch of her shingled frame house across the road from the Atlantic Ocean in July 1988. It is situated precisely eight-tenths of a mile from Walker's Point. She has prepared a salad with lobster doubtless pulled out from one of the pots next to the Point. It is so fresh and sweet it melts on our tongues.

"What did you eat when you were kids?" I ask.

Without hesitation she responds. "Cereal. Hot cereal in the winter. Sausages and hominy and pancakes on Sunday. Big wonderful spaghetti dishes and salad and french bread for Saturday lunch. For Sunday we'd have roast beef and roast potatoes, and vanilla ice cream and chocolate sauce. Then they [the parents] would lie down on the sofa in the library and listen to the Philharmonic. Mother would read and knit. The kids would all go do whatever. I'd go make fudge, to try to please the brothers and make them notice me."

"It was a very ordinary life," Nancy continues. "The press tries to build up all this Greenwich estate and everything. Have you seen the house? It's a nice brown-shingled house, kind of like this one. Couple of acres, max. . . .

George Bush . . . may have picked up the deeper sense of Christian teachings. Witness his reaction one day at the Greenwich Country Day School. He was nearly 12. With his parents and brothers and sister he was watching visitors' day activities. When the obstacle race got under way, all at once everyone started to laugh at a fat youngster who got caught trying to crawl through a barrel; everybody except George Bush. His mother looked at him and saw he was crying. George walked out onto the field, pulled the trapped lad out of the barrel and ran the rest of the race at his side.

In the fall of 1936, at the age of 12, George Bush left home. In fact, his mother took him away to Andover, Massachusetts, and installed him in Phillips Academy. Known as "Andover," this was one of the country's largest all-male college preparatory schools. . . .

The details of his achievements are manifold. Some examples from the Andover Yearbook of 1942 for George "Poppy" Bush are: President of Senior Class, Chairman of Student Deacons, President of Greeks, Captain of Baseball and Soccer, Johns Hopkins Prize as well as member of Varsity Basketball Team, Editorial board of "The Phillipian," Society of Inquiry, Business Board of the "Pot Pourri," Manager of Basketball, Deputy Housemaster, and so on.

There is considerably more, but the natural leadership he acquired at Andover was most important in terms of his career to come. Unlike the usual ambitious people in any organization, Bush never electioneered; he simply let relations with others take their course. This inevitably rendered him the man they wanted to be their chief.

He never asked for credit and as a result earned it, according to Class of 1934's Colonel John Hill. Hill remembers the school's ethos was to be laid back about what you were accomplishing. You would try to give the impression that you weren't really doing much – a direct translation of British understatement. Hill recounts an event that Bush never mentioned to anybody. One afternoon an Andover senior was roughing up a scrawny, homesick new boy – Bruce Gelb. He tells the story. His brother Dick Gelb had been in Andover ahead of him. At the start of a school year Dick was confined to a wheel chair due to an injury. A schoolmate took advantage of Dick, badgering and tormenting him. When Dick recovered his health he got his revenge by beating hell out of the bully, says Bruce.

By the time Bruce arrived at Andover, the bully was still there – in his final year – and he bore a family grudge against the Gelbs. To get even, he soon began to pick on Bruce. One day he told him to move a big stuffed arm chair. Bruce tried, but could carry it only a few feet. At that moment, Bruce recalled the time his best friend in an earlier school was being hazed by older boys, and he, Gelb, had bitten the hand of the toughest one. Encouraged by the memory, Bruce stoutly told the Andover bully that he just couldn't lift that chair any more.

Whereupon the bully put a hammerlock on him. Suddenly, Bruce heard a voice say, "Leave the kid alone!" The bully promptly released Gelb and slunk off.

Gelb asked some boys who had witnessed the scene, "Who was that guy?"

"Oh," chorused the others, "That was Poppy Bush. He's the finest guy in the school. He's a great athlete and everybody loves him."

"At that point," Gelb recalls now, "he became my hero and has been ever since. Nothing makes me a more willing loyalist than a guy who sticks up for a little kid and puts a bully down. Bush has friends like me all over the U.S. and the world," says Gelb. "The reason we stay his friends is that he is still George Bush. He knows who he is. Some people forget where they come from and all the people they have known along the way." . . .

Some who knew the senator [President Bush's father] at Kennebunkport found that he was a bit stand-offish with local tradespeople and year-round neighbors – "Miners" they call themselves. Not so George. He talks to everyone regardless of station. Anyone who lives there and has dealings with the Bushes is apt to find himself invited for food or drink at Walker's Point.

These people seem not to be impressed by the glitz, glitter and glamor of Bush, the international celebrity—though these elements can enhance the love and affection that one human may feel for another. With Bush, however, there appears to be a reason for each individual "Mainers" fondness, gratitude or admiration.

For example, one of the numerous Hutchins in town lost her husband and Bush called her in Florida until he finally got through to her at midnight, interrupting his own high-level meetings in order to do so.

Another Hutchins, a lobster wholesaler named Sonny, spoke to me about Bush in clipped, even New England sentences while convalescing from a hurt back. Bush and the locals deal with each other in a relaxed way, he said. After all, "We've always had famous people come here in the summer – like Booth

Tarkington, Kenneth Roberts; we talk with them and that's the end of it." The message is clear: There is no fanfare. You either fit in or you don't.

"Last week, Bush was here. He and Mrs. Bush were walking over the bridge in town and I tooted and waved and kept right on going. He's just one of the people when he's around here. He goes to church with all the people in town who go to the church up there; he's one of the natives."

QUESTIONS TO THINK ABOUT

1. What kind of a guy was Dan Quayle in college? Should he have had to take the political science exam that included the theory section for which he was unprepared?

2. What aspect of the movie *The Candidate* interested Quayle the most? Regardless of your personal support or criticism of Quayle, suggest some of the reasons why the press had such a field day with him since he first came into the national spotlight.

3. Was Eleanor Roosevelt an asset to President Roosevelt during his time in office? Why did her commitment to social activism not end when FDR died in 1945?

4. Explain what is meant by the president's "pastoral role" toward people who call or write to the president at the White House. Does it ever help to call (202) 456-1414?

5. Why might the young Jefferson's lengthy academic preparation and his unwillingness to enter the real world quickly be healthy signs of great future success? Would your parents accept your decision to become a serious perennial student, deferring a job and other adult responsibilities for a few additional years?

6. In what ways is President Bush's upbringing similar to or different from the average American kid's? Does Kennebunkport sound like an appealing place to you?

7. Why do people less successful than Bush – the boys he protected from ridicule and bullying, and the locals of Kennebunkport – feel loyal to him?

8. How did music and politics provide many of the same kinds of rewards and satisfaction in the life of the young Bill Clinton?

9. Describe the "magnetic pull" that Clinton felt for Washington, D.C., beginning with his trip there to attend Boys Nation in 1963.

10. Compare and contrast your own early experiences, determination, and serendipities with those of George Bush and Bill Clinton.

8 | The Executive Branch

Bureaucrats are often the target of the American public's criticism and, sometimes, even hostility. The bureaucracy is perceived by many citizens to spend enormous amounts of money on programs that have no clear goals and that never succeed in any measurable way. Bureaucrats push piles of paper around, draw good salaries, and get many benefits, while taxpayers struggle to make ends meet. Americans get mad at the bureaucracy when it works well and when it doesn't.

Stories of bureaucratic success do exist, however. In the 1960s, one executive-branch agency took on a challenge more tangible and dramatic than the usual bureaucratic project. The National Aeronautics and Space Agency (NASA) convinced the Congress, the president, and the American people that it could land an American on the moon. For NASA, all the factors for success were present. The technology was in development, the financial resources were available, and the Soviet Union's early achievements in space motivated the American people to support Apollo. Most important, W. Henry Lambright writes, James Webb was NASA's leader. Webb made all the right administrative decisions in organizing a complex and costly venture.

The lesson of Webb's leadership is that a government agency can be run well and can reach its goal. The lesson also is that there are setbacks along the way. By the late 1960s, public support for NASA was not as strong as it had been earlier. A tragic fire killed several astronauts, the Vietnam War was demanding increasing amounts of money, and the focus of the nation had changed from adventure in space to poverty among America's poor. Ironically Webb resigned from the agency months before Apollo made its journey.

W. Henry Lambright
"James Webb and the Uses of Administrative Power"

Without a doubt, James E. Webb is one of the giants of American public administration. He served as Truman's budget director and undersecretary of state. But it was as administrator of the National Aeronautics and Space Administration under presidents Kennedy and Johnson that he established his reputation firmly and indelibly. While not particularly well known by the general public, among professionals in government he is today a "Washington legend." For those who wish to know how to accomplish great deeds through public policy, bureaucratic veterans cite Webb's example. He managed America to the moon and, in so doing, left a legacy of actions and memories that have caused him to be the focus of innumerable awards and testimonials. For example, in 1982 the Smithsonian Institution created the James E. Webb Fellowships to provide training for young persons interested in the administrative aspects of institutions like the Smithsonian, devoted to the increase and diffusion of culture and knowledge; and in 1983 a special fund and lectureship for Excellence in Public Administration was established in his name by the National Academy of Public Administration.

Webb was a forceful man who used his administrative power to the fullest. At the height of the space program, the system he headed utilized thirty-five thousand civil service employees and four hundred thousand contract workers in twenty thousand separate companies. He fought hard for the resources to accomplish the tasks assigned to NASA in the National Aeronautics and Space Act, NASA's basic legislative foundation. He was responsible for billions of dollars, yet he eschewed personal publicity and many of the perquisites of office. He turned down the limousine he could have had and made a black checker cab his symbol during his seven-year tenure at NASA. . . .

. . . He succeeded where it counted most. Not long after he left, Apollo landed on the moon, and world history changed. Perhaps better than anyone before or since, Webb married science, technology, management, education, and politics in pursuit of a monumental goal. President Kennedy made the Apollo decision, but Webb was the single most important shaper of that decision. After the decision, he was the dominant individual in making sure that decision was implemented. . . .

When Webb joined NASA [in 1961], it was still in its formative years. NASA had been created in 1958 as a response to Sputnik, launched by the Soviet Union in 1957, and subsequent Soviet "firsts." There was consensus that the United States needed a strong space program. The major decision of the Space Act of 1958 was that the program was to be run by a civilian agency. This was a decision made primarily by President Dwight Eisenhower.

There was also a sense that this had to be a vigorous agency. It was to be independent, not part of another organization, and run by a single administrator rather than a commission (as was true of the Atomic Energy Commission). The basic building block upon which it was formed was the National Advisory Committee for Aeronautics (NACA), created in 1915. This was an assemblage of large national laboratories devoted to basic and applied research in aeronautics, a nucleus of approximately eight thousand scientists and engineers. Transferred from the Army to NASA during the Eisenhower years were the Army Ballistics Missile Agency team, headed by Wernher von Braun (forty-three hundred employees), and the Jet Propulsion Laboratory, managed by the California Institute of Technology (twenty-four hundred employees).

The first administrator of NASA, T. Keith Glennan, an engineer and previous president of the Case Institute of Technology, had as his deputy (and only other political appointee in NASA) Hugh Dryden, formerly head of NACA. They hired Robert Seamans, an engineer and former Massachusetts Institute of Technology professor, as associate administrator and de facto general manager.

The NASA administrator had a legislative mandate that was remarkably broad and simple: to "plan, direct, and conduct aeronautical and space activities"; to involve the scientific community in these activities; and to widely disseminate knowledge and information concerning aeronautical and space activities. He also had the authority to hire hundreds of new employees at salaries above civil service levels, without regard to the usual personnel classification restrictions. . . .

Webb's first decision was to ask the president to retain Dryden as the number-two man at NASA. He then asked Seamans to stay as associate administrator. This made for maximum continuity in the agency's senior management. Under Glennan, the three had served as a de facto senior management triumvirate. Webb made explicit what had been implicit: NASA would be run by a team, and Webb said so.

The three men would make the major decisions together. No one of the three would act to do violence to the strongly held views of either of the other two. Webb would later say: "This was a policy which intentionally put us in chains. We bound ourselves in these hoops of iron." The idea was cooperation at the top in the processes of analyzing a problem or opportunity and also in the decisions concerning projects, patterns of organization, and personnel assignments. This method wedded different kinds of expertise and made sure that those below knew that top management had examined in depth and was together on a particular issue, so that no one could make end runs or play one off against the other. Below these senior officials were very able, ambitious, hard-driving men. They fell into two categories. One included the headquarters program managers (e.g., of manned space flight, space science, space applications), and the other included the directors of the various large laboratories, or as NASA called them, centers. One of these individuals, von Braun, was better known by far, nationally and internationally, than Webb, Dryden, or Seamans.

In terms of emphasis, the division of labor was obvious. Seamans handled most of the day-to-day management matters; Dryden dealt with the engineering and scientific communities; and Webb focused on the overall organizational and larger administrative and political problems. Webb understood his special role in relating NASA to its political environment. As he wrote later: "The environment is not something apart from the [large-scale] endeavor; it is not just something in which the endeavor operates and which it needs to adjust; it is an integral part of the endeavor itself. . . . The total job (managerial job) encompasses external as well as internal elements, and success is as dependent on effectiveness in the one as in the other."

Webb's emphasis on a "triad" leadership may have been especially important in a science and technology agency. Webb, a man untrained technically, gained legitimacy in decision making within NASA (and probably outside) to the degree that he cloaked his own policy preferences in the mantle of senior associates who were technically trained. Certainly, Webb guided the triad in directions he regarded as wise for the agency as a whole. . . .

Webb inherited an agency that knew what it wanted to do. The issue for Webb was not what *could* be done but what *should* be done. He knew that this was a decision only President Kennedy and Congress could make. He knew that Kennedy was already getting advice on space from two other sources: Vice President Johnson, who wanted the United States first in space as soon as possible, and Kennedy's science adviser, Jerome Wiesner, who represented the scientific community's view. This view opposed manned flight programs because they cut into the budgets for unmanned, science-oriented programs. . . .

On 12 April [1961], however, the Soviet Union launched Yuri Gagarin as the first man in space, and Chairman Nikita Khrushchev boasted: "Let the capitalist countries catch up with our country!" The U.S. reaction was one of complete chagrin and frustration, especially in Congress. Kennedy defended the U.S. program, as did Webb, but the propaganda advantage gained by the Soviets was huge. Then on 19 April it became known that the Bay of Pigs invasion of Cuba was a disaster. America's spirits – and Kennedy's – sank to a new low. On that date the president turned to Johnson and asked him to make recommendations for a U.S. space program that would make the U.S. first in space.

Johnson talked with many in industry, Congress, and the executive branch, but the man on whom he relied most was Webb. In discussions with Johnson, Webb realized that it was possible to recommend a program beyond anything NASA had thus far proposed to an administration. New technology programs involving an Apollo spaceship had been recommended to Eisenhower and Kennedy in March; however, the goal of a moon landing and return had not been made explicit. In this respect, Webb was more cautious than Dryden and some other senior NASA managers. Webb was not about to propose a scheme that went "beyond what I thought Kennedy was willing to approve."

Now the opportunity was there, and Webb made the most of it. He told Johnson that placing a man on the moon was something the Soviet Union could not do with the technology it now had. With enough money, NASA could develop the technology to surpass the Soviets. It could be done within the decade. Johnson spoke with Senator Kerr, head of the Aeronautical and Space Sciences Committee. Kerr told him "that if Jim Webb says we can land a man on the moon and bring him safely home, then it can be done." At Johnson's direction, Webb and Secretary of Defense McNamara prepared a memorandum the centerpiece of which was the option of a manned lunar decision. Johnson passed this on (with his endorsement) to Kennedy on 29 April.

Webb now spoke with Johnson, Wiesner, and leaders in the administration and Congress about the requirements for carrying out such a decision. With Johnson, who was fully in favor of the decision, Webb emphasized the need for political support over the long haul, once the mood of crisis had faded. In talks with Wiesner, representing a community unenthusiastic about manned programs in general, he emphasized that he would make certain that there would be more to the program than space spectaculars; there would be a program of genuine scientific and technological value. Webb and Johnson both spent many hours with key legislators in Congress emphasizing the need for support.

On 5 May, the first U.S. manned space flight, with Alan Shephard, proved successful. Kennedy announced at a press conference that day that he planned to undertake "a substantially larger effort in space." . . .

NASA had to move quickly. Industry would be the key performer, and NASA's centers would provide technical management as well as research and development. Similarly, NASA would work closely with universities through grants and contracts. Webb spoke of an R&D partnership, through which NASA would get the job done. Its partners would be also a constituency from around the country, one that could help bolster political support for the agency.

By the end of 1961, Webb's first year as administrator, NASA had negotiated many of the key Apollo contracts. These included the award of the largest of all peacetime contracts, for the Apollo command and service modules, to the North American Aviation Corporation. The man who at the University of North Carolina had signed thousand-dollar checks, and at Sperry, million-dollar checks, now was responsible for contracts costing billions. An elaborate structure was established to weigh the merits of these contract awards, but ultimately, the big decisions were made by Webb, Dryden, and Seamans.

In addition to letting major contracts for developmental work, Webb spent the months following the Kennedy decision augmenting the capacity of his own organization. In one thirty-day period, from 24 August to 23 September, NASA selected Cape Canaveral, Florida, as the site for a new center and "space port"; picked a government-owned ordnance plant in New Orleans for fabrication of launching vehicles; hired new managers at various levels; and reorganized the agency to strengthen top management's leadership and control over program offices and centers. Perhaps the biggest decision in this period was to create a new manned-spacecraft center to undergird and help manage Apollo.

This center happened to be located outside Houston, Texas, in the district of the congressman who oversaw NASA's budget. . . .

Webb was acutely conscious that important sectors in the scientific community were not fully behind Apollo or him. He was also aware that there was a concern that America was not graduating enough scientists and engineers to meet its needs. It was clear to Webb that NASA should do its part in the educational expansion taking place. It would support university research in the space field through interdisciplinary institutional grants. It would help universities to better help NASA by providing facilities (buildings) without the usual matching requirements. This effort – the Sustaining University Program – was launched in the name of Apollo. It reflected Webb's desire to use his honeymoon to do what had to be done to make the United States preeminent not only in space but in science and technology generally. Also, Webb hoped that the university program would prove to the scientific community that Apollo was going to be an asset to space science, not a draw of resources.

When Webb took charge of NASA, he said he hoped to be as innovative in management as NASA would be in science and technology. For some critics, he was too innovative. But, with budget soaring, he responded to the call to get America moving in space. The SUP and technology utilization efforts were small relative to Apollo. In Webb's view, however, they were important in broadening the understanding of space and enabling NASA to play a greater role for social and economic development on earth. . . .

There comes a point when an organization and its leader must look beyond its present mission to new missions, especially if the existing mission has a finite lifetime. Webb had the problem of advising the president and Congress as to not only what NASA would do for post-Apollo but when and how to sell the program. The selling of Apollo in 1961 was expedited by a political environment that was ripe, made ripe by the competition of a series of Soviet firsts. There was a growing national consensus that the United States had to "do something." NASA careerists planned Apollo as the "natural" technical goal for the agency. Webb contributed mightily to translating the technologists' goal into a presidential objective of restoring national pride and power. Congress was fully ready to go along, as the absence of debate on Kennedy's decision made clear. But in the latter 1960s, when Webb was trying to define and promote a post-Apollo program, the political environment had changed.

First, NASA's own success made a difference. During the 1960s, America began to do quite well in space, while the Soviet Union seemed to lose much of its early momentum. Second, the nation and President Johnson were increasingly distracted from space by two other even larger national efforts: the Great Society and the Vietnam War. Third, at a time when gaining support for post-Apollo was most critical, Apollo was yet to be completed. Fourth, the overall space budget was suffering cutbacks in a period of general financial stringency, and the NASA priority had to be to spend its diminishing resources to maintain Apollo rather than to establish post-Apollo efforts. . . .

On 21 August 1967, Johnson signed a congressional bill that drastically reduced the post-Apollo programs. Johnson stated that ordinarily he would have opposed such cuts, but circumstances had changed, and "we must moderate our efforts in certain space projects." . . .

On 16 September 1968, Webb spoke with the president and then announced his decision to retire from NASA, effective 7 October 1968. In his announcement, Webb said that the retrenchment meant that the United States would be in second place for years to come. . . .

In 1969, NASA did send men to the moon and return them safely to earth. As the administrator in charge of NASA during the 1960s, Webb's place in history is assured. The goal that mattered most was achieved. Achieving that goal was an extraordinary administrative as well as scientific and technological success. It was also a political success, for necessary funds had to be obtained from the White House and Congress every year.

Webb significantly influenced the original presidential decision, thus providing for his agency the long-term mission it needed. He also made certain he controlled the agency as it implemented the mission, establishing an executive secretariat to provide him with a constant flow of information concerning the pattern of decision making as it developed throughout NASA. He made certain that he and his senior associates were in charge. This meant that no one got between him and the president. It also meant that the strong-minded center directors and program managers had to work within the approved lines of endeavor. There was to be no czar, not even for Apollo. Every few years there was a reorganization that affected power relationships, preventing NASA's becoming too "settled." From Webb's point of view, a certain amount of disequilibrium was good. Nor, really, did Webb make himself a czar. He was an "organization man," if ever there was one.

While he was clearly the man at the top, Webb also gave credit and glory to others. This was evident by his willingness to share authority with Dryden and Seamans, who formed with him a "collective leadership." It could also be seen in his willingness to let astronauts, managers such as Mueller, Gilruth, Pickering, Newell, Silverstein, Debus, and von Braun, and many others throughout the organization participate in decision making and enjoy public recognition. As NASA succeeded in the 1960s, it did so as an organization. Indeed, it did so as an organizational system. Webb spoke of a research partnership, a government-industry-university team. When he discussed the NASA workforce, he included the contractors and grantees in his numbers. When he spoke of liquidating capability, he meant capability outside NASA, as well as scientists and engineers in the NASA centers. . . .

What makes an exceptional administrator? Most people who worked for Webb (or observed him) point to a man with an extraordinary ability to enthuse large groups of people and get them moving in a common direction. This is leadership. And it may require certain settings. . . .

What is important about Webb's administrative style is that he combined a sense of control (what it took to be in charge) with a sensitivity to "organizational nurturing." He consciously thought about how to strengthen the capacities of his organization to do its job. Participation in decisions was one method. Reorganization that kept NASA alert, responsive, and adaptive was another. What was needed at one time was not necessarily what was needed at another. In 1961, Webb reorganized to bring power to top management; in 1963 he reorganized to let it slip back to the program offices and centers. Later, there were other reorganizations as part of administrative strategy. . . .

Teaching was a third administrative mechanism. By *teaching* I mean a constant effort to improve other administrators in the practice of management and political action in Washington. He would take the time to talk with his staff and managers about managerial-political activities. He showed them how they could turn problems (e.g., congressional inquiries) into opportunities (ways to win friends in Congress). He read books about administration and brought outside scholars inside to study the NASA organization and techniques. He wanted his organization to be as open and innovative as possible. He felt that his managers could learn from being studied, just as those doing the studying could learn from NASA.

Nothing Webb achieved would have been possible without great personal energy, stamina, determination, intelligence, and optimism. Where do great administrative leaders come from? Are they born or made? The physical and mental energy have to be in the genes. The optimism and enthusiasm, as well as political and administrative skills, obviously are acquired along the way. Webb had a series of experiences in government and business from which he learned and grew as a public administrator. He understood the inseparability of his inside and outside roles. When the 1960s came, and the United States looked for leadership in space, it needed an uncommon man to chart a course and see it through. Webb was ready.

QUESTIONS TO THINK ABOUT

1. How did NASA head Webb use teamwork in running the agency in the years leading up to the moon landing?
2. Was there support for NASA's plans in the Johnson administration, the Congress, and the public? What international events affected NASA's program plans?
3. Do most executive-branch agencies today have the reputation for innovation, teamwork, and success that NASA did during Webb's time of leadership?

9 | The Judiciary

Once on a federal court, judges have life terms. Only impeachment for high crimes and misdemeanors can remove a federal district court judge, a judge of the U.S. court of appeals, or a Supreme Court justice. Tenure for life protects judges from political pressure in their decision making. But to pretend that the judiciary is a branch of government free from political considerations is hopelessly naive. Federal judges are nominated by the president. Their nominations must be confirmed by the Senate. If the Supreme Court has been termed the "storm center" of American politics, then the Senate Judiciary Committee is where every storm starts.

Since 1968 Republican presidents have named every new justice to the Supreme Court. Slowly, with each appointment, the views of the Court have changed considerably from the liberalism of the 1960s to the conservatism of the 1990s. The Supreme Court, as David Savage notes, has been "turning right."

Savage introduces some of today's justices in their less formal moments. He then traces the Court's consideration of the 1991 case of *Ronald Harmelin v. Michigan*. Harmelin was sentenced to life in prison for drug possession under a very tough Michigan law designed to make a significant impact on the state's drug problem. Was the sentence cruel and unusual punishment? The Supreme Court's verdict reveals the emerging positions and alliances on the Supreme Court of the 1990s and beyond.

David Savage
From *Turning Right*

Just after 9 A.M., young Senate staffers hurried to work along First Street on Capitol Hill and took no notice of the gray-suited figure who strolled by. Nearly every morning, the chief justice went walking on the streets near the Court. Usually, he was alone, but occasionally a clerk accompanied him. Rehnquist's perennially sore back tightened up if he sat too long, and the walking helped.

It helped, too, with making decisions, he said. "I began to realize that some of my best insights came not during my enforced thinking periods in my chambers, but while I was shaving in the morning, driving to work, or just walking from one place to another," he wrote.

In his early years on the Court, Rehnquist wore long sideburns and was often casually attired in Hush Puppies and a sport coat. He drove to work in a well-worn Volkswagen. As chief justice, however, he began to trim the now-graying sideburns, to wear gray suits with fashionable green ties, and to arrive at the Court each morning in a long black limousine. On winter days, he donned a fedora and a dark overcoat for his morning walks. Still, in the hot days of the Washington, D.C., summer, when the Court was in recess, Rehnquist abandoned decorum. Strolling along the sidewalk in a white short-sleeved shirt and a broad-brimmed straw hat, he looked like a State Department official who had been assigned to Central America.

Rarely was he recognized on the street. On days when the Court was in session, hundreds of visitors would line up on the plaza, waiting their turn to walk up the long steps and to sit in the courtroom for 15 minutes. On occasion, before the 10 A.M. gavel sounded, Rehnquist would stroll past the lineup of visitors and not a head would turn. While most Washington politicians and government executives are drawn irresistibly to a bank of microphones or a TV camera, the justices prefer to be unseen, unheard, and unknown.

Sometimes, they succeed even beyond their own wishes. A few weeks after being sworn in, Anthony Kennedy was stopped on the Court steps by a young couple with a camera in hand. They asked the new justice to snap a photo of them standing before the edifice of the Supreme Court. He kindly complied and walked on, entirely unrecognized. John Paul Stevens, with his shock of white hair and bow ties, liked to walk out onto the Court steps in the afternoon to soak up some sun, but on one occasion he was perturbed to see tourists wave to him to move aside so he would not block their photos of the building.

Sometimes, their names are better known than their faces. During one summer break, [Justice Antonin] Scalia and his wife piled their three youngest children into a van to drive cross-country to Los Angeles, where the justice was to teach law for several weeks. At the end of a long, hot day of driving, Scalia pulled into a motel and handed the desk clerk his credit card.

As she finished with his registration, she handed the card back and said, "Thank you, Mr. SKALLyuh."

"It's skuLEEuh," he corrected.

"Oh," she brightened, "like the Supreme Court justice."

"Yes," smiled Scalia.

The motel clerk aside, relatively few Americans can tick off the names of the justices. In the midst of the 1988 term, the *Washington Post* polled 1,005 persons to test their knowledge of courts and judges. Some 54 percent of those questioned were able to name the judge on TV's "The People's Court," Joseph Wapner. Asked to name the chief justice of the United States, only 9 percent named Rehnquist. Justice O'Connor was by far the best known, with a 23 percent recognition, while the others trailed Rehnquist with a single-digit response. As a college football star in the fall of 1937, the name of Byron "Whizzer" White was known nationwide. Now, after nearly three decades on the Court, only 3 percent of those surveyed could identify him.

Actually, Rehnquist and his colleagues are content to be virtually anonymous. While most Washington figures believe that power is linked to "visibility" and their "name recognition," the justices adhere to the opposite view. In their view, their rulings carry a special power because they are the pronouncements of nine somewhat mysterious black-robed figures.

In the fall of 1988, Rehnquist was especially pleased to have the Court and the justices stay out of the news. The term had ended in late June on a quiet note, and most of the justices quickly left the heat and glare of Washington for a summer of teaching and relaxation. Scalia took off for a teaching assignment in Greece; Kennedy went lecturing in England and Austria. Blackmun and Stevens returned to the Aspen Institute in Colorado, where each led a two-week seminar to further explore the large concepts of justice and equality. White was drawn to his native Colorado as well, where he enjoyed fly-fishing and golf. Rehnquist went to his Vermont vacation home to write, paint, and relax.

Throughout the summer, the chief justice, an avid fan of American politics, kept his eye on the developing race for the presidency. The next occupant of the White House would probably shape the direction of the Court through the early years of the twenty-first century, he knew. In July, Thurgood Marshall turned 80. He had already outlived all the predictions, but how much longer could he go on? In his chambers, Marshall joked often about his predicted demise. Should he die at his desk, he told his clerks, "Just prop me up and keep voting." He also offered his own prediction: "I expect to die at 110, shot by a jealous husband." . . .

The case of *Ronald Harmelin* v. *Michigan* [in the 1990-91 term] did not pose an issue of legal complexity. It raised a straightforward question of justice and fairness. Does the Constitution require that the punishment fit the crime? The Eighth Amendment forbids the use of "cruel and unusual punishment," and those words had been interpreted to mean that the punishment must generally fit the offense. For example, while a life prison term was not in itself cruel and unusual punishment, it would be deemed so for a parking violation. However, the new wave of stiff sentences for drug crimes forced the Court to reconsider whether these punishments were cruel and unusual.

In 1963, Harmelin served with the Air Force as an honor guard at the funeral of President John F. Kennedy. Two decades later, he had sunk far. He was a cocaine addict, a pool hustler, and a part-time drug dealer, "purely small time," he says. In the early morning of May 12, 1986, he became a big-time dealer, at least in the eyes of the law.

About 5 A.M., two Oak Park, Michigan, police officers spotted a car enter the parking lot of a motel and then leave a few moments later. When the 1977 Ford Torino did not come to a full stop at a red light before entering the road, the officers flashed their lights. The car pulled over, and Harmelin got out. As he was being patted down, he told the officers he had a gun strapped to his ankle but also had a permit to carry it. He did not, however, have a permit to carry the marijuana cigarettes they found in his pocket. Harmelin was arrested and his car impounded. In its trunk, police found a gym bag with $2,900 in cash and 673 grams of pure cocaine, more than 1½ pounds. The cocaine was said to have a street value of more than $60,000.

Harmelin was convicted of drug possession, but his sentence for his first offense came as a shock: life in prison without the possibility of parole. His attorney described it as "death in prison." Harmelin had run afoul of the nation's stiffest sentence for drug possession.

To crack down on drug kingpins, Michigan lawmakers had mandated a life sentence for anyone caught possessing more than 1½ pounds of cocaine or heroin. It did not matter why the defendant had the drugs – Harmelin says he was "doing a favor for a friend" by delivering the cocaine to a dealer near his apartment. Nor did it matter whether the conviction was his first or his tenth. Because Michigan has no death penalty, Harmelin could have gunned down a dozen persons on the street – including the two officers who stopped him – and received no harsher treatment from the Michigan courts.

His appeal, filed from his prison cell, noted that "Ronnie had absolutely no criminal record, [had] harmed no one, did not display viciousness [or] an inability to reform," yet he was imprisoned like an ax murderer for "possessing a substance one can buy freely and legally on the streets of Peru." His appeal arrived at the Court on April 2, 1990.

Since the early 1970s, the justices had relied almost exclusively on the clerks to screen the appeal petitions. There were simply too many to keep up with, at least if the justices also wanted to read the briefs and write opinions in the cases currently being decided. To spread the workload among the clerks, the justices set up a "pool" system whereby the petitions were divided among seven of the nine chambers (not including Brennan or Stevens). For each appeal, a single clerk was assigned to read it, write a memo summarizing the case, and recommend whether it should be heard. These memos were then circulated around the building. Usually, the justices looked through the petitions themselves in the small percentage of cases that were recommended for review. (On average, the Court agreed to hear about three percent of the appeals.)

Stevens, predictably, had his own system. His clerks scanned the petitions and recommended the ones the justice should read. During the previous 33 terms, Brennan, alone among his colleagues, reviewed all the appeal petitions himself. He represented the last of a great tradition. A civil rights plaintiff whose case was thrown out of court, a Death Row inmate who was facing execution, or a hard-luck prisoner such as Harmelin could count on the fact that at least one justice of the Supreme Court would personally read the appeal. Brennan knew what he was looking for, and he could go through the appeals more quickly than his young clerks. Also, Harmelin's was just the kind of case he was looking for. Just a few weeks after his appeal arrived, the Court had announced that it would hear the case of *Harmelin* v. *Michigan*. However, unfortunately for Harmelin, Brennan was no longer on the bench when the case actually came before the Court on November 5, 1990.

Nonetheless, Brennan and Lewis Powell had left behind one precedent that would help him. In 1983, the Court – on a 5-4 vote – overturned a life sentence given a petty criminal whose sixth conviction arose from bouncing a $100 check. This punishment does not fit the crime, the narrow majority said in *Solem* v. *Helm*. That ruling overturned a 1977 opinion written by Rehnquist declaring that the Constitution does not demand that the punishment fit the crime. By 1983, Blackmun had switched sides, giving the liberals a slim majority. The five-member majority had ruled that the Constitution demands that a criminal's sentence "be proportionate" to the severity of the crime. Harmelin's attorney relied on the *Solem* v. *Helm* precedent, but would the Rehnquist Court abide by it?

Carla J. Johnson, a Detroit lawyer, volunteered to represent Harmelin. She had also defended him in the Michigan courts. "I felt so strongly about his case, I took it for free," she said. From his prison cell, Harmelin had filed what is known as a "pauper's petition." Usually, the Court requires that those who file appeals pay a $300 fee and submit 40 copies of printed briefs, which can cost several thousand dollars. Hiring a topflight law firm to prepare the appeal can raise the cost to more than $30,000.

From prisoners and the poor, however, the Court will accept a single copy of a petition, along with a photocopy of the lower-court opinion they want to challenge. Each term, a dozen or more "pauper's petitions" are granted a review, many of them in death-penalty cases. Then, the justices ask an attorney to represent the petitioner by filing briefs and making an oral argument. The Court pays the attorney's expenses – travel and printing – but does not pay for the lawyer's work. It is an honor enough, apparently, to appear in the Supreme Court.

For Carla Johnson, it was her first such honor. Facing the justices, she stressed that the Michigan law was intended to nab drug kingpins, but mostly it snares "first-time offenders." The kingpins are usually too smart to carry drugs themselves. They rely on "mules" to do it for them. Juveniles who do not know the law are recruited. As Harmelin put it in one interview; the law mostly snares "idiots like myself."

"Michigan is way out of line with every state in the Union," Johnson said. "What are you going to do next, cut off their arms?" She geared her argument in part to Scalia's opinion in the juvenile death penalty case. There, Scalia had said this severe punishment was not "cruel and unusual" because a few other states would allow the execution of a 16-year-old. In this case, however, no other state would impose life imprisonment without parole for drug possession, Johnson pointed out.

Scalia was unmoved. "Maybe Michigan has a bigger problem with drugs," he said. "Isn't a state entitled to feel more deeply about a problem that can cause a loss of human life? Why can't they say, 'By George, we're going to put a stop to it'? Why is that wrong?"

Because this punishment is "grossly disproportionate" to the crime, she responded. Harmelin is not a rapist, a murderer, or even a thief, yet he is being punished more harshly than persons convicted of those crimes in Michigan. Also, according to *Solem* v. *Helm,* such a grossly disproportionate punishment is unconstitutional, she insisted.

Rehnquist leaned forward to his microphone and patiently waited for attorney Johnson to finish her point.

"Well, Ms. Johnson, *Solem* v. *Helm* was a 5-4 decision," the chief justice intoned, and it essentially overturned an earlier 5-4 decision on the same subject. "Do you think the Court has reached equilibrium on this issue, or do you think more changes might take place?" he asked, to laughter in the courtroom.

She had run into realpolitik Supreme Court style. Yes, *Solem* v. *Helm* was a clear precedent, but the chief justice disagreed with it, and the votes may have changed since then. Johnson groped for an answer and then responded directly. "I don't think the Court should treat stare decisis too cavalierly," she told Rehnquist.

Oakland County prosecutor Richard Thompson cast doubt on the notion that Harmelin was an innocent dupe. The 673 grams of cocaine is a lot. "That is the equivalent of 1,200 hits on the street," he said. Moreover, when Harmelin was arrested, he also had with him a beeper and a coded address book, besides the cash and pistol. "This is a guy who knew what he was doing," the prosecutor said. He said he suspected Harmelin was probably "a major supplier to mid-level dealers."

The Bush administration also filed a brief in support of Michigan. The case played on two favorite themes of the Administration and the Rehnquist Court: getting tough on crime and deferring to the decisions of state legislatures. Michigan lawmakers are entitled to conclude that the "distribution of drugs is not a victimless crime, but is in fact equivalent to a violent assault both on the users of the drugs and on others who suffer the consequences," the Administration brief said.

Nonetheless, Stevens challenged the argument that Harmelin can be considered a drug dealer. He was convicted only of drug possession. Under the Michigan law, that alone is enough to trigger the life prison term. "Suppose a grandmother is keeping a suitcase for her grandson, who is the 'mule,' and it contains cocaine. He's gone for the weekend. She keeps it for him. Life without parole?" he asked the Michigan prosecutor.

No, not necessarily, because that may not be considered "possession" because she did not know of the cocaine, Thompson replied.

Stevens continued. "Ok, the grandson says, 'I hate to tell you this grandmother, it's cocaine in there. Keep it for me for the weekend,' " he said. Will that trigger the law?

Not necessarily, he responded again. The prosecutor has some "discretion" on whether to bring charges. However, once the charges are brought, judges and the court system have no discretion. Anyone found guilty of possession of the large amount of cocaine must be sentenced to life in prison. No exceptions.

For the Court, Harmelin's case posed another stark choice. Does the Constitution put *any* limits on the increasingly stiff penalties in the war on drugs? Is it cruel and unusual punishment to impose life in prison without parole for first-time drug possession? Must the punishment fit the crime, or can a state use stiff penalties to send a message that it will not tolerate drugs? To judge by their questions, the chief justice could count on O'Connor, Scalia, and Kennedy. Marshall, Blackmun, and Stevens were likely to vote to reverse the sentence. The outcome then depended on White and Souter. . . .

The term had been a miserable one for Marshall. Without Brennan, he stood little chance of prevailing in any major case, whether on civil rights, criminal law, the death penalty, or free speech. Before, most of the cases stood 5-4, and there was always a chance that White, O'Connor, or perhaps even Scalia might switch sides. Now, the margin was typically 6-3. Now, a vote switch by White, O'Connor, or one of the others made no difference. Rehnquist still had a conservative majority. The chief justice was in almost complete control.

For months, Marshall's wife and doctor had been urging him to retire. His eyesight was failing, his breathing was labored, and walking demanded a major exertion. Why continue on simply to cast meaningless dissenting votes? By late June, Marshall had made up his mind. June 27, the last day of the term, would be his last day on the bench. Just a year before, his wife had come to the courtroom on the last day of the term to hear Brennan deliver the opinion upholding affirmative action. Now, she was back again, but for quite a different reason.

Brennan showed up, too. He had come downstairs from his chambers when the term had opened on the first Monday in October. Now, he came back to hear the reading of the final decisions. As he entered the room, he looked rejuvenated. He smiled and waved to friends. He shook hands with a procession of lawyers and Court employees who filed past his seat. His head bobbed as he searched for more friends in the audience. He looked to be thoroughly enjoying himself – but not for long.

The chief justice announced that Scalia would deliver the court's opinion in *Harmelin* v. *Michigan*. By a 5-4 margin, Harmelin had lost. He would remain behind bars for life because of the cocaine he had carried in his trunk. Such a sentence did not violate the Eighth Amendment's ban on cruel and unusual punishment, the majority ruled.

Scalia's opinion was long, historical, and sharp in its conclusions. "We conclude from this examination [of history] that *[Solem* v. *Helm]* was wrong. The Eighth Amendment contains no proportionality guarantee," he said. The punishment need not fit the crime. No matter how severe the punishment for drug possession, the Court would not intervene.

Brennan, his face now frozen, glared at Scalia as he read on. At the other end of bench, Kennedy turned to O'Connor and shook his head slightly, drawing a nod of recognition from her. Though Scalia spoke with utter confidence, his opinion in reality did not represent the views of the majority. Only Rehnquist had signed it. Once again, Scalia had written a sweeping opinion but did not draw a majority to his views.

Kennedy refused to join Scalia's absolutist opinion. In his second full term, he had split away from Rehnquist and Scalia on occasion. Early in the term, he had written an opinion for the Court overturning a conviction because the suspect's *Miranda* rights were violated. In two rulings, he had insisted that the Constitution forbids any racial discrimination in selecting juries. His separate opinion in the *Harmelin* case reached the same result as Scalia and Rehnquist but wrote a different rule of law. Because of "the pernicious effects of the drug epidemic in this country," Michigan lawmakers can impose a life sentence for drug possession, he agreed. Nonetheless, the Constitution demands that the Court consider whether such sentences are "grossly disproportionate" to the crime. This one is not, he concluded, but a truly "extreme" sentence can be declared unconstitutional. O'Connor and Souter joined Kennedy's opinion.

Once again, White, the hard-liner on crime, found himself dissenting, along with Marshall, Blackmun, and Stevens. Life in prison for a first-time conviction for drug possession *is* cruel and unusual punishment, he declared....

The last of the opinions was read, and Rehnquist nodded toward the marshal, who promptly banged his gavel and announced that the "honorable Court" was now adjourned until the first Monday in October. Nothing was said of a pending retirement. Indeed, the chief justice did not know that another change was imminent.

The justices were due to gather in the conference room once more to dispose of the pending appeals. Marshall waited until then to break the news. His many vows to serve out his "life term" had convinced most that Marshall would never announce his retirement – but those predictions were wrong. He had told

Brennan first of the news. At the conference table, he told the others he planned to quit after 24 years. The next week, he would turn 83 years old. His eyesight was failing. So were his legs. His breath came in pained puffs. "I'm old and I'm coming apart," he told reporters the day after his resignation was announced. Perhaps what was most revealing at his last press conference was what went unsaid. Though pressed by reporters, Marshall refused to make a single critical comment about the conservative Court or its chief justice.

Still, his resignation added an exclamation point to the term's end. The last of the Warren Court liberals was gone. Rehnquist and the conservatives had control, and now even the voice of liberalism had vanished. . . .

With its two staunch liberals, William J. Brennan and Thurgood Marshall, gone, the Rehnquist Court is setting off on a new course. While its direction is clear, its destination is not. How far will the Court go in rolling back constitutional rights? Will the majority on the conservative Court feel bound by the precedents from a more liberal era? Will a moderate bloc emerge among the Reagan and Bush appointees? . . .

The retirement of Thurgood Marshall and his eventual replacement with Justice Clarence Thomas symbolized for many the final transformation of the Supreme Court. While Marshall had been a crusader for minorities and the poor, Thomas was expected to solidify the new Court's already powerful conservative majority.

QUESTIONS TO THINK ABOUT

1. How well known and well recognized by the public are Supreme Court justices?
2. In what way did the *Harmelin* case demonstrate the philosophical conflicts on the Court? From the facts available, how would you have voted on Harmelin's claim of cruel and unusual punishment?
3. What effect did Justice Marshall's retirement have on the composition of the Supreme Court as it approached the 1992-93 term? In the time that has since passed, from your own knowledge of recent Court decisions, has the Supreme Court continued "turning right"?
4. Evaluate how important political and ideological philosophy should be in a president's choice of a Supreme Court nominee. Is the public aware of the long-term importance of a president's power to nominate federal judges when they vote in a presidential election?

CRITIC'S CORNER

What does this cartoon imply about the political consequences of the Supreme Court's abortion decisions? What role do interest groups play in some Supreme Court cases? How much consensus is there within the Court on the issue of abortion? In your opinion, can the Supreme Court continue to navigate their way through this minefield of bitter controversy successfully?

10 | Public Opinion

"Politics is an art, not a science," say the professors who teach political theory. "Let's move the Political Science Department out of the social science building and in with the English Department's creative writers or with the painters in Fine Arts. Or at least next to the Philosophy Department – better coffee."

"No, politics is a science, not an art," counter the political science statisticians. "We want out of the social science building, too – not enough parking spaces – but let's move the department over near math or engineering to get at their computer facilities."

Politics is an art and a science in Alaska where a twenty-first-century teleconferencing network uses technology to bring citizens closer to their legislators in Juneau. The huge size, scattered population, and severe weather make Alaska the perfect place for the two-way interactive communications system, F. Christopher Arterton explains. Citizens participate in legislative hearings via the LTN (Legislative Teleconferencing Network). They send messages to legislators with LIN (Legislative Information Network) and POM (Public Opinion Message). Others are catching on to the possibilities. The *National Review* magazine and the Heritage Foundation, a think tank, advertise Town Hall: The Conservative Meeting Place. Conservatives nationwide can share ideas and plan strategy through a computerized communications system.

Many Americans today feel that government is remote from them. They are apathetic and cynical. For a great percentage of the citizens who do not vote or even register to vote, politics has lost all appeal. Yet when Ross Perot reached out to people directly on "Larry King Live" in 1992, many responded. Do science and technology have the capability to reinvigorate the art of politics in the United States?

F. Christopher Arterton
From *Teledemocracy*

The state of Alaska has some unique geographical features that isolate part of its population from the bulk concentrated in major cities. A vast expanse of land covering more area than the eastern half of the United States, Alaska is home to fewer residents than Albuquerque, New Mexico. Most of the population lives in either Anchorage, Fairbanks, or Juneau; the rest inhabit more than 200 smaller villages, separated from one another by vast stretches of open land. The difficulty of traveling establishes the need for a communications system that will collapse the large distances. In addition, very different ethnic cultures live side by side in both places. Special efforts must be made to overcome these impediments to political participation lest government become the spokesperson for the dominant culture concentrated in Anchorage and Juneau and not the voice of all the people.

Alaska has been the scene of many innovative experiments in involving citizens in public life, including the project discussed here that consists of two communication vehicles, the Legislative Telecommunications Network (LTN) and the Legislative Information Network (LIN). Formed in 1979 as a result of a report prepared by the Legislative Teleconferencing Network Task Force, originally five sites were linked by a dedicated four-wire circuit for audio teleconferences.

The LTN centers serve legislators in three ways: receiving legislative testimony from citizens, holding meetings with constituents, and arranging special meetings with aides or others helping legislators with their daily work. Legislative hearings are the most common use. Comments provided by citizens over the system are taken as formal testimony and legislators can listen and cross-examine witnesses just as though they were in the hearing room.

As one might expect, many legislators approached the concept of the LTN and LIN with initial skepticism. Larry Golden, the consultant who wrote the final report for the task force, was instrumental in alleviating the concerns of legislators worried about control over the process, the productive use of their time, and access to the network. Anticipating the political implications of such a system, Golden's idea was to graft the LTN onto the existing political structure with as little disruption as possible. The LTN was only intended to be an extension of the legislative process, not a method of securing direct democracy or altering the system in other ways.

Arranging for a teleconference follows a fairly routine scheduling process on a first come, first serve basis within the priorities noted above (hearings, constituent meetings, other business). The LTN staff asks for at least two weeks notice so they can notify their workers in the field who will then alert the community to an upcoming event. Although there are still a few holdouts, most legislators use the system, quite a few on a frequent basis.

When the legislature is in session, the LTN averages around three teleconferences per day. Most hearings are arranged by the chairman and the ranking minority member of the appropriate committees. However, if a legislator or a group of legislators feels that public sentiment on a particular issue demands a public airing, a teleconference often results. At times, special interest groups that are in touch with legislative activity in Juneau may be able to muster enough support to launch a teleconference. If the legislators are flexible enough and if considerable interest focuses upon one issue, a series of teleconferences can be held. This was true, for example, when the state was deciding whether to award a dividend to citizens from the extra money collected from Prudhoe Bay or to use these funds for new projects.

Charity Kedow, executive director, and Kathy Baltes, manager of LTN, reported that network usage reached saturation levels during the 1984 legislative session; from then on it became necessary to choose between competing users. When prioritizing teleconferences, the LTN will follow seniority rules established for the Alaskan legislature.

The legislators also decide which parts of the state should be included in a teleconference. Since each member has an interest in appealing to a particular district or to particular groups in the state, tension over which sites should be included in the teleconference can occur, especially if the number of sites requesting time stretches beyond the practical limit for conducting an effective meeting. This situation rarely arises: Most teleconferences do not evoke a huge outpouring of citizen interest.

Anyone at a growing number of sites is free to listen to any teleconference, regardless of whether they are scheduled to speak or not. If the subject matter provokes unscheduled listeners to add their thoughts, they can call up the LTN center in Anchorage or use a "back channel" computer network to request permission to speak. According to Kathy Baltes, the staff member principally responsible for the teleconferences, it is very rare for such a request to be denied. So while LTN staff put the practical limit of participation at six sites and legislators often choose the sites they think will be most important to receive feedback from, no one is excluded from talking simply because legislators or the LTN staff overlooked them.

Both Larry Golden and Dave Hammock, a consultant to the LTN, maintained that allowing every site to listen in on every teleconference was vital to establishing the system's integrity. Secret meetings, behind-closed-doors politics, are not possible on the LTN, so that, in theory, universal access will keep elected officials accountable to Alaskan citizens.

There are two other uses of the teleconferencing system. First, most legislators also hold regular teleconferences with their constituents to field complaints or questions and to explain actions the legislature has taken. As distinct from legislative hearings, the electronic office hours offer the citizen the opportunity to define the agenda. Because the format is less structured, extended discussion and debate is more likely. Reportedly, the participants in these constituent teleconferences come more often out of direct, individual interest than as representatives of an interest group or lobby organization.

Second, in order to draft legislation or hammer out compromises, representatives sometimes use the system to conduct working sessions, especially when the legislature is not in session. These usually involve small numbers of legislators and experts discussing issues in great detail. Though anyone on the system can listen in, the nature and substance of these meetings discourage most from doing so.

To complement the LTN, the state of Alaska also funds the Legislative Information Network (LIN) that provides citizens with pertinent and timely information regarding state government. A computer network allows citizens to trace the legislative history of any bill, to follow legislative development in particular subject areas, and to obtain copies of reports or bills. (The same computer network serves to coordinate the teleconferences, allowing the staff to exchange information on a "back channel.") Sites that combine the functions of the two networks are referred to as Legislative Information Offices (LIO); currently, fourteen LIOs staffed by full-time information officers dot the state while four other LIOs function on a part-time basis. Ideally, Alaskans who participate in teleconferences will also use the LIN to learn both the substantive and procedural issues affecting the topics in which they are interested.

Another important feature of the LIN allows citizens in distant locations to send their opinions on various legislative matters to legislators in Juneau through an electronic mail system. A concerned citizen can send a Public Opinion Message (POM) to a legislator or group of them through a computer network. The ease of using this system has made it very popular. When employed with the LIN, citizens can keep track of legislators' behavior on issues and prod them when they deviate from the citizen's own ideas.

Once it became clear that the LTN and LIN fulfilled a political need of legislators and citizens to communicate with each other, additional sites were gradually added. Besides the 18 Legislative Information Offices already mentioned, there are 28 full-time teleconference centers (LTN only) plus an additional 26 voluntary teleconference centers located in the homes and offices of people who have agreed to store and operate teleconferencing equipment for other people in the village.

Undoubtedly the most important reason for successful operation of the network lies in the efforts of those who run it. The crucial link in the system is provided by the field managers who actually run the scattered information offices and telecommunication centers. Not only do these people maintain the communications hardware but they also advocate its use to villagers who might be mistrustful of government, apathetic toward politics, or unaware of political disputes. If the field manager feels that village fishermen should be alerted to a bill concerning tax deductions for the purchase of business equipment, for example, he or she contacts the appropriate fishermen and informs them of the upcoming hearing. If the computer prints the requested information in the form of minutes of a committee hearing, the field manager often helps translate the information into a form that is useful for the citizen.

Thus the field manager walks a delicate tightrope between having to be strictly nonpartisan and yet wanting to stimulate interest in political issues so that the network receives use. Kedow and Baltes both said they selected the field managers with great care, trying to make sure that the new recruits move easily in the social and political circles of the communities they will be serving. Very often, the person chosen will be a former bartender, teacher or other central figure in the community who knows the intimate details of life in the community yet has managed not to alienate factions of the community.

Let us examine the quantity and quality of citizen participation. Alaska's small population is one of the most salient factors in state politics. Each representative has approximately 10,000 people in his or her district; the number of voters is much less. Very often, legislators know a high percentage of their constituents on a personal basis. In state races, elections are highly competitive. Moreover, the fact that many Alaskans work in subsidized or regulated industries also means that they appreciate the importance of speaking up for what they want.

Evidently, the LIN and LTN proved to be very popular within a short period of time. Legislators discovered that Alaskans wanted a greater voice in government and were willing to use the network. . . .

Even though only a few individuals can speak at each teleconference, some citizens find the discussions interesting or important enough that they will attend just to listen and be counted in the audience. One teleconference on highway regulations affecting trucking, for example, attracted over fifty truckers and their families, filling one site. Most of these only listened. Of course, their presence is noted and reported to the legislators in Juneau over the computer network. . . .

In turning to the role of political elites, we must distinguish between how legislators use the system and the strategies of interest groups. Legislators can request that their constituents be heard on a particular teleconference and then notify people in the district of the opportunity, thus appearing to perform a public service for these people. In our talk with Representative Cowdrey, he openly described his efforts to be sure that interests with which he agreed were represented in the teleconference testimony. For example, if one of his committees was organizing a teleconference on oil pricing, he would alert some groups—in this case forestry interests—that normally might not pay attention to these matters but could well have a narrow interest in this particular bill.

Interest groups have begun to use the network in fairly sophisticated ways. For example, when the state was conducting teleconferences on regulating boxing, a political consultant with a side interest in boxing rounded up a busload of boxers and took them to the LTN site. Nobody opposed to boxing showed up, so virtually all the testimony the committee heard was in favor of abandoning state regulation of the sport. The same political consultant mentioned that several local church groups had publicized the LTN to their parishioners as a way to have their voices heard in Juneau on matters of interest to the churches.

Both Representative Cowdrey and Baltes admitted that the LTN could be used by lobbyists, enabling them to back up their position papers with popular support. Walter Parker, a former telecommunications official with the state, noted that the fishermen have used the system very effectively in pressing for support of their troubled industry. According to rough estimates we received from the LTN staff, about 30%-40% participate as individuals, while 60%-70% are affiliated with some group or organization. Even so, the LTN allows legislators to reach *members* of these groups rather than their lobbyists or organizational staff in Juneau. Moreover, the percentage of those participating under their own volition appears to be substantially higher during constituent meetings (as opposed to hearings) but the overall number of participants is often correspondingly lower.

The LTN has exerted an important influence on government accountability of Alaskan politics, a political structure that was necessarily closed to most citizens because of geography and climate. Certainly the LTN allows a widening of the pool of witnesses and greater diversity in viewpoints. This may force legislators to consider the broader public interest as well as the narrow concerns of directly affected groups. In the same vein, because they are open at all sites the teleconferences serve an educational role by demanding more sophisticated and well-thought out testimony from interest groups whose positions are also made more public and widely distributed among the citizens. Now they must sell their positions publicly to a more diverse, larger, and informed audience.

Some observers of Alaskan politics claim the networks also enhance the position of incumbents as against their opponents. The agenda for the LTN/LIN is controlled by legislators who can choose whether to attend or skip a hearing depending on how comfortable they feel with the subject matter. If the legislator plays his card correctly, the LTN and LIN can effectively showcase his or her talents.

One must also note that opposing groups can more easily generate effective counterpublicity. They can seek information at the LIN about a legislator's record and then publicize their findings to the voters. Lobbyists and interest groups who have come to recognize the importance of the LTN/LIN have devised communication channels of their own in order to take political advantage of the system; these channels can be adopted to help opposing candidates.

In a more discreet way, the LTN and LIN have altered the political topography of the state. Because these networks offer such quick and easy contact with locations all over Alaska, legislators have expanded their political activity beyond their own districts, particularly as it relates to work they do to fulfill committee obligations. Lawmakers now seek opinions from a cross-section of the Alaskan population, and the networks have increased their familiarity with various interest groups in the state. One cannot, however, ascertain whether the presence of the LTN/LIN had sparked additional political mobilization in Alaskan politics outside of the networks.

In the final analysis, the intelligent manner in which the LTN and the LIN was grafted onto the existing political structure accounts for its success. The tacit endorsement of these systems by legislators using the system confers a legitimacy that encourages serious participation by all parties.

QUESTIONS TO THINK ABOUT

1. Why is Alaska well-suited for a teleconferencing network between citizens and their legislators?
2. Explain why some critics believe that the LTN and LIN networks are actually a vehicle for strengthening the voice of already strong interest groups rather than allowing more citizen input. Do you agree with these critics?
3. In what way does teleconferencing fulfill the same role as TV talk shows like "Larry King Live" and radio call-in programs? Would you favor nationally televised issue debates and instantaneous electronic public-opinion surveys? What are the benefits and the dangers of such an idea?
4. Do you think the conservatives' phone-linked computer network, Town Hall, featured in the Critic's Corner on the next page, is successful? Are conservatives well organized and well coordinated in their political activities?

CRITIC'S CORNER

Let's face it: Leftist organizations are so . . . coordinated. They're so . . . "networked." Just ask Robert Bork.

When it comes to "networking," conservative organizations have made big leaps in recent years. But too often, when a conservative organization engages in a policy battle, it can find itself fighting alone. Without allies.

Until now.

The *new* TOWN HALL, the computer-based conservative meeting place, is the locus where conservative organizations assemble and coordinate their policies, ideas and strategies—with the immediacy and intimacy they've never before enjoyed. TOWN HALL is an easy-to-access, secure setting where conservative groups and individuals can "network" with each other. TOWN HALL is a friendly and affordable conservative "inner sanctum" where the "Right" groups can plot, debate and plan—either internally or with other groups—on how to win that policy fight. Together.

TOWN HALL turns your phone-linked computer into a huge office building that only conservatives can enter. It's a place where your organization maintains a secure, private "office" suite: where a group can hold conferences between far-flung national, state and local affiliates, or communicate via our state-of-the-art electronic mail system. Where

you can research a critical issue and gain immediate access to important policy papers in the TH library, or allow individuals in different states to work together—at the same time— on an organization publication or direct mail piece.

And while TOWN HALL lets your organization network internally, our computerized piece of real estate is also the setting where your group can network with other conservative groups—the same groups which would have helped in that last policy fight, but which your organization couldn't coordinate with quickly enough—whenever you want, 24-hours-a-day.

Now with TOWN HALL—a joint project of National Review and The Heritage Foundation, two trusted conservative institutions—your organization, whether it be a Washington-based monolith or a small-but-dedicated local outfit, can conference with other conservative groups or individuals, share information and ideas, market products and publications, poll conservatives, and much, much more.

TOWN HALL's functions are endless. So when your group opens a TOWN HALL office, you'll not only increase your access to the rest of the conservative movement, you'll increase productivity.

TOWN HALL
The Conservative Meeting Place

To open your organization's office, or to get more information about TOWN HALL, contact Jeanne Allen, TOWN HALL Executive Director, at 1-202-546-4400. To open an individual account today, call 1-800-441-4142. Or maybe you'd like an online tour. Just dial by modem 1-800-648-6964.

A Project of NATIONAL REVIEW and THE HERITAGE FOUNDATION

11 | Interest Groups

The United States was a kid once, and it had parents like all kids do. The founding fathers, who probably could have used help from founding mothers, did a good job at birth and in childhood, although they covered over some big problems like slavery. America's founding dads gave a lot of warnings to their young. "Avoid entangling foreign alliances," said George Washington. James Madison told the young nation to be home by midnight, except on weekends, and to fear "faction" – any group that seeks to promote its interests above those of the rest of the citizenry. His fear was mostly of a poor unpropertied majority who might try to overwhelm the wealthier propertied minority. (Was this founding father of democracy, like many parents, a little bit hypocritical in fearing majority rule?) Madison's idea to prevent the domination of any one group was to encourage *many groups* to arise and compete with one another. Thanks for suggesting interest-group politics, Mr. Madison. It was a good idea.

Then America, like all kids, grew up to discover that times change. New problems arise that parents could not foresee. Two hundred years after Madison's warning, interest groups have become a big business in American politics. In fact, many of them represent big business. Interest-group lobbying today usually involves a sophisticated organization and lots of money. Associations representing over 8,000 special interests are registered in Washington. They have staff, headquarters, and computer equipment that enable them to lobby effectively for their positions. Interest-group political action committees (PACs) give money to candidates at election time. Their leaders meet with presidents and legislators. They befriend executive-agency bureaucrats. Lobbyists use many interesting techniques to win support. In the chapter on Congress, you may recall Senator James Eastland's request that the Cotton Council, Mississippi's most powerful interest group, bring a new supply of Chivas Regal to his office (chapter 6).

Not all interest groups in America are equally privileged in the resources they have available to them. William Greider recounts the efforts of "Janitors for Justice," a group of hard-working low-paid people who clean up Washington, D.C.'s corridors of power after work ends each day. The janitors make very little money and lack any job benefits. Only by taking to the streets together and making their plight known to people directly – often with some embarrassment – do the janitors feel that they will be heard.

Like "Janitors for Justice," organizers of interest groups on the local grass-roots level do not have exciting jobs, complete with PAC funding and computerized mailing lists. In his interviews with ordinary people, Studs Terkel found Maria Elena Rodriguez-Montes in Chicago. Her special interest is toxic waste, her group is made up of neighborhood people, her headquarters is her home, and her methods involve working at the deepest layer of the grassroots. Note Rodriguez-Montes's use of the kids' sticky fingers as a sure-fire lobbying tactic.

William Greider
From *Who Will Tell the People*

The quality of democracy is not measured in the contentment of the affluent, but in how the political system regards those who lack personal advantages. Such people have never stood in the front ranks of politics, of course, but a generation ago, they had a real presence, at least more than they have now. The challenging conditions they face in their daily lives were once part of the general equation that the political system took into account when it decided the largest economic questions. Now these citizens are absent from politics – both as participants and as the subjects of consideration.

These citizens are not the idle poor, though many hover on the edge of official poverty and virtually all exist in a perpetual condition of economic insecurity. These are working people – the many millions of Americans who fill the society's least glamorous yet essential jobs and rank at the bottom of the ladder in terms of compensation. A large segment of working-class Americans has effectively become invisible to the political debate among governing elites. They are neither seen nor heard nor talked about.

Their absence is a crucial element in the general democratic failure of modern politics. . . .

Like other citizens who have lost power, the humblest working folk have figured out how politics works in the modern age. They know that their only hope is "rude and crude" confrontation. To illustrate this reality, we turn to a group of citizens in Washington, D.C., who are utterly remote from power – the janitors who clean the handsome office buildings in the nation's capital. In a sense, they clean up each night after the very people and organizations that have displaced people like themselves from the political debate. While they work for wages that keep them on the edge of poverty, their political grievances are not heard through the regular channels of politics.

Like other frustrated citizens, the janitors have taken their politics, quite literally, into the streets of the nation's capital.

In late afternoon on a warm June day, while the people in suits and ties were streaming out of downtown office buildings and heading home, a group of fourteen black and Hispanic citizens gathered on the sidewalk in front of 1150 Seventeenth Street Northwest and formed a loose picket line. They were the janitors who cleaned this building every night and, though hardly anyone noticed or cared, they were declaring themselves "on strike" against poverty wages.

"Fire me? Don't bother me one bit. Can't do worse than this," Lucille Morris, a middle-aged black woman with two daughters, said. She was passing out picket signs to hesitant coworkers, most of them women. "Hold 'em up!" she exhorted the others. "Let 'em know you're tired of this mess."

Others grinned nervously at her bravado. An older Hispanic woman dressed in work clothes started into the building and was intercepted by one of the strikers, "She says she's just going in to use the bathroom," Leila Williams reported, "but she's coming back out." Williams, a sweet-faced grandmother who lives with her sixteen-year-old grandson in one of the poorest wards of southeast Washington, was wearing a bright red union tee-shirt that proclaimed: "Squeeze Me Real Hard – I'm Good Under Pressure."

"No one is working – this building isn't going to get cleaned tonight," the organizer from the Services Employees International Union announced with satisfaction. "And nobody's going to get fired," Jay Hessey reassured. "The company can't find enough people to do these jobs at this pay."

"I've been here eleven years and I still get the same pay the newcomers get – $4.75 an hour," Lucille Morris said. "We be doing like two people's work for four hours a night. We don't get nothing in the way of benefits. You get sick, you sick. You stay out too long, they fire you."

"One lady been here for fourteen years and she still get five dollars an hour for doing the bathrooms," Leila Williams added. "They give you another quarter an hour for doing the toilets. When we pass inspections, you known, they always treat us. They give us pizza or doughnuts, like that. We don't want no treats. We want the money."

The SEIU, a union that mainly represents people who do society's elementary chores, launched its "Justice for Janitors" strategy nationwide in 1987 and has staged scores of similar strikes in downtown Washington as well as other major cities. Because of the way federal government now regulates the workers' right to organize for collective action, regular union-organizing tactics have been rendered impotent. So the workers mostly stage symbolic one-night walk-outs to grab attention.

The real organizing tactic is public shame – theatrical confrontations in-tended to harass and embarrass the owners and tenants of the buildings. The janitors will crash the owner's dinner parties and leaflet his neighborhood with accusatory handbills. They will confront the building's tenants at social events and demand help in pressuring the owners.

They, for instance, targeted Mortimer Zuckerman, the real-estate developer who owns *The Atlantic* magazine and *U.S. News & World Report*, with a nasty flier that declared: "Mort Zuckerman might like to be seen as a public citizen, responsible editor, intellectual and all-around good guy. To the janitors who clean his buildings, he is just another greedy real-estate operator." They hounded Zuckerman at important banquets and even in the Long Island Hamptons at celebrity softball games, in which he is a pitcher.

The owners and managers of some five hundred office buildings in Wash-ington have developed an efficient system that insulates them from both unions and higher wages. Each owner hires an independent contractor to service the building and the competitive bidding for contracts is naturally won by the firm that pays the least to the janitors. About six thousand workers – most of them black or Hispanic – are left without any practical leverage over the arrange-ment. When the union signs up workers and demands its legal right to bargain for a contract in their behalf, the building owner promptly fires the unionized cleaning contractor and hires a new own who is nonunion. Old janitors are fired, new ones are recruited, and the treadmill continues.

This management device keeps janitors like Lucille Morris stuck perma-nently at the same wage level year after year, hovering just above the legal minimum required by law, a wage level that provides less than $10,000 a year at full-time hours.

But these janitors do not even get full-time work from their employers. By doubling the size of the crews, the contractors can hold the workers to a four-hour shift each night and, thus, legally exclude the janitors from all of the em-ployee benefits the firms provide to full-time employees – health insurance, pensions, paid vacations, paid sick leave. The law protects this practice too.

In order to survive, these women and men typically shuttle each day be-tween two or three similar low-wage jobs, all of which lack basic benefits and other protections. Some of the janitors, those who are supporting families, qualify as officially poor and are eligible for food stamps, public housing, or other forms of government aid. In effect, the general taxpayers are subsidizing these low-wage employers – the gleaming office buildings of Washington and their tenants – by providing welfare benefits to people who do work that is nec-essary to the daily functioning of the capital's commerce.

In another era, this arrangement might have been called by its right name – exploitation of the weak by the strong – but in the contemporary politi-cal landscape that sort of language is considered passé. Exploitative labor practices are subsumed under the general principle of economic efficiency and the consequences are never mentioned in the political debates on the great social problems afflicting American cities. The government may authorize welfare for the indigent, but it will not address the wages and working conditions that impoverish these people. . . .

For the city of Washington, the political neglect constitutes a social irony, for many of these janitors live in the same troubled neighborhoods where the vicious street combat over drugs occurs. The community is naturally horrified by the violence among the young drug merchants and, without much success, has deployed both police and National Guard to suppress it. Yet the city is oblivious to the plight of the janitors – the people who are working for a living, trying to be self-supporting citizens and must live in the midst of the dangerous social deterioration.

Economists might not see any connection between these two social problems, but any teenager who lives in one of the blighted neighborhoods can grasp it. One group of poor people, mostly young and daring, chooses a life of risk and enterprise with the promise of quick and luxurious returns. Another group of poor people, mostly older men and women, patiently rides the bus downtown each night, and in exchange for poverty wages, they clean the handsome office buildings where the lawyers and lobbyists work. When the janitors stage their occasional strikes, they are harassing the very people who have helped block them out of governing issues – the policy thinkers, the lawyers and lobbyists and other high-priced talent who have surrounded the government in order to influence its decisions.

By coincidence, one of the tenants at 1150 Seventeenth Street, where they were picketing, was the American Enterprise Institute, the conservative think tank that produces policy prescriptions for the political debates of Washington. When the service-employees union organizers approached AEI for support, their request was brushed off, but AEI has had quite a lot to say about minimum-wage laws and their supposedly deleterious effects. In recent years, AEI has published at least nine different scholarly reports arguing against the minimum wage. This position faithfully represents the interests of AEI's sponsoring patrons – the largest banks and corporations in America.

But the SEIU organizers insisted they were not trying to make an ideological point by picking on AEI. The real target was the building owner, which operated a dozen downtown buildings in a similar manner. Besides, they explained, most of the ostensibly liberal policy groups in Washington are no different, from the janitors' point of view.

Indeed, the next strike was planned against another building, also owned by the Charles E. Smith Management Company, which served as the home of the Urban Institute, a liberal think tank that specializes in studying the afflictions of the urban poor. The Urban Institute, though presumably more sympathetic to the working poor, has also published scholarly pamphlets questioning the wisdom of laws to improve their wages.

The Urban Institute scholars are regarded as a liberal counterpoise to such conservative institutions as AEI but, in fact, the liberals are financed, albeit less generously, by the same business and financial interests that pay for the conservative thinkers – Aetna Insurance, $75,000; Chase Manhattan Bank, $15,000; Exxon, $75,000; General Electric, $35,000; Southwestern Bell, $50,000 and so on. The commonly held illusion in Washington politics is that supposedly disinterested experts contend with each other over defining the "public good" from different viewpoints. Yet many of them get their money from the same sources – business and financial interests.

Like other tenants, officials at the Urban Institute insisted the janitors' pay was not their problem. It was a dispute for the cleaning contractor or the building owner to resolve. The SEIU organizers were twice turned down in their efforts to meet with the Urban Institute's officers, so they went out to picket their private homes and tried to crash the institute's banquet for its board of directors.

"Isn't it the same kind of issue any time you pass someone on the street who's homeless?" asked Isabel V. Sawhill, a senior fellow at the institute who is an authority on the "underclass" and related social questions. "It's hard to get involved as an individual in all these microdecisions to change the system. It can't be done at that level. Laws and policies have to be changed."

But these weren't exactly distant strangers one passed on the street. They were the very people who cleaned the office each night, carried out the trash, vacuumed the carpet and scrubbed the sinks and toilets.

"Actually, we never see them," Sawhill allowed. "I do sometimes see them, I admit, because I hang around late, but most people don't."

The janitors, it is true, were mostly invisible. Despite several years of flamboyant efforts, the janitors' campaign had gained very little presence in the civic consciousness of Washington. Public shame is not a terribly reliable lever of political power. For one thing, it only works if widely communicated, and the major media, including *The Washington Post*, had largely ignored the fractious little dramas staged by the janitors.

"People are yawning at them," said Richard Thompson, president of General Maintenance Service, Inc., the largest employer of low-wage janitors. "If there were really a justice question, people in this city would react. There are a lot of government and city government folks who wouldn't stand for it."

The janitors thought they would embarrass both local politicians and congressional Democrats when they targeted a strike at the new shopping complex in Union Station, which is owned by the federal government. Instead, the janitors were fired and commerce continued without interference from the government. Though the Democratic party is ostensibly sympathetic to people like the janitors, Democrats also rely on the real-estate industry as a major source of campaign money.

After an hour or so of picketing on Seventeenth Street, the janitors got into vans and drove over to a museum at New York Avenue and Thirteenth Street

where a local charity was holding its annual fund-raising gala. The strikers had
no quarrel with the charity, but they did wish to embarrass David Bruce Smith,
a young man who is an officer in his grandfather's real-estate company and was
serving as chairman of the benefit dinner.

The women in red tee-shirts and the union organizers spread out along the
sidewalk and began giving handbills to any who would take them. "Talk with
David Bruce Smith," the leaflet asked. "The Janitors Deserve Some Benefits
Too!"

The encounter resembled a sidewalk parody of class conflict. As people began arriving for the event, an awkward game of dodging and ducking ensued
between the black janitors and the white dinner guests in evening dress.
Women from the charity dinner stationed themselves at curbside and, as cars
pulled up for the valet parking, they warned the arriving guests about what
awaited them. The black women came forward offering their leaflets, but were
mostly spurned, as people proceeded swiftly to the door.

"Look, we are a charitable organization and this is political," a man complained bitterly to the union organizers. "People are going to see this and say,
what? Are you trying to embarrass me? They're coming here to enjoy themselves."

Jay Hessey reminded him of the constitutional right to petition for redress
of grievances. Three D.C. police cars were on hand in the event the janitors violated the law by blocking the doorway or waving placards. It's unfair, the official sputtered, to target an organization that is devoted to charitable activities.
It was unfair, the janitors agreed, but then so is life itself. Some people get
valet parking. Some people get an extra quarter for cleaning the toilets.

As tempers rose, Hessey stood toe-to-toe with the angry officials and re-
buffed them with an expression of utter indifference to their distress. Hessey's
colloquial term for the janitors' rude theater – "In your face" – was the essence
of their politics. Cut off from the legitimate avenues of political remedy, the
janitors had settled on what was left. Like it or not, fair or unfair, people were
going to consider, at least for a few uncomfortable moments, the reality known
to these janitors.

Most of the guests followed instructions and darted past the demonstrators
to the door, but this greatly amused Lucille Morris and Leila Williams and
their companions. It had taken considerable courage for these black and Hispanic cleaning women to stand on a sidewalk in downtown Washington and
confront well-to-do white people from the other side of town. Once they were
there, the women found themselves enjoying the encounter.

It was the white people who turned grim and anxious. Without much success, the black women followed couples to the doorway, urging them to read
the handbills. An elegantly dressed woman in silk turned on them and snapped:
"You know what? For three hundred dollars, you should be able to enjoy your
evening!"

When a mother and daughter streaked past Leila Williams, refusing her handbill, she called after them: "All right, ladies. But you might be standing out here yourself sometime."

"That's right," another janitor exclaimed. "The Lord gave it all, the Lord can take it away."

Their exercise in public shame was perhaps not entirely futile. The elegant woman in silk evidently thought better of her harsh words to the black women because, a few minutes later, she returned outside and discreetly asked them for a copy of their leaflet. She mumbled an expression of sympathy and promised to help, then returned to the banquet.

The janitors may lack formal educations and sophisticated experience with finance but they understand the economic situation well enough.

They know, for instance, that unionized janitors in New York City or Philadelphia will earn two or three times more for doing the very same work. They know that in Washington the federal government and some major private employers, like *The Washington Post* and George Washington University, pay nearly twice as much to janitors and also provide full employee benefits. They know, because the union has explained it for them, that janitorial services represent a very small fraction of a building's overall costs and that even dramatic pay increases would not wreck the balance sheets of either the owners or the tenants.

The problem, as they see it, is not economics. Their problem is power and no one has to tell the janitors that they don't have any. Collective action is the only plausible means by which they can hope to change things. But even the opportunity for collective action has been gravely weakened for people such as these.

The janitors' predicament provides a melodramatic metaphor for a much larger group of Americans – perhaps 20 million or more – who have also lost whatever meager political presence they once had. These are not idlers on welfare or drug addicts, though they often live among them. These are working people, doing necessary jobs and trying to live on inadequate incomes.

These Americans have been orphaned by the political system. They work in the less exalted occupations, especially in the service sector, making more than the minimum wage but less than a comfortable middle-class income. Most have better jobs and higher wages than the Washington janitors – office clerks, hospital attendants, retail salespeople – but are trapped by similar circumstances. Among health-care workers, for instance, one third earn less than $13,000 a year. Some occupations that used to be much higher on the wage scale – airline stewardesses or supermarket clerks – have been pushed closer to the low end by the brutal giveback contracts that labor unions were compelled to accept during the 1980s.

The incomes of the group I'm describing range roughly upward from the poverty line (around $10,000 for a family of three) to somewhere just short of the median household income of around $35,000. "Working poor" does not accurately describe most of them but then neither does "middle class." The poor still suffer more in their daily lives, of course, but even the poor are represented in politics by an elaborate network of civic organizations.

If one asks – Who are the biggest losers in the contemporary alignment of governing power? – it is these people who are economically insecure but not officially poor. During the last generation and especially the last decade, they have been effectively stripped of political protections against exploitation in the workplace. Neither party talks about them or has a serious plan to address their grievances. In the power coordinates that govern large national questions, these people literally do not exist. . . .

After many weeks of pressure and rude confrontations, the D.C. janitors found that some people do respond to the tactics of public embarrassment. After twice rebuffing them, officials at the Urban Institute agreed to support the janitors' plea for better wages. Mortimer Zuckerman also evidently had a change of heart, for his real-estate company abruptly agreed to bargain with the union for contracts at three buildings. The Charles E. Smith Company retreated too after the expressions of community concern generated by the janitors' appearance at the charity dinner.

These breakthroughs for "Justice for Janitors" might be taken as heart-warming evidence that "the system works," as Washington political columnists like to say. But the real meaning was the contrary. The janitors' union, like others, has figured out that the way politics gets done nowadays is not by electing people to office or passing bills in Congress. Politics gets done by confronting power directly, as persistently and rudely as seems necessary.

For all its weaknesses, the irregular methodology exemplified by "Justice for Janitors" has become the "new politics" of the democratic breakdown. Other labor unions, large and small, have adopted similar strategies designed to "shame" corporations into accepting decent labor relations. They confront prominent shareholders at public gatherings or testify against the companies at zoning hearings and before government agencies. They assemble critical dossiers on a corporation's environmental record that will shock the public and drive off consumers. These and other corporate-campaign strategies are sometimes effective in forcing a company to respond to its workers. Like the "Justice for Janitors" campaign, however, the tactics are driven by the workers' essential weakness, not the potential power that lies in their collective strength. In the present circumstances, what else works?

Studs Terkel
From *The Great Divide*

Maria Elena Rodriguez-Montes

"I was born with an excessive amount of energy. My daily schedule is very busy. People ask me, How do you do it? I don't know. God gave me something."

To say she is active in her community and city is to say Babe Ruth was a baseball player. She serves on a dozen or so committees, among them: Board of Trustees of the City Colleges of Chicago; chairman, UNO [United Neighborhood Organization, a citywide community action group], Southeast Branch; director of Illinois Fiesta Advocativa . . .

She is petite, delicate-featured, offering the impression of a china doll. She is twenty-nine, a mother of three children, twelve, eight, and six. "I was seventeen when I got married, a senior in high school. I don't have a formal education. I think of going back to school. My parents were migrant workers. There were seven of us. I'm the pickle in the middle.

"I'm a person who was born and raised on the Southeast Side of Chicago, two blocks from where I now live."

Five years ago, August 1982, an organizer from UNO knocked on my door. He was knocking on a lot of doors, trying to get people to fight the proposed landfill for the neighborhood – 289 acres, for toxic waste. Waste Management, the company, is the largest in the world.

Two hundred and eighty-nine acres, in comparison to sixteen acres in Love Canal. Two, three blocks away from the school our kids go to. It scared me.

Would you be willing to host a small meeting at your house? Sure. Four people showed. We called others. A couple of weeks later, there were thirty, meeting in the basement. We had expected twenty at most. There was an interest. People who had just bought homes in the area were afraid the property values would go down. Senior citizens were scared. The smell was bad already, and it was going to get worse with this.

We identified IEPA [Illinois Environmental Protection Agency] as responsible. At the first meeting with them, they said talk to the alderman, talk to the mayor, talk to USEPA [United States EPA]. Passing the buck. It was somebody else's problem, not ours.

About thirty of us went to the governor's office downtown. How can we get these guys to respond? Our strategy was: We'll take our kids down, with taffy apples. The kids were grabbing things, getting all the furniture sticky. The secretaries and staff were getting real upset – (laughs) – how else would we get their attention, unless we disrupted formal office procedure?

This was our first action. It was kinda scary. I had never been so assertive before. I was the spokesperson. I said to this guy, the state director of EPA, we're not leaving. Of course, our kids are running around with their sticky taffy apples.

He got the governor on the telephone and wanted me to go in the next room to talk to him. I said, "I'll talk to him over the phone with these people present." So every time the governor said something to me over the phone, I would turn to my people and ask them, "What do you think?" The governor agreed to come to our meeting. It was our first victory, our first sense of power.

He didn't show, but sent the IEPA director. There were about two hundred people. We demanded a study of contamination in our soil, water, air. And no permit issued to Waste Management until the results were in. They agreed. Again, we felt it was a tremendous victory. People by this time were feeling good.

It wasn't a great study. Yes, we have cancers higher than in other parts of the city. Yes, we have a lot of lead around. Yes, we have a lot of toxins in the air. "But you're not really at that much of a risk."

Congressman Washington was running for mayor and needed the Hispanic vote. When he was elected, we had a big meeting at St. Kevin's Church. Six hundred people showed up. I was chairing the meeting. It was my debut as a community leader.

The mayor came out with the kind of speech you expect from a politician, okay? It was many, many words. He talked wonderfully and the people applauded. They thought he had said something, but I knew he hadn't. He was shaking people's hands as he was walking away.

I remember feeling angry. Did he really think he was fooling us? I called out, "Mayor, will you please come back here? We're not done with you yet, buddy." (Laughs.) I said, "You spoke a long time, but you haven't answered any of my questions. I'm going through them, one by one, and I want an answer to each one." You don't normally speak to a mayor like that, but I wanted somebody to be accountable. Why not the mayor?

"Will you look at that zoning permit, and if possible revoke it? Yes or no?" He'd look at me: "Yes, Mrs. Montes." (Laughs.) "Will you, as soon as you get back to City Hall, look at those contracts?" We went through them all. "Final question – let me make this clear – will you keep this company out of our neighborhood? Yes or no?" He said yes.

I remember I grabbed him, hugged him, and kissed him on the cheek. The whole crowd was standing and applauding. It was the best thing ever happened to us. It was great. We got a real commitment that day. The mayor did put a moratorium in effect.

It does not allow any new landfills in the city of Chicago. Waste Management is still out. Waste Management is still thinking of coming in the neighborhood. I personally will not allow it.

We took two hundred people and jammed the annual stockholders' meeting of Waste Management. Sisters of Mercy, who own some stock, gave us their proxies. They stopped us at the door, but we created such a ruckus that their stock went down three, four points the next day.

We knew we had to aggravate them. So we formed a human chain that didn't allow the garbage trucks into the landfill. We had a big sign: THE MUCK STOPS HERE. We're talking about the Dan Ryan Expressway, okay? Trucks were backed up for miles. A week later, we brought double amount of people and our kids, too. Again, we backed the trucks up for miles.

They brought in the paddy wagons. It was scary because none of us had ever been arrested before, okay? We had people there who weren't willing to be arrested and certain ones who were willing to go all the way. The police got very confused and arrested the wrong people. They arrested one little girl of four or five. I was the last one they took away.

We were singing all the time: "All we're asking is give South Deering a chance." I remember saying, "If we don't get to see the president, we'll be back. I don't care if we have to go to his house, his church, or the school where his kids go." These things made us all the tighter.

I may have got some of this energy from my mother. She was active in bringing in bilingual education. She was PTA president. She worked hard forming youth groups in the community. She was in everything.

Two years ago, when my daughter was ten, she organized an action. My children go to a magnet school, so they're bused. The driver was drinking. He'd stop, go to a bar, and leave all the children in the bus. My daughter and another leader decided they weren't going to allow this to continue. They organized thirty, forty kids on the bus and decided to go see the principal. The person at the top. They all marched into the principal's office and requested a meeting then and there. She came out, they explained the situation and made demands. The principal was impressed. They made a difference: the driver was fired.

Maybe I'm not always at home, not as much as I should be, as much as some parents are, but I'm giving them a vision. I'm an example to them that as individuals, we can make a difference in life.

There's a young lady that I just recently met. She reminds me of myself when I was younger. Her mother said, "I want you to be her mentor." I want this young lady to feel the way I feel now, okay?

QUESTIONS TO THINK ABOUT

1. What is the only way, according to Greider, for a group of citizens to make their needs known to those in positions of power and to the public?

2. Describe some of the complaints made by "Justice for Janitors." Why is the plight of the working poor particularly paradoxical for those who live and work in Washington, D.C.?
3. Why was the issue of the toxic-waste landfill one that produced grassroots citizen activism in Chicago?
4. Do well-organized, well-financed interest groups use the same tactics in lobbying as groups like the Washington janitors or the Chicago neighborhood activists against toxic waste? Can groups with few resources be successful in reaching their goals?

CRITIC'S CORNER

WAYNE STAYSKAL
Courtesy Tampa Tribune

" I THOUGHT HE WAS A MEMBER OF A SPECIAL INTEREST GROUP...
BUT I FOUND OUT HE'S ONLY A VOTER ! "

What does this cartoon imply about the importance of everyday voters to members of Congress? What does it say about the relationship between interest groups and legislators in Congress? How do you feel about the lobbying activities of special interest groups such as the National Rifle Association, the tobacco industry, etc.? Do you think it is ethical for members of Congress to receive large campaign contributions from interest groups?

12 | Political Parties and Elections

Every candidate who has run for office, from town council to state legislature to the presidency, has campaign stories indelibly inscribed in her or his memory. Ordinary voters usually don't know all the details about these inside stories. Part of the fun of working on a political campaign is being involved in the behind-the-scenes dramas that occur during a candidate's run for office.

Campaign stories can be triumphant or tragic. Politicians and political scientists learn important lessons from both kinds. After Gerald Gardner's quick look at 1952 and 1956 Democratic presidential nominee Adlai Stevenson's dilemma, Christopher Matthews offers two upbeat stories describing how both Jesse Jackson and Ronald Reagan have proven themselves to be adroit campaigners. In 1990 Dianne Feinstein made a run for the governorship of California. Feinstein had formerly been the Democratic mayor of San Francisco, and the time seemed right for her to take on Republican Pete Wilson. Celia Morris chronicles Feinstein's losing effort, as huge sums put into mass media did not pay off in the end. Interestingly, one of the candidate's most successful strategies involved small house parties where person-to-person campaigning occurred. Feinstein's 1990 campaign reveals the variety of techniques used in modern elections. Feinstein ran again in 1992 for the Senate and won; Senator Tim Wirth left the Senate in 1992, disillusioned with political life, as his account reveals – 1992 was a big year for "new blood" in the Congress.

Despite the high-tech world of politics today, there's plenty of room for you to get over to your state representative's headquarters – the un-air-conditioned rented room above the noisiest bar in town – and start stuffing envelopes!

Gerald Gardner
From *The Mocking of the President*

Though the McCarthy era of communist witch-hunts cast a pall over satire in America during the [1952 and 1956] Eisenhower-Stevenson campaigns, there were some wags who were willing to sink their barbs into Adlai Stevenson. A columnist for a Boston daily wrote, "I originally liked Stevenson because he was so direct and straightforward in his speeches and told you exactly what he meant. But then I lost faith in him. What I didn't like was that he was so direct and straightforward in his speeches and told you exactly what he meant."

Christopher Matthews
From *Hardball*

[Jesse Jackson]

In 1987, Jesse Jackson showed how it's done.

Speaking to an elite black-tie fund-raising audience in Washington, D.C., he paid tribute to Senator Bill Bradley of New Jersey. Jackson said that Bradley was one of his personal heroes "because of his fight against racial stereotyping. Bill Bradley triumphed against great odds to become a basketball star. He had to reach these goals despite the handicap of race and family background. We all know the Bill Bradley story: how the young white man from the right side of the tracks came to one day become a professional basketball player.

"His neighbors were riding him, and his friends laughed at him, but he persevered. Bill was determined to succeed until at last he broke the chains of race-conscious behavior to join the front ranks in the great American sport of basketball." The crowd, still giddy at the subject matter, was beginning to erupt.

"When Bill first spoke his dream out loud, his guidance counselors at school tried to discourage him, to break his spirit. Finally one of them took him aside and told him the facts of life: 'Bill, you must accept the fact that it's got nothing to do with your ability. It doesn't matter how many points you score or how loud the cheers are. You can't go to the top, because you are *white.*'"

As Jackson spoke this last, blunt word the audience of establishment Democrats went stone silent. The candidate had accomplished his dramatic objective. He was admitting that he faced tremendous odds in his campaign for

President. But he was saying that the problem was not his radical positions or his divisive statements but his race, pure and simple.

It was . . . masterful. . . . The well-heeled crowd walked out of the Hilton that night thinking that Jackson had told a great joke with an ironic premise. But he had done more than that. He had laid the conceptual foundation for his second campaign for the Presidency. Sure, he had a vulnerability as a candidate, but he, Jesse Jackson, could not be blamed for that vulnerability. . . .

[Ronald Reagan]

President [Reagan] took his TelePrompTer with him wherever he went, but it would be a mistake to ascribe the Great Communicator's skills to technology alone. He was, first of all, a skilled and professional performer who did not skimp on rehearsal time, spending vital hours at the front of the White House family movie theater mastering his material. By the time he delivered his speeches, his command was so great that TV viewers could not even see the pupils of his eyes pause on the TelePrompTer screen; his rotation was so smooth that it looked to all appearances as if his eyes were locked on his audience, not on the words being projected on the glass.

Above all, he never forgot that he himself, not "supply-side economics" or "strategic defense," was the most important product. Backstage monitors were there to help him appear more "regular" and less regal. The space-age TelePrompting and those contacts of his made him more *personal* in his broadcasts.

When Reagan used such techniques, he was positioning himself with enormous science, establishing himself in the public mind not as an aloof head of government but as the man next door. Every action was designed to make him appear close to the people and distant from the government. Where his predecessors identified themselves with the attainment of government power, Reagan posed as a visiting citizen. . . .

The climactic moment [of the 1980 Republican Convention] came as Reagan appeared to end his prepared remarks. He paused on the platform, looked out to the convention floor and to the millions at home, and announced that, in the best Hollywood tradition, he was throwing away the script.

"I have just thought of something that is not part of my speech," Reagan said in his best husky-intimate voice, "and I am worried whether I should do it."

He paused again, and followed through with a beautifully composed tribute to America as the refuge of those "who yearn to breathe freely." Then the clincher: "I'll confess that I'm a little afraid to suggest what I am going to suggest. I'm more afraid not to."

He then asked for a moment of silent prayer for the great "crusade" he was now beginning.

Reagan's finale was the hit of the convention. It had drama, suspense, even a Hitchcockian twist at the end, all of which dynamized the politics of the occasion. It allowed Reagan to do what he likes to do most: portray himself as an amateur among professionals, a citizen among politicians. Only later would it get out that the finale had been written well ahead of time. The closing remarks, which had been purposefully deleted from the texts given to the press, were on his three-by-five cards all the time.

Celia Morris
From *Storming the Statehouse*

Dianne Feinstein would win the Democratic nomination for governor of California because she was a woman with a rich husband and because the television camera loved her. True, she was a viable candidate because she was smart, hard-driving, ambitious, and compassionate. But as a bright red splash against a background of battleship gray, she appealed to voters in a state in which political power has become balkanized.

The challenge Feinstein confronted fueled the widely held suspicion that women get their chance at office only after men have mucked up politics so badly it is hardly worth trying and may indeed be impossible. By 1990, the great golden promise of California had begun to dull, and voters who bothered to pay attention were both confused and angry. (The majority had given up on the political process altogether.)

The cry that had emboldened adventurers for over a century–"Go West, young man!"–had brought more people to California in the 1980s than at any time in its history, but nobody knew quite what to do with them, or more precisely, how to pay for them. The infrastructures of the state were falling apart, and the mechanisms that people had used to address and solve their collective problems had broken down. The erosion of political order, ironically, gave Feinstein a chance to win high office that she exploited with a stalwart competitor's glee. . . .

Political power had become balkanized, and the operative term to describe the consequence was "gridlock." The common word is "stuck." Cars were stuck on freeways; bills were stuck in committees; legislators were stuck in office.

A woman with an appetite for governing–for making things work and watching people strive–saw, for all practical purposes, a vast field with no horizon. And nobody could say No to her running for governor. The breakdown of political order meant, among other things, that there was no recognized succession of political power and authority and therefore no one who could give or withhold permission when Dianne Feinstein began thinking about running for governor. But if nobody was in a position to hinder, no one was sure to help either. . . .

Though she had been considered for the Democratic vice-presidential nomination [in 1984], she had held no position higher than mayor of a medium-sized city [San Francisco], and City Hall does not ordinarily have the power necessary to catapult someone to the highest office in the state. She had no ties other than to the Democratic party that would provide a statewide political infrastructure. She was not a labor Democrat, nor a club Democrat, nor an ethnic Democrat – and she had never been involved in the California women's movement.

But television had changed American politics forever – especially in California, which might as well have invented media – and Dianne Feinstein was a candidate who showed to advantage on television. The state had long since taught the rest of the country to expect unusual things: since the early 1960s, California had dumbfounded observers by electing a tap dancer and a sleepy linguist to the United States Senate and giving an affable if mediocre actor a platform from which to rise to the presidency. In so mercurial an atmosphere, a woman governor whose only apprenticeship had been as mayor would not seem wholly out of line.

Nor would anything in California's political party structure work against Feinstein. Since parties are relatively weak there, the Democratic party is not a principal vehicle for setting the policy agenda, for fund-raising, for recruiting new and promising candidates, or for appealing to new voters. . . .

Because the advent of television politics had made the electoral process stunningly expensive, such new legislators as there were tended to come from the ranks of Sacramento staff who had mastered that process and cozied up to the power structure and the lobby, rather than community activists who were fighting for causes like the environment. The political game had been self-referential: electoral politics was now merely about electoral politics. Voters had grown disgusted with the typical California politician because they thought he or she was merely holding on to power – not to do anything with it but simply to have it.

The legislature had come to seem a battleground for special interests. The insurance industry and the trial lawyers, for instance, had used campaign contributions to influence legislators to fight each other to a standstill over bills regulating insurance coverage so that no such bills were likely to emerge in the foreseeable future.

This unpleasant and unproductive situation, if it did little else, gave Dianne Feinstein the chance to go before the voters and insist that she was different: she represented change. If she knew very little about state government, she nevertheless was not tainted with Sacramento. She was *not* the typical California politician. . . .

Faced, then, with an opponent [Senator Pete Wilson] whose resources were virtually unlimited and a massive and largely indifferent electorate, Feinstein was confronted with a key question: how could she catch and hold the voters' attention? The obvious answer was through the media.

Although California is fortunate in having one of the country's world-class newspapers, the *Los Angeles Times,* it reaches fewer than one-third of the households in its region. Its political reportage typically begins on page 3, yet surveys suggest that three-quarters of even *Times* readers seldom make it past page 1. Feinstein staffers were convinced, furthermore, that the *Times* was preoccupied with the mechanics of the race rather than the issues.

Vicky Rideout, for instance, who had moved to Feinstein's campaign from [primary-opponent Attorney General] John Van de Kamp's to be issues director and chief speech writer, was well positioned to appreciate her dilemma. "The political reporters around here are ridiculous," Rideout said disdainfully a few days before the election. "They poked fun at Van de Kamp for trying to run an issue-oriented campaign, and now they write that the candidates won't talk about issues. The very next day [after a reporter or columnist has so complained] we'll give a totally issue-oriented, substantive speech, and they won't be there to cover it."

[Advisor] Darry Sragow summarized Feinstein's exasperation with the print media: "The *Times* probably won't cover a press conference, and people probably aren't going to read [a story about] it anyway." If this was true of the *Times,* no other newspaper (with the possible exception of the *Sacramento Bee,* which serves an audience of political junkies) could be expected to do better.

Then there is television. Roughly half of California's 30 million people live within range of the Los Angeles media market and a quarter within range of the San Francisco media market. San Diego and Sacramento split the difference, to make four media markets that reach about 88 percent of the voting public.

So what about television news? According to Sragow, "The budgets of the TV news bureaus have dropped dramatically, [and] there's not a single TV news bureau in Sacramento." Since network television is a commercial proposition, "the people who run the news media, whether electronic or print," as consultant Bill Zimmerman puts it, "are in the ratings business." Together the network news programs have a rating of 40 percent—if Zimmerman is correct, MacNeil/Lehrer "doesn't even register in terms of a percentage of the total audience"—which means that less than half the voting population looks to television for news. So instead of dwelling on less sensational developments, the media report murders, rapes, fires, and natural disasters that capture people's attention.

Therefore, a man paid to reach the voters, as Sragow was, had a problem. Concluding that "generating news doesn't work" and observing that "electronic entertainment, in one form or another, is [our] main leisure activity," Sragow decided that the best time to reach California voters was at eleven o'clock at night with thirty-second television ads interspersed between programs and the segments of programs. "It's the only chance we have," he said, and "that's the reason we have to raise such obscene amounts of money."

Sragow's consolation was that "anybody who's different breaks through the information barrier more readily [and] a woman's different. . . .

The other way to reach voters is through grass-roots organizing, but because California has more than 13 million voters and twenty-six thousand precincts, the conventional wisdom goes against spending money on a field operation. To make it work, it is necessary to target carefully and find thousands of canvassers who will hit the streets and dial the phones largely because they have faith in what they are doing. So a candidate needs, on one hand, a political organization that believes that grass-roots efforts matter and is willing to find the money to pay for them, and on the other, organizers who believe that electoral politics matter.

Feinstein knew that an effective grass-roots operation *can* be mounted in California, however, and can make the difference in a tight election. . . .

Within the Feinstein campaign, there was only one major project that reached out systematically to touch real people, and that was Jean O'Leary's Feinstein 1,000 – an effort to hold a thousand house parties all around the state to raise money for Feinstein while showing people with modest means that if they organized, they could create political change as effectively as people who could write $1,000 checks. Its publicly stated goal was $1 million, or $1,000 for each house party – a figure O'Leary thought realistic had she been able to get under way in June.

A Van de Kamp supporter with impressive organizing credentials, she had worked for twenty years in national politics and had not only gone to every national Democratic convention during those two decades but had served as a whip at the last one. Her major organizing experience, however, had been as executive director of both the National Gay and Lesbian Task Force and the National Gay Rights Advocates.

After Feinstein "slaughtered" Van de Kamp, O'Leary had called Duane Garrett, the Feinstein campaign chair, to ask for a job, and he "advised her to do fund-raising," claiming that "the party was going to do the fieldwork." Garrett subsequently called [Feinstein's husband] Dick Blum to say, "She's outstanding, give her anything she wants," but even though O'Leary was "extremely persistent," because of the campaign's reorganization and Feinstein's two-week vacation, she was not on the staff until August.

The device that would combine fund-raising and political outreach had come to her in a flash: "House parties would be the only thing within the campaign that would look like a field operation." But the north/south problem that plagues California organizing insinuated itself into O'Leary's plans. During the primary, a program called the Feinstein 500 had been organized in San Francisco. Since O'Leary was in Los Angeles and supported Van de Kamp, she knew nothing about it. According to someone who worked closely with her,

O'Leary called the San Francisco office the day before she was to be officially appointed, and the man at the other end said, "Who the fuck are you?"

O'Leary can be abrasive – as she herself put it, "People do get pissed off at me a lot!" – but this time she was caught off guard. A series of conference calls between O'Leary, [fund-raiser John] Plaxco, and Blum ranged in and out of shouting matches and finally resolved the incipient territorial dispute in favor of O'Leary and the south.

The plan that O'Leary was able to implement involved working through the Democratic party structure to pull in volunteers who had a "natural affinity" for the campaign. Using the 1988 precinct captains' list, which included seventy-five hundred names, she called on elected officials and contributors as well, but many of the one thousand people who had signed up to be hosts dropped out after they found out they would have to work at it. "We'd given them explicit instructions about how to do it," O'Leary said, "but those didn't always work."

The house parties were casual receptions, several of which Feinstein attended in San Francisco on October 14, the first Sunday they were scheduled, and they continued until the election. O'Leary liked meeting the half-million-dollar target, and she was all the more pleased because her planning time had been telescoped. "The best thing was making a miracle happen," she confessed. "If we'd started in June, it wouldn't have been a miracle. It would have been an organizational feat. Starting in August, it was a miracle!"

Unfortunately for Feinstein, it would be one of the few. . . .

Some things were still working for Feinstein: *women for:*, the influential newsletter that had supported Van de Kamp in the primary now came out for her, albeit reluctantly, "since a 'No Recommendation' would be, in essence, a vote for Wilson." Perhaps the most telling of Feinstein's endorsements, however, came from the *Sacramento Bee,* which had written so slightingly of her while endorsing John Van de Kamp in the primary. She had done her homework, and now the *Bee* could write that she had "worked successfully to overcome her unfamiliarity with state government and to sharpen her analysis of state issues." She had also developed an agenda "as sensible as the problems are severe, and she has shown increasing passion for getting to it."

But the Republicans were simply outclassing and outworking the Democrats. Having discovered that 80 percent of the people the Republican party registered between June and the close of registration in October were likely to vote – and to vote Republican – they had been pouring money into registration since June to get 250,000 new Republicans on the rolls, and they were clearly coming close to target. (In the Berkeley postmortem, one Republican operative put it bluntly: "We gained something like three hundred thousand registrations on the Democrats because so many of their people fell off the rolls and they never went out to replenish them.") The GOP outspent the Democrats by four to one on Get-Out-the-Vote strategies, putting $5 million into getting absentee ballot applications to every registered Republican. Furthermore, former President Ronald Reagan, Vice-President Dan Quayle, First Lady Barbara Bush, and former First Lady Betty Ford were merely the most illustrious Republicans who beat the political bushes with Wilson, while Kennedy was the only Democrat of comparable stature who stumped for Feinstein.

The operative word was "weary." Less than a week before the election, the *New York Times* ran a half-page article dissecting a political ad with a negative message and proclaiming that "swaying voters is less an orchestrated symphony of manipulation than a last-minute improvisation of sounds and symbols." So much for the vaunted expertise of media consultants. Eight people out of ten in an *LA Times* poll said they did not believe ads anyway. . . .

Despite Feinstein's claims that Wilson was dramatically outspending her, Cathleen Decker of the *LA Times* reported that the two candidates had raised and spent almost the same amount of money. But as Sherry Bebitch Jeffe of the Claremont Graduate School observed, Feinstein had not ignited the public enthusiasm in the general election that she had in the primary, and a few days before the election, Jeffe gave the edge to Wilson: "I have not seen her give people a strong enough reason to vote for her." . . .

On the Sunday before the election, the *Los Angeles Times* published predictions from nine experts, every one of whom came down for Wilson. One wrote, "DiFi lost much of her outsider status" and blamed "the excessive particularism of her attacks on Wilson," which made them easy to refute. Another said she "came across as the money candidate, saddled with husband Richard Blum." Yet another claimed that her "positive 'star quality' image faded fast over the summer when her negative TV ads matched Wilson's." . . .

Pete Wilson won the precinct vote on election day by 19,000 and the absentee vote by 247,000. . . .

In the end, Feinstein's bright red splash against a sea of battleship gray had proved superficial. Her experience as a woman had given her no more spacious or compelling a vision than Wilson's, and the thirst Darry Sragow had discovered in four years of focus groups would not be slaked in this gubernatorial campaign.

Or perhaps it was simply that neither the candidates nor the campaign professionals they hired had ever learned how to talk about much of anything in a way that moved the electorate. As the *San Francisco Examiner* would say about their one debate, "Most of the time, both candidates spoke an insider-ish jargon that made them seem like they have spent the last year in a hermetically sealed space capsule talking only to political junkies, rather than campaigning up and down the state listening to the concerns of real people."

Except for the "grabber ad," the one that began with the shot of Feinstein on the steps of City Hall and the voice-over that rang out "Forged from tragedy!" her ads for the most part did not work. As consultant Pacy Markman put it, her "advertising [was] mediocre. There was a way to take the fact that Pete Wilson took more money from the S&L people than any other senator and make a powerful argument, but they just did a bad job of it. They took a good idea and blew it." According to the *LA Times* poll, a fraction more voters thought Feinstein's ads ineffective than otherwise (46 percent to 45 percent), while 48 percent though Pete Wilson's did the job they set out to do – 8 percent more than those who turned thumbs down.

Though her ads made the point that Dianne Feinstein was competent and forceful, they showed her in so many different hairstyles and clothes that her image was muddled. Her own campaign staff referred to her preachy demeanor in two ads as Church Lady I and Church Lady II, and as A. G. Block of the *California Journal* put it, "She can be pretty smarmy: she can come off as the aunt who folds her hands and smiles while she tells you bad news because she knows what's best for you."

In the Berkeley postmortem, a Wilson aide observed that, ultimately, the media blitz may have made no difference: "What we did didn't move our numbers very much, what you did didn't move our numbers very much, and your numbers kept going up and down and up and down." [Campaign manager] Bill Carrick lamented that "the real lesson of this campaign" was "that the paid media didn't matter." For consultants who would leave a campaign with almost $2.7 million for a year's work, not counting whatever cut they got off the top of the media buys, this may have been less discouraging than for their boss. . . .

Nevertheless, Dianne Feinstein had run a remarkably close race against the most formidable candidate the California Republicans could offer. With a final donor list of sixty-six thousand, she had proved that she could raise record-breaking amounts of money and convince many interest groups to make an investment in her career that they would be reluctant to write off. According to campaign chair Duane Garrett, by the end of the campaign she had learned so much "she really was running as almost the optimal candidate." When the shouting and hoopla wafted away, then, it remained possible that if Feinstein could learn the lessons of her loss, she had a shot at an impressive political future.

[In 1992 Dianne Feinstein won a Senate seat from California.]

Tim Wirth
"Diary of a Dropout"

When I decided this spring not to run for a second term in the United States Senate, I surprised not only my colleagues, friends, family and staff, but also myself. I had come to Congress from Colorado in 1974 as one of the 75 post-Watergate Democrats elected to the House of Representatives. After 12 years in the House and five nail-biting reelection campaigns, I narrowly won the Senate seat Gary Hart had vacated. This year I was favored to win a tough race, and despite occasional twinges of private doubt, I was basically drifting into my reelection campaign on automatic pilot. I hoped that my second Senate term would bring more satisfaction than the first.

But in one week those illusions came apart. After 18 years on Capitol Hill, the prospect of another term in office had lost its bright glow.

I am leaving the Senate now because I have become frustrated with the posturing and paralysis of Congress. I even fear that the political process has made me a person I don't like.

Looking back at the climactic week of my political life, I can put my decision and its causes into the kind of order that immediacy obscures but hindsight permits.

Monday, March 30, was a banner day for the Wirth fundraising machine. In the morning, my wife, Wren, and I flew from Colorado to Houston, where we secured more than $70,000 in campaign contributions from executives of the natural-gas industry – apparently close to a single-event record for a non-Texan politician.

It was done in style, at a crowded reception in the grand River Oaks house of Oscar and Lynn Wyatt, a marble-floored approximation of a French chateau. The mansion, called Allington, is a big drawing card in Houston, and few upwardly mobile Houstonians would pass up a chance to see and be seen on the premises. Oscar Wyatt, a self-made tycoon with a stiletto tongue, had spent nearly six months returning one call for every four that I made to him. Once we actually talked, though, he quickly agreed to be my host, along with Mike Walsh, the new head of Tenneco and an old friend of mine from the days when we were both admissions officers, he at Stanford and I at Harvard.

Through my legislative work on energy issues, I had come in contact with Oscar, whose Coastal Corporation owns about 5 percent of all American gas and liquid pipelines, and Mike, who left the presidency of the Union Pacific Railroad to take over Tenneco, a huge conglomerate with major difficulties. In the Senate last February, I had helped pass a major energy bill that promoted natural gas and encouraged the gas industry to end its dependence on oil. The big reception in Houston was a way for the energy industry to say thank you by helping me raise part of the $4 million war chest I thought I'd need for the fall campaign.

I knew that raising so much money at a single event from a single industry would expose me to more of the attacks that the Colorado press has been making for years. The fact that natural gas is a major Colorado industry, that I have long used it to fuel my Jeep and that for years I have been pushing it as an environmentally sound domestic-energy source would not take the sting out of the inevitable headline: "Gas Magnates Bankroll Wirth Campaign."

The story would fail to note, of course, that I have received almost no support, financial or otherwise, from Detroit auto makers, whom I have angered by pressing for safety and fuel-efficiency improvements, or from the oil industry, whose legislative efforts to open the Arctic National Wildlife Refuge to prospecting I helped defeat this year. But when I take money from friends, people who are not only constituents but whose interests I see as coincident with national interests, I can count on an ugly story about being in the pocket of big contributors.

It was probably just as well that no reporters were in the room in Houston, where earlier in the day I gave a talk to a group of Coastal employees. Journalists would certainly have loved the way Oscar Wyatt had got the group to start asking me questions. Recalling the time his father had taken him to a carnival where one of the sideshows was a kissing pig, Oscar said, "C'mon, you only get one chance to kiss the pig, so you better get with it."

Tuesday, March 31, I spent a good part of the morning on the telephone, working on three big fund-raising events scheduled for May in Philadelphia, New York and Los Angeles. Back in 1974, as I faced the problems of financing my first race, a wise friend in Denver told me, "If you don't have enough confidence in yourself to ask for money, you don't belong in politics." I learned that lesson early and lived by its corollary: "If you don't ask, people have an absolute chance of not saying yes."

I had become very good at asking, but all the time it took to raise funds was time not spent talking with constituents, not tending to legislative business and not actually campaigning. That style of grass-roots, country-courthouse politics was, for me, more myth than memory.

Unhappily, the first loyalty of any candidate is too often to self and reelection, rather than to any broad political organization or community of likeminded activists. The problem is not merely the power that big givers – interest groups as well as individuals – may gain over the elected officials they help; it is the fragmenting of what the parties used to provide: financial, organizational and even ideological support.

The Republicans, with the patronage power of the White House in their hands, can still deliver some of those rewards and exact some discipline in return. Democrats, revolting against Tammany-style corruption or Chicago-style big-city machines, have by and large become independent operators. As a result, the Democratic Congressional leadership has few weapons it can deploy to exert control. On every important vote, the Senate Majority Leader, George Mitchell of Maine, has to go out on the range and try to roundup 57 straying heifers – the Democrats whose numbers give them theoretical control of the body.

The weekly Democratic caucus luncheon today epitomized our inability to work as a team. Held on the second floor of the Capitol, these sessions are scheduled to start at 12:30, but seldom get going before 1:15. And, for the most part, little of substance can be discussed because any controversial positions will be leaked to the press before we've finished digesting lunch.

The March 31 caucus was supposed to discuss two pending bills, one on health research and the other on financing international programs. But the talk was all about Senate perks, the fees we should pay to exercise in our seedy gym, the rationale for maintaining the Capitol physician's office and pharmacy and the hours the Senate restaurant should stay open when we're in night session. These petty matters had come to have immense political importance because of the incredible uproar over the misnamed, misrepresented "bank" in the House of Representatives.

The House bank scandal, devastating in its effect on the other side of the Hill, threw the Senate into a panic too. It did not seem to matter that no taxpayer or depositor lost a penny. What got fixed in the public mind was that Congress had grown arrogant and out of touch. Yes, many Representatives did overdraw their accounts, a few repeatedly and for large amounts, and yet no check bounced, no overdraft fees were assessed. The House bank, really more an old-fashioned, though poorly administered, cooperative, became a symbol of the special privileges all politicians supposedly get in Washington.

It was a great story for the news media, one that glibly portrayed public servants as rip-off artists. Droves of reporters went after the details with a slavering intensity rarely shown for more complicated, more important stories like the budget deficit, the $400 billion in hot checks that the government is writing this year. The gap between what comes into the Treasury and what goes out constitutes the biggest overdraft in world history and has paralyzed the government. But that scandal has received little attention compared with the furor generated by the House bank.

It was already "Topic A" some weeks earlier when Wren and I went to a ghastly mob-scene dinner in the ballroom of the Washington Hilton, where once a year the radio and television correspondents gather in evening clothes to celebrate themselves and the unspoken (but true) assumption that they are at the top of the power brokers' ladder in Washington.

On the way into the dinner, we had run into Representative Thomas J. Downey of New York, a close friend and a man clearly in agony. Tom is one of the most effective, decent, conscientious legislators I know, brilliant and incredibly hard-working. But he is a representative who overdrew his account. "I just came down here to help people," he told us. "That's all I ever wanted to do." It was painful to see a man of such talent so plaintive.

At the Democratic caucus luncheon in the Senate, the House bank preempted everything else. The talk turned immediately to how to handle our own perceived vulnerabilities (the gym, the doctor's office, the Senate restaurant), and degenerated into a round of suggestions for ways the "perks" issue could be turned against the Republicans in the executive branch. It would be easy, we could see, to tar the other guys with the brush they were using on us.

Unhappily, politics was consuming us all. A basic reason our institution was in trouble, I said, was that we were too often engaged in trivia and not performing the work for which we were elected. I said we needed to focus on national policy matters, on passing an energy bill through both Houses of Congress, on campaign-finance reform.

Another gathering that night brought the political realities of 1992 into even more depressing focus. Wren and I drove across the Potomac to McLean, Va., for a supper-and-strategy session at the home of Chuck Robb, the Virginia Senator who is chairman of the Democratic Senatorial Campaign Committee. Chuck and his wife, Lynda Bird, Lyndon Johnson's daughter, had invited each of the 16 Democrats from the Senate class of 1986 who would be running for reelection in November, and 12 had come with spouses and a smattering of senior staff to talk about the coming campaign.

At any time during the year, it is difficult to get three, let alone a dozen, senators in the same room at the same time. This night could have given us a rare opportunity to exchange serious ideas and to learn from each other. We should have been able to let our hair down and talk frankly about what we stood for and where we thought the country was going.

Instead, we were told by two prominent figures in Washington political circles – to no one's surprise – that Americans are angry at the government and those who work in it. Everyone was tired, and so was the talk. I don't recall any mention of the global environmental crisis or America's wasteful energy appetites, and only glancing reference to health costs, education and defense-industry conversion. Questions and comments were few and dispirited, most concerned with ways of using careful polling, target groups, and narrow issues – in other words, ways to get reelected.

I thought of Hickory Hill, a mile or so down the road, the home in which Robert F. Kennedy held regular seminars in the sixties to examine national and international problems. Bobby Kennedy, with his passion and intellect, had been my model for what public service should be. His assassination had a profound effect on Wren and me. We had stood in Union Station in Baltimore as his funeral train came through, weeping with the crowd. We came away profoundly saddened and changed.

More than anything, Kennedy's death had propelled us into elective politics. Looking around the gathering of my colleagues, I wondered what had happened to our zeal. How could we be wasting our time like this when there was so much to do, in the old Kennedy phrase, to get our country moving again? Angry and frustrated, we drove home.

Wednesday, April 1, was an ordinary Senate day, chopped up into the usual rushed 15-minute encounters with Colorado constituents and special-interest groups from outside the state. It was also yet another futile day of pushing for some movement in my long battle to designate more than 650,000 acres in Colorado as wilderness. The project had been stymied for years by the flat-out opposition of Senator William L. Armstrong, my Republican counterpart until he retired in 1990.

Hank Brown, the Republican who replaced him, did not have the same set-in-concrete, Sagebrush Rebellion convictions against protecting public land.

After intense negotiations last year, Hank and I had worked out what we thought was a decent compromise. Instead, we discovered we had ignited significant controversy.

At issue was the legal status of water rights, which are fundamental to controlling this scarce resource in the region. Water rights have been the cause of violent feuds and political finagling for generations. In 1985, the Sierra Club brought an old and bitter controversy to the surface by suing the Forest Service in federal court to try to reserve water rights for all designated wilderness areas – thus pitting developers against conservationists. Since the court did not fully resolve the issue, my Colorado wilderness areas bill became the vehicle both sides wanted to use to write their interpretation into binding law.

Hank Brown and I worked out a way to finesse the issue. In addition to adding 75,000 acres to the original request for wilderness status, our bill would have prohibited dams and other diversion structures in the new preserves, in effect protecting the water as it flowed through.

To many environmentalists in Colorado, who had been among my strongest supporters, that concession was an act of betrayal. They would not accept my argument that the wilderness we would save was worth far more than the shaky precedent our compromise might set.

That was the stalemated situation on April 1. During the day, I tried to talk the issue through once again with Representative George Miller of California, an old friend and Morris K. Udall's successor as Chairman of the House Interior Committee. I also spent much of the afternoon as chairman of a routine hearing on one of Hank Brown's special projects – to make the Cache la Poudre River in his backyard a National Water Heritage Area, extending a courtesy to him that grew naturally out of our collaboration on the wilderness bill.

All of this effort amounted to just more wheel-spinning on a project that should have been wrapped up 10 years ago. I was trying to work the bill through the House – and getting nowhere. I was losing heart. If, in our strong and affluent democracy, we had so much trouble preserving this small portion of God's creation, how in the world could we expect Brazilians or Malaysians to protect their millions of acres of rain forest?

The day left me drained – not an unusual feeling – and acutely aware of how hard it had become to get past square 1 on the Capitol Hill battlefield. The environmentalists have a clear and defensible position, but at the end of the day, where is the progress? On this issue, in which Wren and I and my staff had invested so much time, we were not only getting nowhere, but were being eaten up by our own political supporters.

Thursday, April 2, was the day the roof began to fall in. That afternoon, I learned that Senator Kent Conrad of North Dakota, who had been elected with me in 1986 and had been at the Robbs' dinner the night before, had gone to the Senate floor to announce that he would not be running for reelection. His decision was a shocker. Here was a talented young senator, stunning everyone by cutting off what looked like an extremely promising political career. When I heard the news, I felt compelled to go over to his office and talk to him. Why? I wanted to know. "I just didn't like to go to work in the morning," he told me. "It is so frustrating. The budget is out of control, and I think I'm wasting my time and my life."

At home that night, I told Wren about my conversation with Kent. Wren replied that I'd been saying the exact same thing. "For weeks," she said, "you've been saying that we shouldn't have done this again."

She was right. On automatic pilot that afternoon, I had reviewed the draft of the statement I was planning to use 10 days later to announce my intention to run again – words I would deliver at a series of stops on a well-orchestrated campaign swing around Colorado.

Now my own manual control came back on. Thoughts flooded in, especially of scary false medical alarms Wren and I had each been through in the previous six months. Our reactions in both cases had shocked us. Before our diagnoses turned out to be wrong, we had each said to the other: "Well, if the news is bad, there's one bright side. We won't have to run again."

The truth was that I dreaded the campaign that lay ahead and, almost as much, the likelihood of winning it, of having to spend another six years like Kent Conrad, hating to go to work every morning. Discussing the race with my staff, I had told them that since the Republicans were going to do everything they could to beat me – their Colorado party chairman had publicly described his job as "attacking his [my] character" – I would have to reply in kind.

It was going to be a vicious fight. The substance of five years in the Senate, of 17 years in the Congress, of real achievements rung up for Colorado, would be ignored, irrelevant.

I felt an intense disdain for the man I would probably have to face, State Senator Terry Considine. His reborn-right-wing policies and right-to-life stridency were contrary to my deepest beliefs. Recently, reviving an old Communist-baiting cliché, he told a good friend of mine that we environmentalists were like watermelons: green on the outside, pink on the inside. I was certain I would defeat Considine, but I was equally sure it would be a long and ugly fight. With the news media all too ready to treat rumor as news and unattributed accusations as truth, I knew I would be subjected to unending Republican attacks. I would have to counterattack. Indeed, I was already armed with a great deal of unflattering material about my likely opponent.

Negative campaigns work. That is why there are so many of them and so few politicians running on their records or on the issues. I believed I could win that kind of campaign, but in tearing down my opponent, wouldn't I inevitably end up diminishing myself?

Another worry was the impact of such a campaign on our children. Our son, Christopher, 24, and our daughter Kelsey, 22, recent graduates of Stanford and Harvard, respectively, had grown up in politics, but this was the first campaign they would work full-time. How would the intense personal attacks affect them?

I tried to sort out what was really important to me. As we talked that night, Wren reminded me what a psychologist friend had said to her about the effects of waging the kind of campaign I was heading into. "If you have a mature, integrated personality, you can't just split off a piece of it and go out and do something that you intrinsically feel is wrong." Wren repeated the psychologist's words. "That is a betrayal of self. When you destroy someone, you destroy a part of yourself, too. And if you keep on doing it, you become a deadened, hollow man."

Friday, April 3, brought all the doubts to a head. The day started with an 8 A.M. memorial service for John Heinz, the Republican Senator from Pennsylvania who had died in a helicopter crash exactly a year earlier. We had been high-school friends and basketball teammates. Married but neither of us yet in politics, we became much closer, a foursome with our wives.

When Jack was already a congressman and I was running for the first time, the Heinzes incurred the wrath of their Republican brethren by sending me a substantial campaign contribution. When Jack ran for the Senate in 1976, I returned the favor; the pro-Heinz interview I gave *The Philadelphia Inquirer* drew complaining phone calls from top Pennsylvania Democrats. Ten years later, it was Jack's turn again when I ran for the Senate. He was chairman of the Republican Senate Campaign Committee, whose mission was to defeat Democrats wherever possible. When Jack came to Colorado, the stop he made in an obscure corner of the state managed to fulfill his party obligation without doing damage to me.

Jack radiated good spirits, boundless energy and an innocent conviction that he could make the world a better place. He and his wife, Teresa, shared Wren's and my passion about the environment. We worked and vacationed together; our children became close friends. We competed on the tennis court and collaborated in committee rooms, especially on Project 88, a major initiative we had written to address environmental problems through economic incentives. Our friendship had made possible my most productive activity in the Senate, and Jack's death took much of the joy out of my life there. Speaking at his funeral the year before may have been the most difficult thing I have ever had to do.

What was most important, in retrospect, was that our work on the environment had been completely nonpartisan—something I have rarely found in the Senate. Partisanship can be healthy, but during the Reagan and Bush years, it had risen in intensity to become an overwhelming polarizing force.

In the Senate, more and more issues are provoking divisions along strict ideological lines. The Republican contingent has grown increasingly conservative, led by a cadre of vocal rightwingers, like Phil Gramm of Texas and John McCain of Arizona. In reaction, the Democrats in the Senate have drifted left of center, courting a whole range of special interests in a frantic effort to hold voting blocs and financing sources.

As a result, bipartisanship has been replaced on the Senate floor by endless bickering and an increasing number of meaningless votes, usually on symbolic amendments offered to embarrass the opposition. How many times should we have to count the yeas and nays on Robert Mapplethorpe and the National Endowment for the Arts, or on flag burning, or on such mischievous and misconceived ideas as the Constitutional amendment to balance the budget? Meanwhile, the real issues get lost. The deficit looms larger. Campaign-contribution abuses grow. The government in Washington, paralyzed by division, falls further into disrepute.

In personal terms, Jack Heinz's death left me with no allies in the Republican camp, no one with whom to explore ways through the logjam. On my own side of the aisle, my Democratic colleagues were all, like me, free agents who did occasionally band together, only to be demoralized by repeated Presidential vetos.

All that I had lost and missed so much came back to me in St. Alban's Parish that morning. Wren and I sat in pews behind the Heinz family, surrounded by many of our closest friends. The setting was familiar. Our children had been confirmed here. Next door was the Washington Cathedral and the Bethlehem Chapel, where Wren and I had been married. It should have been a consoling place, but I felt my sadness turning only to anger, especially as I watched my Republican colleagues take their places across the aisle in the pews reserved for senators. As I watched, I realized how few of them I connected to, personally or politically. I even resented them for intruding on my grief over Jack's death.

The chief celebrant at the service was Jack Danforth, the Republican Senator from Missouri and an ordained Episcopal minister. Danforth had given a moving homily at the funeral services a year ago in Pittsburgh and Washington. He had since emerged as the chief sponsor of Clarence Thomas's nomination to the Supreme Court and had doggedly managed Thomas's eventual confirmation.

For me, as for many Americans, the Thomas confirmation hearings had been a degrading spectacle, demeaning to the nominee, his accuser and the Senate. Early on, well before the Anita Hill charges came to light, Danforth had brought Thomas by my office, and, after nearly two hours of discussion and considerable research, I had been one of the first senators to announce against Thomas. After watching the conduct of the members of the Senate Judiciary Committee – their attacks and apparent lack of preparation – I felt embarrassed to be a member of the Senate. Yet here I was taking communion from Jack Danforth. By the end of the service, I was furious – furious at the stupid accident that took Jack Heinz away from us, furious at the life I was leading.

Later that day, I was scheduled to speak briefly at a luncheon seminar given by the Environmental Defense Fund, and to introduce William Reilly, the head of the Environmental Protection Agency. I had written out a scathing attack on the Bush administration's policies, from its hypocrisy on wetlands to its weasely response to the emerging crisis of global climate change.

But as food was served, I toned down my remarks and, in the end, found myself giving Reilly a nice introduction. What I did not say but actually felt was that he is a decent man who has let himself become compromised – by losing so many policy battles inside the administration and yet staying in office. The feeling, I realized, was not far from the view I was beginning to hold of myself.

Before lunch, I had called Carter Eskew, a partner in the prominent political consulting firm of Squier, Eskew & Knapp. Over the months, I had shared much of my discontent with Carter, who, besides being my campaign's chief media adviser, is also a friend. He was probably the only person who had a window onto Wren's and my misgivings about what we were doing. I told Carter to expect Wren and me to drop in on him that afternoon. We arrived about 2:30. I talked nonstop; Carter and Wren just listened.

I surprised myself with the clarity of my analysis. I saw myself about to go through seven months of horror – a negative campaign that would be hurtful to all concerned. And for what? To spend another six years in an institution that didn't work? To continue an insane life that required me to spend the vast percentage of my time doing things I did not want to do?

Carter did not try to argue with my decision. If he was shocked, he did not show it. Maybe he assumed that I just needed to let off a little steam. Later, he did say that he never thought I would really quit. But the more I thought about running, and the more I spelled out my reasons against it in Carter's office, the easier the decision became.

After about two hours, Wren and I left; I had to catch a plane for a number of meetings on another insane weekend schedule in Colorado, and she was going to Pittsburgh for the weekend to visit Teresa Heinz. We agreed to make lists – reasons to stay in the left-hand column, reasons to leave in the right. We talked in between meetings all weekend, and the analysis all leaned one way: It was over.

From then on, it simply became a matter of telling our children, our family and our close friends, as well as getting the announcement made as quickly as possible. Within 72 hours – by Tuesday evening, April 7 – the story had leaked to the press. Tom Brokaw got Teresa Heinz out of the tub to find out if the reports were true. On Wednesday morning in front of my office in Denver, I made it official. We were free.

Had I not already made up my mind by Friday night, a question that my son, Chris, put to me over the telephone would have clinched the internal debate. "Who really wants you to run?" he asked. "Who out there is just desperate to have you stay in the Senate?"

The question stopped me cold. Here I was, running around from constituency to constituency like the proverbial beheaded chicken, beseeched for beneficences and castigated for a catalogue of calamities.

All of a sudden, it occurred to me that I didn't have to put up with this any more. I could say, like another politician who should realize that his time has come to retire from elective office, "Shut up and sit down." I could leave the field to younger, more enthusiastic knights, as I was 18 years ago.

One reason the Senate had become such a dispiriting place to work was that most of its members felt the same impotence I did in the face of the staggering deficits that had turned the United States government into a holding operation, rather than an arena for innovation.

A few days after my formal announcement, Wren and I came back to Washington and met for a kind of therapy session with my Senate staff, people I admired enormously and knew I had disappointed. One of them was candid about her reaction to my retirement. "This is incredibly out of character," she said. "You are competitive. You are fighters, and for a lot of us, it's hard to see people we hold up as fighters decide not to fight anymore."

I tried again to explain – the institution, the growing frustration, the money chase, the imminent bitter and destructive campaign, Jack's death, becoming someone I didn't like – and admitted that I, too, was astonished. The place I had thought represented all that was good about this country – the United States Senate – was no longer the place for me.

As usual, though, it was Wren who put our future in proper perspective. "The next fight," she told the staff, "is the one that's really going to count. It's the fight for the future, for our kids, for their kids. What we have to do is take some time off, flush the knots out of our heads and then come back. And it won't be politics as usual, because the environment isn't a political issue; it's the most fundamental issue."

And remember, I thought to myself, there's more than one venue for fighting the fight that counts.

QUESTIONS TO THINK ABOUT

1. What dilemma does the amusing story about 1952 and 1956 presidential candidate Adlai Stevenson's issue-based speeches reveal? What lesson might today's presidential candidates have learned about direct and straightforward campaign messages?
2. Would Jesse Jackson's joke about Bill Bradley be as effective with all audiences as it was at the elite fund-raiser? How great a factor do you think a candidate's race is in the minds of American voters?
3. Why was Ronald Reagan called the Great Communicator? What was appealing to the convention delegates about his "ad-lib"?
4. Identify some of the facts of political life in California that made Dianne Feinstein a good candidate for the governorship in 1990.
5. What basic strategies did the Feinstein campaign decide on to get the

most out of the funds they had available? Which of the strategies worked well? Which did not? What tactic did Feinstein's Republican opponent Wilson use with much success?

6. In what ways could Feinstein's 1990 loss have been important preparation for her 1992 Senate race? How can a losing candidate turn that loss into a positive experience for the future?

7. Did Senator Wirth decide not to run for reelection because of policy disappointments, campaign pressures, or personal factors?

8. How did Senator John Heinz's death in 1991 affect Wirth's attitude toward staying in the Senate?

CRITIC'S CORNER

RALPH DUNAGIN
Courtesy Orlando Sentinel

"WE JUST SPENT $12 MILLION TO CONVINCE THE POOR PEOPLE YOU'RE NOT RICH!"

In what way is this cartoon ironic? How does it poke fun at campaign strategy making? What does it imply about the class background of members of Congress? Have you seen, in recent elections, politicians fight an "upper-class" image?

13 | The Media

When Douglass Cater called the press the "fourth branch of government," he meant that it has great power to check the actions of the legislative, executive, and judicial branches. By investigating and exposing the inner workings of government, the press empowers ordinary citizens. It provides the people with important information that they could not discover on their own.

Cater's "fourth branch" is an apt designation in another way. Today's emphasis on a candidate's personality, appearance, and lifestyle applies equally to professional newspeople. Reporters have been transformed into celebrities in much the same way that candidates have. There are numerous examples of network news correspondents who have covered presidential primaries, only to have the crowds pursue the famous reporters and ignore the little-known candidates. Before the rise of television news, reporters had less celebrity status and fewer of the problems that come with fame.

Here are the stories of three journalists from different eras and different media. First, veteran reporter Russell Baker recalls the 1960 incident that spurred him to leave his *New York Times* reporting job for a career as an author and editorial page columnist. Then, long-time United Press International reporter Helen Thomas remembers what it was like to cover the Kennedy White House. She describes a relaxed, open relationship between President Kennedy and the press. Despite First Lady Jacqueline Kennedy's dislike of reporters, the atmosphere that prevailed in those years helped Thomas handle the intense demands of the White House beat with confidence.

The third story is a less happy one. When she died in a car accident in 1983, NBC's Jessica Savitch was near the top in TV news. She anchored the network's coverage of the 1980 national conventions in addition to many other choice assignments. Gwenda Blair pieces together some of Savitch's experiences, revealing the story of a talented young woman under great pressure to succeed. The price that Savitch paid for success was tremendous insecurity, damaging involvement with illegal drugs, and much personal unhappiness.

Russell Baker
From *The Good Times*

My fatigue with the reporter's life became apparent slowly through an accumulation of small incidents.

[*New York Times* Washington Bureau chief] Scotty Reston and I were headed across Farragut Square to lunch one day when two cars ran together a half block behind us on K Street. Police reporting had made me a connoisseur of auto accidents. Some people could tell a fake Rembrandt from the real thing; I could tell a run-of-the-mill fender bender from a real accident.

On hearing the crash, I glanced back briefly without seeing much. I didn't have to. Heavy traffic was moving at such a crawl that the crash couldn't have done much human damage.

"Just a fender bender," I told Reston without breaking stride toward lunch.

"Let's see what happened," Reston said, turning and hurrying back toward the source of the bang.

I started to say nothing could possibly have happened, let's go get lunch, but Reston had already put distance between us, so I tagged along, amused by his boyishness.

Here was the most influential newspaperman in Washington running to a minor accident. Even if there were blood, Reston was wasting time. Newspapers didn't devote much space anymore to death by car. It was too commonplace. *The New York Times* was certainly not going to report Washington's traffic fatalities. Why didn't we just go to lunch?

After on-site inspection assured Reston the accident was indeed routine, we did go to lunch, but as we crossed Farragut Square, I realized this trivial incident contained a message I ought to heed. It dramatized the difference between a great reporter and a reporter who would never be special.

The great reporter was never too big to investigate the faintest hint of news. He went through life fueled by a bottomless supply of curiosity. When fenders banged, his very soul needed to know what happened, and he was powerless to go blithely off to lunch until he was sure he wasn't walking away from a story.

The great reporters took nothing for granted. That was true not just of Reston, but of Tom O'Neill, Phil Potter, Bill Lawrence, Harrison Salisbury, Homer Bigart, and a half dozen other veterans who were superstars of the trade. They had reporting in their genes. Most reporters lost the passion for it by middle age, but the precious few seemed just as fervid about it at sixty as they'd been the first day they walked into a newsroom.

The more I thought about that car accident, the gloomier it made me. My amusement at Reston dashing to the scene told me very plainly that my passion for reporting had faded with age.

Hearing two cars collide, Reston instinctively heard the possibility of news. Sure, it might be just a fender bender, but if you walked away without checking, how could you be sure one of the passengers wasn't the secretary of state with a bump on the head so bad he'd forgotten who he was? My instinct, by contrast, was to make an unwarranted assumption – "just a fender bender" – that wouldn't spoil the prospect of a pleasant lunch.

When a reporter avoids a possible story because he'd rather eat lunch, it is time to think about doing something else.

After the political excitements of 1960 . . . I returned to the Capitol to discover that I had had enough of the Senate. I knew how it worked now. I knew pretty much what it would do in most situations. I even knew what most of the senators would say when they rose to speak. I now looked on most Senate doings as little more than high-level fender benders.

I had loved covering the Senate when everything was new and strange. It was like attending the best graduate school of political science in the world. When you had a question, you called the appropriate senator off the floor, and he came out and talked to you. You got one-on-one lessons from masters like Lyndon Johnson, Styles Bridges, Everett Dirksen, Richard Russell.

When you stop learning, though, even the best school may feel like the end of the line. In 1961 I was thirty-six, had been fourteen years in the business, and was restless. I had begun to think of myself as grown-up. I had decided that while reporting was a delightful way to spend a youth, it was not a worthy way for a grown man to spend his life. At least not for this grown man. The indignities of the reporter's life no longer seemed like fun, but just indignities.

I was sitting on a marble floor in a corridor of the Senate Office Building one day when I experienced a moment of vivid inner clarity and realized that I was sick of it.

With a half dozen other reporters, I was covering a meeting of the Armed Services Committee. The committee usually met in private, doors locked against the public. Doing public business in private was common practice at the Capitol, so reporters spent a lot of time idling outside closed doors. Afterward, a couple of senators usually came out to posture for television and issue hollow, misleading, or deceptive accounts of what had happened.

Sitting there, looking down the long marble tunnel toward the elevator, I thought of my father. Maybe it was the marble that did it. He had been a stone mason. I thought:

"Here I am, thirty-six years old. When my father was thirty-six he had been dead three years. Still he managed to build something, to leave something behind that can still be seen, touched, used. Given three years more than my father had, how have I used the time? I have built nothing worth leaving and don't even know how. Instead, I spend my life sitting on marble floors, waiting for somebody to come out and lie to me."

From that moment on, I was emotionally ready to end my reporting days. What else could I do, though? I seemed caught in a job toward which I would become progressively more contemptuous as it became a familiar, then boring, series of annual routine events. This was the fate of too many aging reporters.

When I was full of youth's sassy zest, I had often facetiously declared that most reporters by the age of forty should be hanged if they refused to step aside and let youth replace them. Now I confronted the tiring reporter's destiny myself.

Helen Thomas
From *Dateline: White House*

Actually, I, in effect, assigned myself to cover the White House after the Kennedy inauguration. I was sent over to cover the President going to church on a Sunday, the day after the inauguration, and I just stayed on, reporting every day until my editors automatically assigned me there.

I have to confess that after I was assigned to cover John F. Kennedy and his family in the President-elect period, I was like the woman who came to dinner. I did not want to leave. I had a ringside seat to instant history and I didn't want to give it up.

Heavily bundled up against the cold that snowy Sunday morning, I got in a "pool" car in the motorcade with Kennedy when he decided to attend mass at his parish church, Holy Trinity, a couple of blocks from his N Street home. He hadn't broken with the routine of his past life. As we rode down N Street, Kennedy stopped his driver, got out of the car, and picked up the newspapers on the doorstep of the Georgetown home where he had lived for many years. Then he knocked on the door of a neighbor, Ben Bradlee, then with *Newsweek*.

Suddenly, on impulse, Kennedy decided to walk to church. I hopped out of the press car and trudged behind him in the snow. After mass, we went back to the White House. Later in the afternoon, Kennedy, looking over his new offices, popped into our messy press room, and we chatted about light things, the weather and the newspapers he regularly read, *The New York Times* and the *Washington Post*. . . .

[First Lady] Jackie [Kennedy] made me and all reporters feel like intruders. She seldom spoke to me in the three years she was in the White House although we saw each other often. She had no sizzling hostility toward reporters in those days, she just ignored us, regally. But she was totally, completely aware that we were there. Once she returned from Hyannis Port, Massachusetts, with a German shepherd puppy her father-in-law had given her. The press knew she had named it Clipper and sent her a note on Air Force One asking what she would feed it. "Reporters," she scrawled. . . .

I was a regular on the White House reporting team by now and, when not covering Presidential news, I would often team up with Fran Lewine to zero in on Jackie. In all fairness to Mrs. Kennedy, I'll admit we were insatiable, and so were our editors. We interviewed customers and merchants in those elegant stores and salons along posh Worth Avenue where the Kennedys shopped in Palm Beach. (That's the first time I ever saw a hardware store with wall-to-wall carpeting.) We interviewed Jackie's hairdresser, her pianist, her caterer. I even interviewed the owner of the local diaper service. We were called the diaper detail; but, then, so were the agents who protected the Kennedy children.

Secret Service agents went overboard (sometimes literally) to do Jackie's bidding, in the name of security. They served as chauffeurs, servants, nannies, swimming and water skiing companions, and, at times, they seemed embarrassed at the lengths she would go to avoid the press. I always knew that when the agents shoved us around, orders had come from the top. . . .

Jackie's war of independence from the press never ceased. During her first year in the White House, she gave a luncheon for the press and arranged matters so that she would sit near friends and women writers who were not on the daily "Jackie" beat. And when she gave a press reception in Paris and was mobbed by the foreign press, she snubbed American newswomen. A *Women's Wear Daily* reporter inquired whether she read that paper. Jackie said coolly, "I try not to."

Jackie once impishly suggested that women reporters be held at bay by Presidential aides holding bayonets. She told Kennedy, jestingly I presume, that he should find a foreign assignment for me. She also wanted to relegate women reporters covering a White House State dinner to a post behind the potted palms. . . .

We were exhausted keeping up with Jackie's energetic forms of relaxation. As we trailed her, we tried to blend in with the local scenery, although I'm sure we didn't. I, for one, was strictly an indoor girl and preferred spectator sports. In Middleburg, we wore slacks and bulky sweaters and mingled with the horse set in the tavern at the Red Fox Inn, picking up local gossip about life-styles in Jackie country. (Never, before Middleburg, had I heard of a drug store that sold only horse medicine.)

Jackie never acquired a taste for politics. But as First Lady she captivated men who ran the world – de Gaulle, Nehru, Ayub Khan, Haile Selassie – even Khrushchev. In the White House she was called "the queen" and she was a regal, imperial First Lady if there ever was one, certainly with the press.

"She would be more at home in Buckingham Palace," we would mutter.

Toward the end Jacqueline began to enjoy her position on the pedestal and to comprehend more fully what she meant to the country. But she never came to terms with White House correspondents. Even though she had been an inquiring photographer herself for the old *Washington Times-Herald,* she deeply resented prying White House reporters, particularly prying female reporters. We were the thorn in her crown. Jackie was charmingly at ease with men, children, and animals. She was constantly on guard with women of the press.

The irony is that Jackie Kennedy unwittingly gave a tremendous lift to me and many other women reporters in Washington by escalating our beat, covering the First Lady, to instantaneous front-page news. Eleanor Roosevelt had made front-page news before her with her liberal activism, but Jackie, in her diametrically different fashion, was news twenty-four hours a day. She, her husband, and her children set a new and dizzying high in First Family newsmaking. One biting quip from Jackie or a spill from a horse could launch a thousand headlines. There was a mystique about her, in and out of the White House. . . .

The tempo at the White House, under the influence of both Jackie and JFK, was definitely upbeat. Chiefs of state landed in helicopters on the South Lawn where Caroline Kennedy and nursery school friends played on trampolines and swings in the tree houses. The movie theatre ran cartoons. I broke the story that Jackie was setting up a nursery school in the solarium on the third floor for Caroline, and had integrated it with one black student, the young son of Deputy Press Secretary Andrew Hatcher. . . .

Caroline and her brother John, Jr., were the joy of Kennedy's life. He would come out of the Oval Office, clap his hands, and they would come running, along with all their little friends. Kennedy like to show them off, and even had photographs taken when Jackie was not around.

Caroline's most quoted remark was made when she was three years old and wandering around the White House. "Where's your Daddy?" she was asked.

"He's upstairs with his shoes and socks off, doing nothing," she said. . . .

Unlike the First Lady, the President maintained an easy camaraderie with the press. He liked the press – well sometimes. He realized that our constant probing was a direct reflection of the prevailing public mood, one he could never get from his aides. He considered us a necessary, abrasive force, although there were times when he undoubtedly wanted to banish us to Siberia. . . .

President Kennedy knew that effrontery and aggressiveness are the marks of the conscientious newsperson. A speed-reader, he used to devour the wire service reports and some ten daily newspapers. Nothing escaped him – he even read the "women's pages" and the society columns. He would observe mournfully, "I'm reading more and enjoying it less." He relished the daily banter with the press. Kennedy had a burning curiosity; he wanted to know all the major news and all the trivial gossip about the people around him.

Shortly after Tom Elliston, a reporter for the U.S. Information Agency, became the father of twins, Kennedy spotted him sitting in the lobby outside the President's Oval Office. Kennedy was en route to an important conference but he stopped and asked the new father, "What did you do, sneeze?"

In my work with UPI in those days, when I wasn't Jackie-watching, I was constantly trailing or questioning Kennedy. Sometimes I guess I was rather brazen in my questions. But he was relaxed about it all. He was an inveterate tease and quipster himself.

"Helen would be a nice girl if she'd ever get rid of that pad and pencil,"

Kennedy told [Press Secretary Pierre] Salinger early in the game. From Palm Beach on I had followed him with pad and pencil, openly writing down everything he said. He had apparently tired of the scrutiny.

On one occasion, Salinger decided to call reporters and photographers into the Oval Office for a picture-taking session. I was the only member of the writing press in the lobby at the time and I marched into the President's office – the lone "pad and pencil" reporter amid the covey of cameramen.

Kennedy looked up, surmised the situation at once and said, "Well, if it isn't Miss Thomas of the Universal Press."

Both "Lucky" Pierre and I have total recall of the telephone call I made to him at three o'clock in the morning to find out whether one of Caroline Kennedy's hamsters was dead. An AP story had just come through saying so and my editor had ordered me to match the story. Pierre could not have been more tolerant, but I had to wait for my answer (yes, the hamster was dead) until later in the day. . . .

Kennedy's essential intellect and wit allowed him to look both at life and people with detachment and compassion. He let the world in on his jokes and he lampooned everything and everyone, including himself. Of his job as President he said: "The pay is good and I can walk to work." Of his wife he said, when Jackie dressed in a large flamboyant hat to greet a visiting head of state, "What are you trying to do, ruin my political career? Take it off!" Of his Vice President, composing a birthday telegram to Johnson, who was known for his super-sensitivity, he admitted, "This is worse than drafting a state document." And of Nikita Khrushchev, with whom he had had an unnerving cold-bath meeting in Vienna, he said thoughtfully, "He has his good days and bad days, too."

Kennedy was chummier with the press than any other President I have covered because, in a sense, he was one of us; that is, one of our generation – the first President born in the twentieth century. He knew about our deadlines, problems, policies – and about our shenanigans. For one thing, he knew full well that reporters satirized members of the handsome Kennedy clan at every opportunity. The President provided a convenient target with his youthful looks, that unruly shock of hair, his Boston accent, the awkward jab of the forefinger when he answered questions. So was Jackie, sometimes the ultra-sophisticate and sometimes the wide-eyed little girl with the Marilyn Monroe voice.

Gwenda Blair
From *Almost Golden*

Savitch felt under such pressure that she had to reserve every bit of psychic capital for herself; there was nothing left over for [her husband, Mel] Korn. In addition to anchoring the Sunday night broadcast, she was busy with weekend news reports, news digests, *Prime Time Saturday*, speaking engagements, and constant public appearances, often to pick up the awards that continued to shower down on her. She had to do just as much flying in, just as much setup time, just as much fighting over copy, but nothing she did was noticeable or important, and none of it added up to a coherent body of work.

Putting the shine back on her journalistic credentials was particularly important during the negotiations on her contract, which was due to expire at the end of summer. Convinced that she needed more firepower to get the best deal, Savitch decided to supplement Don Hamburg and hired Richard Leibner, a well-known agent for television newscasters whose client list included Dan Rather, Diane Sawyer, Andrea Mitchell, and Ed Bradley. Items began appearing in the gossip columns to the effect that Savitch was busy talking with CBS and ABC. "The peacock's tail could get to look quite bedraggled unless NBC blocks some of that disgruntled and unhappy talent from taking flight," Liz Smith wrote in the *New York Daily News* on May 29, 1980.

Savitch also arranged to talk to RCA chairman Edgar Griffiths about her new contract. Beforehand, she and Korn spent a weekend figuring out an agenda for the meeting and hammering out a wish list. "We wanted a very direct discussion about the problems she was having and how she could enhance the news if given broader opportunities," Korn said. "They had her running around on the magazine show, which was a ridiculous scene." According to [president of NBC News] Bill Small, Griffiths never contacted him about Savitch's contract, but the fact that she had tried to go over the heads of the news division caused her stock with [NBC executive] Dick Salant to sink even lower. Doing so, Salant said, was "a no-no," something that was "generally regarded as unforgivable" and "would have gone over very, very badly." In the end, Savitch did not get any sort of commitment to anchor *Nightly News*, but she did get a significant raise, to $265,000 for the first year of the new contract, $285,000 the second year, and $300,000 the third and final year.

In 1980, NBC decided that it needed a woman in a visible position during the Republican and Democratic National Conventions, scheduled for Detroit and New York, respectively. Bill Small took a calculated risk and put Savitch on the podium, the position that offered the most visibility but required the least reporting. It was a position to which Small felt a personal connection. He claimed to have been the first to see it as a television position, back when he was CBS Washington bureau chief and had told those planning the network's coverage to put a correspondent with a mike up on the platform. Because Washington politicians tend to dominate the podium, it made sense to use the D.C. bureau chief as producer for the podium correspondent; Small himself had served in that capacity for Harry Reasoner in 1968 and for Daniel Schorr in 1972. Now, in 1980, it seemed to him only fitting to tap the new head of NBC's Washington bureau, Sid Davis, to produce Savitch. "I picked her because she was an aggressive, go-getter reporter," Small said, adding that "some eyes did roll" – including, apparently, those of Sid Davis, whom Small described as "reluctant" to accept the assignment.

It was a make-or-break proposition, and Savitch was scared stiff. There was ample reason. Since the early days of television, the conventions were thought to set the agenda and the relative positions of ABC, NBC, and CBS for the next four years. Although the conventions had steadily diminished in political importance, the networks continued to put huge effort and expense into them. In 1980, NBC hired Henry Mancini, one of Hollywood's priciest composers, to compose theme music for the network's coverage. Everyone from the network went, able-bodied or not, equipped with fat little loose-leaf notebooks whose covers had special caricatures by *The New York Times*'s Al Hirschfeld of the anchors and correspondents – Savitch looked like a giraffe-necked Lauren Bacall wearing a necktie – and were packed with capsule descriptions of noteworthy delegates and the phone numbers of their hotels. (The notebooks were not of sterling accuracy; the title page listed the wrong dates for the Republican convention.) NBC customarily spent so much on this and other convention paraphernalia that the news operation usually took three years to get back in the black, or near it. As a result, extra-heavy pressure was on the reporters, who had to shine at the conventions if they were going to get anywhere. Savitch felt the burden. "Jessica was to be the equal of Chancellor and Brinkley," Wallace Westfeldt said. "They're the jazz boys – they had done it so often they could do it in their sleep. But Jessica didn't know what to say and hadn't been told what to do."

The assignment was again mismatched to her talents. True, she would be seen on the screen every time the camera panned the podium, but the podium was the place that required the most academic-style knowledge of partisan politicking and parliamentary maneuvering. "You can't do much enterprise reporting if you're on the podium," said Wally Pfister, a veteran producer who had worked at all three networks. "You have to be more of a producer of thumbsuckers. It's the best seat in the house, but in fact you're in splendid isolation." Worse, the podium correspondents were surrounded by monitors and worked in such close quarters that they were acutely aware of each and every time they were scooped by one another. Savitch would be under merciless scrutiny.

Political conventions are angels-dancing-on-the-head-of-a-pin affairs, nightmares of detail with delegations from the fifty states and the District of Columbia and Puerto Rico and the Virgin Islands and Guam and God knows where else, all selected and governed by different rules, in a maze of floor fights and platform planks and caucuses and dark horses and favorite sons, and Savitch was literally sick with worry. Once again she interviewed everyone she could, took the parliamentarians of both parties out to lunch, reviewed tapes and scripts from past conventions, and filled her file box with three-by-five cards. To build up her strength she wore small weights around her ankles and went jogging with Chewy. According to Westfeldt, the late producer Stuart Schulberg told him that at one pre-convention rehearsal, Savitch rushed off during a break. "Stuart heard racking sobs from inside the ladies' room," Westfeldt said. "He stopped outside the door and asked if he could help. When he discovered it was Jessica, he took her to his office and sat her down. She told him how scared she was, and he arranged for NBC political consultants to brief her."

As Savitch plowed through her cram course in the political system, Korn had trouble accepting that the only time she might be able to see him was during the weekend, when they visited the huge houses Korn's friend John Sculley, at the time president of Pepsi-Cola, maintained in Connecticut and Maine. Korn was also dismayed by Savitch's accelerating use of cocaine, which she claimed to need for sex, and the way she kept calling to renew prescriptions for painkillers. Matters came to a head one summer weekend at the Sculley place in Maine, when Korn raged at Savitch for constantly ducking into the bedroom or the bathroom to snort cocaine. He told her he was deathly afraid that the Sculleys would find out. He told her she would destroy her career. He told her she should know about drugs from covering the wrecked lives of athletes who used them. She ignored him. The coke, he told one friend, was like a third person in the room with them, and the third person was the biggest of all. It was the last weekend Korn and Savitch spent together. . . .

Inside the convention was media madness, a barrage of floodlights, snapping camera shutters, and shrieked journalistic inquiries. On the raised podium, Savitch and the other reporters assigned to the rostrum were kept from thrusting their noses everywhere by a picket-style fence that was three feet high. Despite being penned in, Savitch aggressively button-holed every important Republican that passed within arms' reach, and was constantly shouting "Come to me!" at the control booth. "She had done her homework," Davis recalled. "She knew all the parliamentary rules and never slipped up explaining them in simple English." Nonetheless, her performance did not draw raves. "Jessica Savitch, the podium reporter for NBC, should slow down when she talks," wrote Kay Gardella in the *New York Daily News* on the third day of the convention. "She's good but her high-handed manner can be offensive. There's a cutting edge that needs blunting." Jim Wooten, a former *New York Times* reporter who had joined ABC in 1976 and was that network's podium correspondent, was even less impressed. "I was up, the new kid on the block, and Bruce [Morton, the CBS podium correspondent,] was kind of bored because he'd done it so many times before," Wooten said. "But Jessica was two or three beats behind, saying the obvious, adding almost nothing to NBC's reporting of the events." . . .

During the convention, all three networks hosted press receptions. That sponsored by NBC was a brunch, and was held late one morning. When Nancy Collins, then a *Washington Post* reporter, arrived, she saw Savitch sitting all alone and went over to say hello. "I went up because she seemed so lonely," Collins said. "She seemed thrilled to be talking to somebody." As Collins moved around the room speaking to acquaintances, she noticed that Savitch was still by herself, and invited the podium correspondent to accompany her. "It was very poignant," Collins, now a *Today* correspondent, recalled. "Here I was, not even in television at the time, taking one of the stars of the show around with me as I worked the room." . . .

Contractually obligated to do her bidding, the members of her coterie formed a warm, unthreatening, loyal wall between her and the increasingly hostile outside world. Their job was to make her look good and to keep her happy, and they worked well and successfully at it. All attention would focus on Savitch, with total concentration on such matters as new eyeshadow possibilities, a piece of jewelry she might wear on the air, whether her hair needed bleaching. All this was examined and discussed and debated in endless, minute detail. She was extremely particular. The staff had to follow her into the studio when she did the updates, but while there they had to be silent as stone. Savitch enforced a communal attachment to Chewy, asking her little circle to fetch the dog and babysit the dog and walk the dog. In return for their obedience, she was, on the whole, excessively kind. She sent cards, bought wine and presents, dispatched her limo for trips to sick mothers, and often sent out for food for everyone from Hurley's or Hatsuhana, an expensive restaurant on West 49th Street. (Savitch herself barely touched the food.) When one makeup woman got married, Savitch lent her the dress she had worn when she married Donald Payne.

Certain members of the circle appeared to have a particular responsibility: to be sure that Savitch had the recreational chemicals for which she had an increasing appetite. They did their work well, in that they were never found out. Savitch did her part, too; she was rarely directly seen with drugs, and was never caught in the act of using them at NBC. "Drugs were there all along," said one member of the circle. "Jessica would go to the bathroom or for a walk with [one of these people] to do coke. Sometimes I had to take her to the bathroom, but she wouldn't let me go in."

During this time Savitch took a trip on which she was to be joined by a friend a few days later. Just before leaving, the friend, who insisted on complete anonymity, received a phone call from Savitch, who asked if the friend would mind going to Savitch's apartment, where a package was to be waiting. Would the friend bring the package, which contained one of Savitch's favorite garments? The package was not there. Concerned because the errand was making her late for the plane, the friend called the person who was supposed to have sent the package. The person told the friend under no circumstances to deliver anything to Jessica Savitch. Soon afterward the package arrived at the apartment. The friend slit it open. It contained a scrap of cloth and a large sandwich bag full of white powder.

Furious, the friend left a phone message for Savitch: I am coming, but without the package. There's been trouble, the friend said. When the friend arrived, Savitch was in a state, her hair disheveled, her strapless top askew, her heels flapping. The friend explained calmly that the package had arrived, but that it had been ripped, and that inside there was nothing but an old rag, which the friend had left at Savitch's apartment. Relieved, Savitch flew to the phone and called one of her minions. "Everything's all right," she said. "Use what you want, but send some to me by Federal Express." A package arrived the next day.

In the interim, Savitch was without chemical stimulation for twenty-four hours, a situation that at the time she found difficult to withstand. She called a doctor out of the phone book, put on her best anchorwoman voice of authority, and explained that she'd recently had an operation and needed a painkiller. She disappeared for a little while, and came back glassy-eyed and in better spirits. Shortly afterward, the friend ended the acquaintanceship with Savitch. "During the last year I knew her," the friend said later, "she aged so much it was frightening. She had this horrible anorectic body and her skin looked terrible, with these sores that wouldn't heal. The last time I saw her, she didn't look like Jessica Savitch but like a much older relative."

No one in broadcasting could fail to know what an enormous risk drug-taking is to both health and reputation, and yet, between the cocaine and the prescription drugs, Savitch apparently took quite a lot. If the drugs were supposed to make her feel good, they were a resounding failure. Again and again, friends and co-workers spoke of seeing someone who looked as if she rarely if ever felt anything even approaching good. If she took them to stop feeling bad, they were also a failure, as she seemed to feel bad most of the time. What Savitch seemed to feel worst about was that she had lost her lifelong battle to be taken seriously, that she had reached the top only to be dismissed as a bimbo. . . .

It seems clear that much of her distress stemmed from two overwhelming, paradoxical anxieties. The first was the fear of failure; the second, the fear of success. Savitch radiated composure on air, but her co-workers saw someone so fundamentally unsure of herself that it seemed she could never believe that she was a legitimate success, that every accomplishment was not fortuitous and each triumph not illusory. No matter how many times she was profiled in the magazines, or how many bravos greeted her speeches, Savitch always feared that her career might vanish, just as other precious things and people had in the past. No matter how successful she became, every gain served ultimately to remind her only of all she had to lose – she knew full well how fleeting show-biz fame can be. Worse, she was convinced that on some level she deserved to have everything taken away. The scorn she encountered at NBC served to heighten the sense of inauthenticity that permeated her life. She had been told so many times that she was a glossy fraud, a paper-thin construct of blond hair and a tooth-some smile, that it is no surprise she came to suspect it might be true. . . .

At one point, Savitch was asked to give a speech in the Parker Lecture Series, established in the 1960s in memory of George S. Parker, the founder of Parker Brothers, the toy manufacturers, in Salem, Massachusetts, the company base. The program, which sponsored a public address every eighteen months, favored news figures, and Walter Cronkite, Dan Rather, and Eric Sevareid had already appeared there. The first woman so honored, Savitch was to be paid $5,000, in return for which she was to attend a black-tie reception, speak for thirty minutes and answer questions for another thirty minutes, and then go on to a public reception. Before the speech, Savitch waited backstage at Salem High School, nervously folding and unfolding the pages of her speech. [Documentary producer] David Fanning, who had accompanied her, heard a loud buzz from the other side of the curtain. Peeking out, he saw a stage completely empty except for a small podium with a little light, and over a thousand people waiting for Savitch to appear. It was, Fanning thought, a terrifying prospect: "She was about to have to step out in front of those people and be as wise as Walter Cronkite or what they thought Walter Cronkite should be. To give them wisdom and answer their questions about the world, to be that person she seemed to be on the news every Saturday night." Fanning thought later that her performance was extraordinary. The actual speech had very little content, but her answers to the questions that followed – for example, would Teddy Kennedy run for president in 1984 – were deft. "She was making it up as best she could, which people accepted because they needed to accept it. I had real sympathy for her at that moment."

QUESTIONS TO THINK ABOUT

1. Do you think it was difficult for Russell Baker to leave his job as a reporter? Why was he willing to take a career risk by changing jobs at that time in his life?
2. What techniques did President Kennedy use to maintain good relations with the press? Might Jack and Jackie Kennedy have played "good cop, bad cop" with reporters?
3. Apart from her professional goal of covering Jackie's activities, what personal feelings do you think Helen Thomas had toward Mrs. Kennedy? Consider how attitudes like Mrs. Kennedy's toward female reporters may have contributed to the women's movement of the late 1960s. Would Jacqueline Kennedy Onassis likely hold the same view of women members of the press today?

4. What different pressures affected wire-service correspondent Helen Thomas in 1960 and TV news reporter Jessica Savitch in 1980?

5. Do you feel that Savitch's colleagues and personal friends did enough to help her deal with her drug problem? Today, ten years later, might Savitch have found more support? What similarities exist in Savitch's story and the stories of some young, well-known athletes of today?

6. Compare Baker's decision at age thirty-six to shift career paths with Savitch's, at the same age, to push ahead despite her unhappiness. Why did each make a different decision? Their personalities? The public fame and recognition of television as compared with the print media? A gender difference? The expectations of the 1960s versus the 1980s?

CRITIC'S CORNER

What does this cartoon imply about how exciting it is to watch American government in action on C-SPAN? Is important governmental policy making always supposed to be entertaining? Is C-SPAN worth watching even if it does sometimes put you to sleep?

14 | Civil Liberties and Civil Rights

Civil liberties and civil rights are a passionately felt topic in American government. The Bill of Rights contains individual freedoms that cannot be infringed on by other citizens or by government. Civil liberties are as controversial as they are important. The American judiciary is frequently faced with tough decisions on how to balance individuals' rights and society's welfare. Abortion, flag-burning, and censorship are examples of the different kinds of civil liberties issues that courts hear.

In 1990 popular music provided the courts with a classic censorship dilemma when the Miami rap group 2 Live Crew sang about subjects that some Florida public officials believed were obscene. Edward de Grazia's long and detailed study of obscenity and the First Amendment includes the story of the 2 Live Crew controversy. He quotes various people about their personal reactions to the group's lyrics and its freedom to sing them. Journalists, Crew members, fans, jurors, scholars, and other performers each see the issue from their own points of view. Opinions vary on whether 2 Live Crew was spreading dangerous filth about women, or whether the white power structure was trying to silence the legitimate voices of American black men. In this case, the First Amendment let 2 Live Crew be "As Nasty As They Wanna Be."

Edward de Grazia
From *Girls Lean Back Everywhere*

In 1957, for the first time, the Supreme Court spoke to the question of whether literature dealing with sex was meant to be protected by the First Amendment; the Court said that literature was protected, but that "obscenity" was *not*. The justices defined "obscenity" much as [federal] Judge [John M.] Woolsey had [in 1933], subjectively, in terms of its ability to arouse the "average person's" prurient interest in sex. Then, in a 1964 case involving Henry Miller's erotic novel *Tropic of Cancer,* the wise and courageous Justice William J. Brennan, Jr., produced a more objective and much more liberal rule by which the freedom of literature and other arts might be measured.

In fact, the rule that Brennan announced (referred to in this book as "the Brennan doctrine") was so generously fashioned to protect literature and art that it led to the freeing of hard-core pornography. In order to ensure freedom for valued cultural expression the Supreme Court had found it necessary to free what was "obscene" as well. It did this by effectively (although not formally) abandoning the effort to define what in a literary or artistic context was undefinable – "the obscene" – and providing an efficient, because nearly absolute, defense for expression "not utterly without" literary, artistic, scientific, or other social value. Thus the Court made it close to impossible for prosecutors to prove that targeted literary or artistic works were obscene but easy for defense lawyers to demonstrate that the works of literature or art created or disseminated by their clients were entitled to First Amendment protection.

Soon the Court's critics found in the Brennan doctrine grounds to blame the Court for the "tides of pornography" that were now "seeping into the sanctity of the home." The spread of pornography was cited as evidence not that entrepreneurial capitalism had made sex a multibillion-dollar industry, but that the Supreme Court had mocked the founding fathers' intentions with regard to freedom of the press.

In 1973, the Court's new chief justice, Warren E. Burger, redefined obscenity in a way he hoped would be more palatable to conservative opinion, and this led Brennan and three others who had served on the Warren Court (Stewart, Marshall, and Douglas) to disassociate themselves from Burger's position and move into deep dissent. At that point Brennan, disdaining Burger's effort to fashion an improved definition of "the obscene," called for the abandonment of attempts to define and suppress obscenity through law. It was plain to Brennan that people who express themselves through literature and art could not be fully safe from government control unless the Court constrained government to forgo any attempt to punish purveyors of pornography and obscenity to adults.

The wisdom of Brennan's 1973 position (which he reiterated frequently in dissent) recently was confirmed when the director of a Cincinnati art gallery, the leader of a Miami rap music group, and the owner of a Fort Lauderdale record store all found themselves arrested under the Burger Court's revised definition for showing, singing, and selling what police officials and prosecutors claimed was obscene because in their judgment it did not qualify as "serious" art, or even art. Splendid as Brennan's achievements of the sixties were, they have not dispelled fears that literature and art can subvert and even destroy deeply entrenched political and religious values. And they have by no means discouraged ambitious public officials and zealous religious leaders from invoking the law to suppress artistic expression they find repellent. . . .

In Miami, in June 1990, Luther Campbell, the leader of 2 Live Crew, was arrested for singing and playing "obscene" songs; thereafter he was acquitted by jurors who, aided by experts, felt they knew artistic expression when they heard it. But in Fort Lauderdale, record-store owner Charles Freeman, who was arrested around the same time for selling a recording of the same music – the 2 Live Crew album *As Nasty As They Wanna Be* – to an undercover sheriff, was convicted by a jury that failed to see the serious artistic and political value that many other people saw in the songs. Yet the First Amendment has for the past twenty-five years been put forward by the Supreme Court as a barrier to this sort of censorship. One had hoped the issue was settled. . . .

Liz Smith [Columnist, formerly at the New York *Daily News,* now at *Newsday.*]: In my time I've had a lot to say about how sticks and stones can break one's bones; but words can never hurt. . . . And this column has been an active defender of First Amendment rights and also the right of others to say anything they like about those in the public eye. I've always felt if we in the press offend, at least it is better than suffering suppression, censorship, etc.

But a July 2 column by John Leo in *U.S. News & World Report,* which I clipped and put aside before I went on vacation, has me on the ropes. . . .

John Leo: the issue at the heart of the controversy over the rap group 2 Live Crew is not censorship, artistic freedom, sex or even obscene language. The real problem, I think, is this: Because of the cultural influence of one not very distinguished rap group, 10- and 12-year-old boys now walk down the street chanting about the joys of damaging a girl's vagina during sex. . . .

The popular culture is worth paying attention to. It is the air we breathe, and 2 Live Crew is a pesky new pollutant. The opinion industry's advice is generally to buy a gas mask or stop breathing. ("If you don't like their album, don't buy it," one such genius wrote.) But by monitoring, complaining, boycotting, we might actually get the 2 Live Crew Pollutants out of our air. Why should our daughters have to grow up in a culture in which musical advice on the domination and abuse of women is accepted as entertainment?

Liz Smith: So, is censorship the answer? The performance of 2 Live Crew – so violent, so anti-female – forces an almost involuntary yes! But once you censor, or forbid or arrest the real culprits, how do you deal with other artists who "offend"? Where do you draw the line? This is a tough one. But the average child isn't likely to encounter the kind of "art" that the National Endowment is trying to ban. Kids are not all over art galleries and theaters. But pop music assails them at every level and at every moment of their lives.

What I *would* like to see is every responsible, influential and distinguished black activist, actor, and role model – Jesse Jackson, Spike Lee, Whoopi Goldberg, Arsenio Hall, Eddie Murphy, Diana Ross, et al. – raising his or her voice to decry the horrible "message" of 2 Live Crew.

I would advise famous and caring whites to do the same, though they may be accused of racism. However, the issue goes far beyond race. Clips of 2 Live Crew in concert show that the audiences are not exclusively black by any means. What they are is young and unformed and dangerously impressionable.

Debbie Bennett [2 Live Crew publicist]: It's nice to see that Liz Smith is keeping racism in America alive and kicking. She's so stupid it's unbelievable. She wrote that since kids don't go to art galleries or see shows with people like Karen Finley, obscene art is okay. But since they listen to music, 2 Live Crew should be banned. Way to pass judgment on every teenager in America.

—

In an account of the 2 Live Crew members' trial that appeared in *The Village Voice,* Lisa Jones reported what two teenaged black women, courthouse fans of Luther Campbell, had to say about the prosecution and the music:

Antoinette Jones (18): They're just giving Luke a hard time because he's black. He's trying to make a living like everyone else. If someone wants to listen to his music that's their business. What do they think music is? They're acting like music is a gun.

Latonia Brooks (17): [Their lyrics] do have to do with sex and body parts, but when they rap, they put it all together. It's not like a man on the street saying dirty words to you. Their music makes sense. What they're saying is the truth. That's what most people do in bed. I don't, but that's what most other people do in bed.

—

Unlike the jury that convicted the record-store owner Charles Freeman for selling the "obscene" album, 2 Live Crew's jury was not all white; it found all three Crew members not guilty. Two of the (white) jurors told reporters why they had voted to acquit.

Susan Van Hemert (Juror): I basically took it as a comedy.

Beverly Resnick (Juror): This was their way of expressing their inner feelings; we felt it had some art in it.

—

The verdict came after four days of testimony during which the jurors "spent hours" listening to, and occasionally laughing at, two garbled tape recordings of a performance by the group that had been made by undercover deputies from the Broward County sheriff's office. The tapes, one of which had been enhanced by the police to eliminate background noise, were the prosecution's only evidence.

Defense lawyers Bruce Rogow and Allen Jacobi won the case by producing expert witnesses to testify about the artistic and political values in the group's songs, a strategy like the one that defense lawyers in the Cincinnati Mapplethorpe case had successfully used. One of the 2 Live Crew witnesses, *Newsday* music critic John Leland, gave an annotated history of hip-hop music. Another, Duke University professor and literary critic Henry Louis Gates, Jr., placed the music in its African-American oral and literary tradition. Gates explained the "signifying," and the use of "hyperbole" and "parody"; he described why it was that artistic works like *As Nasty As They Wanna Be* were not to be taken literally. This probably was the evidence which persuaded the jury that there was at least a reasonable doubt that the music was obscene.

Gates said that the Crew's lyrics took one of the worst stereotypes about black men – that they are oversexed animals – and blew it up until it exploded. He also suggested that the "clear and present danger" doctrine that judges still sometimes used to justify the suppression of speech was not applicable to the Crew's music.

Professor Henry Louis Gates, Jr.: There is no cult of violence [in this music]. There is no danger at all [from] these words . . . being sung.

—

The Crew's chief lyricist defended the group's music, and its success, on essentially political grounds.

Mark Ross (aka Brother Marquis): The bottom line is getting dollars and having your own. It's really a black thing with us. Even though people might say we're not positive role models to the black community, that if you ask us about our culture, we talk about sex, it's not really like that. I'm well aware of where I come from, I know myself as a black man. I think I'm with the program, very much so. You feel I'm doing nothing to enhance my culture, but I could be destroying my culture, I could be out there selling kids drugs.

—

Performers and purveyors of rap music, like curators of art galleries, are engaged in the communication of images and ideas through artistic means. Because of this, interference with their work by policemen, prosecutors, or judges violates the freedoms guaranteed under the First Amendment. No one can intelligently suggest that the country's musicians and distributors of music are not as entitled to be free in their professional activities as its writers and booksellers and museum curators are. The only constitutional limitations permissible with respect to songs are also applicable to books, paintings, photographs, films, and the other arts, as to all speech and press–which is to say, the restraints ought to be limited in their application to persons who use music intentionally to incite others to crime or violence, or who force nonconsenting or captive audiences to listen to it.

Purposeful disseminations to children of music that may be deemed "obscene" *for them* (in the constitutional sense mentioned in *Miller* v. *California*) would raise different questions. When 2 Live Crew played Fort Lauderdale, they were not arrested and charged with inviting or alluring minors to hear their sexually explicit songs, playing to "captive audiences" of persons who did not wish to hear what was played and could not escape it, or intentionally inciting the men in the room to rape or sexually abuse women. They were charged with singing lyrics that policemen, prosecutors, and lower court judges had heard about, decoded, and decided were not art, but were obscene. . . .

Holly Hughes: A solo performer and writer of theatre skits, she demonstrates how her mother imparted the " 'Secret meaning of life' by displaying her body and placing her hand up her vagina" in a skit titled "World Without End." Her works are less concerned with male-female sexual relationships than "she is with lesbian desire," said a review of another work, "Dress Suits to Hire." I think the same judge that outlawed 2 Live Crew would probably have outlawed me, and Karen Finley [A regular at NEA-funded avant-garde theatres such as the Kitchen and Franklin Furnace Archive, she smears her nude body with chocolate and with bean sprouts symbolizing sperm in a piece entitled "The Constant State of Desire." Miss Finley also coats make-believe "testicles" with excrement and sells it as candy. In one monologue, she spreads her legs and puts canned yams into her body. . . .]. I think they outlawed them because black men making money outside of the system and having power and having control of their own voice is very threatening. Even if their work is sexist . . . you don't get rid of anything you don't like by censoring it.

QUESTIONS TO THINK ABOUT

1. Describe the Supreme Court's position on the First Amendment as it pertains to obscenity during the 1960s. Did the Court retain that view in the 1970s and beyond?
2. Do you believe that obscenity, which sometimes is in the form of pornography, causes violence and other antisocial behavior?
3. Are there ways other than censorship to counteract the lyrics of 2 Live Crew's songs?
4. What racial issues are involved in the 2 Live Crew controversy? In your opinion, are there age, culture, race, or gender differences that explain people's differing views of what is art and what should be censored?

CRITIC'S CORNER

"PRESIDENT?... NO, CHILD, BUT YOU CAN GROW UP TO BE FRONT-RUNNER!"

What does this cartoon say about race relations in the United States today? In answering this question, consider how this cartoon can function as both an indictment of racial prejudice and as an acknowledgment of the advances made in civil rights. Would this cartoon have been conceivable in the 1950s or 1960s?

15 | The Economy and Public Welfare

Just as the American ideology of liberal individualism faces a tough test when confronted with the realities of politics in the United States today, it, too, faces a tough test with economic realities. Individualism, competition, private property, and limited government are basic components of American economic thought; strong government, big corporations, and a wealthy elite are not. Political scientist Kevin Phillips, a well-known conservative, believes that he speaks for the true tenets of liberal individualist economics. An economic populist, he favors free competition among hard-working individuals with only limited governmental intervention in economic life. He opposes "bigness," whether it be in the form of huge corporations or powerful government. He rejects established elites.

In his article, Phillips looks back critically on the Reagan years, the 1980s, assessing them as a time of economic polarization in America: a rich upper class grew and prospered, while average Americans struggled to make ends meet. As a modern populist, Phillips favors a system that rewards the industrious "little guy." Reagan Republicans promised to stand up for ordinary Americans but actually helped the rich get richer, charges Phillips. Not all observers agree with Phillips's data or with his conclusions. His book has created quite a controversy between liberals and conservatives because of its harsh judgment of the 1980s and its predictions for the future of American politics.

For the poor who got poorer in the 1980s or 1990s, government assistance programs are designed to provide a "safety net" for all citizens. They guarantee that no matter how bad times get for any individual or family in America, the basics to sustain life – food, shelter, clothing – will be available. Then, when better times arrive, those who received government help will be able to take advantage of new opportunities. As is true with all public policies, welfare works imperfectly. Some healthy, able-bodied adults get by on welfare without working. A few recipients cheat by claiming that they are supporting more children than they really are. Others never get off welfare; the next generation of the family inherits welfare dependence. However, public assistance is probably no more imperfect than other government programs such as the insurance on deposits in failed savings and loan banks. The savings and loan bailout will cost taxpayers many times more than welfare does.

Homeless Americans lack even the safety net of public housing, food stamps, and other payments. They avoid criticism from mainstream society by not taking welfare, but they don't avoid getting stepped on by busy commuters rushing to and from work each day. The homeless live beneath the public-welfare safety net, on the streets, in subways, in bus terminals. A few eat in soup kitchens run by churches. They wear rags. Census-takers have trouble finding and counting them. The homeless have few advocates, especially after the recent death of Mitch Snyder, their best-known spokesman. Many Americans ignore homeless people, or believe that they live the way they do because they choose to. Journalist Mort Rosenblum, returning to the United States after working abroad, talked to a group of the homeless in New York City and discovered the same fear, hope, and humor in them as in all Americans.

Kevin Phillips
From *The Politics of Rich and Poor*

This is a television nation. Maybe it's time for a mini-series about the *second* American Civil War. This time it would not be North versus South. This time it would be the haves versus the have-nots: Harlem against the Yupper East Side, Beverly Hills against Compton, the suburbs against the inner cities, the displaced against the entrenched. This time it would not be neat and territorial. This time it would be guerrilla war, in neighborhoods, in cities, with block against block until people walked across the gulf and discovered the unique idea of sharing.

–Benjamin J. Stein
Columnist and Former Republican
White House Aide, 1987

Society matrons, Wall Street arbitrageurs, Palm Beach real estate agents and other money-conscious Americans picking up the newspaper *USA Today* on May 22, 1987, must have been first bewildered and then amused by that day's lead story. In describing a new Louis Harris & Associates survey of the attitudes of upper-bracket citizens, reporter Martha Moore summed up the typical interviewee as "rich. Very. He's part of the thinnest economic upper crust: households with incomes of more than $100,000 a year. Only 1.2 million households in the USA have that kind of dough, 1.9% of the population."

Statistics like these clouded the true peaks of wealth in the polarized late 1980s. So did talk about eliminating Social Security benefits for the $50,000-a-year "rich." Households with annual incomes of $100,000 and net worths of $500,000 – the threshold for Louis Harris's study – were only the upper-middle class of late-Reagan-era America, commercial and professional cupbearers to the genuinely monied. In Wichita, Kansas, or Beaufort, South Carolina, they would have been local gentry – of a sort. In high-priced Manhattan, though, they might have been a young accountant and his teacher wife, reluctantly planning to sell their cramped cooperative apartment and move to the suburbs. Yet a surprising number of late-1980s polls and comments contributed to what was a truly flawed perception – that circa 1988 "rich" somehow started at $50,000 or $100,000 a year, and that gradations above that were somehow less important. The truth was that the critical concentration of wealth in the United States was developing at *higher* levels – centimillionaires, half-billionaires and billionaires – provocative enough to resummon the spirits of American populism. . . .

For the first time in U.S. history, millionaires were economic nobodies as mega-wealth ballooned out of sight. By the late 1980s a person couldn't be a serious millionaire with just $1 million in *assets*; $1 million in annual *income* was what it took. As for *rich*, old-line money managers and private bankers generally agreed that $10 million in assets or two or three successive years of several million dollars in annual income was at least entry-level. *Over a hundred thousand Americans still qualified.*

Economic change had rendered the term "millionaire" all but meaningless, something that median-income families earning $30,000 a year rarely understood. The price explosions of the Carter years in agricultural commodities, oil and farmland had minted millionaires out of Idaho potato growers, Oklahoma oil wildcatters and Ohioans with three hundred fifty fertile acres, and then the Reagan years finished the process by reestablishing a more familiar wealth boom in financial assets and professions. Bare-bones millionairedom, its ranks fattened from six hundred thousand Americans in 1981 to roughly one and one half million in 1989, was becoming no more than middle-class. Purchasing power was deteriorating along with status. To replicate the over-the-counter clout of $1 million in 1913 required progressively larger sums: $2.02 million in 1920, $1.38 million in mid-Depression 1935, $2.43 million in 1950, $3.18 million in 1965, $8.32 million in 1980, and almost $12 million on Election Day, 1988. . . .

Riches must be judged in the context of their times. More than inflation is involved. If the country's wealth has grown, so has what a rich man can do with it.

Besides increasing the enjoyment of wealth, new technology and leisure time also spur *further* wealth creation. Economist Milton Friedman has pointed out that "historically, rising income has transformed what one generation thought of as a luxury into what the next sees as a necessity." Meanwhile, this process of turning former luxuries into everyday commodities also becomes a vehicle of watershed changes in new fortunes – from John Jacob Astor's beaver hats and Henry Ford's model T automobiles to the computers, cable systems, videocassettes, gourmet foods, fashions and luxury real estate developments of 1980s mega-money.

The 1980s were another of these watersheds in which, at first, public understanding and perceptions trailed far behind the new magnitudes of wealth accumulation. Table [1] plots the extraordinary escalation of all four relevant asset-holding classifications: millionaires, decamillionaires, centimillionaires and billionaires. . . .

Table [1]

Year	Millionaires	Decamillionaires	Centimillionaires	Billionaires
1981	600,000			?
1982		38,855	400	13
1983			500	15
1984			600	12
1985	832,602		700	13
1986			900	26
1987	1,239,000	81,816	1200	49
1988	1,500,000	100,000	1200	51

. . . Tables [2] and [3] show that as of 1988 the major new fortunes in finance were being made not by the pedigreed Yale clubmen manning partners' desks at Brown Brothers Harriman or Dillon Read, but by buccaneers – corporate raiders and leveraged buyout specialists, latter-day Goulds and Insulls. And once again the rewards had increased spectacularly. Back in 1981 the financial community's biggest earners had made five to ten million dollars a year. By 1986, however, the top dozen incomes ranged between $35 million and $125 million, in 1987 between $25 million and $100 million and in 1988, between $50 million and $200 million a year. If anything, these figures were probably understated – like the estimate that Michael Milken made $60 million in 1987 when his compensation actually totaled $550 million. Equally significant, the cutoff point for the financial community's "top 100" in 1987 was $4 million of compensation. And this in the year when the stock market had crashed! In order to keep the 1987 list "from becoming a Goldman Sachs yearbook," *Financial World* had to set up a special, *separate* listing for the estimated forty-eight Goldman partners making at least $4 million that year. To make the 1987 or 1988 lists long enough to gather in everyone in the financial community draw-

Table [2] 1987 Billionairedom

Industry and Name	Estimated Net Worth (in billions $)
Real Estate	
Alfred Taubman	$2.5 Bil
Jay & Robert Pritzker	1.5
Harry Helmsley	1.3
The Marriott Family	1.3
Donald Bren	1.2
Samuel LeFrak	1.0
Communications	
Samuel & Donald Newhouse	7.5
John Kluge	3.1
Anne Cox Chambers & Barbara Cox Anthony	2.5
Rupert Murdoch	2.2
William & Randolph Hearst	1.5
Katharine & Donald Graham	1.1
Walter Annenberg	1.1
Computers	
David Packard	3.0
Ross Perot	2.5
William Hewlett	2.0
William Gates	1.2
Retailing	
Sam Walton	8.7
Leslie Wexner	2.4
Milton Petrie	1.1
Donald Fisher	1.0
Food and Drink	
The Mars Family	5.0
Edgar & Charles Bronfman	3.6
The MacMillan Family	2.9
John Dorrance	1.5
August Busch	1.3
John Lupton	1.3
William & Joseph Coors	1.2
Michel Fribourg	1.2
Ernest & Julio Gallo	1.0
John Simplot	1.0

Table [3] Financial World "Wall Street 100 Index" (in million $)

Calendar Year 1986		*Calendar Year 1987*	
Michel David-Weill, Lazard Frères	$125	Paul Tudor Jones, Tudor Investment Corp.	$80–100
George Soros, Soros Fund Mgt.	$90–100	George Soros, Soros Fund Mgt.	$75
Richard Dennis, C&D Commod.	$80	George Roberts, KKR	$70
Michael Milken, Drexel*	up to $80	Henry Kravis, KKR	$70
J. M. Davis, D. H. Blair	$60–65	Michael Milken, Drexel*	$60
Jerome Kohlberg, KKR	$50	Michel David-Weill, Lazard Frères	$54
Henry Kravis, KKR	$50	Jerome Kohlberg, KKR	$35
George Roberts, KKR	$50	John Weinberg, Goldman Sachs	$32
Ray Chambers, Wesray	$45–50	Donald Carter, Carter Organization	$32
William Simon, Wesray	$45–50	Theodore Forstmann, Forstmann Little	$30
M. Steinhardt, Steinhardt Partners	$40	Ray Chambers, Wesray	$28
E. Johnson III, FMR Corp.	$35	Reginald Lewis, TLC Group	$25

Calendar Year 1988

Michael Milken, Drexel	$180–199
Gordon Cain, Sterling Group	$120
Henry Kravis, KKR	$110
George Roberts, KKR	$110
Robert Bass	$100
Paul Bilzerian, Singer Co.	$80
Irwin Jacobs, Minstar Inc.	$75–100
Michel David-Weill, Lazard Frères	$65
Peter Peterson, Blackstone Group	$50–60
Richard Rainwater	$50–60
Joseph Schuchert, Kelso & Co.	$50–60
S. Schwartzman, Blackstone Group	$50–60

*Now known to have been substantially underestimated.
Source: Financial World Magazine

ing at least $1 million in compensation, experts indicated, would have required several thousand listings.

Paper entrepreneurialism – mergers, acquisitions and junk bonds – was the key to the swollen 1986 – 88 earnings list. A few people were making huge sums for owning or managing major mutual funds, but most of Wall Street's big money came from restructuring and repackaging corporate America. Selling stock to retail clients, investment management firms or mutual funds paid well; repackaging, remortgaging or dismantling a Fortune 500 company paid magnificently.

The public policy changes of the Reagan era, from antitrust to deregulation, helped make all this possible. Just before the 1988 election, James O'Leary, retired chief economist of the New York-based United States Trust Company, complained about how the merger-buyout craze had been unleashed: "In recent years, we have gone hog wild on deregulation. The antitrust laws aren't being enforced anymore, opening this thing up to abuse. And a few days earlier, Martin Lipton, the New York lawyer who reportedly received history's largest legal fee for advising on a corporate merger, nevertheless complained that "we and our children will pay a gigantic price for allowing abusive takeover tactics and boot-strap, junk-bond takeovers. . . . As with tulip bulbs, South Sea bubbles, pyramid investment trusts, Florida land, REITs, L.D.C. loans, Texas banks and all the other financial market frenzies of the past, the denouement will be a crash."

But the money to be made brought even skeptics aboard the gravy train, working to put more and more companies "into play." Between 1980 and early 1988, the cumulative value of mergers, acquisitions, takeovers and leveraged buyouts, friendly and hostile, exceeded two thirds of a trillion dollars. . . .

As the decade closed, the distortion of American wealth raised questions not just about polarization but also about trivialization. Less and less of the nation's wealth was going to people who produced manufactures or commodities. Services were ascendant – from fast food to legal advice, investment vehicles, data bases and videocassettes. New heyday wealth has always been scorned for representing unfamiliar or unfashionable vocations or sectors – the "beer barons" of Victorian England are an example. Similar disdain applied to late-1980s fortunes made in everything from candy bars to pet food, cosmetics, cable television and electronic games. The mounting concentration of wealth in the service industries, however, raised a larger problem. It was one thing for new technologies to reduce demand for farmers, steelworkers and typists, enabling society to concentrate more resources on health, money management and leisure. But the distortion lay in the disproportionate rewards to society's economic, legal and cultural manipulators – from lawyers and investment advisers to advertising executives, merchandisers, consumer finance specialists, fashion designers, communicators, media magnates and entertainment promoters. Unfortunately, heyday biases in these directions are as American as apple pie. As disposable income concentrates even more strongly than usual in the hands of the upper 10 to 20 percent of Americans, vocations dealing in short-term objectives and satisfactions profit. Humdrum activities and long-term objectives suffer....

> If your daughter's in cotillion
> And your son's enrolled at Choate
> And your wife is worth a million
> I'm sure to get your vote
> Gridiron Club Parody of George Bush, March 1988

> That the Great Divide between rich and poor in America has widened is perhaps the most troubling legacy of the 1980s.
> *Business Week,* September 1989

> Our biggest fear is that the Democrats surface with a leader who is able to capitalize on the theme of economic populism.
> GOP Pollster Vincent Breglio, 1989

By the time of Bush's inauguration in January 1989 the triumph of Upper America was both complete and precarious – precarious because its success was becoming so obvious. Widespread resentment over extreme wealth was inevitable, though still unfocused.

As 1989 unfolded, so did a new wave of conspicuous consumption. By April many stock market indexes had regained their October 1987 pre-crash levels. Spring sales at Sotheby's and Christie's set records, including $4 million for Andy Warhol's painting of Marilyn Monroe. The world's most expensive automobile, a 1931 Bugatti Royale, had sold at auction in 1987 for $9.8 million; in spring 1989 the price rose again. From Bel-Air to Beverly Hills, entertainers, movie executives and foreign investors rolling in money gave Southern California a new real estate term: "tear-downs" – the replacement of old homes with $5–30 million kitsch palaces including tanning parlors, motorized chandeliers, petting zoos and heliports. In late summer lavish multimillion-dollar birthday parties for financier Saul Steinberg and publisher Malcolm Forbes – his was complete with charging Moroccan cavalrymen – added to a sense of excess.

Financial players were becoming as reckless as they had been in 1929. Soon after Reagan left office, undercover FBI agents moved into Chicago's commodity trading pits, where rigging had become rampant. Massive indictments followed by summer. Insolvent, recklessly managed savings and loan associations, centered in Texas and the Southwest, promised to cost the American taxpayer $200 billion before the end of the 1990s. In New York, where Drexel Burnham, the nation's fifth-largest securities firm, had agreed to pay an enormous fine as part of a settlement of criminal securities fraud charges, federal prosecutors also indicted its prize employee, Michael Milken, the originator of junk bonds, themselves increasingly in disrepute and default. When government figures showed that Milken had actually earned a stunning $550 million in 1987, even billionaire David Rockefeller suggested that "such an extraordinary income inevitably raises questions as to whether there isn't something unbalanced in the way our financial system is working."

George Bush had earlier told a newspaper interviewer that he didn't like "this fast-buck stuff," and on Inauguration Day he would repeat his concern:

> In our hearts, we know what matters. We cannot only hope to leave our children a bigger car, a bigger bank account . . . and what do we want the men and women who work with us to say when we're no longer there? That we were more driven to succeed than anyone around us?

But just what change Bush could or would represent was not entirely clear. In 1988 he had briefly tried out a populist image – eating pork rinds, campaigning with country music star Loretta Lynn, speaking to a succession of police and sheriffs' rallies. And when he first got to the White House, he laid out a horse-shoe pitch. Yet the America Bush truly represented was that of old multigenerational wealth – of trust funds, third-generation summer cottages on Fisher's Island and grandfathers with Dillon Read or Brown Brothers Harriman – which accepted the economic policy of the Reagan era despite its distaste for its arriviste values.

That was clear in the people Bush selected for his cabinet. The secretaries of state, treasury and commerce – James Baker III, Nicholas Brady and Robert Mosbacher – were old Bush friends, graduates of the best private schools, second- or third-generation multimillionaires with a collective net worth of about $250 million. As treasury secretary in 1987-88, Baker had insisted on Latin American debt-repayment policies benefiting Chemical Bank, in which he had several million dollars' worth of stock. He claimed sentimental reasons for holding his stock, which came to him in a merger between Chemical and the Texas Commerce Bank, founded by his grandfather. The ethical embarrassments of Bush's upper-class associates were a far cry from those of Ronald Reagan's hustling middle-class friends and aides, but the political evolution was simple enough: in two decades of presidential control, the Republicans had evolved from "cloth coat" Middle Americanism under Richard Nixon to aggressive new-money capitalism under Ronald Reagan and finally to the old-money, Episcopal establishment under George Herbert Walker Bush.

Mort Rosenblum
From *Back Home*

Finding the homeless is no trick in New York. Let your attention wander, and you'll trip over them.

At the Gucci end of Fifth Avenue, at Fifty-Third Street, a gaily colored poster advertised the Broadway production of *Les Misérables*. A few steps below the street was a scene beyond even the fevered mind of Victor Hugo. As I climbed down to the subway station, it took a physical effort to penetrate the stench of vomit and urine. Inert little bundles lay side by side along both walls. Occasionally one would twitch or turn fitfully. It was like the worst part of Port-au-Prince, but for two differences: There was none of the lively street life that lightens the load of misery in the Haitian capital; also, it was the middle of the afternoon.

No one paid attention to the spike heels and silk-stockinged legs that picked their way over the bodies. A transit cop, with no alternative to offer, surveyed the scene indulgently. Once a good-natured custodian slapped a wall near one group, and they all shuffled to their feet, scooping together their few rags of clothes, tattered blankets and cardboard mattresses. When the man moved on, they quickly remade their beds and went back to sleep. Those farther away did not bother to wake up.

One man, somewhere between seventeen and thirty, with filthy dreadlocks, lay lifeless under a threadbare khaki blanket. The sum total of his life was thrown loosely into a tattered plastic trash bag, a small one, tucked under his head. He had cruddy boots but no laces. A few guys had no possessions at all, not even the strip of grimy cardboard others used as mattresses. They may have had clothes somewhere else; I wouldn't bet on it. A few men were upright. One young black with vacant eyes held out a battered paper cup, without much conviction. I surveyed their faces, looking for the spark that might initiate an interview. There was nothing.

This was March, and it wasn't warm yet. After making a point of not blocking them out, I found the homeless in every underground passage. And the crazies. At Penn Station I watched a man in a brown suit stiffened with filth, young and able-bodied. He was absorbed in a fierce fistfight with a plastic trash barrel, and he was losing.

In every other industrialized society someone has thought of the bottom layers of the underclass. We offer something only to people who meet our strict criteria. Elsewhere varying safety nets provide medical care, housing, job retraining and family allowances. A homeless European can usually find a bowl of soup and a bed. In America down-and-out is a desperate business.

New York treated the crisis like an emergency, squandering millions by overpaying crooked landlords of welfare hotels unworthy of the rats and cockroaches they sheltered for free. Even for those who qualified, waiting lists for public housing averaged eighteen years. On the street some New Yorkers were generous. Others howled about the menacing eyesores that polluted their neighborhoods. From time to time, kids amused themselves by splashing gas on ragged human bundles and setting them afire.

I saw a piece in *The New York Times* suggesting muted outrage that a Soviet documentary focused on the poor and homeless. But no foreigners, however friendly, fail to notice them or shake their heads at our version of the human condition.

One Sunday morning I drove slowly through the far end of the East Village, looking for people with nowhere to live. Finding them was easier than I expected. On Ninth Street, heading west toward Second Avenue, two guys shuffled and staggered under a huge wooden structure the way ants carry home outsize burdens. It looked too worthless to have been stolen, and the guys looked too poor to be thieves. It was, in fact, firewood. The men were from a Rainbow communelet, part of a New Age hippie movement, that was having its usual fifty or so homeless to lunch.

Their tiny settlement was on a weed-grown lot, temporarily vacant, behind a bent and rusty tin door. A ragged tarp was strung over an open fireplace and a cleanly swept expanse of dirt. Some broken chairs showed signs of doubling as beds. The only dwelling was a rudimentary canvas tepee for two. Purple morning glories and sunflowers grew wild.

Caleb Beacon and his wife, Cascadas, seemed to be the heads of the household, although they took pains to explain everyone was equal. Caleb had done the world. He's been a hippie in the London production of *Hair*; he'd played the flute in Johnny Carson's studio orchestra. Tattoos decorated his bare white biceps, and he wore a gaily colored crocheted Rasta hairnet. Cascadas had a nice smile and bad teeth.

I shook hands with a half dozen people around the fire. There was Red, who was black. He was a carpenter whose last boss took over his tools and Red's wages. "I got a self-destructive streak," Red said with a shy grin. "I guess I did too much wine and things. Sometimes I think I'm too sensitive for this world."

Manny was Hispanic and Italian. "He's our Woporican," Caleb announced. Manny smiled as though he had heard that one before; his T-shirt announced: "I Don't Give a Shit." "He used to have a job until he tried to stop some guy from getting mugged," Caleb added. Manny had worked for the city, cleaning up parks. He saw three Polish youths robbing an old man. He drove them off, flailing his spiked stick which was supposed to be only for spearing trash. They reported him, and he was fired for attacking citizens with municipal property. I did not check out the story, but Manny's eyes teared as he told it.

William Birdwell, Bird, wore a beret, a black raincoat and the owlish look of a Left Bank poet with writer's block. He had thought a lot about the injustices of society and the human price of others' greed. His basic message was that corporations and authorities wanted people to be beaten down, attached to their jobs and afraid to be different.

I brought up the word "homeless."

"I'm not homeless," Bird said. "I live on the planet."

"My home is my heart," Manny added.

Red snorted. "You're lying. I'm homeless."

I spent some time with Sunrise, a handsome but street-battered young man who announced, with a laugh, that he was a wanted criminal. His crime was sleeping out in front of the White House. Sunrise was part of the nuclear protest group that keeps a permanent vigil in "Peace Park," across Pennsylvania Avenue from the President. The cops took him to court for illegal camping.

Sunrise found he could no longer make a living by playing guitar for handouts. "In Washington you get arrested for playing on the street," he said. "It's the same on Bleecker Street. I see us heading towards martial law, and people are going to be railroaded into the system."

He shook his head, puzzled. "It's really scary. They are turning everybody into robots. You see people walking down the street with sad expressions. They don't turn their head one way or the other. They wear the latest styles, but what do they really have? Robots. Zombies."

The mood picked up when Stagger Lee stumbled into the fireplace. He repeated Sunrise's theme: "As soon as you start doing things for free, not supporting the system, they want you in jail. They want you dead. People like us are already gone, just living day by day."

And then Caleb: "Anything you do that makes you free, they want you in chains."

Stagger was all rough tattoos and incoherence until he pulled me aside. "You know where I can get poems published?" he asked. "I got a few things I'm working on." I asked if he had them written down. "No, but they're up here," he said, tapping his forehead. For the next fifteen minutes he declaimed moving and delicate verse about mystical Peruvian ladies, failing light and, mostly, living on the street.

The little kitchen served meals for free to anyone who wanted them. Cascadas and the others scrounged ingredients, paying token amounts to neighborhood grocers, who were regularly generous. They preached ideology of the Temple of the Rainbow. Drugs were energetically discouraged. "Shit, people got enough problems without that," Caleb explained.

One regular was a burly black man with a booming laugh. He wore huge earrings, a straw hat over a turban and a Monte Alban Mezcal "Eat the Worm" T-shirt. He and Stagger Lee and I did a rousing harmony of "My Girl" until none of us could remember any more of the words.

Another was Daniel Eggink, who wore a tie. Four years before he and his wife, a country singer, had brought their seven kids to New York from Haight-Ashbury in San Francisco. Their old car was stolen on the street, along with everything they owned. Now he printed greeting cards, using his daughter's drawings. He was the group's philosopher-spokesman.

The real problem in an increasingly desperate society, he said, was fear. "A third of the people are only one paycheck away from the other side of the line. They begrudge the homeless for not being next to them at their miserable jobs." People who might be of help ignore the homeless, he said; "The cruelest and most superficial people are those who've gone to college." And big business made it worse: "Corporations appropriate the land of marginal people and then defoliate. They want a dependent population, to keep people ignorant. New York is for the rich; if you make less than seventy-five thousand dollars, New York is not for you."

Daniel reflected a minute and concluded: "Basically the middle-class dream is a failure. We have all been robbed of being able to take the mud and transform it with our dreams to meet basic needs and sell the excess. Once you could be poor with dignity. Now that is no longer possible."

I asked if he was worried about a new policy allowing street people to be carried off for psychiatric treatment. He was not.

"In New York dead bodies are swept right up," he said. "As long as you're alive, they'll let you rot in the street under the guise of freedom. If you don't even have the control not to foul yourself, you need help."

That was just before Joyce Brown [a homeless person temporarily hospitalized involuntarily in October 1987 for chronic schizophrenia] was carted to Bellevue and had to fight hard to get out. Cleaned up, she was an instant media star. She did the talk shows, lectured at Harvard and took a job. A little later someone spotted her panhandling again, and she explained she'd run a little short of cash.

I mentioned her to a doorman I'd befriended, and he curled his lip. "You see, she's back on the street. That just goes to show you." I nodded, but I wasn't sure what that was supposed to show me. What I saw was a huge number of people in desperate shape, and they were inching steadily farther away from America's fabled taps of milk and honey.

QUESTIONS TO THINK ABOUT

1. In what way does Phillips believe that Reagan administration policies led to the fortunes made in the 1980s?
2. Do you see a difference between the sources of income found in Phillips' Table 2 and Table 3?
3. Is Phillips critical only of the money made by the wealthy during the 1980s, or is his criticism deeper?
4. Identify at least five reasons why a person might fall through the safety net and end up on the street, homeless.
5. Why are homeless people treated with more indifference in the United States than in other industrialized nations?
6. For what reasons might the homeless resist attempts by local, state, and federal agencies to help them?
7. According to Daniel Eggink, which groups in America are most hostile to

the homeless? What does he say about the attitudes of college graduates?
8. Does America's liberal individualist ideology support or condemn, or both support and condemn, the gap between the very rich and the very poor?

CRITIC'S CORNER

SAFETY NET

©1985 HERBLOCK

From your reading of *The American Polity,* what governmental programs make up the "safety net"? What is the cartoonist criticizing? Who do you think are the people that now fall through the safety net?

CRITIC'S CORNER

How does this cartoon depict taxpayers? Public officials? Why is the congressman shown as an anthropomorphized pig? How has the tax system affected the spirit and vitality of average Americans, according to the cartoonist?

16 | America in the World

The dissolving of the Soviet Union into independent republics, the fall of communism in Eastern Europe, and the end of the cold war have brought relief and optimism to all Americans. The threat of nuclear war no longer seems as real as it did in the past. NATO and the Warsaw Pact are not poised for confrontation in Europe. The Third World has ceased to be a battleground for U.S.-Soviet competition. While the post-cold war world still contains danger and conflict, the opportunities are more and better than in the past. Who could mourn the end of the cold war?

The CIA could. America's premier intelligence-gathering agency may find itself a victim of its own success. With Soviet communism no longer the enemy, the need for inside information, secret infiltration, and covert missions has diminished. Loch Johnson asks the question, "Now That the Cold War Is Over, Do We Need the CIA?" He finds the answer to be a clear yes.

The role of the CIA will change greatly in coming years, but threats still exist and intelligence must be gathered. The CIA will have to adapt to the new challenges of America in the world, as will all citizens who, unsuspectingly, grew up believing that the future will be like the past.

Loch Johnson
"Now That the Cold War Is Over, Do We Need the CIA?"

Espionage isn't what it used to be. Consider that for over forty-five years, the national security efforts of the United States have been designed to thwart the global expansion of the Soviet Union and its communist allies – the so-called containment doctrine.

The United States has deployed ships and soldiers around the world and aimed twelve thousand strategic nuclear warheads on targets from Moscow to Minsk. We have peered into the Soviet heartland with sophisticated reconnaissance satellites and ringed the perimeter of the USSR with electronic listening devices. Our spies have pilfered top secret documents from safes within the Kremlin itself.

Presidents have unleashed the Central Intelligence Agency (CIA) to fight communism in the back alleys of the world. Its weapons have included secret propaganda, political manipulation, economic disruption, and paramilitary (warlike) operations ranging from assassination plots against foreign leaders to large-scale "secret" wars.

On their side, the Soviets [did] . . . their best to spy on the United States and disrupt our attempts to influence global affairs. The KGB, the chief Soviet intelligence agency, proved to be a ruthless adversary in this hidden and undeclared World War III.

Now, suddenly, the CIA and the KGB have run into a hitch: the end of the Cold War. . . .

. . . Once cut off from the West by an iron curtain, today Moscow is practically as accessible to Americans as London and Paris. Further, the Warsaw Pact – once a knife-point against the jugular of Western Europe – has been thrown into the furnace of history, replaced by upstart new regimes struggling for freedom and democracy.

These startling developments, predicted by no one, have led to clamors in the United States for sharply reduced spending on national security – a longing for a "peace dividend" in a time of budgetary stress. Certainly much can be cut among large-item, strategic weapons systems, as the two leading military experts in Congress, Sam Nunn (D) of Georgia and Les Aspin (D) of Wisconsin, have spelled out. Yet, as the war in the Persian Gulf has underscored, this nation will need to have a diverse (and, unfortunately, costly) array of conventional weapons at hand – from the smart bombs that so impressively invited themselves through closed doors in Baghdad to the modern tanks and airlift capability that may again be called on in the future to deter aggression in the Middle East or elsewhere.

Moreover, in the longing for a peace dividend in the aftermath of the Cold War, it should not be forgotten that the nation's intelligence budget merits protection. The reason is simple: threats to the United States remain plentiful, even if the [former] USSR is now a friend. Too often these lingering dangers have been ignored as a result of America's fixation on the Soviet peril.

Although the intelligence mission ought to be retained as a budget priority, new ways of spending these resources are warranted. No longer must the United States dedicate 50 percent of the strategic intelligence budget to intelligence operations against the Soviet Union, as was the case throughout most of the Cold War. Now it must concern itself with other more pressing dangers, outlined below. . . .

. . . Consider how important it is for the United States to have information from overseas about other matters touching our daily lives – not always very gently.

It is hard to tell in advance what nation – large or small, friend or enemy – may pose a threat to our security in the future, as Iraq's bellicose behavior underscored. It is clear, however, that the United States has sometimes been quite unprepared to react to dangers, often because its leaders lacked good information about global events.

For example: regardless of how one evaluates the U.S. military operations against Grenada (1983) and Panama (1989), the interventions were based on shoddy information. The chief rationale for the invasion of Grenada – an alleged threat against American medical students studying there – was never verified; neither the CIA nor any of America's other intelligence agencies had espionage agents on the island. (The medical school's administrators later denied any threat.) Upon landing, U.S. troops had to acquire maps of the island at local service stations, so lacking was the military intelligence.

In Panama, the American military commander leading the operation to apprehend its unscrupulous dictator, General Manuel Antonio Noriega, was astonished to find the Panamanian troops well armed with advanced weaponry – another dangerous intelligence failure.

Grenada and Panama are small nations located right next door to the United States. Harder still is the task of knowing what is happening in countries thousands of miles away. Islamic fundamentalists . . . held American hostages for years . . . (chiefly in Lebanon), but the United States [failed to learn] their precise location or the plans of their captors. Nor did the United States have much information about where its prisoners of war were being kept in Kuwait and Iraq during the Persian Gulf War, the exact whereabouts of the Iraqi leader (Saddam Hussein), or much about the resolve of Iraqi troops hidden in bunkers – though much of the intelligence about Iraqi military movements was first-rate, pouring into U.S. decision councils from dozens of "platforms" (satellites and aircraft) gliding high above the sands of Iraq and Kuwait.

Iraq openly proclaimed that it has chemical and biological weapons; but the outside world knows little about its ability and intentions to use them. Nor do we know, with much precision, to what extent U.S. bombing during the Persian Gulf War managed to destroy the plants where they were manufactured. The proliferation of advanced weaponry around the world must be tracked more closely by American intelligence. Accurate data on the worldwide flow of weapons may lead, one hopes, to renewed international efforts in the United Nations (and elsewhere) designed to curb the sale of sophisticated arms, which have made regional disputes so dangerous to world peace.

Illegal drugs pose another threat to the United States. The Bush administration has declared the drug scourge Public Enemy No. 1. Every year some five thousand to six thousand ships ply the waters from Colombia and Peru to the United States, each carrying two hundred to three hundred containers (many with freight originating in nearby landlocked Bolivia). A comparable number of airplanes make this same trip annually. Efforts to monitor this transportation for contraband – not to mention the drug traffic from other countries (with Turkey high on the list) – presents an intelligence problem of staggering proportions. So far, only about 10 percent of the illegal drugs are intercepted as they stream across U.S. borders.

Some would argue that America's declining economic strength presents the greatest threat to the United States since the decline of the Cold War. They see an important new role for the CIA and other intelligence agencies in secretly gathering economic intelligence to share with American industry in its struggle against foreign competition – especially the Japanese.

Such a role would not be entirely new. The CIA has been interested in knowing more about the decisions of the Organization of Petroleum Exporting Countries (OPEC) ever since 1973, when secret price fixing sent gasoline prices spiraling upward. The CIA has also closely monitored Soviet crop production and oil supplies over the years, among other things. Sometimes the relationship between the CIA and American industry has been startlingly close and controversial. In the 1960s, for instance, the CIA joined in a secret alliance with a U.S. corporate behemoth, International Telephone and Telegraph (ITT), to overthrow the president of Chile, Salvadore Allende, before he could move to nationalize the company's holdings (an operation that failed, though it probably helped to weaken Allende, who was eventually toppled by an internal right-wing coup).

Widespread economic spying on one's major allies is an even more contentious matter than covert interference in the affairs of smaller, developing nations. Here intelligence experts, as well as chief executive officers in the private sector, are of two minds.

Some in each group argue for a greater CIA role, as part of a national industrial strategy. If the CIA can help give American industry a competitive edge by finding out about trade deals and negotiating positions, so much the better. Major companies already perform their own industrial espionage but, argues this side, they need help. In addition, other nations – including U.S. allies – have been spying on U.S. companies for years. (KGB activities of this sort . . . actually increased during 1990, according to former CIA director William Webster.) So, continues the argument, it is time for Americans to use whatever means we have for discovering others' commercial secrets.

Others in the CIA, as well as inside the boardrooms of U.S. industry, are less quick to accept this espionage mission. They worry about disrupting alliance relations if the spies are caught (as some inevitably are). They are skeptical that the CIA is well equipped for this kind of espionage; and they believe that industry can handle this task pretty well itself anyway. They wonder, too, how this information would be distributed. Which industries would benefit in the United States? Could the identities of the CIA's spies and their methods be kept secret? Mostly, they see this approach as insignificant compared to the more deep-seated causes of America's ailing manufacturing capabilities.

This brief list of spy missions for U.S. intelligence barely scratches the surface. Terrorism will continue to be a problem. Indeed, experts fear that the war in the Persian Gulf may have as one of its end results the spawning of a whole new generation of anti-American terrorists operating out of the Middle East. On another front – of obvious relevance to long-range security interests of Americans and everyone else on this small globe where all life is connected – some ecologists hope that the CIA can turn its impressive satellites toward monitoring the changing condition of the world's rain forests and other environmental concerns.

Beyond the list of collection targets lies the vital task of *analyzing* what all the information means. Too often analysis has been the neglected stepchild of the intelligence agencies. The new collection priorities will require the training of specialists to appraise the rising tide of information about once-ignored nations. As former CIA Director William E. Colby observed in 1990, "When Cold War secrecy and contest made information hard to come by, except by fascinating secret operations and technological triumphs, and produced a demand for action-minded paramilitary and political warriors, the analysts took a back seat." Now, he concludes, "The new era will put them where they should be: at the center of the intelligence process."

So, while some savings in the national-security budget should be possible in this new era of . . . *rapprochement*, the intelligence budget should be separated out from the weapons budget. The United States needs more intelligence (and steady attention to its conventional capabilities for deterring aggression by renegade nations in the developing world); but the United States can safely reduce spending on strategic weapons systems. This reduction can be carried out without undermining the still-necessary posture of mutual assured destruction (MAD). The place to begin, as many authorities have advocated (America's premier statesman, George F. Kennan, among them), is with a 50 percent reduction in strategic nuclear warheads, carried out simultaneously in both the United States and the [former] Soviet Union – all carefully monitored by "national technical means" (NTM, that is, modern surveillance instruments such as satellites), as well as by on-site inspections.

Budget-planners should make sure, however, that any increased funds for the CIA are channeled almost exclusively toward arms control monitoring and other information gathering, not into its "dirty tricks" department. With few exceptions, the CIA's covert actions have done more to harm than to help America's interests abroad. In contrast, the CIA in its role of information-gatherer has proven itself, despite the inevitable errors, indispensable to those who make decisions in Washington.

This is not to say that covert action should be abandoned altogether. The United States needs to maintain a capacity for secret operations in emergency situations. Indeed, members of the United Nations (UN) Security Council should consider the establishment of a UN-directed "SWAT team" – *small, multinational, acting under proper authority, and carefully supervised* – to conduct quick paramilitary strikes against chemical-biological (CB) and nuclear-weapons facilities in the hands of outlaw regimes and terrorist factions. When diplomatic initiatives fail to curb the outlaws, this approach may arguably serve as a better alternative – in extreme cases of CB or nuclear threats – than a full-scale military invasion, with all the loss of civilian lives that option usually entails.

"The winds and waves are always on the side of the ablest navigators," observed the great British historian Edward Gibbon. Skillful navigation depends on taking one's bearings carefully. Without a robust intelligence service able to monitor events around the world (not just in Moscow), the United States would find itself condemned to steerage beneath cloudy skies. The Cold War may be over, but the U.S. need for accurate information about the world remains acute.

QUESTIONS TO THINK ABOUT

1. What problems did the dissolution of the Soviet Union present for the CIA?
2. List some of the possible CIA projects that exist in today's world. Can the CIA be effective in taking on any of them?
3. How could the CIA prevent the need to use overt military force against America's enemies in the coming years?
4. Will the same kind of personnel be needed by the CIA in the 1990s and beyond as were needed in the years of the cold war? What specific skills will be of special interest to the agency in the future?

CRITIC'S CORNER

What implications does this cartoon carry about America's commitment to cleaning up the environment? Is the American government more concerned about image or action on environmental issues? Based on the cartoon, how do you think the other participants at the Earth's Summit reacted to what was perceived as a degree of American indifference?

The Study Guide

1 | Social Change and Political Response

Viewing America through a Young French Traveler's Eyes

Begin by reading all of chapter 1.

Why has Professor Ladd decided to open his book on American government by featuring the ideas of a long-dead Frenchman? The reason is because Alexis de Tocqueville's *Democracy in America* is *the* classic work on American government. "Classic" in this context means a work that is a landmark on the subject, one that has stood up over time as being significant. Throughout *The American Polity* Professor Ladd will cite many classic books by footnoting them and by listing certain works at the end of each chapter. However, if you could choose only one classic book on American government, most political scientists would agree that it would be Tocqueville's *Democracy in America*.

You can figure out a good deal about Tocqueville and *Democracy in America* from reading Professor Ladd's opening pages and from your own knowledge of U.S. and world history. Start by trying to answer the following questions:

Who was Alexis de Tocqueville, how old was he when he visited America, and what social class did he belong to?

What events in France would have influenced Tocqueville's desire to visit America? What did he hope to investigate while he was here? What were his long-term reasons for studying the United States?

When did Tocqueville visit, who was president, and what was the nation like in those years? From the picture in the text, speculate on how Tocqueville reacted to his experiences and the people he met in the United States. If Tocqueville had visited the United

States at a different time, would he have made the same observations?

Alexis de Tocqueville is regarded primarily as a political scientist, yet he studied many other facets of American life – social, religious, moral, educational, economic, geographic – and believed that all these facets were interrelated. Be sure you can explain how Professor Ladd describes the links that Tocqueville believed connected all facets of American life. In other words, why does Professor Ladd say that Tocqueville wanted to "see the system as a whole"?

What three main observations did Tocqueville make about American society? Write them down, using three simple words or phrases. This is not the last time you will see these features of American life mentioned. At the start of chapter 3 Professor Ladd examines the portion of the nation's heritage derived from European classical liberalism (which he also calls *liberal individualism*). When you read chapter 3, think back to what you learned about Tocqueville and his ideas in this chapter.

Putting Tocqueville to the Test of Time

What three observations did Tocqueville make about American society? Tocqueville claimed that individualism, equality, and democracy were three social and political features that characterized the United States then. Professor Ladd discusses both continuity and change in chapter 1. Test out Tocqueville's observations for continuity and for change.

Individualism. Professor Ladd comments that individualism was an important principle of American life and remains so today. Give an example. From his discussion give an example in which the rights of individuals can conflict with the rights of society.

Equality. Does Professor Ladd use the term *equality* to mean "equality of opportunity" or "equality of result"? The two ideas are very different. Give an example from the book to suggest that the United States has not fulfilled the promise of equality for all.

Democracy. Has American government always been as democratic as it is today? Should it be more democratic? You will have a much clearer personal view of the answer to these questions after you have finished this course. From Professor Ladd's discussion in this chapter, give an example of the kind of controversies that exist today about the degree of American democracy. You will encounter a debate about how democratic American democracy really is at the end of chapter 4. When you get there pay special attention to the theories of elitism and pluralism. A raucous class discussion may start – or, if it doesn't, you should start it! File away your knowledge of Tocqueville to use as evidence in support of your views.

To gain a little more insight into the Frenchman's reaction to America, read the two short excerpts for chapter 1 in the "Cases" section of this *Study Guide.** You will be reading Tocqueville's diary entry about a native American, written while near Detroit, followed by an excerpt from journalist Richard Reeves's recent conversation with black inner-city Detroit residents. Both observers were gathering their own evidence on individualism, equality, and democracy in America.

Assessing Political Change in the United States

Professor Ladd concludes chapter 1 by dividing American history into several periods. Why does he call them sociopolitical periods? This section offers a mini-review of U.S. history if a few details have faded from your memory since your junior year in high school. You need to know the terms that Professor Ladd applies to each sociopolitical period, the approximate dates of each period, and a few characteristics of each. Complete the sentences below, but do not try to memorize all the historical details Professor Ladd uses to illustrate each era.

1. The _____, from _____ to _____, was

   characterized by farming as the main occupation, _____

   as most people's educational achievement, and _____ as

   the most significant level of
   government. What important regional differences existed between North
   and South during this era?

2. The _____, from the 1860s to the 1910s, was

   characterized by _____ as the growing occupation,

   _____ in population, and eventually

   _____ in the size of government. What areas of life
   did government become more involved in during this era?

---

*The "Cases" section of the *Study Guide* contains short excerpts that let you look into the nooks and crannies of political science. The books and articles from which the excerpts are taken focus on interesting people, unusual events, and strange moments in politics that serious political science might overlook. Try using a few tidbits from the cases on your exam's essay questions.

3. The industrial state, from _____ to _____, was

characterized by the emergence of _____ as a powerful
group in the American economy and in politics and a dramatic

_____ in the size and role of government.
What do statistics reveal about the spending of the federal (national)
government versus state and local governments beginning in this era?

4. The _____, from _____ to the future, is
characterized by the increased importance of technology, knowledge, and
an economy based on services. This is the sociopolitical period you will
read about in the next chapter. It is the era you are living in now and will
be living in into the twenty-first century. It is the era that college courses
like this one are preparing you to take an active part in.

Sample Test Questions

MULTIPLE CHOICE—SELECT THE *BEST* ANSWER

1. Alexis de Tocqueville came to the United States from France in 1831 to:
   a. flee the French Revolution.
   b. observe an old democracy in action.
   c. study how a young democracy worked.
   d. design the Statue of Liberty.
2. The three main features of American life that Tocqueville observed were:
   a. individualism, equality, and democracy.
   b. liberty, equality, and fraternity.
   c. financial inequality, social equality, and hypocrisy.
   d. financial inequality, social inequality, and feudalism.
3. The American belief in equality of opportunity is found in all of the
   following cases *except*:
   a. black Americans' struggle for civil rights.
   b. women's desire to be accepted in jobs that were traditionally held by
      men.
   c. students' use of education to raise their socioeconomic status.
   d. bankers' demands for exceptions to FDIC insurance regulations.
4. A reliance on technology and knowledge characterizes the sociopolitical
   period termed:
   a. the rural republic.   c. the industrial state.
   b. the industrializing nation.   d. postindustrial society.

5. The size and scope of the national government's power, exercised especially through spending, grew most during the sociopolitical period termed:
   a. the rural republic.
   b. the industrializing nation.
   c. the industrial state.
   d. postindustrial society.
6. The nation was dominated by agriculture in the sociopolitical period termed:
   a. the rural republic.
   b. the industrializing nation.
   c. the industrial state.
   d. postindustrial society.
7. Large cities containing a rapidly growing population developed within the sociopolitical period termed:
   a. the rural republic.
   b. the industrializing nation.
   c. the industrial state.
   d. postindustrial society.
8. By "social change and political response," Professor Ladd means that:
   a. As the American people and their way of life have changed, the political system has changed to meet new needs.
   b. As political change has been initiated, the American people have adapted to what the government has decided.
   c. People do not change; only institutions change.
   d. Americans are politically and socially responsive to all kinds of change.
9. Alexis de Tocqueville believed that the various aspects of American life – social, religious, moral, economic, and political – were:
   a. unrelated.
   b. dominated by politics.
   c. interrelated.
   d. in conflict.
10. American democracy, Alexis de Tocqueville believed, could be clearly contrasted with:
    a. French democracy.
    b. American authoritarianism.
    c. aristocracy.
    d. Russian communism.

TRUE/FALSE

11. Alexis de Tocqueville believed that equality and democracy were political trends that would eventually develop throughout the world.
12. The rights of the individual never conflict with the rights of society.
13. Political change usually leads to social change rather than the other way around.
14. During the period when the United States was industrializing rapidly, few differences between North and South existed.
15. The government's response to the Depression brought the United States fully into the industrial-state period.

ESSAYS

16. What were Alexis de Tocqueville's main observations about the United
    States in the 1830s in his book *Democracy in America*? Are some or all of
    these observations valid today? Is there potential conflict among the
    values that he saw as characteristic of the American people?
17. Trace the sociopolitical periods delineating American history. Mention
    the key features of each era. How did each era's problems eventually lead
    to the next era? In your analysis, try to use the concept of social change
    and political response as your theme.

ANSWERS

Multiple Choice

1. c	p. 3	6. a	pp. 8-9
2. a	pp. 4-5	7. b	p. 9
3. d	pp. 6-7	8. a	pp. 7-8
4. d	pp. 11, 13	9. c	p. 4
5. c	pp. 11-13	10. c	pp. 4-5

True/False

11. t	p. 5	14. f	p. 9
12. f	pp. 5-6	15. t	p. 11
13. f	pp. 7-8		

2 | Postindustrial Society

In some ways this chapter is Professor Ladd's toughest. It has two focuses: First, Professor Ladd explains the difficult and abstract notion of a postindustrial society, the sociopolitical period that the United States has just entered. Your political science professor might save this part of the chapter until the end of the course because it seems "futuristic." Second, Professor Ladd offers a lot of important data that describe the ethnic and cultural makeup of the American people. Here you encounter the first of the (possibly dreaded!) charts, graphs, and tables. This part of the chapter is a must before you go on to learn about the government of the American people.

What Is the Postindustrial Era?

Begin your study of chapter 2 by reading Professor Ladd's brief summary at the end of the chapter. This summary of what postindustrialism means will help you read the first half of chapter 2 more quickly. Now read from page 14 to page 32. Who coined the term *postindustrialism*?

The discussion of postindustrialism opens with the mention of the mass media. As you study the specific features of postindustrial society, try to make a broad connection between the mass media and the postindustrial era.

Table 2.1 is unusual and interesting. Professor Ladd cites statistics there to show how the United States has changed in fifty years. Can you speculate on a common factor behind these various changes? Do more cars mean more divorces? Be prepared to mention at least one specific change that occurred as America moved from an industrial society to a postindustrial society. Next, the chapter takes up a serious consideration of what the term *postindustrial society* means. Professor Ladd identifies five characteristics of the era. You should be able to answer the questions below. If you can't, look back at the text.

Technology. Is technology new to America? How is technology's role different in postindustrial America than it was in earlier times? How is technology tied to educational institutions? What is research and development (R & D)? How does the United States compare to Japan in R & D? Based on Figure 2.2, what trends can you spot in R & D spending?

The Knowledge Base. Why is knowledge so important in postindustrial society? Who must have it, why must they have it, and how do they get it? Compare two sets of statistics: those from Figure 2.4 on higher education in the United States, Britain, France, Germany, Japan, and Sweden, and those from Figure 2.3 on higher education in the United States in 1970 and 1989. How do Americans feel about spending many tax dollars on education in a knowledge-based society?

Occupations: The Service Economy. Remembering back to chapter 1 and the nation's earlier sociopolitical eras, what were the main occupations in the rural republic? In the industrializing nation? In the industrial state? What occupations do most (72 percent) of the people have in a postindustrial society? Give specific examples. Categorize (a) your mother's and father's occupations, (b) your political science professor's, (c) the occupation you plan to pursue after graduation. What is a bureaucrat? Bureaucrats will come up for more discussion in chapter 8, so you have a little time to organize your thoughts on this topic.

Mass Affluence. What does Professor Ladd mean by the existence of mass affluence in a postindustrial society? Are all Americans rich? Approximately what percent are at or below the poverty level? What factor in particular prevents countries in Africa, Central America, and southern Asia from achieving higher levels of prosperity?

In the early 1990s the United States experienced a severe economic recession, as all of you probably remember from your high-school years. Despite the recession, the United States remains a very prosperous nation. Which other nations does Professor Ladd mention as being very prosperous?

New Class Relationships. Describe the socioeconomic classes in the United States during the industrial period. Which class was very strong and active? Is that class as strong now? What has happened to organized labor in Professor Ladd's estimation? Do educated, postindustrial professionals fit into older class designations, such as "working class" or "middle class"? Professor Ladd ends his discussion here, but if you have taken a sociology course and are interested in socioeconomic class issues, you might want to develop your own theory about what class conflicts may occur and which class may dominate in postindustrial American society.

The Ethnic and Cultural Composition of the United States

Demographics are the statistics that describe a group of people in terms of factors like religion, age, race, ethnicity, gender, income, region. Demographics are also a hot political topic. The United States is a nation of many different ethnic, racial, and cultural groups. Is it a melting pot as once was thought? Or is it a multicultural society in which each group must guard its uniqueness? The campus debates on "political correctness" involve these conflicting images of America.

Read the rest of chapter 2, from page 32 to page 40. You cannot possibly memorize all of the demographic data that Professor Ladd sets forth there, but some especially important facts should be mastered. As for the rest, remember that there is a wealth of demographic information in chapter 2 of *The American Polity* that you can footnote and use in many future term papers. Rather than sell the book back after the semester, keep it and get more than your money's worth from it in the future!

Using the text, especially the figures and tables, cite and explain a statistic given for each of the following areas and the demographic groups listed below:

Regarding ethnicity, cite a statistic given for the English, Scottish, and Welsh; Latin Americans; and Asians; explain it.

Regarding race, cite a statistic given for whites, blacks, and Hispanics, and explain it.

Regarding religion, cite a statistic given for Protestants, Catholics, and people of other religions, and explain it. (Take a careful look at Figure 2.9. Avoid the trap of misreading the figure. Which is the largest Protestant denomination? How do you determine the total number of Protestants?)

Regarding socioeconomic status, cite a statistic given for whites, blacks, and Hispanics, and explain it.

So much for basic demographics. Two complex topics remain: economic inequality and regional attitudes. More than statistics are required to make sense of these topics.

ECONOMIC INEQUALITY

Look back at the socioeconomic differences among racial groups that you observed above. Clearly, differences exist. What happens to the differences when families with both a working wife and a working husband are compared across racial groups?

Equality of opportunity or equality of result? In chapter 1 Professor Ladd discussed America's commitment to the former, not the latter. Equality of opportunity means that economic mobility must exist. Does it? Consult Table 2.5. What is the key determinant of mobility? In chapter 1 the centrality of individualism to the American creed was also explored. Look at the question asked respondents in Table 2.4. Do all racial groups believe in individual effort as the key to success? Do all income groups? They do.

Equality of opportunity does not mean equality of result: The statistics in Figure 2.14 reveal that the 20 percent of America's wealthiest families earned 44 percent of the nation's wealth, while the poorest 40 percent earned 15 percent of the wealth. There is much disagreement about the distribution of wealth during the 1980s while President Reagan was in office. For a strong opinion, read the short excerpt by Kevin Phillips in chapter 15 of the "Cases" section of the *Study Guide*. Look for Ross Perot in Phillips's Table 2.

While you are taking a break to read a case excerpt, you may enjoy the two personal stories of mobility in America in chapter 2 of the "Cases." The first features Elizabeth Colton's account of 1988 Democratic presidential candidate Jesse Jackson. You will gain new insight into his fight for equality for black Americans after you learn about his own origins. Then read the frightening Katherine Newman story of downward mobility. This is not what upper-middle-class kids expect: Read and think carefully, study hard, for you must be prepared to rely on yourself in the uncertain world of the postindustrial future.

REGIONAL DIFFERENCES

Figure 2.10 is one of Professor Ladd's best. It shows visually what has happened to regional differences in income. From your past study of U.S. history you will remember the great differences that once existed among regions. Do these differences exist today? Which regions have the highest per capita income?

Now look at Figures 2.11 and 2.12, which contrast party identification and regional attitudes in the 1940s and in 1990-91. Again, the picture is clear from the charts. What has happened to the sharp differences in regional attitudes over fifty years?

Finally, Professor Ladd points out a particularly interesting phenomenon in the United States – bicoastal liberalism. Using the data in Figure 2.13, answer the following questions:

1. In what regions is sex between unmarried people most frowned upon? Where is it most accepted?

2. What region most strongly supports a woman's legal right to have an abortion? What region opposes legal abortions most strongly?

3. Is there any region where a majority believes that women should stay home while men run things? What region most reflects that view? Where do the fewest feel that way?

Bicoastal liberalism is a fascinating subject, one that would make a good topic for a term paper. Consider bicoastal liberalism a bit more, perhaps in terms of where you live, where you go to school, where you plan to live, and how accurately these statistics (which measure population overall) reflect the attitudes of individuals you know personally.

Sample Test Questions

MULTIPLE-CHOICE—SELECT THE *BEST* ANSWER

1. Over the past fifty years in the United States, the number of all of the following has increased, *except*:
   a. automobiles   c. divorces.
   b. public transportation.   d. telephones.
2. What is true of the District of Columbia, Iowa, North Dakota, West Virginia, and Wyoming, according to the 1990 census?
   a. All gained population.   c. All lost population.
   b. All gained a Senate seat.   d. All were geographically
                                              relocated by Congress.
3. Which of the following is *not* an example of an occupation in the service economy?
   a. teacher   c. bureaucrat
   b. attorney   d. machinist
4. The nation that measures highest in per capita income today is:
   a. the United States.   c. Greece.
   b. Japan.   d. Haiti.
5. In terms of median income, statistics place racial groups in the United States in the following order:
   a. blacks highest, then Hispanics, then whites.
   b. Hispanics highest, then blacks, then whites.
   c. whites highest, then blacks, then Hispanics.
   d. whites highest, then Hispanics, then blacks.
6. Bicoastal liberalism means that:
   a. All liberals live along the Atlantic and Pacific coasts.
   b. Attitudes along the New England, Middle Atlantic, and Pacific coasts tend to be more liberal than attitudes in central regions of the United States.
   c. Liberal attitudes spread outward toward the coast from the central regions.
   d. Most bisexuals are liberals.

7. Economic mobility is correlated most with which factor?
    a. region   c. education
    b. religion   d. ethnicity
8. In a postindustrial, knowledge-based society, research and development takes place in all of the following settings, *except*:
    a. the home.   c. universities.
    b. private industry.   d. government.
9. Which of the following classes was especially strong during America's industrial era?
    a. the robber barons   c. the working class
    b. the bourgeoisie   d. the small farmers
10. Recent immigration to the United States has come largely from all of the following parts of the world *except*:
    a. southern Europe.   c. Central America.
    b. Asia.   d. South America.

TRUE/FALSE

11. Mass affluence means that most of a nation's people do not have to worry about obtaining the basic food and shelter necessary for life.
12. Levels of education in America have gone down because spending for education has diminished.
13. In a service economy most people will make a living by becoming servants to the wealthy.
14. Overpopulation is a major factor in the poverty of third world countries.
15. Because Americans do not attend church services in large numbers, their religious beliefs have likewise lessened.
16. Working class people are the strongest group in the postindustrial era.
17. Income differences among whites, blacks, and Hispanics decrease when only families with two working adults are compared by racial group.
18. Regional differences in income have consistently lessened over time in America.
19. Regional differences in social and political attitudes are nearly nonexistent in the United States today.
20. A majority of all racial, ethnic, religious, age, and income groups feel that working hard and exercising individual initiative are the best ways to get ahead in America.

ESSAYS

21. Describe the main features of postindustrial society. Which kind of individuals and groups will benefit from the changes that postindustrialism brings? Who will be hurt? Using the idea of social change and political

response, what general changes in American politics can you predict for the postindustrial era?

22. Considering various demographic features of the American people – such as religion, age, race, ethnicity, gender, income, and region – would you describe the nation as more of a melting pot or more multicultural? How great are the economic differences among racial and regional groups? What are the attitude differences among these groups? Back up each of your statements with at least one specific piece of evidence (a statistic) that substantiates your view.

ANSWERS

Multiple Choice

1. b p. 15	6. b p. 35	
2. c p. 16	7. c pp. 38-39	
3. d p. 24	8. a pp. 19-20	
4. a p. 28	9. c pp. 28-31	
5. d p. 33	10. a p. 32	

True/False

11. t pp. 25-26	16. f p. 29
12. f pp. 21-22	17. t p. 33
13. f pp. 23-25	18. t pp. 34-35
14. t p. 26	19. f pp. 35-36
15. f pp. 32-33	20. t pp. 36-38

3 | The American Ideology

In chapter 3 Professor Ladd delves deeply into the ideas underlying the American creed introduced in chapter 1. To start, read the whole chapter. Keep in mind that the first part of the chapter involves historical and philosophical ideas. Near the end, Professor Ladd uses the example of Henry Ford to illustrate the application of the creed in the early twentieth century. Professor Ladd concludes by examining the issue of the existence of a single creed in contemporary American society.

Classical Liberalism

The reason for the American Revolution of 1776 is portrayed somewhat differently in *The American Polity* than it usually is in U.S. history books for younger students. In the past you might have envisioned the American Revolution as having been a unique, one-time/one-place event. How does Professor Ladd see the American Revolution in its origin and relationship to other revolutions? Younger students also tend to see the American Revolution as a physical act of rebellion. What kind of revolution was it really?

Interestingly, the ideas behind the American Revolution came from Europe. From what country? From what person? What term does Professor Ladd apply to these ideas? Note the irony in the source of the American ideology.

The term *classical liberalism* (also called Liberalism, with a capital L) describes America's ideology. *Liberal individualism,* notes Professor Ladd, is another phrase you can apply accurately to America's creed. As Professor Ladd points out, classical liberalism is *not* the same thing as today's liberalism. In fact, classical liberalism is the creed embraced by today's conservative. If these abstract notions seem confusing, do not worry because very soon you will be on firm ground with the meat of American government – Congress, the presidency, the judiciary. If the abstract ideas intrigue you, consider taking a course in political philosophy or theory. There you trace Western history (usually from

Plato through Marx) in terms of major political ideas. While not directly applicable to job-hunting skills, philosophy and theory is great stuff that will stay
with you forever.

If you concentrate hard for a short time on the next part of this chapter, you
will grasp the difficult idea of classical liberalism. You might strengthen your
grasp by listing the six major tenets of classical liberalism, a philosophy pre-
scribing change in the aristocratic society of the 1600s. Where have you seen a
list like this before? (Remember Alexis de Tocqueville and what he saw in
America?) Be prepared to explain briefly each of the following tenets of classical liberalism:

individualism
freedom
equality
private property (capitalism)
popular choice in government
limited government

In particular, consider how these six elements are interrelated. How is individualism related to private property? How is freedom related to popular choice
in government? As you consider these questions you can see more easily how
the recent revolutions in Eastern Europe and the former Soviet Union were in
part inspired by these same ideas.

To demonstrate your understanding of classical liberalism answer these
questions based on points that Professor Ladd makes:

For what socioeconomic class is classical liberalism especially
suited?

Why did historian Louis Hartz call America a "fragment society?"

Why is equality the single most important tenet of American ideology in its ability to unlock (un-Locke!) the rest of the creed?

What particular need did the creed fulfill for the United States according to British writer G. K. Chesterton?

And now back to Tocqueville.

What impact did Tocqueville predict that liberal individualism
would have eventually on the rest of the world?

Professor Ladd concludes his explanation of classical liberalism with an admission: The American creed is not perfect. Be ready to criticize the creed;
using his arguments, consider the following:

Have all groups in America been successful in terms of the creed's
promises?

Are citizens who do not follow the tenets of the creed accepted fully by others?

Has the United States, a nation that embraced classical liberalism from its start, always had a good understanding of other nations' struggles to achieve liberal individualism?

Henry Ford

What action did automobile company owner Henry Ford take in 1914 concerning wages? What did he do subsequently about car prices? Why did he do these things? Relate Ford's decisions to the individualism, freedom, equality, and capitalism (belief in private property) advocated in the American creed.

Eighty years after Henry Ford's decision there is evidence both for and against the creed's success. Certainly not all business owners embraced Ford's line of thinking in the 1980s. The short chapter 15 excerpt by Kevin Phillips in the "Cases" section of the *Study Guide* exposes the fact that the wealthy got wealthier in the 1980s. Refer back to Figure 2.14 in chapter 2 on the distribution of wealth in America over time. Or read about the savings and loan scandal. True, American ideology never promised equality of result, but it did promise equality of opportunity. Has it made good on its promise? On the other hand, look back to Professor Ladd's Table 2.3 in chapter 2. In what nation is per capita income the highest? There is still room for a lot of debate eighty years after Henry Ford.

One American Creed?

When Professor Ladd calls an ideology a "constrained" set of beliefs, he means that the elements of the ideology all fit together into one cohesive idea. Review the six basic beliefs of America's liberal individualist creed. Are they "constrained"?

How do children and new citizens learn about the creed? Use Professor Ladd's term to describe the process.

The chapter on the American ideology closes by considering whether one unified American creed still exists. Scrutinize the photo on page 57. From the photo, your own knowledge, and Professor Ladd's discussion, assess in light of the American creed the Los Angeles police's treatment of Rodney King and the jury's verdict in the King case. In chapter 2 you learned about the many demographic variables that describe Americans: religion, race, ethnicity, gender, income, age, region. Which variables are potentially most divisive to the nation?

The debate on your campus about political correctness is part of a larger debate in America about the creed. At what point do multicultural forces threaten to explode the "melting pot"? Professor Ladd's view is optimistic. Go back to chapter 2 to locate one specific set of data (a figure or a table) that supports the view that most Americans share belief in one unified American creed.

Not all nations follow liberal individualist beliefs. Our leading economic competitor, Japan, is built on an ideology of collectivism rather than individualism. To learn something about a contrasting ideology take a quick look at the excerpt for chapter 3 in the "Cases" section of the *Study Guide*. James Fallows describes the Japanese ideology, then urges Americans to be *More Like Us*.

Sample Test Questions

MULTIPLE-CHOICE—SELECT THE *BEST* ANSWER

1. The American creed's classical liberalism came from:
   a. Greece.
   b. Rome.
   c. Europe, particularly England.
   d. Russia.
2. All of the following are important parts of classical liberal thought *except*:
   a. collectivism.
   b. private property.
   c. democracy.
   d. freedom.
3. Henry Ford raised wages in his auto factory in 1914 because:
   a. unions pressured him to do it.
   b. all other company executives believed it would increase profits.
   c. Ford felt that higher wages would increase his workers' buying power and make the company stronger in the long run.
   d. government regulations forced Ford to take the action.
4. All of the following trends could destroy the unifying role of the American creed, *except*:
   a. ethnic group identities outweighing individualism.
   b. linguistic differences, the absence of a common language.
   c. differences in the application of justice for whites and blacks.
   d. further immigration into the United States.
5. Political socialization is the process by which:
   a. Americans become resigned to economic inequality.
   b. children learn elements of the American creed.
   c. schools teach children the facts of American history.
   d. immigrants learn to speak English.
6. Classical liberalism was first developed by the philosopher:
   a. John Locke.
   b. Everett Ladd.
   c. John Adams.
   d. Henry Ford.

7. The greatest difference between the American and the French revolutions is that:
   a. they were inspired by differing beliefs about equality.
   b. the French Revolution was one single event, while the American Revolution had its origin in ideas that had long been accepted.
   c. the American Revolution meant many things to many different people, while the French Revolution had a unified rationale.
   d. they had differing beliefs about aristocracy.

8. What attitude have Americans often shown toward citizens who do not go along with the basic ideas of the American creed?
   a. They have exiled them.
   b. They have isolated and rejected them.
   c. They have tolerated them.
   d. They have idolized them.

9. The limited government mentioned in classical liberalism means all of the following, *except* that:
   a. government should be restrained in its intrusion into people's lives.
   b. individual rights should be protected from government control.
   c. government should never be involved in any aspect of people's lives.
   d. the citizens should decide how much power the government should wield.

10. The socioeconomic class that is most likely to embrace a liberal individualist philosophy is:
    a. the peasantry.   c. the middle class.
    b. the aristocracy.   d. the wealthy.

TRUE/FALSE

11. The Englishman G. K. Chesterton believed that the United States did not share a creed or an ideology.
12. Historian Louis Hartz finds America to be the perfect role model for small nations undergoing revolutions in recent times.
13. Classical liberalism places the individual at the center of political, social, and economic life.
14. Scholar Leon Samson once observed that equality and democracy were elements common to both socialism and the American ideology.
15. Historian Arthur Schlesinger believes that the diversity of ethnic and racial groups in America is disappearing rather than increasing.

ESSAYS

16. Discuss the major components of classical liberalism, mentioning the origin of the philosophy in European history. How suited was classical liberalism to America at the time of the Revolutionary War? What kinds of

social and economic problems exist in the United States today to call into question the validity of the liberal individualist creed? Use at least two specific examples to illustrate challenges to the creed today.

17. Is it essential for the whole American population to accept the creed? To receive equality of opportunity within the creed? Equality of result? Use the example of Henry Ford in 1914 and that of black Americans today to comment on how the gap between the promise and the reality of the American creed is continuously being narrowed.

ANSWERS

Multiple Choice

1.	c	p. 47	6.	a	p. 47
2.	a	p. 47	7.	b	pp. 48, 50-52
3.	c	pp. 54-56	8.	b	p. 53
4.	d	p. 57	9.	c	p. 47
5.	b	p. 59	10.	c	p. 47

True/False

11.	f	pp. 50, 53
12.	f	pp. 53-54
13.	t	pp. 47, 51-52
14.	t	pp. 49-50
15.	f	pp. 57-58

4 | The Constitution and American Democracy

Many of you who have a good background in U.S. history will be able to move quickly through pages 61-77 of chapter 4, because that part of the chapter reviews the writing of the U.S. Constitution. Save your energy because you will need it to give full attention to Professor Ladd's discussion of Greek democracy and, particularly, theories of the distribution of power in America, one of the most interesting underlying themes of an American government course.

The Constitution

This is review for those of you who studied U.S. history recently and were conscientious students. If you are shaky on constitutional history, use this opportunity to learn the basics. You may find the topic more interesting as a background for U.S. government than you did as straight American history.

As you read pages 61-77, look for the following terms identifying the people, dates, places, events, and ideas associated with the writing of the U.S. Constitution:

> American Revolution, 1775-1781
> Declaration of Independence, 1776
> Articles of Confederation, 1777; main weaknesses
> Constitutional Convention, 1787
> Alexander Hamilton
> George Washington
> James Madison
> Virginia Plan
> New Jersey Plan

Great Compromise
three-fifths compromise

(These topics are explored in detail at the start of chapter 5.)
James Madison
separation of powers
checks and balances
branches of government
Federalist Papers No. 10 and No. 51
faction
"Ambition must be made to counteract ambition."

Federalists
Antifederalists
ratification, 1788
Virginia
New York
congressional and presidential election, 1789

Be sure that you can trace the chronology and major themes in the making of the U.S. Constitution. As you can see from Professor Ladd's discussion, it is often easier to remember historical events if you memorize only the key details and concentrate on understanding the overall significance of the events. Less is more.

Professor Ladd gives a nice glimpse into the personality of America's first president, George Washington. First, read about his inauguration in Box 4.2. Why was President Washington loved by "all ranks of people"? What past twentieth-century presidents would be received in a similar way? Would any modern presidents be accorded this degree of respect? As you read Professor Ladd's analysis of Washington, be prepared to comment on:

Washington as a charismatic leader,
Washington as a revolutionary and a conservative,
Washington's commitment to returning to private life.

President Washington's desire to serve in government and then return to private life raises a large issue for later chapters on Congress and the presidency. Washington and other early American political figures envisioned ordinary citizens serving in government for a time, then going back to private life. Many of today's professional career politicians start off in government right after school, maybe as a legislative aide. They remain politicians their whole lives, even staying in Washington, D.C. as lobbyists after leaving public office. They live totally "inside the beltway," with little connection to the American people whom they serve. Not George Washington; perhaps politicians should study Washington's model closely even today.

Greek Democracy and the American Polity

Pick up your reading with page 78 and read through page 86. Democracy is a form of government first developed in ancient Greece, although those of you who have studied ancient history know that Greek democracy did not have the same meaning as democracy does today. For example, the Greeks had slavery, whereas the United States gave up slavery after 1863. In Greece not everyone could vote, while in the United States the franchise was extended in the twentieth century to include all citizens over eighteen.

The Greek philosopher Aristotle (who looks like a typical political science professor in the statue on page 79) studied governments based on who rules in whose interest. You can grasp Professor Ladd's discussion of Aristotle easily when you see his governmental categories shown in a chart.

	bad – in the interest of the ruler(s)	good – in the interest of all
rule by one person	tyranny	kingship
rule by a few people	oligarchy	aristocracy
rule by many people	democracy	polity

By titling his book *The American Polity* Professor Ladd has told you much about his vision of U.S. government. The United States is *not* a democracy and does not want to be! The United States is a polity. You have now come upon a crucial theme in the course, one that will tie together all the coming chapters. Read page 79 carefully. Define a polity. Who rules? Who is protected? What two conditions did Aristotle suggest were necessary for a polity? Do not go on until you grasp the difference between democracy and polity, and fully understand the latter.

Now jump ahead 2000 years from Aristotle to Madison in 1787. He knew the difference between a democracy and a polity, and designed for the United States a polity. Again, define a polity. Who rules? Who is protected?

How does the issue of school prayer illustrate the tension inherent in a polity? Professor Ladd uses school prayer to show the conflict between majority rule and minority rights. On pages 81-85 you encounter the dilemma facing a polity, you begin to study the Bill of Rights (an important topic in chapter 14), and you learn about one Supreme Court case before you read about many in chapter 9. As you read, pay particular attention to:

First Amendment
establishment clause
Engel v. Vitale (1962)
New York Regents' prayer

attempts to amend the Constitution by two-thirds, by three-fourths
public opinion polls on prayer in schools and on amending the Constitution to allow school prayer
Wallace v. Jaffree (1985)
Lee v. Weisman (1992)

You should be ready to answer an essay question exploring the philosophical
reason for adding the Bill of Rights to the Constitution; the difference between
a democracy and a polity; and the way the school prayer issue illustrates the
tensions within a polity. Take a moment to read about Gregory Watson, "The
Man Who Would Not Quit," in chapter 4 of the "Cases" section of the *Study
Guide*. He found Madison's "lost" Twenty-Seventh Amendment (Box 4.1),
which was finally ratified by three-quarters of the states in 1992.

Professor Ladd ends his discussion of the Constitution by updating the dis-
tinction Aristotle drew between a democracy and a polity. At the time of the
writing of the Constitution, the framers were fearful of too much democracy—of direct rule by the people, of the mob. (Madison's concerns in this area
will be explained in depth at the start of chapter 5.) However, over the two
hundred years of American ~~democracy~~ polity, the people have come to be
more trusted; reforms making democracy more direct and more representative
of majority views have been enacted. Once again, reach back to your knowledge of U.S. history to the Progressive movement: the era, the regions, the
supporters, the views. What do each of the following progressive reforms allow? direct primary? referendum? initiative?

Power

Pages 86-91 hold the key to the most interesting aspect of American government: Who really holds power in the United States? On this question Professor Ladd can give you no answer; neither can your instructor, the graduate
assistant, the kid slumped next to you in the lecture hall, nor your parents. Only
studying all the information that lies ahead in *The American Polity* can help you
to answer this question for yourself. An answer without support is worthless.
Likewise, knowing all the material on American government in the text without
drawing a conclusion about who really rules is boring and useless. As you
plunge into the heart of *The American Polity*, keep in mind the question asked
by political scientist Robert Dahl: "Who Governs?" There are three possible
answers, with many shades of gray in between.

The People. Classical liberal belief in individuality, freedom, equality, and popular choice in government all support, in theory, rule by the people. Reforms
made during the Progressive era, that remain part of American government
today, do too. But ask yourself these kinds of questions in later chapters: What

percentage of eligible American voters actually vote? How are congressional elections funded? Who supplies executive agencies with much of their information at oversight hearings?

A Power Elite. It has been decades since President Eisenhower warned Americans of the "military-industrial complex," decades since C. Wright Mills wrote *The Power Elite* in which he identified a "triangle of power" that quietly controlled America. In the past years Marxist scholars like Michael Parenti, who labeled American democracy "democracy for the few," have witnessed the failure of Marxism as practiced in Eastern Europe and the former Soviet Union. The theory of a power elite running America seems long dead. Yet consider Professor Ladd's discussion about wealth in the United States, about the mass media's influence, about the size of certain institutions in American society – universities, corporations, government. Consider your own experiences. What kind of job does your mother or father hold? What college do you attend? Who pays? Where are you headed in life compared to others of your age group? What factors have helped you or held you back? Are you a member of the power elite, or are you challenging it?

For a glimpse into elitism in America, read the short excerpt in chapter 4 of the "Cases" section of the *Study Guide.* Robert Christopher describes the lofty Council on Foreign Relations, but he titles his book *Crashing the Gates.* For a dramatic crashing of elite gates, look back to the excerpt in the cases for chapter 2 in which Elizabeth Colton reveals the young Jesse Jackson.

Groups, through Pluralism. Many contemporary political scientists (but not all) take the position that power is held by interest groups. Groups include many different citizens in the political process. The groups vary in influence as issues change – strong on some, disinterested on others. They compete. They balance each other out. They forge compromises. Interest-group politics is called *pluralism,* one of the most difficult concepts when first encountered, but important in political science. Look for evidence of pluralism as you dig deeper into American government. Do people join interest groups? Are groups influential at election time through PAC contributions? Are groups important to members of Congress? Is the bureaucracy concerned with groups' needs? How many groups could be listed? Hundreds? Thousands? Many of them will already be familiar to you. Can you match the following interests with their interest groups?

_____	a. environmentalists – land	1. NOW
_____	b. the right to choice on abortion	2. Gray Panthers
_____	c. the elderly	3. Greenpeace
_____	d. militant elderly	4. NRA
_____	e. environmentalists – sea	5. NAACP

_____	f. the right to own guns	6.	Sierra Club
_____	g. preventing abortions	7.	AARP
_____	h. civil rights	8.	Operation Rescue

If you decide by the end of the course that you are a pluralist, you are in good company. As you will see in the next chapter, Madison was a pluralist. But be aware that many criticisms of pluralism have been made. Do all citizens have the same chance to join an interest group? Do they have the same assets to use towards persuasion? (For example, do the homeless have computerized mailing lists to communicate efficiently with their membership?) As Professor Ladd asks, do clear policies emerge from a system based on so much compromise? Under pluralism does what is good for the whole nation ever get considered or just what is best for small, powerful, organized special interests?

Sample Test Questions

MULTIPLE-CHOICE—SELECT THE *BEST* ANSWER

1. How similar is the American Constitution of the 1990s to that written in 1787?
   a. It is identical.
   b. It is very similar, with some amendments added.
   c. It is quite different, with amendments that have changed the structure of government to meet the needs of postindustrial America.
   d. It is totally different, after the most recent constitutional convention.
2. Before the Constitution was ratified in 1788, the United States was governed by:
   a. the Articles of Confederation.
   b. the British House of Lords.
   c. separate state constitutions.
   d. the Declaration of Independence.
3. All of the following are features of the U.S. Constitution as James Madison designed it *except*:
   a. checks and balances. c. presidential supremacy.
   b. separation of powers. d. representation.
4. Aristotle set all of the following as conditions for a good government by the mass of people *except*:
   a. a total majority rule.
   b. a large majority of the people having middle-class status.
   c. protection of the minority's interests.
   d. wealth spread fairly evenly among the people.

5. In *Engel v. Vitale* (1962), the Supreme Court:
   a. declared the First Amendment unconstitutional.
   b. declared the New York Regents' prayer unconstitutional.
   c. overturned a past decision requiring mandatory school prayer.
   d. substituted a moment of silence in place of the school's prayer.

6. Among the Progressive era reforms that increased direct democracy were all of the following *except*:
   a. direct primary.
   b. initiative.
   c. impeachment.
   d. referendum.

7. Political scientists such as C. Wright Mills and Michael Parenti believe that:
   a. America is ruled by a tiny elite to advance its own interests.
   b. many interest groups compete to formulate government policy in the United States.
   c. majority rule, with each person having one vote, decides issues in American politics.
   d. foreign governments own and control the U.S. government by bribing public officials secretly.

8. Which of the following best describes George Washington's role in the early years of the nation?
   a. He was a great general, but a poor political leader.
   b. He created legitimacy for the new government by accepting the institutions as they had been designed.
   c. He strengthened the nation by his personal charisma, which was able to take the place of poorly designed governmental institutions.
   d. He let many citizens down by refusing to stay on in government as president for life, choosing instead to return to Mount Vernon.

9. Slaves were counted in the 1787 Constitution for the purposes of representation in the House of Representatives by the provision in the :
   a. three-fifths compromise.
   b. Great Compromise.
   c. Virginia Plan.
   d. New Jersey Plan.

10. Pluralist thinkers believe the key players in American politics to be:
    a. Supreme Court justices.
    b. the mass of poor people.
    c. the military-industrial complex.
    d. interest groups.

TRUE/FALSE

11. Aristotle used the terms *democracy* and *polity* interchangeably, their use today depending on the Greek-to-English translation.

12. Neither elite nor pluralist theorists believe that American politics is controlled by the people as a whole.

13. George Washington was the primary author of the ideas behind the Constitution.
14. Current public-opinion polls on school prayer support the views of the Supreme Court in *Engel v. Vitale* (1962).
15. The clearest explanation of the principles underlying the Constitution is found in the *Federalist Papers*.

IDENTIFICATION—DISCUSS BRIEFLY

16. Great Compromise
17. three-fifths compromise
18. Federalists versus anti-Federalists
19. Articles of Confederation
20. George Washington

ESSAYS

21. Describe the method that Aristotle developed for classifying governments into different categories. Which category best fits the government of the United States? Use the specific example of school prayer to show the tensions that exist between the majority and the minority inside the American political system.
22. Compare the elite theory of how power is distributed in America with the pluralist theory. In what ways do the two views clash? What do they share in their interpretations of American politics? Using your knowledge about the writing of the Constitution in 1787, offer an opinion based on evidence as to whether the framers of the Constitution were elitists or pluralists.

Answers

Multiple Choice

1.	b	pp. 61, 74		6.	c	pp. 85-86
2.	a	pp. 65-67		7.	a	pp. 88-89
3.	c	pp. 69-71		8.	b	pp. 74-77
4.	a	pp. 78-79		9.	a	pp. 69-70
5.	b	p. 81		10.	d	pp. 90-91

True/False

11. f   p. 78
12. t   pp. 86-91
13. f   pp. 67, 69
14. f   pp. 81-82
15. t   p. 71

Identification

16. In the Constitution, states were given representation in the House of Representatives according to population, which pleased the large states; Senate representation by two senators for each state satisfied the small states. p. 69

17. In the Constitution of 1787, slaves were counted as three-fifths of a person for the purposes of representation and taxation. pp. 69-70

18. Federalists, led by Alexander Hamilton, favored a strong national government and backed the Constitution, which provided it. Anti-Federalists wanted to preserve the power of the state governments. Yet the two groups agreed on many basic governmental ideas. p. 72

19. The Articles of Confederation were the first form of government for the United States after the American Revolution. Almost all power resided in the states. The Articles' weaknesses became apparent after a few years because the national government – the Congress – could not levy taxes, support an army, or establish a uniform currency. pp. 65-67

20. After leading the American army during the Revolutionary War, George Washington joined in the effort to call the Constitutional Convention in 1787. He presided over the convention and in 1789 became the United States's first president. He did not wish to remain in public life indefinitely, however, and often expressed his desire to return to private life at Mount Vernon. pp. 74-77

5 | The American System of Divided Government

Madison's *Federalist Papers* No. 10 and No. 51

To begin the study of chapter 5 on divided government, read pp. 97-99. Before going any further into the chapter you should understand what divided government is, who came up with the idea, and why he devised this plan for the United States. In American history or civics courses you took when you were younger, what two phrases were always used to describe the system of divided government?

Along with chapter 5 (or perhaps earlier, with chapter 4 on the Constitution) your professor may have asked you to read James Madison's *Federalist Papers* No. 10 and No. 51 printed in the back of *The American Polity* on pp. A20-A28. This is probably the most important reading in the course – and the toughest! It is a primary source, a document written in 1787. "Publius" did not have a simple or modern writing style, yet the ideas are clear if you dissect the argument systematically. Open to p. A20 and follow along with Madison's thinking as he, at age thirty-six, wrote articles (along with Alexander Hamilton and John Jay) for the New York newspaper to persuade the state legislature to ratify the new Constitution. The key terms from these two *Federalist Papers* are:

faction
mischiefs of faction
less than a majority
majority
liberty
sown in the nature of man
unequal distribution of property
enlightened statesmen

republic
representation
large republic
compound republic
separate and distinct exercise of the different powers of government
federal system (federalism)
multiplicity of interests

Read through these two documents once. Using the list above, underline key phrases in which Madison states each part of his argument. Then analyze the two essays with some assistance from the following summary:

In designing a Constitution to take the place of the Articles of Confederation, Madison's main fear was "faction" (p. A20), by which he meant a group of people who unite to try to impose their wishes on other citizens (p. A21). In 1787, Madison's concern centered mostly on the majority, which he saw as a mass of poorer people who would try to gain political power for themselves. He feared a minority less, because he felt that it could be easily controlled through the election process (p. A22). Today, however, Madison's fear can be interpreted more generally: He feared any single group, no matter how few or how many, that seeks to get what it wants at the expense of the rest of the citizens. All citizens' rights and interests must be protected.

Madison thought of two ways to stop the "mischiefs of faction" (p. A21). The first was by removing its causes. Faction could be eliminated by doing away with liberty (p. A21), but since liberty is essential to American politics that will not work. Nor can people overcome the tendency to form a faction. People are by nature self-serving and join with others who have the same interests that they do (p. A21). These shared interests, Madison felt, are usually based on money. In the United States wealth is not distributed equally, and thus a faction will always form based on a group's amount of wealth relative to the wealth of others (p. A22). Perhaps Americans can rely on "enlightened statesmen" (p. A22) to remove faction. No, Madison warns, because there may not always be good and capable leaders in positions of power!

Faction cannot be removed, Madison concludes; it can only be controlled (p. A22). Yet in controlling the danger of faction, the strengths of democratic participation must not be lost. Madison's solution is to divide governmental authority at every point, to separate powers as many ways as possible, to check and balance each political institution. The United States should be a republic, with representatives who would provide a buffer between the voters and the policies of the government (p. A23). The nation should be as large as possible so that many officials, representing many diverse interests would all have a say (pp. A23-A24). The branches of government should be independent from one another (pp. A25-A26). The national and the state governments should share power through the federal (federalism) system (p. A26). The ultimate solution to faction, Madison concludes, is a multiplicity of factions (p. A27). When there are many groups competing for power, no one group with a single interest can dominate.

Look back for a moment to the very end of chapter 4. Reread Professor Ladd's discussion of pluralism. Does Madison seem a little more modern now?

In addition to Madison's perceptive warnings and brilliant solutions, he is also very quotable. Try using a few of these lines, footnoting them to Madison of course, when you are in class:

"Liberty is to faction what air is to fire. . . ." (p. A21)

"Enlightened statesmen will not always be at the helm." (p. A22)

"Ambition must be made to counteract ambition." (p. A26)

"If men were angels, no government would be necessary. If angels were to govern men, neither external nor internal controls on government would be necessary. In framing a government which is to be administered by men over men, . . . you must first enable the government to control the governed; and in the next place oblige it to control itself." (p. A26)

Understanding Divided Government in Action: Case Studies

Separation of powers is not just a theory from the *Federalist Papers*. A little more than two hundred years later, separation of powers can be seen in action every day in American politics. Professor Ladd gives three examples: the 1989-90 executive versus legislative battle over a bill that would have allowed Chinese students to stay in the United States; the 1991 congressional resolution backing President Bush's decision to use force against Iraqi President Saddam Hussein who had invaded Kuwait; and the fight in 1991 over President Bush's Supreme Court choice, Clarence Thomas, whose nomination was to be with the "advice and consent" of the Senate.

Read Professor Ladd's case studies from pp. 100-7. Then list all the ways in which these examples reveal the separation of powers and checks and balances in American government. Here are some of the checks shown in the case studies that should be on your list for divided government.

bill passed by the House of Representatives
bill passed by the Senate
conference committee
presidential veto
House override of the veto by two-thirds vote
Senate upholding of veto
president as commander-in-chief
congressional power to declare war

House and Senate joint resolution
presidential nomination of federal judges
Senate's advice and consent

Notice that some of the checks in the list were mentioned by Madison and are formal parts of the Constitution. Others that should be on your list, such as political party competition, are additional checks that have grown up over time. Professor Ladd emphasizes an important factor in recent American politics: Divided government is made all the more divided when the presidency is controlled by one party and the Congress by the other, a situation that marked U.S. government over much of the past decades, until President Clinton's inauguration in January 1993.

When you finish chapter 5, you are really just beginning your study of divided government. The whole American government course revolves around divided powers. At the end of some of the upcoming chapters in this *Study Guide*, you can take a "Madison test": grade the nation on how well separation of powers has worked to protect the rights and interests of all Americans.

Problems with the System of Divided Government

Professor Ladd next takes up the debate between those who think that divided government works well in the United States today and those who feel it should be altered, possibly by constitutional amendment. Read pp. 107-14 to identify these two points of view. Make two lists: one against divided government and one for it. Did you include most of the following?

AGAINST DIVIDED GOVERNMENT

1. It is difficult to hold an official or a branch of government accountable for a policy since power is dispersed so widely.

2. The president has a hard time enacting policies because of congressional opposition, sometimes from within the president's own party.

3. Separation of powers makes government move slowly and inefficiently, which was no problem in the 1790s but which is a major liability in the 1990s.

FOR DIVIDED GOVERNMENT

1. Negative reaction to FDR's proposal to expand the size of the Supreme Court in 1937 is an example of the public's support for separation of powers.

2. Deadlock, inaction, and standoff may prevent impulsive action, particularly when there is no genuine agreement on a proposed policy.

3. The British parliamentary system, which concentrates power within one branch, has been criticized for a lack of checks on the majority party and the prime minister.

4. Battles among branches of government, such as between the president and the Congress over control of foreign policy or over the line-item veto (which, if enacted and held to be constitutional, would give the president the power to veto certain parts of a budget bill instead of rejecting the whole budget) are part of the ongoing struggle intended by the authors of the Constitution so that "Ambition . . . [is] made to counteract ambition."

What reforms have been suggested to modify the separation of powers system? Professor Ladd describes several ideas. Be sure you can explain two of these ideas: (1) having voters elect the president and member of the House of Representatives together as a party team, (2) allowing the president to choose half the cabinet from the Congress, (3) permitting the president to dissolve the Congress and call new elections, or (4) permitting the Congress to remove the president and call a new election.

Federalism as an Important Part of Divided Government

Professor Ladd devotes the last part of chapter 5 to the second of the two major expressions of divided government in the Constitution: federalism. Along with separation of powers among the three branches of government, federalism separates power between the national government and the state governments. The most difficult part of understanding federalism is understanding the word itself. Because the word *federal* is used today to indicate the national (Washington, D.C.) government, it is easy to misunderstand what *federalism* means. Federalism is the division of power between the national government and the state governments. If you encounter a term such as federalism that is not clear to you, try using the glossary at the end of *The American Polity*. Professor Ladd gives short, clear explanations of key terms that can be very helpful when encountering many new ideas at one time.

Read the section on federalism on pp. 114-28. Here is an outline of the section, including all the key concepts. Remember that the outline only highlights important ideas; it does not summarize all the material you should be familiar with.

I. Federalism in the Constitution
   A. States' powers
      1. Senate
      2. Constitutional amendment

3. "Reserve clause" – Tenth Amendment
   a. *National League of Cities v. Usery* (1976)
   b. *Garcia v. San Antonio Metropolitan Transit Authority* (1985)
4. Restrictions of Fourteenth Amendment

B. National powers
1. "Necessary and proper clause" – Article I, section 8
2. Fourteenth Amendment

II. Development of federalism
A. States' rights – John C. Calhoun and nullification
B. National government's power
1. John Marshall's Supreme Court – *McCulloch v. Maryland* (1819)
2. FDR's New Deal
3. Civil Rights

III. Federalism today
A. Grants-in-aid
B. National dominance – 55 mile per hour speed limit
C. The Reagan reversal
D. States' importance
1. Divided government – a check
2. Needs of a diverse population
3. Experimentation with programs on the state level

Federalism may seem like a rather dry topic in American government, especially when compared to upcoming chapters on the presidency, interest groups, and elections. Yet if you go on to take a political science course in state and local government, you will learn many interesting things about federalism, like how layer cake federalism is different from marble cake federalism; why federalism today is sometimes called *permissive* or even *coercive* federalism; who really controls the national/state relationship; who has most of the money; what the differences are among project, categorical, block, and revenue-sharing grants; and what innovative programs are being developed in the "laboratories of democracy." For a taste of the style of state politics, take a moment to read Texas Governor Ann Richards' autobiographical account. Her start in state politics is chronicled in the excerpt in chapter 5 of the "Cases" section of the *Study Guide*.

Sample Test Questions

MULTIPLE CHOICE—SELECT THE *BEST* ANSWER

1. Divided government includes all of the following features *except*:
   a. separation of powers among branches.
   b. federalism.
   c. bicoastal liberalism.
   d. checks and balances.

2. The most extreme states' rights position ever espoused in the United States was:
   a. grants-in-aid.
   b. nullification.
   c. civil rights.
   d. state banks.

3. The ongoing struggle between national power and state power can be seen in all of the following *except*:
   a. the conduct of foreign policy.
   b. *Usery* and *Garcia.*
   c. the "reserve clause" and the "necessary and proper clause."
   d. the 55 mile per hour speed limit.

4. The main difference between the divided government of the United States and Britain's parliamentary system is:
   a. the existence of political parties in the United States but not in Britain.
   b. the number of citizens who can vote in elections.
   c. the gender of the executive, which in Britain can be female but in the United States must be male.
   d. the number of branches of government.

5. Public reaction to FDR's 1937 plan to "pack" the Supreme Court by adding more justices was one of:
   a. indifference.
   b. support.
   c. hostility.
   d. panic.

6. By a compound republic, James Madison meant that
   a. The United States should rejoin England.
   b. Power should be divided between the central government and the states, and among the three branches.
   c. The United States might compound its problems by trying to draft a new Constitution.
   d. The combination of Madison, Hamilton, and Jay was a good one for writing about the Republican party.

7. A line-item veto, if enacted and upheld as constitutional, would give the president the power to:
   a. strike out parts of a budget bill while keeping other parts.
   b. deny aid to some AFDC recipients but allow it for others.
   c. let the president remove 50 percent of the Congress once in a term.
   d. veto a bill without Congress being able to override the veto.

8. In *McCulloch v. Maryland* (1819) the Supreme Court ruled that:
   a. "Separate is inherently unequal."
   b. setting up a national bank was "necessary and proper."
   c. McCulloch had the right to remain silent and the right to counsel.
   d. Maryland deserved the "equal protection" of the Fourteenth Amendment.

9. All of the following are grant programs cut by the Reagan administration *except*:
   a. revenue sharing.   c. job training.
   b. defense.   d. urban development.

10. Which new expression of separation of powers emerged as significant during the 1980s?
    a. Democrats controlled the Congress, Republicans the presidency.
    b. Americans fought in the Persian Gulf War, while the European allies paid for it.
    c. The Senate turned down the president's choice for a cabinet position.
    d. The president used a line-item veto to curb spending.

TRUE/FALSE

11. All possible reforms in America's system of separation of powers involve a change to a parliamentary system.

12. A proposed constitutional amendment must be approved by three-fourths of the state legislatures.

13. States have no ability to influence the Congress over issues like the 55 mile per hour speed limit.

14. The fight between President Bush and the Congress over the Chinese student immigration bill was mainly a clash over which branch controls foreign policy.

15. James Madison believed that representation damaged a democracy.

16. Federalism in America is weak today because the states are not willing to experiment with new ideas.

17. The House of Representatives is an expression of federalism.

18. The Senate is an expression of federalism.

19. The American system of divided government includes the Senate's right to give "advice and consent" to the president when proposing Supreme Court nominees.

20. Divided control between the Democratic and Republican parties was an important aspect of separation of powers specifically written into the Constitution.

ESSAYS

21. Paraphrase briefly and simply James Madison's arguments in *Federalist Papers* No. 10 and No. 51. (To do this, female or male, you must put on a wig unless you have long hair already.) Include as many of the terms listed on pp. 235-36 in this *Study Guide* as possible. Be sure to include Madison's specific warnings and his solutions.

22. Discuss the importance of federalism in American government. How has federalism changed over time? What trends are apparent in federalism today? In your answer, use Professor Ladd's discussion of the controversy over the 55 mile per hour speed limit to illustrate the way in which federalism divides power in American government.

23. What are the benefits of separation of powers in government? What are the liabilities? Be specific in mentioning the good and bad points. Illustrate your answer by referring either to Professor Ladd's example of the Emergency Chinese Immigration Relief Bill or the Persian Gulf War Resolution. Conclude your essay by describing at least two proposals for changing the current American system of divided government. Express your own view on whether these changes would be helpful or dangerous.

Answers

Multiple choice

1. c	pp. 97-98	6. b p. 98
2. b	p. 118	7. a pp. 113-14
3. a	pp. 115-17, 125-26	8. b pp. 118-20
4. d	pp. 107-10, 112-13	9. b pp. 123-24
5. c	pp. 110-11	10. a pp. 103-4

True/False

11. f	pp. 109-10	16. f pp. 127-28
12. t	pp. 115-16	17. f p. 115
13. f	pp. 125-26	18. t p. 115
14. t	pp. 100-3	19. t p. 99
15. f	pp. 85, 99	20. f pp. 103-4

6 | Congress

Read This Before Reading Chapter 6

Chapter 6, Congress, begins the section of the course that Professor Ladd calls "Governance." Governance is the heart of an American Government course, since it is in this section that you will learn about the three branches of government. You will study the basic role that each branch carries out, how they must work together to get things done, and how their powers overlap and check each other. Congress is the first branch you will study: The authors of the Constitution put the Congress in Article I.

You will want to divide your reading of the Congress chapter into three parts. First, search the chapter for Professor Ladd's observations on the attitudes that the American people have about Congress today. Look for discussions on incumbency, ethics, and public dissatisfaction with Congress. Second, identify the changes that took place in Congress in the mid-1970s and that remain important today. "Congressional individualism" and "spreading the action" are two key concepts to look for in your reading. Third, be sure to spot the specific information about Congress that the chapter mentions. Use the following list as a guide. As you can see, there are a lot of details to learn in this chapter. They will become easier to remember when you see how the facts connect up to reveal the operation of Congress.

> socioeconomic characteristics of legislators
> bicameralism
> Congress
> House of Representatives
> Senate
> filibuster
> cloture
> unanimous consent
> Rules Committee

Congressional Record
suspension of the rules
discharge petition

seniority
standing committees
select committees
joint committees
conference committees
subcommittees
how a bill becomes law

staff expenses
party unity voting
Speaker of the House
majority leaders
minority leaders
whips

power of the purse
CBO
budget committees
Gramm-Rudman-Hollings
sequestration

legislative oversight
GAO
legislative veto
joint resolution of approval or disapproval

Read chapter 6; Underline, highlight, make notes in the margins or take notes in a separate notebook.

Read This after Reading Chapter 6

Chapter 6 is loaded – lots of big ideas and lots of facts. Before you worry about what you have missed, look at all you know. If you have cable, turn the TV on to C-SPAN (Cable Satellite Public Affairs Network). You may see a live floor debate in the House of Representatives, or you may have tuned in a committee hearing. Watch for half an hour, and see if you can identify these ten key congressional concepts in action:

1. Which chamber is meeting? Or what kind of committee is meeting?
2. What subcommittee reported out or is hearing the bill being discussed?
3. In what document is the floor debate being recorded?
4. Who in the leadership is mentioned?

5. What legislators, from what states, are talking?
6. Is the issue under discussion a budget issue? Is the Congress performing its oversight role?
7. Are any special rules in effect during the floor debate or the hearing?
8. Does party unity seem to exist on the issue under debate?
9. Can you see staff talking with legislators during the hearing?
10. If you are watching a floor debate and the chamber is not full, where might the rest of the legislators be?

Try to watch C-SPAN whenever you have some free time. It is great preparation for spending a semester in Washington, D.C., as an intern for a representative or senator. Now back to chapter 6. (Of course you can leave C-SPAN on in the background as you study American government!)

You can find the places in chapter 6 that you need to reread by answering the following questions. Look back to your underlining and notes to help with the answers. Go slowly; there is a lot of material here.

1. What is bicameralism? Going back to chapter 5, tie bicameralism to checks and balances, and to federalism.
2. How is the House of Representatives different from the Senate (a) in composition, (b) in number of rules, (c) in tone and atmosphere? Use these specifics in your answer: "statesman"; Rules Committee; filibuster; 435 members; unanimous consent; two-year terms; discharge petition; districts equal in population; cloture; 100 members; suspension of rules; six-year terms; small states.
3. Describe the socioeconomic characteristics of legislators. Do they look like their constituents in education, occupation, wealth, race, ethnicity, gender? Who are your home state's senators? Your representative in the House?
4. How important is the committee system in the Congress? What are the functions of standing, select, joint, and conference committees? Who gets to be the chair of each standing committee? Sketch out how a bill becomes law, including the roles of House and Senate standing committees, subcommittees, the Rules Committee, the president. Reread Professor Ladd's description of the passage of the 1988 Trade Bill to see your chart in action.
5. Name the leadership positions and the leadership groups in the House and in the Senate. Who is the Speaker of the House today? What Speaker in history was called Boss or Czar?
6. Is party unity strong in Congress today? What is a party-unity vote? How does each party organize itself in the House and in the Senate to try to achieve party unity? Be familiar with the most important and most recent information from Figures 6.7 and 6.8.
7. What is "congressional individualism"? Explain the changes that took place in the 1970s involving presidential and congressional power. What

kind of people were elected to Congress in the mid-1970s? Use references to: seniority; Vietnam and Watergate; staff; "spreading the action"; the number of subcommittees; mass media; party unity.

8. In what ways did Vietnam and Watergate motivate the political individualists (former House Speaker Tip O'Neill calls them "Watergate Babies") who ran and won in the early and mid 1970s? In the early 1990s, almost twenty years later, have congressional individualists changed the public's perceptions of Congress for the better? What ethics problems and policy failures have plagued Congress in the 1990s?

9. How much money is available to members of the House for staff expenses? To senators? How is the increase in congressional staff related to congressional individualism, to the reassertion of congressional power in the 1970s, and to incumbency in the 1980s and 1990s?

10. In what ways has Congress tried to control spending as part of its "power of the purse"? Trace its strategies, citing the CBO, budget committees, Gramm-Rudman-Hollings, and newer sequestration rules. How successful have these attempts been?

11. What is legislative oversight? How does the GAO assist? This topic will be discussed further in chapter 8 on the executive branch.

12. What was a legislative veto? Why did Congress like it? Why did presidents not like it? Why did the Supreme Court declare it unconstitutional in the *Chadha* case (1983)? How does a joint resolution of disapproval (or approval) take the place of a legislative veto?

This is a good time to take a break from the serious study of Congress by reading a few personal observations on this branch. the "Cases" section of the *Study Guide* offers you short excerpts form Christopher Matthews on the young Congressman Lyndon Johnson and former Senator James Abourezk's recollection of legendary southern senator, James O. Eastland. Then Mark Bisnow and John Jackley, two "Hill rats" who came to Washington as interns and worked as congressional staff aides, share some inside stuff that might be interesting to you if you are planning to try D.C. yourself.

To complete your understanding of chapter 6, consider the issues Professor Ladd opened the chapter with: incumbency, ethics, and public dissatisfaction. Why have almost 98 percent of all incumbents been reelected? Consider factors such as staff, as well as PAC contributions and the media, which Professor Ladd will discuss later in the book. Do lapses in congressional ethics, such as the 1992 bank scandal, relate to incumbency? This is a controversial question in American government that you should think about as the course progresses. Several political scientists have recently written books about the professional politician who selects herself or himself for a career in politics at an early age and stays in politics as a long-term, full-time occupation. They are hardly the citizen-legislators from many different walks of life whom the designers of the Constitution envisioned as our representatives.

Finally, how has the American public reacted to ethics problems? In the 1990s, the public has offered its opinion in several ways. Look at Figure 6.2, which compares how much confidence the public has in major American institutions. The military does quite well (although just half the public has a great deal of confidence in it), while only 10 percent of the people have a great deal of confidence in Congress. Note that corporations and law firms are not loved either. Figure 6.3 elaborates on the sources of people's dissatisfaction with Congress. In Figure 6.1 Professor Ladd reveals a paradoxical aspect of the public's dissatisfaction. How do voters feel about their own members of Congress?

By 1992 legislators were also reacting to public opinion. Using the data in Figure 6.4, tell how many senators and representatives chose not to run again? Be ready to name at least three reasons for these retirements. Professor Ladd hastens to mention that incumbency will remain a strong force in congressional elections. Yet the election of many freshman senators and House members will have an impact, just as it did when the Watergate Babies arrived in the 1970s. Can you speculate on the types of people, the political views, and the kinds of changes that the "Bounced Check Babies" will have brought into Congress in the 1990s?

Sample Test Questions

MULTIPLE CHOICE—SELECT THE *BEST* ANSWER

1. Which type of congressional committee is responsible for reconciling differences in House and Senate versions of a bill?
   a. a joint committee
   b. a subcommittee
   c. a select committee
   d. a conference committee
2. Congress is assisted in preparing and analyzing budgetary questions by the:
   a. OMB.
   b. CBO.
   c. AFDC.
   d. Democratic Caucus.
3. When sixty senators vote to end a filibuster, the rule invoked is called:
   a. amendment.
   b. cloture.
   c. unanimous consent.
   d. suspension of rules.
4. The main difference between past Gramm-Rudman-Hollings budget cuts and newer sequestration rules involves:
   a. whether cuts are made in the whole budget or just in certain categories of spending.
   b. who makes the cuts, the Supreme Court or the Congress.
   c. the actual percentage of the cut made in the entire budget.
   d. the recent use of a congressional veto to make cuts.

5. In terms of socioeconomic characteristics, legislators differ from their constituents in all of the following ways *except* that:
   a. they are wealthier.
   b. they are more religious.
   c. they are from occupations needing high levels of education.
   d. they are "more male" and "more white" than their constituents.

6. The House Rules Committee puts conditions on a bill before it goes to the floor that dictate:
   a. who will pay for the appropriation.
   b. what subcommittee will hold hearings.
   c. how many amendments can be offered.
   d. whether a filibuster will be allowed.

7. Which of the following best describes the process by which the 1988 Trade Bill was passed?
   a. bribery
   b. compromise
   c. presidential mandate
   d. strict party-unity voting

8. When members of Congress "spread the action" beginning in the 1970s, all of the following resulted *except* that:
   a. the House and Senate began to share responsibility for the passage of laws.
   b. less emphasis began to be placed on the seniority system in committee assignments.
   c. the size of congressional staff increased.
   d. more subcommittees were formed.

9. An account of all the speeches made on the floor of the House of Representatives is contained in:
   a. the GAO report.
   b. the *Congressional Record.*
   c. *The American Polity.*
   d. Woodrow Wilson's *Congressional Government.*

10. Legislative oversight empowers the Congress to check:
    a. the executive branch.
    b. the Supreme Court.
    c. the CBO and GAO.
    d. the Speaker of the House.

TRUE/FALSE

11. In public opinion polls, the American people rate the Congress very highly as an institution they respect.

12. The Senate has more rules than the House of Representatives, because it is easier to get 100 senators to abide by strict rules than it is to get 435 House members to comply.

13. Party unity voting in Congress is below 60 percent.

14. More women and more black Americans have been elected to the Congress in recent years.

15. Committee and subcommittee chair positions are allotted to the parties based on their election percentages in the House and Senate.

IDENTIFICATION—BRIEFLY DESCRIBE THE FOLLOWING TERMS

16. whips
17. bicameralism
18. power of the purse
19. select committee
20. discharge petition
21. $754,000-$1,760,000
22. legislative veto
23. Thomas Reed and Joseph Cannon
24. Democratic Caucus and Republican Conference
25. thirty years old/twenty-five years old

ESSAYS

26. Assess the complexity of "how a bill becomes law." In your answer, explain the process that takes a bill from its initial step to its final passage. Include specifics such as the effects of bicameralism, the committee system, the Rules Committee, filibuster, cloture, the conference committee, the presidential veto. To conclude, discuss how the process of a bill's becoming law reflects the checks and balances in place throughout American government.

27. How important is party unity voting in Congress today? Describe how the Democrats and Republicans organize themselves inside the House and Senate. Mention the changes that occurred in the relative power of the president and the Congress in the 1970s, and how these changes affected party unity voting. Finally, relate the reelection of incumbents to the ongoing Democratic dominance of Congress.

28. What is the attitude of the American people toward Congress? Toward individual members of Congress? Describe the ways in which incumbency, ethics problems, and public distrust of Congress are related. What trends are evident in the election politics of the 1990s that might improve the image of the national legislature?

THE MADISON TEST

If you wish, test Madison's ideas, set forth in the previous chapter, against what you've learned about Congress. What feature of the U.S. Congress do you think best exemplifies the principle that Madison used in formulating the Constitution? What feature of Congress do you think violates Madisonianism most dangerously today? (There is no single correct answer.)

Answers

Multiple Choice

1. d   pp. 145-46
2. b   p. 165
3. b   pp. 142-43
4. a   pp. 166-68
5. b   pp. 156-58

6. c   pp. 143-44, 147
7. b   pp. 148-52
8. a   pp. 146-48
9. b   pp. 144
10. a   pp. 168-69

True/False

11. f   pp. 133-37
12. f   pp. 141-43
13. t   pp. 153-55
14. t   pp. 156-58
15. f   pp. 148, 153

Identification

16. Each party in each chamber has a whip, who, as a member of the leadership, is responsible for trying to line up votes for the party's position on each bill. pp. 154-55
17. Bicameralism describes the two-chambered legislature of the American Congress. Bills must pass both the House of Representatives and the Senate before going to the president for a signature. The two houses are very different in their norms and procedures. pp. 140-41
18. The legislature's constitutional power to tax and to spend is often termed "the power of the purse." p. 164
19. A select (or special) committee is formed either in the House or in the Senate, usually to investigate a special problem that does not clearly come under the control of an existing standing committee. Some select committees are made up of members from only one party to carry out tasks for that party. pp. 145-46
20. In the House, a discharge petition can be voted by a majority in order to force a bill out of a committee that has held onto it for more than thirty days. p. 144
21. Each senator gets between $754,000 and $1,760,000 for staff salaries, depending on the size of her or his state. p. 153
22. Declared unconstitutional by the Supreme Court in *Chadha* (1983), the legislative veto was a provision included in certain bills by which the president was authorized to take an action that the Congress could then "veto." Currently, the Congress can have some control over the executive branch by a joint resolution of disapproval (or approval) in which both

houses vote on an executive-agency action and send their resolution to the president for a signature. pp. 169-70

23. Reed and Cannon were strong Speakers of the House during the 1890s. p. 159

24. The Democratic Caucus and the Republican Conference are the party organizations in the House that manage the internal party affairs of the chamber and try to encourage party unity voting on issues. The Senate has similar party leadership groups. pp. 154-55

25. To be in the Senate a citizen must be thirty years old, while a House member must be twenty-five years old. p. 156

7 | The Presidency

Chapter 7 presents you with two opportunities: to learn about the presidency as an office of government and to study some presidents close-up through Professor Ladd's analysis. The two topics are intertwined throughout the chapter. By the end of chapter 7 you will be familiar with several twentieth-century presidents but, more importantly, you will be familiar with the demands of the office of the presidency. During your lifetime you will be able to apply this knowledge to many different presidents. A good way to begin chapter 7 is to reread Professor Ladd's discussion of George Washington on pp. 74-77. Washington's example is all too easy to forget two hundred years later.

The Paradox of the Presidency

Read pp. 173-75. What are some of the paradoxes and contradictions inherent in the office of the presidency? How did President Kennedy view the office? What does Professor Ladd mean when he describes both the power and limits of the office?

Is the president a lone individual in the executive branch? (In chapter 8 you will learn about the complex branch the president leads.)

How much does the personality of the person elected president influence the way the office works? Greatly, says Professor Ladd, as you will see.

President George Bush and President Bill Clinton

Read pp. 175-81. While your own assessment of Presidents Bush and Clinton has much to do with your personal political views, you should be ready to comment on Professor Ladd's analysis by answering these questions.

1. What does Figure 7.1 reveal about former President Bush's popularity with the American people? Note in particular the differences in his

popularity rating during the Persian Gulf War in the winter of 1991 and during the 1991-92 recession.

2. Did President Bush have strong political views and a clear idea of how he wanted to change the United States? How did President Bush combine a firm belief in individualism and competition with a desire to bring all Americans into the mainstream of society? As president, was he always able to reconcile these views? How did a commitment to individualism, smaller government, and equal opportunity for all make President Bush seem weak at times?

3. How are President Clinton's youth and the era in which he was brought up important factors in his view of the presidency? In what way did Americans' desire for change help him win in 1992?

4. How was President Clinton's reputation as willing to compromise an asset in his winning the 1992 Democratic nomination? How can such a trait continue to be an asset or become a liability for him as president?

The Office of the Presidency

Read pp. 181-98. An outline of this part of the chapter will help you pick out the key points. Keep in mind that the outline below only highlights main ideas; you must take the responsibility for finding out what each entry means.

I. Election of the president
   A. Electoral College
      1. how each state's electoral votes are determined and cast
      2. direct vote for pledged electors
      3. effect on campaign strategies
   B. House of Representatives vote if there is no electoral-college majority.

II. Major constitutional checks on the president
   A. President as commander in chief checked by Congress's power to declare war
   B. President's power to negotiate treaties, nominate ambassadors and judges of federal courts checked by Senate's power to give advice and consent
   C. President's power to veto a bill passed by both houses of Congress checked by Congress's power to override a veto by a two-thirds vote
   D. President's power to carry out laws checked by Congress's ability to pass laws and to oversee their execution
   E. Impeachment of the president for high crimes and misdemeanors by impeachment charges brought in the House and a trial held in the Senate

       1. Andrew Johnson
       2. Richard Nixon and Watergate

III. Responsibilities of the president
    A. Clinton Rossiter's famous list
       1. Chief of state
       2. Chief executive
       3. Commander in chief
       4. Chief diplomat
       5. Chief legislator
       6. Chief of party
       7. Voice of the people
       8. Protector of peace
       9. Manager of prosperity
      10. World leader
    B. Responsibilities involving external political skills
       1. Campaigning
       2. Speech making
       3. Communicating ideas
       4. The example of President Reagan
    C. Responsibilities involving internal political skills
       1. Persuading others to give support
       2. Managing the executive-branch bureaucracy
    D. Policy responsibilities

IV. The institutional presidency (Professor Ladd's term for the staff offices
    directly under presidential control)
    A. Growth during FDR's administration in the 1930s
    B. Executive Office of the President
       1. White House staff
          a. circular versus hierarchical staff setups
          b. chief of staff
             1. example of President Reagan and James Baker
             2. example of President Bush, John Sununu, Sam Skinner,
               and James Baker
          c. Political life inside the inner sanctum of the West Wing
       2. National Security Council (NSC)
       3. Office of Management and Budget (OMB)
       4. Vice presidency

End your study of the office of the presidency by looking for a moment at
the classic photo on p. 196. You are viewing a solemn moment in American
history.

Take a break after reading all this material on the presidency, by reading the short excerpts in the "Cases" section of chapter 7 of the *Study Guide*. These excerpts on the vice presidency are not intended to trivialize the office or to make fun of any individuals. But who can resist Garry Wills' or W. Lance Bennett's Dan Quayle (a political science major in college) stories?

After you recover from these excerpts, try Peter Hay's brief look at first lady Eleanor Roosevelt. Then read Bradley Patterson's account of the little-seen work and workers in the White House.

The Exercise of Presidential Power

Read pp. 198-206. Political scientist Richard Neustadt's well-known characterization of presidential power as the power to persuade sets the tone for the last part of chapter 7. Be sure you understand Neustadt's thesis.

Professor Ladd concludes by touching on the strengths, weaknesses, and persuasive powers of past presidents: John Kennedy, Lyndon Johnson, Richard Nixon, Jimmy Carter, and Ronald Reagan. Sometimes presidents who were once thought to be less than great in office are reevaluated by historians and political scientists. Presidents Herbert Hoover, Dwight Eisenhower, and Richard Nixon fall into this category. Glance at the photo on p. 204. Any comment? Look at Table 7.1 to see how the American people rate recent presidents. This data is very interesting, you must admit, whether or not you would make the same assessments. Do Americans make simple judgments about presidents? Who is especially respected for foreign policy? For domestic policy? Who is thought least moral? Who is considered best overall? Can you offer your own explanation for the public's perception of President Kennedy almost thirty years after his death?

Professor Ladd mentions James David Barber's controversial book, *The Presidential Character,* an extremely interesting and unusual work that classifies twentieth-century presidents by personality types. Barber uses his theory to try to predict behavior in office based on the president's character as formed in youth. *The Presidential Character* is worth a look especially if you like both psychology and politics. For now, catch glimpses into the personalities of three American presidents in the "Cases" section of the *Study Guide*. This chapter's excerpts feature Fawn Brodie on Thomas Jefferson, Charles Allen and Jonathan Portis on Bill Clinton, and Fitzhugh Green on George Bush. All three take a Barberesque approach that may interest you.

Sample Test Questions

MULTIPLE CHOICE—SELECT THE *BEST* ANSWER

1. A characteristic of George Bush as president has been his:
   a. lack of energy due to poor health.
   b. clear vision for major policy change.
   c. ease in dealing with people.
   d. confrontational approach toward opponents.
2. A president who relies on a hierarchical style in running the White House places a lot of authority in:
   a. his or her mate.   c. the Congress.
   b. the chief of staff.   d. political scientists.
3. Which agency in the Executive Office of the President is responsible for putting together the president's budget proposals?
   a. Office of Management and Budget (OMB)
   b. Congressional Budget Office (CBO)
   c. The vice president's staff
   d. Impoundment Bureau
4. All of the following presidents gave their vice presidents considerable responsibility *except*:
   a. Franklin Roosevelt.   c. Jimmy Carter.
   b. Dwight Eisenhower.   d. Ronald Reagan.
5. All of the following sit on the National Security Council *except*:
   a. the president.   c. the secretary of defense.
   b. the vice president.   d. the Speaker of the House.
6. The twentieth-century presidents rated most highly overall by the American public are:
   a. Richard Nixon and Gerald Ford.
   b. Franklin Roosevelt and John Kennedy.
   c. Ronald Reagan and George Bush.
   d. Harry Truman and Jimmy Carter.
7. If no presidential candidate wins a majority of the electoral vote in the November election, the vote for president goes into:
   a. the House, with each representative having one vote.
   b. the Senate, with each state having one vote.
   c. the House, with each state delegation having one vote.
   d. the House and then the Senate, with a two-thirds vote required to win.
8. All of the following presidents have undergone significant revisions in the way historians and political scientists originally assessed their time in office and the way they are now assessed *except*:
   a. Herbert Hoover.   c. Richard Nixon.
   b. Franklin Roosevelt.   d. Dwight Eisenhower.

9. Political scientist Richard Neustadt believes that a president's power comes from the power to:
   a. command.
   b. punish.
   c. persuade.
   d. wage war.
10. All of the following presidential appointments need the advice and consent of the Senate *except*:
   a. Supreme Court judges.
   b. federal district court judges.
   c. the chief of staff.
   d. the cabinet secretaries.

TRUE/FALSE

11. Andrew Johnson was the only American president ever impeached.
12. President Andrew Johnson was removed from office after his impeachment in 1868.
13. President Richard Nixon was removed from office after his impeachment in 1974.
14. When Clinton Rossiter describes the president as chief diplomat, he means that the president can negotiate and ratify treaties independent of any check on presidential power.
15. When a president is rated low in performance during his administration, history usually judges him to be poor.
16. Jacqueline Kennedy was present at the swearing-in of President Kennedy's successor, Lyndon Johnson.
17. Electors of the electoral college are pledged to vote for the presidential candidate with the most popular votes in the state.
18. President Reagan's strength was in external political skills such as campaigning and speaking.
19. President Bush's approval ratings were almost unchanged through his years in office.
20. Dan Quayle was one of the most experienced, polished vice presidents ever to be selected.

ESSAYS

21. Contrast a president's need for external political skills with the need for internal political skills. Are both skills likely to be found in one person? Use specific examples from President Hoover, President Nixon, President Reagan, and President Bush to illustrate the differences between external and internal political skills.
22. What factors affect a president's popularity among the American people? Does popularity shift significantly during a leader's term or terms? Explain how the judgments that Americans express in polls about past presidents reflect the same changes and complexity of opinion found in polls during a president's time in office.

23. Explain the concept of the institutional presidency. When did it begin? Offer five examples of the institutional presidency as it functions today. Then discuss how the large staff increases that Congress provided for itself beginning in the 1970s (examined in chapter 6) were in part a response to the institutional presidency and the need to preserve separation of powers.

THE MADISON TEST

In *Federalist Paper* No. 10, Madison warns Americans not to rely on individuals elected to public office to protect the polity, because "Enlightened statesmen will not always be at the helm." Was his warning correct? Has the United States relied too much on individuals, or has the political system proven to be stronger than any individual leader? What are your views?

Answers

Multiple Choice

1. c	pp. 175-80	6. b pp. 203-6
2. b	pp. 191-92	7. c p. 182
3. a	pp. 194-95	8. b pp. 201-3
4. a	pp. 195-98	9. c pp. 198-99
5. d	p. 194	10. c p. 183

True/False

11. t	pp. 183-84	16. t p. 196
12. f	pp. 183-84	17. t p. 182
13. f	pp. 183-85	18. t pp. 187, 205
14. f	pp. 183, 186	19. f pp. 178-79
15. f	pp. 201-6	20. f p. 198

8 | The Executive Branch

The executive branch, bureaus, independent agencies, cabinet-level depart-ments, executive agencies, bureaucracy, civil service, administration, regulatory commissions, foundations and institutes, boards: These terms appear through-out chapter 8. Still, you can readily attack the chapter with just two simple ideas in mind: First, chapter 8 is a continuation of chapter 7. The executive branch is part of the presidency. The president's constitutional duty is to carry out laws; the executive branch does this on behalf of the president, and second, all of the organizations listed above do basically the same thing. While there are many types of executive-branch agencies, all exist to carry out the presi-dent's constitutional responsibility for executing the laws passed by Congress. You will learn the differences among types of agencies, but their basic purpose is the same.

The executive branch is a very important part of American government be-cause it is here that most citizens have contact with government. Not many people attend presidential state dinners, call senators to chat, or argue cases before the Supreme Court. But all citizens pay taxes to the IRS and probably have had a hassle or two with that agency; everyone eventually collects Social Security; lots of people apply for passports or get government-backed mort-gages. Citizen contact with the executive branch on the state level is even more common. When did you last stand in line at the Department of Motor Vehicles in your home state?

Because the executive agencies are within the president's branch of govern-ment, one might assume that the president controls these agencies. But this is only partly true. Surprisingly, the executive agencies can also act as a check on the president.

What Makes Up the Executive Branch?

Read pp. 208-23.

The executive branch is huge. With fourteen cabinet-level departments and sixty other independent agencies, the executive branch employs about 3 million people. One cabinet-level department alone is the single largest employer in the United States. Which one? Another cabinet-level department spends more money than any other public or private organization in the United States. Which one? Figure 8.2 will help you envision the size and cost of government today. (Remember that state and local governments have large bureaucracies too.) To master the material in chapter 8, you must understand the structure of the federal bureaucracy, remember the different types of agencies, be able to list their functions, and offer some examples.

INTERAGENCY MEMO

To: Professor Ladd's American government students

From: *Study Guide* author

Re: Structure of the federal bureaucracy

Prepare your responses to the outline questions that follow. Do not consult others. You may use the textbook. Your answers should be neatly typed or printed in triplicate in black ink only (only kidding—you can use green). Do not fold, spindle, or mutilate.

You will receive a bonus for each correct answer in the form of good grades in American government, the respect of your professor, the envy of your peers, and self-satisfaction.

I. Cabinet-level departments
   A. How many cabinet-level departments existed in 1789?
      1. Name each original cabinet post.
      2. Which department grew most over the first hundred years?
      3. Did the cabinet-level departments employ many people?
   B. How many cabinet-level departments exist today?
      1. Name them all.
      2. Name the department that employs the most personnel today (Figure 8.2).
         a. How many does it employ?

b. How many altogether?
3. Name the department that spends the most money today (Figure 8.2).
   a. How much does it spend?
   b. Why so much?
4. Name the cabinet department that interests you the most.
C. Who heads cabinet-level departments?
   1. Who appoints the secretaries and undersecretaries?
   2. Name two current cabinet secretaries.

II. Independent Agencies (Figure 8.3)
A. Why, in general, are certain agencies classified as independent?
B. Does the president have complete control over them?
   1. Independent agencies
      a. Who appoints the head?
      b. Name two independent agencies.
   2. Foundations and institutes
      a. Are foundations and institutes ever involved in political issues?
      b. Name two foundations and institutes.
   3. Independent Regulatory Commissions
      a. Who heads independent regulatory commissions?
      b. For how long?
      c. How much political control over these organizations does the president have?
      d. Name two independent regulatory commissions.

Who Controls the Executive Branch?

Read pp. 223-29.

The bureaucracy executes laws passed by Congress, spending money appropriated by Congress, for the benefit of various groups of citizens. Bureaus are run by rules, Professor Ladd mentions, so their jobs should be clear cut.

Go back to Madison, to separation of powers, to letting "ambition counteract ambition." As Professor Ladd says on pp. 228-29, the agencies are the "hub" of policy making. Many political players figure in the executive-branch game. Who are the potential players? Ascertain who is involved in the executive branch controversies that Professor Ladd describes.

When you can answer the questions below, you will have a good grasp of who really controls the executive branch.

1. Paperwork Reduction Act of 1980
   What was the issue underlying the passage of the Paperwork Reduction Act?

Who is involved from the president's office? From the executive agencies? From Congress? From interest groups affected by the act? How are the political parties involved?

How are OMB, executive orders, and deregulation involved in this act?

2. The Department of Housing and Urban Development, and its secretary, Jack Kemp

What is HUD responsible for?

Who appointed Kemp secretary of HUD?

What program did Kemp push hard for?

Who opposed his ideas?

How did the Democratic Congress react to Kemp's ideas?

What happened to Kemp's ideas for programs after the 1992 Los Angeles riots?

3. Federal Reserve Board

What issues is the Fed involved in?

What kind of executive agency is the Fed? How close is it to the president?

Who heads the Fed? How many people make up the board of governors? How long do they serve?

The overall picture that emerges from Professor Ladd's examples is one of competition among many players for influence in the executive agencies. Does this fit Madison's picture of letting "ambition counteract ambition"?

You can clearly see the congressional/presidential struggle over the control of the agencies in action during oversight hearings. An oversight hearing is not a hearing on a proposed bill, but rather a chance for the Congress to check up on how well the executive branch has carried out a law that has been on the books for years. Oversight is one of the least known but most important functions of Congress because oversight allows Congress to monitor how well taxpayer dollars, appropriated by the Congress and actually handed out by the executive agencies, are being spent. It is a significant congressional check on the executive. Watch some oversight hearings on C-SPAN when the House of Representatives (the Tuesday to Thursday Club) is not in session live.

THE IRON TRIANGLE

Professor Ladd discusses the "symbiosis" that can develop between agencies and the interest groups affected by the agencies' administration of laws. Sometimes "iron triangles" form. You are about to discover one of the most interesting hidden feature in American government.

An iron triangle (sometimes called a subgovernment) includes: members of a congressional subcommittee, an executive agency, and private interest groups.

Iron triangles form naturally inside government, Professor Ladd notes, because of the shared policy interests of all three players. Why are they seen as "grubby and self-serving" by critics, according to Professor Ladd? Are they always bad? Be ready to cite an example of an iron triangle by either borrowing from Professor Ladd's examples or devising one from your own knowledge of American government (and your political imagination).

On one hand, as you have seen, agencies are engaged in congressional/presidential tussles. On the other hand, they are locked into cozy iron triangles. Caught in the middle of these swirling patterns of political interaction is the bureau chief. You might want to reread pp. 227-28 to remind yourself of the dilemma facing the bureau chief who is the head of an office inside an agency. A bureau chief has two loyalties, loyalties that often pull in opposite directions. Cabinet secretaries or agency heads, appointed by the president to follow a clear policy course, demand that the bureau chief implement the new policies. Members of Congress and interest-group leaders know the bureau chiefs well and may have a different idea than the agency head about what constitutes sound policy. The agency employees themselves have been around a long time – much longer than the president and this president's new ideas – and they will be there far into the future; sometimes they pull their bureau chief another way, toward doing things the old "agency" way. This conflict can be difficult for a bureau chief. Yet it also works as a Madisonian check on power (although one he probably never anticipated.) So paradoxically agency personnel themselves can be a strong check on presidential power over the president's own executive-branch agencies!

Civil Service: The Merit System

Some of you will undoubtedly become civil servants. You will work for government on the national, state, or local level. How many federal employees are there currently? Read pp. 229-37 to finish chapter 8. Here are the key terms you should know:

three million employees
civil service
merit system
Office of Personnel Management (OPM)
GS ratings
veterans' bonus points
pay raises
Senior Executive Service
Senior Foreign Service

Volcker Commission
Pendleton Act

4,500 employees
Plum Book
political appointees

When you can answer the questions below, you will be well on your way toward understanding the role the civil service plays in the executive branch.

What problems exist in attracting able young people to government service? Would you consider a career as a civil servant? Why do senior civil servants sometimes leave the agencies to work elsewhere? Do incompetent civil servants leave? Look at the cartoon on p. 235. What is its message about government employees and about firing bad ones? Notice how the cartoon reinforces the negative stereotype about public servants, a stereotype that hurts morale in the agencies.

How has the savings and loan scandal touched the executive branch's reputation? The American people trusted members of Congress, the president, state officials, bankers, and executive-agency regulators with their money. As Professor Ladd emphasizes, "There is more than enough blame to go around." Check out the cartoon on p. 236.

To end on a more optimistic note, go to the excerpt for chapter 8 in the "Cases" section of the *Study Guide*. Former NASA chief James Webb is one of the best examples of good public administrators. The piece by W. Henry Lambright on Webb shows that there is more to public service than entrenched incompetence. If you particularly enjoyed the material on the executive branch, you might want to consider a future political science course in public administration, the academic area that focuses on the agencies in depth.

Sample Test Questions

MULTIPLE CHOICE—SELECT THE *BEST* ANSWER

1. About how many people are employed by the executive branch agencies?
   a. 300
   b. 3,000
   c. 3,000,000
   d. 3,000,000,000
2. A federal regulatory commission is designed to protect the interests of:
   a. businesses.
   b. the public.
   c. the federal government.
   d. the state governments.
3. With less than 1 percent of the jobs in the executive branch coming through political appointments, most federal workers are hired through:
   a. the merit system.
   b. the plum book.
   c. the president.
   d. the Congress.

4. The Civil Service Reform Act of 1978 gave significant personnel authority to the:
   a. Office of Personnel Management (OPM).
   b. Congressional Budget Office (CBO).
   c. General Accounting Office (GAO).
   d. Office of Management and Budget (OMB).
5. Which of the following cabinet-level agencies was not an original one, begun during George Washington's presidency?
   a. State Department.　　　　　　c. Justice Department.
   b. Energy Department.　　　　　 d. Treasury Department.
6. Where do foundations and institutes fit within the executive-branch structure?
   a. They are independent regulatory commissions headed by boards.
   b. They have cabinet-level status.
   c. They are somewhat removed from direct presidential control, but can become involved in political issues.
   d. They are controlled by the Congress instead of the president.
7. The programs advocated by HUD secretary Jack Kemp were designed to aid:
   a. inner-city residents.　　　　　c. college students.
   b. farmers.　　　　　　　　　　 d. endangered species.
8. A small, highly trained group of civil servants who can serve the federal government in any number of different agencies belong to:
   a. the Tuesday to Thursday Club.　c. the Senior Executive Service.
   b. the Plum Book Circle.　　　　 d. the Deeply Rooted 7,000.
9. An iron triangle can develop among all of the following involved in an issue *except*:
   a. the executive agency.　　　　　c. interest groups.
   b. the congressional subcommittee.　d. the federal district court.
10. The most serious concern of the 1989 Volcker Commission was:
    a. the excessive influence of the president over the executive agencies.
    b. the low pay and prestige of government service.
    c. the low pay and prestige of serving on congressional oversight committees.
    d. the unfairness of civil service tests because of veterans' bonuses.

TRUE/FALSE

11. The Office of Management and Budget (OMB) has a lot of influence over the federal regulations administered by the executive agencies.
12. The president can virtually control the policies of the Federal Reserve Board by replacing the head of the Fed and its board members whenever desired.

13. The Department of the Interior is the largest executive agency in terms of personnel because of the size of the national forests it must manage.
14. A cabinet secretary needs the advice and consent of the Senate to take office, as well as the Senate's advice and consent to resign.
15. The American civil service is considered the best in the world in terms of expertise and morale.

IDENTIFICATION—DISCUSS BRIEFLY

16. merit system
17. bureau chief
18. independent agency
19. Pendleton Act (1883)
20. long, set, staggered terms

ESSAYS

21. What is an iron triangle? Who is part of it and how does it function? Describe the role of the executive agency within the iron triangle. How can a bureau chief experience a dilemma about loyalties inside the agency? Mention in your answer: the president, the appointed head of the agency, the civil servants, other players in the iron triangle.
22. How are bureaucrats and civil servants perceived by many Americans? What are some specific reasons for negative perceptions? Cite two attempts that have been made in the past decades to reform the civil service, including an assessment of the soundness of the reforms proposed.

Answers

Multiple Choice

1. c   p. 208
2. b   pp. 222-23
3. a   p. 233
4. a   pp. 235-36
5. b   p. 214

6. c   pp. 221-22
7. a   pp. 212-13
8. c   pp. 231-32
9. d   pp. 227-28
10. b   pp. 232-33

True/False

11. t   pp. 210-12
12. f   p. 214
13. f   pp. 217-18
14. f   p. 213
15. f   pp. 231-33

Identification

16. Almost all the people who work for the federal government's executive agencies acquire their jobs by taking merit exams and receiving GS ratings. Run by the Office of Personnel Management (OPM), the merit system allows civil servants to hold onto their jobs for a long time. Critics charge that incompetent civil servants are too well-protected and entrenched. pp. 233–36

17. A bureau chief is a merit system employee who heads an office within an agency. The bureau chief can become the focus of pressure from several sources: from the political appointee who heads the agency; from the civil servants who work in the agency; and from members of Congress and interest groups involved in the bureau's area of administration. pp. 227–28

18. An independent agency describes any of the executive agencies except the cabinet level departments. Independent regulatory commissions, foundations and institutes, and the many agencies that handle specialized areas of government services are all independent agencies. Some are closely controlled by the president (as are cabinet level departments), while others are more remote from presidential control. pp. 220–21

19. The Pendleton Act of 1883 created the American civil service by mandating merit exams as a condition for employment. Merit system employees received job protection but had to stay out of direct political activity. pp. 233–34

20. The boards that manage independent regulatory commissions consist of individuals appointed by the president for set terms of several years (depending on the agency). The individuals' terms are staggered; because they overlap, no one president can easily dominate the boards by making new appointments. This system is designed to remove independent regulatory commissions from the president's direct political control. p. 223

9 | The Judiciary

The judiciary is a difficult branch of government to study: Concepts like judicial review and judicial intervention are complex. The Supreme Court cases discussed in this chapter are complicated and detailed. The American court system operates with great exactness and precision, and so must you as you complete the branches-of-government part of the course.

Chapter 9 is important to all American government students. If you are considering a career in law, this material will be of special interest to you. A full treatment of the topics in chapter 9, as well as those in chapter 14 on civil liberties and civil rights, is included in the advanced political science course usually titled Constitutional Law. Constitutional Law is always one of the most difficult (and feared) yet interesting courses in the Political Science Department, as some of you will discover in the future.

There are three distinct parts to chapter 9. One part covers important Supreme Court cases; another–the structure of the U.S. legal system; a third–judicial appointments. Despite the multitude of abstract concepts and specific detail in each part, you should work on chapter 9 by first reading the whole chapter. Look for the following key ideas, terms, and names, and underline or make notes on each:

> interpretation of the law
> "storm centre"
>
> *Roe v. Wade* (1973)
> > abortion/trimesters/viability of a fetus
> > right of privacy/national right/state right
> > pro-choice/pro-life
> > effect on number of legal abortions (Figure 9.1)
> *Webster v. Reproductive Health Services* (1989)
> > state regulations/public health facilities/public funds
> > position of Justice O'Connor

Planned Parenthood v. Casey (1992)
    state regulations/parental consent
    undue burden test
    impact on *Roe*
Influence of changed composition of Supreme Court on decisions

Plessy v. Ferguson (1896)
    "separate but equal"
Brown v. Board of Education of Topeka (1954)
    Fourteenth Amendment – "equal protection"
    Chief Justice Earl Warren
    "Separate . . . facilities are inherently unequal." (Box 9.1)

Judicial intervention (judicial activism)
    prisons, mental hospitals, facilities for the elderly, schools, desegre-
        gation plans
costs of insuring individuals' rights

U.S. Supreme Court (Figure 9.2)
U.S. Court of Appeal
U.S. District Courts

jurisdiction
    state and federal courts
    exclusive/concurrent
    original/writ of certiorari/appeal

judicial review
    Alexander Hamilton
    Marbury v. Madison (1803)
    Chief Justice John Marshall

standing
class-action suit
justiciability
caseload

federal judges
    advice and consent of the Senate
    senatorial courtesy/blue slips
    American Bar Association ratings
    gender and ethnic background (Table 9.2)

After you have gone through chapter 9 once, you can use this chapter of the *Study Guide* to master the judiciary chapter part by part.

Supreme Court Cases

Reread pp. 241-52. Professor Ladd prefaces his detailed examination of two major issues that have come before the Supreme Court by alluding to the political nature – though not thought of as political – of the judiciary's work. (Look for a moment at the photo on p. 245. Do these judges look like politicians?) Professor Ladd mentions how important the prestige of the judiciary is. How does this prestige help the Supreme Court enforce its decisions? The issues that come before the Court represent enormously controversial public questions. What did Justice Oliver Wendell Holmes call the Supreme Court? Why?

REPRODUCTIVE RIGHTS

The first issue that Professor Ladd explores in depth is abortion and how the Supreme Court's views on abortion have changed as the times, and the justices on the Court, have changed. Be prepared to discuss the following questions:

1. Who controlled abortion policy before *Roe v. Wade*? What case provided a precedent for *Roe*? What kinds of human experiences brought the issue to the Court in 1973?
2. What was the basic content of the 1973 *Roe v. Wade* decision? On what right was the right to an abortion based, according to the Supreme Court? Describe the trend in the number of legal abortions performed after the Court's decision.
3. What two strong opposing interests emerged from *Roe v. Wade*? State each group's basic position.
4. What changes did *Webster v. Reproductive Health Services* (1989) make in *Roe*?
5. What changes did *Planned Parenthood v. Casey* (1992) make in *Roe*? Has *Roe* been overturned?

Now that you know how the Supreme Court has adjudicated the abortion issue (at least as of 1992), speculate on these questions:

6. If a Supreme Court justice retires and is replaced by a conservative jurist before the next abortion case is heard, what may happen to *Roe*? Which people in the United States would be most affected if *Roe* were overturned?

7. What are your views on abortion? On the federal government's power over abortion? The state governments'? Who should pay for legal abortions for poor women? In 1992, after *Planned Parenthood v. Casey,* the Congress resumed consideration of a "freedom of choice" bill that would preserve abortion as a national right. Do you oppose or favor such a law? Should an issue like abortion be decided by the courts, the legislature, or no governmental institution? You may wish to look ahead to chapter 10 where Professor Ladd presents a complete picture of American public opinion on the abortion issue.

SCHOOL SEGREGATION

The second issue discussed in depth by Professor Ladd is the Supreme Court's memorable decision in the 1954 case *Brown v. Board of Education of Topeka* (see Box 9.1). This was, perhaps, the most monumental case ever heard by the Court. All students of American government should be able to answer the following questions with authority:

1. From your knowledge of U.S. history, what did the 1896 *Plessy v. Ferguson* case claim?

2. What were the facts in *Brown*? What clause in the Fourteenth Amendment was used in *Brown*? Who wrote the decision? (You will learn much more about this justice later in chapter 14.) What was the Court's vote?

3. Why was the judiciary the branch of government that acted to end the segregation of schools by law?

Before you leave *Brown*, you should think deeply about Chief Justice Earl Warren's words: "Separate . . . [is] inherently unequal." This is a classic phrase in American history and government. In Constitutional Law you will study many landmark Supreme Court cases, but perhaps none as important as *Brown v. Board of Education.*

JUDICIAL ACTIVISM

It should now be clear why Justice Oliver Wendell Holmes called the Supreme Court a "storm centre" in American politics. He also said, "I am not God." Holmes was a believer in the philosophy of judicial restraint: The Court should not try to take over the legislature's role in making law; it should interpret the constitutionality of laws without employing judges' personal views on what the laws should be.

Professor Ladd notes that some judges today, especially those who sit on federal district courts or state courts have been accused of judicial intervention and judicial activism, for ordering very specific remedies for problems in prisons, in mental hospitals, in segregated schools, based on their views of what is best for society. Judges virtually "make law," critics say. They spend taxpayers' money with court-ordered mandates, yet they bear no responsibility for raising tax revenue. Review the examples that Professor Ladd offers. Yet consider also the rights of prisoners, patients in state mental hospitals, children in inner-city schools. In some cases only an activist court, not an executive or a legislature, will make it a priority to protect the rights of powerless minorities. How did Aristotle define a polity?

The Structure of the U.S. Legal System

Review the technical terms relevant to the legal system by scrutinizing the outline below. You do not have to know every detail, but you should be able to provide a specific example when asked to.

I. Jurisdiction
   A. concurrent
   B. exclusive
     1. state courts
       ex.:
     2. federal courts
       ex.:

II. Federal court system (Figure 9.2)
   A. U.S. District Courts
   B. U.S. Courts of Appeal
   C. U.S. Supreme Court
   D. specialty courts
     ex.:
     ex.:
   E. movement of cases from state to federal court

III. U.S. Supreme Court
   A. jurisdiction
     1. original
       ex.:
     2. writ of certiorari
       ex.:
     3. appeal
       ex.:

    B. judicial review
       1. Alexander Hamilton
       2. *Marbury v. Madison* (1803)
       3. Chief Justice John Marshall
    C. standing
    D. class-action suit
       ex.:
    E. justiciability
    F. caseload
       ex.:

JUDICIAL REVIEW

The one item in the outline that needs further explanation is the difficult and important concept of judicial review. You have studied judicial review in U.S. history, but you might not remember it because this historical event is much more important as a topic in American government.

In 1803, John Marshall was chief justice of a Supreme Court whose power was severely limited. It lacked the power of judicial review – the right to declare an act of Congress unconstitutional – without which the Court could do little to function as a co-equal branch of government. Why was this power not specifically given to the Court in the Constitution? Legal historians can explain much about the framers' thinking on this. In the long, hot days of summer in Philadelphia in 1787 there was disagreement. Some at the convention, especially Alexander Hamilton, clearly advocated giving the Court the power of judicial review. Others were reluctant because of the power this would give the Court over the Congress.

Marshall, both as a strong Federalist and a Court member, wanted to strengthen the Court in every way possible. He knew he needed to secure the power of judicial review for the Supreme Court, so he took it, in one of the most significant and ingenious court cases ever! Reread Professor Ladd's discussion of *Marbury v. Madison* on pp. 256-58. Look at the portrait of Marshall. Here is a man who knew what he wanted to accomplish in government and found a foolproof way to do it.

From the discussion of the case in the text, you know that Federalist party sympathizers, among them William Marbury, had been nominated for judgeships right before the Federalist president, John Adams, left office. It all happened at the last minute (At what time of night? *Marbury v. Madison* is always identified in U.S. history as the case of the midnight judges.) and the papers never got sent. The new president, Thomas Jefferson, appointed anti-federalists to the positions. Angry, Marbury asked the Supreme Court to issue a writ of mandamus, a power given the Court in the Federal Judiciary Act of 1789 (an act of Congress), demanding that Jefferson's secretary of state, James Madison, hand over the signed but undelivered papers. It was Madison's job to do this because, in the early years of the nation, the executive branch was very small. (How many executive agencies were there? Name them. Taxpayers certainly got their money's worth with the great James Madison both running foreign policy and sending out personnel materials.)

Chief Justice Marshall faced an awful dilemma. If he just said no to Marbury, he would disappoint his Federalist colleagues and do nothing for the weak Court's prestige. Worse, if he said yes to Marbury's request for the papers, Jefferson and Madison would have grinned mischievously and said to the robed justices: "Make us do it." The judiciary had no way to enforce its decision, and the Court would have been in worse shape than before. Here is what Marshall said: Marbury should get his judgeship papers because they were signed and are legal. But the Supreme Court cannot issue the writ of mandamus sought by Marbury ordering Madison to deliver the papers because the section of the Federal Judiciary Act of 1789 that gives the Supreme Court the power to issue such writs is unconstitutional. It gives the Court a power beyond that included in the Constitution.

In *Marbury* Chief Justice Marshall sacrificed a small part of the Supreme Court's power – the power to issue a writ of mandamus. But in sacrificing that small power, he *took* for the Supreme Court what is perhaps the strongest potential power in American government – the power to declare an act of Congress unconstitutional. The Supreme Court today has the power of judicial review because Chief Justice John Marshall took the power for the Court in *Marbury*, setting a precedent for the Court's future exercise of judicial review.

Judicial Appointments

You have already seen how important judicial appointments are: The changing composition of the Supreme Court from the early 1970s to the early 1990s is reflected in the differences between *Roe v. Wade* and *Planned Parenthood v. Casey.*

Reread pp. 262-70. List the steps in the confirmation of a federal judge. Review the three layers of federal courts to which judges are appointed. For lower federal court nominees, be sure you know what the following terms mean: senatorial courtesy, blue slips, advice and consent, Justice Department check, ABA ratings. Study Table 9.2 for a general idea of the gender and ethnic make-up of recent presidents' judicial appointments. Which presidents have been most concerned with appointing women, black Americans, and Hispanic Americans to the bench?

Supreme Court nominations can best be studied by example. In what is rather a stormy ending to the "storm centre" chapter, Professor Ladd elaborates on several recent Supreme Court nomination fights. To understand the role of political ideology in picking a Supreme Court justice, study the Robert

Bork story. Be aware of the Senate's power of advice and consent, and of the partisan (political party) make-up of the Senate. Spend a few moments on the views of law professor and Bork opponent Laurence Tribe in which he contrasts "original intent" (Bork's view of the Court's proper role) with "unenumerated rights" (the view granting individual liberties except where they are denied by the Constitution). This important clash goes beyond the Bork nomination. Use the concepts again when you come to the controversy over civil liberties examined in chapter 14.

Who eventually was confirmed for the seat for which Bork was rejected? Who took the seat vacated by liberal Justice William Brennan? Refer back to the photo on p. 245 to identify these individuals. Finally, who filled Justice Thurgood Marshall's seat upon his retirement in 1991? You might be interested to know that in 1954 Marshall was one of the attorneys representing Linda Brown in *Brown v. Board of Education*.

Before you look over Professor Ladd's account of the Clarence Thomas hearings that conclude chapter 9, pause to read the fascinating account of the current Supreme Court in the "Cases" section of the *Study Guide*. David Savage is a journalist who covers the Court; he shows some of the human side of the Court and presents an account of an agonizing 1991 Court case. Then re-read the section on Justice Thomas' confirmation hearings that you doubtless remember watching (perhaps on C-SPAN). The issues raised were important and the history made will not soon be forgotten, but the anguish of the hearings, evident even in the photos on p. 270, also remains.

Sample Test Questions

MULTIPLE CHOICE—SELECT THE *BEST* ANSWER

1. Judicial review means that the Supreme Court can:
    a. declare a senatorial order invalid.
    b. advise the legislature on the constitutionality of a proposed law.
    c. declare an act of Congress unconstitutional.
    d. invalidate a federal law unless the president vetoes the invalidation.
2. A class-action suit is brought on behalf of:
    a. all citizens similarly affected.
    b. all citizens of the United States.
    c. any citizen who agrees to help pay the attorney's fees.
    d. the federal government.

3. In which pattern do cases move through the federal court system?
   a. from Supreme Court, to U.S. Court of Appeals, to federal district court.
   b. from federal district court directly to Supreme Court.
   c. from U.S. Court of Appeals, to federal district court, to Supreme Court.
   d. from federal district court, to U.S. Court of Appeals, to Supreme Court.

4. *Webster v. Reproductive Health Services* (1989) and *Planned Parenthood v. Casey* (1992) modified *Roe v. Wade* (1973) by returning significant power over the abortion decision to:
   a. physicians.
   b. state legislatures.
   c. women.
   d. Congress.

5. Cases can come to the Supreme Court in all of the following ways *except*:
   a. original jurisdiction.
   b. a writ of certiorari.
   c. appeal.
   d. formal request from the president.

6. Which of the following statements best expresses Robert Bork's judicial position as expressed during his unsuccessful Senate confirmation hearings?
   a. Americans have all the rights granted in the Constitution as well as any other individual rights they wish to have.
   b. Americans have only those rights specifically stated in the Constitution.
   c. Americans have only those rights stated in the Constitution, which the Supreme Court, over time, has upheld as valid.
   d. Americans must give up a right in the Constitution each time they wish to be granted a new right not explicitly stated.

7. In *Brown v. Board of Education of Topeka* (1954) the interpretation of the Fourteenth Amendment that was overturned was conveyed in the phrase:
   a. "separate but equal."
   b. "I am not God."
   c. "storm centre."
   d. "separate . . . [is] inherently unequal."

8. Which of the following justices of the Supreme Court is female?
   a. Justice Scalia
   b. Chief Justice Rehnquist
   c. Justice O'Connor
   d. Justice Souter

9. The Supreme Court must hear a case on appeal when:
   a. Foreign governments sue the United States.
   b. A state's highest court has declared an act of Congress unconstitutional.
   c. A senator has declared bankruptcy.
   d. There is substantial agreement among the American people that the case belongs in the highest court of the land.

10. Senatorial courtesy allows:
    a. the president to reject the Senate's choice for a Supreme Court nomination.
    b. the Judiciary Committee to override the American Bar Association's rating of a potential federal judge.
    c. senators to be pleasant to judicial nominees despite the fact that they disagree on judicial philosophy.
    d. senators from the president's party, in whose state the federal court nominee resides, to express an informal veto if the nominee is unsatisfactory.

TRUE/FALSE

11. The Supreme Court is bound by precedent in all its decisions.
12. For a person who wishes to go to court to have "standing," she or he must be able to stand up in front of the judge for the entire length of the trial.
13. The number of legal abortions in the United States increased after *Roe v. Wade* in 1973.
14. Justice Clarence Thomas is the only black American ever to have sat on the Supreme Court.
15. Bankruptcies are an important part of the workload of the federal district courts.
16. Each successive president since Lyndon Johnson has appointed more women, blacks, and Hispanics to the federal courts than the previous president.
17. *Griswold v. Connecticut* (1965) provided a precedent for *Roe v. Wade* (1973) by interpreting the right to privacy as an unenumerated right in the Constitution.
18. The decision in *Brown v. Board of Education* was made by a close 5-4 vote.
19. Any Supreme Court justice can write a concurring opinion or a dissent, but only the Chief Justice can write the majority opinion.
20. Judicial intervention and activism by state court and lower federal court judges have often been on behalf of powerless minorities.

ESSAYS

21. Describe the process by which federal judges are selected. Include every step from nomination to confirmation. Mention all the political officials involved. Then, using one specific recent example, discuss the kinds of philosophical and personal issues that have surfaced in the appointment procedure.

22. How has the Supreme Court's position on abortion changed over the past decades? Cite specific cases that show the changes. Identify at least two reasons for the Court's shifts.
23. Explain the concept of judicial review. When did it originate in American government, and how? Because the Supreme Court consists of unelected judges, is judicial review a violation of the democratic system?
24. Contrast the judicial philosophies of restraint and intervention (activism). Support or criticize the activist trend of the recent past by citing the circumstances in which activism frequently has been used. Include reference to at least one current court case to substantiate your view.

THE MADISON TEST

How might Madison have felt when *Marbury v. Madison* was decided? What were his feelings as Jefferson's secretary of state and a person involved in the case? As the main designer of the Constitution sixteen years earlier, how might he have reacted to the Supreme Court's power of judicial review? You be the judge.

Answers

Multiple Choice

1. c	p. 256	
2. a	p. 260	
3. d	pp. 254-55	
4. b	pp. 241-49	
5. d	pp. 258-59	

6. b	pp. 265-67	
7. a	pp. 249-51	
8. c	pp. 245, 264	
9. b	p. 259	
10. d	p. 262	

True/False

11. f	p. 252	
12. f	pp. 259-60	
13. t	pp. 243-44	
14. f	p. 269	
15. t	p. 255	

16. f	pp. 263-64	
17. t	p. 243	
18. f	p. 249	
19. f	p. 246	
20. t	pp. 252-54	

10 | Public Opinion

In the coming chapters, which make up the "Participation" section (Part IV) of *The American Polity,* Professor Ladd changes the focus of the book from the institutions that make political decisions to the people who select the decision makers. Even before you start this part of the course, you already know much about participation. Think back for a few moments to the concepts you have encountered in the past nine chapters and how these fit into the issue of participation in the American political process: The U.S. as a *polity* rather than a *democracy*; Madison's fear of faction and his solutions; the on-going debate between elitist and pluralist thinkers about who really rules America. As you study participation in the political process, try to relate your knowledge to what you have learned about the branches of government. Look back to specific events, people, and ideas in the material on Congress, the presidency, the executive branch, and the judiciary that illustrate who participates, as well as how and when they participate in the American polity. In this part of the course you can begin to synthesize all the information you have been learning into your own "big-picture view" of the political system.

You could not have a better guide for the study of public opinion than Professor Everett Ladd. *The American Polity* makes excellent use throughout of public-opinion survey research. The book has a multitude of interesting tables and figures that go beyond what is usually available in an introductory American government text. The reason is evident on the title page. In addition to being a professor of political science, a columnist for the *Christian Science Monitor,* the editor of *The Public Perspective* (a public-opinion journal), author of numerous political science books as well as *The American Polity,* Professor Ladd is also director of the Roper Center for Public Opinion Research at the University of Connecticut. Since Professor Ladd has written a clear, concise, nontechnical explanation of public opinion, you can manage this chapter largely on your own, so the *Study Guide* will offer only a minimum of guidance.

To begin, read the summary at the end of the chapter. There you will find Professor Ladd's main ideas clearly stated. As you read the chapter itself, look for the following topics:

> the public's degree of information about political issues
> manipulation of public opinion
> people's ambivalence on issues
> the measurement of public opinion
> uses and abuses of public-opinion polling

Then, read chapter 10, from start to finish, in one sitting if possible.

Ambivalent? Manipulated? Informed?

The ambivalence Americans feel on subjects of deep importance can be troubling. But this ambivalence is not as simple as it may seem. Having read pp. 276-92 of the text, you should be able to answer the following questions and arrive at your own assessment.

1. What does ambivalence mean? Use either Figure 10.1 or 10.2 to show a specific example of the ambivalence of the American public about government.
2. What are some of the reasons for the public's ambivalence about government? Are people just ignorant and confused, or is ambivalence a sign of the complicated nature of public opinion?
3. How does the environmental issue reflect public ambivalence about the progress in and methods of improving the environment? Use Tables 10.1 and 10.2, as well as Figure 10.3, in formulating your answer. Do not try to memorize the data Professor Ladd offers. Instead, concentrate on grasping the idea he is conveying with his statistics.
4. Likewise, how does the abortion issue reflect ambivalence and complexity in the public's opinion as expressed in Figure 10.4? You might make an interesting connection between the attitudes expressed in Figure 10.4 and the Supreme Court's major abortion decisions, *Roe v. Wade, Webster v. Reproductive Health Services,* and *Planned Parenthood v. Casey,* all of which you studied in chapter 9.
5. Three important names in the study of public opinion are James Bryce, Walter Lippmann, and V. O. Key. Briefly, explain what each one believed about public opinion in America.
6. Could public opinion actually be an expression of views artificially created by those in power – the elite – to make the public think that it favors a certain position, when in fact it is really the position the elite wants the public to favor? Do elites give the public alternatives in governmental

policy that are not really different at all? This creation of beliefs, which are not genuinely the attitudes of those who express them, is called "false consciousness," and it is a Marxist critique of public opinion.

7. How easily can public opinion be manipulated by those in power and by the media? As you read Professor Ladd's discussion of "selling candidates," glance at the photo on p. 284. Think about the excerpt from Bennett's essay on Dan Quayle and the movie *The Candidate* from chapter 7 in the "Cases" section of the *Study Guide*.

8. Is the public well-informed about political issues when it responds to opinion polls? In chapter 6 the *Study Guide* asked you to be sure to find out who your home state's U.S. senators are and who your House of Representatives member is. You have had plenty of time to research it. Are you part of the 28 percent who know or the 72 percent who do not know their rep?

9. What factors could be responsible for the public's "mood swings"? On what kinds of issues do people have stable attitudes and on what kinds of issues do their views change drastically? Professor Ladd will tell you more about the media's role in changing public opinion in chapter 13.

10. How different is the public's understanding of general underlying issues as compared with specific, detailed matters?

Polling: "Must I drink the Whole Bottle in Order to Judge the Quality of the Wine?"

Polling has become an important part of public participation in many aspects of American life. So it is important to know the basics of how public-opinion polls are conducted. An outline of the key points in this section will take you to the end of chapter 10. As always, keep in mind that the outline only touches on the points you need to know about.

I. Who polls?
   A. Gallup and Roper
   B. ABC/*Washington Post;* CBS/*New York Times;* NBC/*Wall Street Journal; Los Angeles Times*

II. How are people polled?
   A. by mail
   B. by telephone
   C. in person

III. Who is polled?
   A. sample, representative of demographic breakdown (quota)
   B. random, with equal probability (e.g., random digit dialing)

IV. Where can polls go wrong?
    A. sample error and inaccurate sampling techniques
    B. poor wording of questions
    C. mistakes in interviewing
    D. press oversimplification of results
    E. Examples
        1. *Literary Digest* fiasco of 1936 (very famous classic incident)
            a. non-representative sample
            b. poor return rate of poll
            c. only one mailing
        2. 1948 Dewey/Truman presidential race
        3. 1992 British election
        4. 1992 Bush/Buchanan New Hampshire Republican primary

V. When are polls accurate?
    A. public well-informed and focused
    B. choices clear
    C. no ambivalence on the issue

Public opinion and polling is an interesting topic that has relevance in many areas of life other than politics. Be alert to polls and poll results when you read newspapers and hear statistics on television news shows, and on election evenings when exit polls are much featured by the networks. For those of you who are intrigued by twenty-first century communications technology, take a look at the excerpts in chapter 10 of the "Cases" section of the *Study Guide*. Alaska is already hooked up for teleconferencing, F. Christopher Arterton reveals. The eye-catching ad from *Policy Review* shows conservatives how to connect with one another. Although these ideas for two-way interactive television may seem strange, do you recall the popularity of on-again/off-again presidential candidate Ross Perot's similar suggestions in 1992?

Sample Test Questions

MULTIPLE CHOICE—SELECT THE *BEST* ANSWER

1. All of the following went wrong with the *Literary Digest*'s 1936 presidential election poll *except*:
    a. The sample was not representative of the American voting public.
    b. The poll was not returned by many of those questioned.
    c. The poll was only conducted once before the election.
    d. The results were changed by the magazine's editors to fit their choice for president.

2. By describing the public as ambivalent, Professor Ladd means that:
   a. The American people are basically ignorant.
   b. The public has mixed feelings on many issues.
   c. The elites mold public opinion as they wish it to be.
   d. People only understand specific policies, never underlying ideas.
3. When using probability sampling, pollsters choose people by:
   a. selecting a location, then picking respondents randomly.
   b. drawing up a precise list of people who fit certain demographic char-
      acteristics.
   c. asking people questions first, then deciding if they should be in the
      sample.
   d. insuring that it is probable that every American will be phoned for an
      answer to a poll question.
4. Writing in the 1920s, American journalist Walter Lippmann was a critic of
   government by public opinion because he felt that:
   a. Polls were not accurate enough, nor taken frequently enough.
   b. Politicians did not follow public opinion faithfully.
   c. People were spending too much time studying issues before being
      polled, thereby eliminating much of their leisure time.
   d. People were not well-educated enough to make specific policy deci-
      sions.
5. The strongest public support for a woman's right to choice on abortion
   comes in the circumstance of:
   a. a family's poor financial condition.
   b. the woman's second thoughts about having a child.
   c. a prognosis that the child might be deformed.
   d. rape or incest causing the pregnancy.
6. When Marxist thinkers call public opinion the product of "false consciousness," they mean that:
   a. People do not know how to answer poll questions, so they lie.
   b. The public's opinions are created for them by elites.
   c. Leaders are fakers for pretending to be conscious of what the com-
      mon person wants.
   d. People are conscious of how elites try to manipulate them.
7. Among the opinions expressed most on the environment is:
   a. a willingness to pay more in taxes for air-pollution reduction.
   b. a willingness to pay a gas tax for pollution-control measures.
   c. a feeling that pollution is becoming worse.
   d. a feeling that jobs cause pollution.

8. The Englishman James Bryce, visiting America in the late 1880s, predicted:
   a. the increased impact of public opinion once polls could be taken.
   b. the loss of public input as Americans became more passive.
   c. the demise of democracy once opinion polls were commonly used.
   d. the rise of elites along with the growth of technology.
9. American public opinion is most clear and stable on:
   a. specific government policies.
   b. basic underlying political views.
   c. abstract, philosophical questions.
   d. issues that create ambivalence.
10. All of the following are methods of polling that have proven successful at various times *except*:
    a. random digit dialing.
    b. using a magazine mailing list as a sample.
    c. quota or representative sampling.
    d. probability sampling.

IDENTIFICATION—DISCUSS BRIEFLY

11. V. O. Key
12. "[Y]ou may fool all the people some of the time; you can even fool some of the people all the time. [But] you can't fool all the people all the time."
13. George Gallup and Elmo Roper
14. "Must I drink the whole bottle in order to judge the quality of the wine?"
15. "Dewey Defeats Truman!"

ESSAYS

16. Discuss the ambivalence among the American people in their expression of public opinion. Offer a specific example of an issue on which polling data shows ambivalence. What effect can ambivalence have on poll results? Under what circumstances is public opinion most volatile (changeable), and when is it most stable?
17. Assess the basic criticisms that have been made of public-opinion polling. Starting with the *Literary Digest* fiasco of 1936, mention three examples of polling failures and why they failed. What factors can cause polls to be inaccurate? When are they most accurate? Include in your answer criticism made by Marxists as well as the very different criticism made by journalist Walter Lippmann.

THE MADISON TEST

Would Madison like the direct democracy of government by public-opinion poll or Perot's proposal for an "electronic town hall"? What about Alaska's teleconferencing network between citizens and legislators? Considering questions like these should help you prepare yourself for the next chapter, which is very Madisonian.

Answers

Multiple Choice

1.	d	pp. 294-97	6.	b	p. 283
2.	b	p. 290	7.	c	p. 280
3.	a	p. 295	8.	a	p. 282
4.	d	p. 282	9.	b	p. 289
5.	d	pp. 290-92	10.	b.	pp. 294-97

Identification

11. V. O. Key was an American political scientist whose classic book on public opinion defined it as "those opinions held by private persons which governments find it prudent to heed." That is, they are attitudes on issues that are public, not private, matters. Key also called public opinion "a mysterious vapor"! p. 281
12. These were President Abraham Lincoln's words about the manipulation of public opinion. p. 285
13. Gallup and Roper were two of the originators of scientific polling techniques. Their organizations remain prominent in public-opinion polling today. pp. 296-97
14. These words of a Belgian mathematician, Adolphe Quetelet, provide the premise that underlies polling: A well-chosen sample will correctly represent all to whom the poll will apply. p. 293
15. The headline "Dewey Defeats Truman!" which appeared on the front page of the *Chicago Daily Tribune* the morning after the 1948 presidential election, signifies the failure of the pollsters to spot a trend away from Dewey in the weeks before the election. Also, the polls were concluded too far before election day. pp. 301-2

11 | Interest Groups

In addition to public opinion, interest groups provide another forum for political participation in America. All on their own interest groups are one of the most exciting topics in American government. Yet the topic will be all the more exciting for you because you will realize with this chapter that you know a considerable amount about American politics and that seemingly diverse areas in the study of American government do fit together. The interest-group material illustrates the way that broad, abstract theories in political science can be explored through specific, easy-to-grasp topics.

Tocqueville and Madison: A Reprise

Read pp. 305-14. What did America's French visitor Alexis de Tocqueville call interest groups? What did Madison call them? Whether you believe them to be the dream or the nightmare of American politics, interest groups flourish today. Why did Tocqueville believe that Americans, who were strong individualists, formed interest groups so naturally?

Why did Madison believe that groups were an inevitable part of American life? Go back briefly to chapter 5 to review Madison's warning about and solution to "faction." Comment on how faction is "sown in the nature of man" and how "[l]iberty is to faction what air is to fire. . . ." Recall that Madison believed "the most common and durable source of factions has been the various and unequal distribution of property." Remember: Madison suggested that one solution to the "mischiefs of faction" are factions (plural!). Explain how factions can balance each other out in a large, diverse nation in which "[a]mbition must be made to counteract ambition" through a "multiplicity of interests." To Madison, while a single faction was bad, many bads make a good.

Thus, pluralism: A quick look back to the end of chapter 4 will reacquaint you with the pluralist power structure in which a system of competing, shifting, countervailing, balancing interest groups is envisioned. Madison was a pluralist, although he did not call his view by that term. Tocqueville placed much hope for the future of American democracy in the strength and vitality of interest groups because they could prevent "tyranny of the majority." Aristotle probably would have approved group politics on the grounds that groups *are* minorities and thus all kinds of minority interests are protected in such a form of government (a polity) from the corrupt rule of the majority (a democracy). Interest-group politics seems to have had some prominent backers early on. But at the end of the chapter the critics of interest-group politics will have much to say.

To debate the existence and desirability of a group-based political system in America, you will need to be able to blend factual material with the broad idea of pluralistic power in America today. Prepare to comment on:

> lobbying
> 14,400 lobbyists
> the case of Michael Deaver
> 8,100 registered groups
> "the tip of the iceberg"
>
> economic interests
>
> business and trade associations
> labor unions
> state and local governments
> special-interest citizen groups
> public-interest groups
> foreign governments
> civil rights groups
> women's groups
> education groups

You are well able to study on your own the basics about the number and types of interest groups in existence. Only a few items on the list need comment.

The ethics problems of lobbyist and former White House deputy chief of staff Michael Deaver is exemplary of a wider issue. As Professor Ladd points out, many former federal officials remain in Washington to lobby. The access they can provide to government policy makers is great; they earn a lot of money lobbying. Does that make lobbying more elitist than pluralistic?

Learn an example of each of the types of interest groups listed above. Take examples from the book or from your own knowledge. Always illustrate with a specific example when you refer to a type of group. Write: public-interest groups such as the Sierra Club; special-interest citizen groups like the National Rifle Association (NRA); interest-groups lobbying for state and local governments, among them the National Governors' Association; business associations, such as the American Petroleum Institute; women's groups, including the National Organization for Women (NOW). You will add depth and interest to your answers by using specific examples.

State and local governments are not usually thought of as lobbyists; rather, they are thought of as being lobbied by state and local interest groups. But layers of government lobby other layers of government for funds for important programs. Professor Ladd also reveals that "the federal government lobbies itself."

Public-interest groups claim to be a bit different from other interest groups because they lobby on behalf of "the public," on issues like health and the environment. Note Professor Ladd's interesting discussion of who participates in these kinds of interest groups. Do you belong to a public-interest group?

Tables 11.2 and 11.3 in the text show only some of the interest groups that address women's concerns and educational issues. Still, most interest groups that are active today do center around economic issues as Madison predicted. Table 11.1 in the text indicates the number of new lobbying groups registered with the House of Representatives in 1991-1992. New corporate groups make up 44 percent and new trade associations 24 percent. As Professor Ladd notes in his discussion, if you add the two together, almost 70 percent of registered lobbyists represent the interests of American business – dramatic, but to be expected in a capitalist society.

Influence of Groups and the Clean Air Act

Read pp. 315-30. When you get to the discussion of the Clean Air Act, do not read for each detail, but rather to see the machinations of interest groups in action. Still, after reading this section you should be familiar with the topics below and be able to answer questions on these topics.

I. Number of members
   An interest group needs members, but size can undermine cohesion.

II. Money
   Staff, communication with members and the public, campaign contributions – all require money. The number of interest-group political action committees (PACs) are shown dramatically in Figure 11.1. PAC money is a big factor in elections, so interest groups will be important in chapter 12, too.

III. Organization
The use of polls, computers, direct mail, and other modern techniques give some interest groups a lot of power. Groups also provide information to policy makers.

IV. Intensity
Numbers, money, and organization do not mean as much as a membership that is singlemindedly devoted to its cause. At elections, some groups "target" hostile legislators with great effectiveness.

V. Alliances
Interest groups create alliances with other groups when a big issue is about to be decided.

With these measures of interest-group influence in mind, study the example that Professor Ladd gives on the 1981-82 and the 1990 debates over modifying the 1970 Clean Air Act. Perhaps most interesting in the account are Tables 11.5 and 11.6 in the text. Look at Table 11.5 to see the two sides engaged in the struggle: the environmentalists versus the corporations. Friends of the Earth and the League of American Bicyclists are typical of the former group, while the latter contains, well . . . just check out the business list! Table 11.6 shows the 1989 PAC contributions to House of Representatives candidates. Yet in the period covered in this account, clean air standards were not lowered, despite the large amounts of money expended by industry. Compromises, the hallmark of a pluralist system, were made. Membership, money, organization, intensity, and alliances all figured into the process.

Not all political decisions are made by this kind of a classic competitive, countervailing interest-group battle. Some issues bring forth no opposition, and an interest group gains its victory with ease. Other times groups move to different arenas. They lobby within the executive agencies for support, but they also lobby the judiciary in a way. For example, groups submit *amicus curiae* briefs to the Supreme Court on occasion to state their views on a case. Can you offer a recent example? (If you can ever slip *amicus curiae* briefs into an essay, you will make quite an impression. They are not in the usual vocabulary of American government students.)

Some Critiques of Interest-Group Politics

Read pp. 330-35 to finish the chapter. Professor Ladd tells you that interest groups are inevitable and desirable, but that they cause problems. From the earlier parts of the chapter you can easily see how groups are both inevitable and desirable. The problematic nature of interest-group politics is more complex. Problems include the following:

1. Big business interests could dominate the system, transforming pluralism into elitism. Early in the twentieth-century the Progressive movement feared this same "group tyranny," as Professor Ladd calls it. Why could big business interest groups influence the political process so profoundly (use the measures of group strength)?

2. Special interests, each with its own narrow agenda, could dominate the system. The "molecular government" that would result could be best illustrated by the many "iron triangles" that form among congressional subcommittees, executive agencies, and interest groups. Was this not Madison's dream – a "multiplicity of interests"? Yes, in a way, but he did not foresee the lack of competition among iron triangles that would constitute true pluralism, nor did he anticipate that what is good for the whole nation would not necessarily result from the sum of what is good for each special interest. Noted political scientist Theodore Lowi is a prominent critic of interest-group politics on the grounds that the "public good" (if there is such a thing) gets lost.

3. Interest groups in theory allow all citizens to participate in the governmental process, yet in reality allow only those groups with resources (membership, money, organization, intensity, alliances) to exert much influence. Political scientist E. E. Schattschneider described the upper middle-class bias of pluralism's interest groups. What segments of society are not easily able to join in interest-group politics as it is played in the United States today? How effective are the computerized mailing lists of the homeless? How well staffed are the Washington offices of the group looking out for the interests of children who receive AFDC payments (a preview of chapter 15)?

If you are a pluralist who believes that interest-group competition is an accurate way to describe the distribution of power in the United States today and that interest-group politics can work well as a way for all Americans to participate in the political system, then be ready to respond persuasively to the three criticisms above. If you plan to remain involved in politics after your success in this course, you should especially consider the following ideas:

1. Public-interest groups are a way to balance the power of large corporate groups. There are public-interest groups in all areas of American life – health, the environment, consumer affairs. They are eager for new members like you.

2. Citizens can monitor their elected officials to see whether they have a sense of the national interest (at least some of the time) or are just special-interest politicians. C-SPAN lets you ferret out iron triangles. Newspaper articles usually tell how your representative and senator voted on important legislation.

3. Interest groups that look out for the poor, the weak, and the disadvan-

taged do exist, but they rely on support from people who are middle-class, strong, and well educated. From children, to the handicapped, to the homeless, to animals, there are groups that want to join in the pluralist fray. People like you must become active on their behalf.

Chapter 11 has brought together important abstract ideas, like pluralism, with the specific material on interest groups in America today. You have seen Madison's warning heeded, and you have seen the nation go perhaps too far in the direction of a "multiplicity of interests." With the example of George Washington, the United States avoided the tyranny of a government run by one person. With the guidance of Aristotle and Madison, tyranny of a majority without regard for the minority was prevented. Do we instead have tyranny of special interests? While you are mulling this over, read the accounts of two atypical interest-group movements in chapter 11 of the "Cases" section of the *Study Guide*. An excerpt from William Greider's *Who Will Tell the People* profiles "Justice for Janitors," while Studs Terkel looks at one average American's fight against the corporate giant Waste Management.

Sample Test Questions

MULTIPLE CHOICE—SELECT THE *BEST* ANSWER

1. Which of the following is closest to the number of interest groups registered to lobby in Washington?
   a. 80
   b. 800
   c. 8,000
   d. 80,000
2. When an interest group "targets" a candidate it means that:
   a. The group focuses resources on the campaign in hopes of defeating the candidate.
   b. The candidate is chosen by the group to receive its PAC money and other electoral assistance.
   c. The candidate is shot at in public by a member of the powerful National Rifle Association (NRA); if the candidate survives, he or she wins.
   d. The candidate is selected to become the head of the interest group that targeted him or her.
3. Political scientist E. E. Schattschneider criticized interest-group politics because:
   a. Too many groups compete.
   b. The poor get too much representation in interest-group politics relative to the little they contribute to the nation's prosperity.
   c. A single elite is formed secretly when interest groups are active.
   d. The poor do not have the same access to interest groups as do wealthier citizens.

4. French visitor Alexis de Tocqueville called interest groups:
   - a. associations.
   - b. pressure groups.
   - c. factions.
   - d. lobbies.

5. The primary way in which an interest group tries to influence the judiciary is through:
   - a. extravagant dinner parties.
   - b. PAC contributions.
   - c. threats.
   - d. *amicus curiae* briefs.

6. More than two-thirds of the interest groups active on the national level represent:
   - a. state and local governments.
   - b. foreign governments.
   - c. business and trade associations.
   - d. the public interest.

7. Which of the following interest groups would be *least* likely to share its mailing list with the others?
   - a. Sierra Club
   - b. Wilderness Society
   - c. National Rifle Association
   - d. Greenpeace

8. The cooperation that often exists among congressional subcommittee members, executive-branch agencies, and interest groups is termed:
   - a. an *amicus curiae.*
   - b. a trust.
   - c. an iron triangle.
   - d. a pork barrel.

9. By "molecular government," former cabinet secretary Joseph Califano means that:
   - a. Interest-group politics works well only in deciding the funding for scientific projects.
   - b. The national interest is like one huge molecule that keeps America united.
   - c. Special interest groups have fractured power in America to the point where the national interest is lost.
   - d. The government is like a molecule and the interest groups are like atoms, all waiting to explode.

10. While James Madison feared any one faction or group that would try to dominate others, how did he feel about many groups?
    - a. He feared them more than he feared one group.
    - b. He felt that many groups would balance one another out, protecting all interests.
    - c. He hoped that computerized mailing lists would solve the problem of groups communicating with one another.
    - d. He realized that the smaller the nation, the more groups that would arise.

TRUE/FALSE

11. All issues that come before the legislature have competing, countervailing interest groups involved in the final decision.
12. One of the most cohesive, unified interests in American politics is organized labor.
13. It has always been illegal for a former federal government official, regardless of her or his former position, to become a lobbyist after leaving government employment.
14. The more decentralized a nation is in terms of national, state, and local layers of government, the more likely it is to have many interest groups.
15. The Progressives of the early twentieth century opposed the dominance of big business at the expense of the influence of the average American.
16. In the 1981-82 and 1990 battles to change the standards of the Clean Air Act, the big splits among the various oil companies' positions helped the National Clean Air Coalition to keep standards strict.
17. A strong sense of individualism, Alexis de Tocqueville believed, would prevent interest groups from forming in America.
18. Corporate and public-interest groups can lobby in Washington, but state and local governments cannot legally lobby for what they want.
19. Political action committees (PACs) contribute more heavily to Democratic than Republican candidates.
20. In presidential elections during the 1980s, union leaders were very successful in getting all union members to vote solidly for Democratic candidates.

ESSAYS

21. Describe Madison's plan for an effective pluralistic system of government. Point out two ways in which modern American pluralism has fulfilled that plan and two ways in which interest-group politics has strayed from the Madisonian ideal.
22. What features make for a strong and influential interest group capable of competing in the national political arena today? For each feature you mention, cite a specific example of an interest group with that strength.
23. Criticize interest-group politics as it exists today in Washington. Mention problems such as: which interests are well represented and which are not; what people serve as lobbyists; iron triangles; and the importance of the national interest in interest-group politics.

THE MADISON TEST

Since this is a very Madisonian chapter, try taking this Madison test: Give your name in a form you do not usually use (Al D'Tocqueville, Jim Madison) to an interest group that is compiling a mailing list. Choose a public-interest or special-interest group you have some sympathy for. Then see what other interest groups get your name from shared mailing lists. Warning: Get a large mailbox or be ready to move away and change your name.

Answers

Multiple Choice

1. c p. 309
2. a p. 319
3. d p. 334
4. a p. 306
5. d p. 330

6. c p. 311
7. c pp. 319-20
8. c p. 334
9. c p. 334
10. b pp. 305-6, 331

True/False

11. f pp. 333-34
12. f p. 316
13. f pp. 308-9
14. t p. 311
15. t p. 332

16. f p. 323
17. f p. 306
18. f p. 311
19. t pp. 317-18
20. f p. 316

12 | Political Parties and Elections

Political parties and elections occupy a central position in the study of participation in the American political system. Chapter 12 gives you a complete treatment of both subjects: Political parties is Professor Ladd's major area of scholarly interest; he is the author of the well-known book *American Political Parties: Social Change and Political Response* and writes numerous articles on the current party system.

In reading chapter 12 you must be aware of the need to focus on important points and key tables. In the short amount of time allotted parties and elections in your course, you could not study exhaustively all the material Professor Ladd presents. So you should treat chapter 12 a bit more like a political science book on a specific subject – political parties and elections – than a textbook that treats only main ideas. Finding the most important information in the chapter, along with some supporting detail, is good practice as you near the end of your introductory course and look forward, if you choose, to advanced classes in political science.

Begin by reading Professor Ladd's summary at the end of the chapter to see the main topics covered in political parties and elections. Then read pp. 337-39, which introduce the chapter. The main topics to be developed in the chapter, borrowing a theme from chapter 1, are continuity and change in the American political system.

Changes to look for:

The New Deal Democratic realignment of the 1930s has given way to the current absence of any one dominant majority party.

The once strong role that political parties played in elections has weakened and the role of mass media has strengthened.

Continuities to look for:

> The basic structure of American political parties, as well as the practices of voting and elections, continues pretty much as it was in the past.

The History of the American Two-Party System

Read pp. 339-46. First become familiar with the history of American political parties. Then see how the parties operate today. Use the outline below as a guide to the important points in this section. But remember you need to search out the details from your own reading.

    I. Origin of American parties
        A. a way for individual citizens to participate (classical liberalism)
        B. oldest system of parties in the world
            1. Hamilton's Federalists
            2. Jefferson's anti-Federalist Republicans (who became Democratic-Republicans before becoming Democrats)

    II. Criticism of parties
        A. not necessary in the Constitution (Madison)
        B. splits nation against unified goal (Washington)
        C. trouble caused by opposition party (Jefferson)

    III. In support of parties
        A. a tie between citizens and their government
        B. create clear issue and policy choices (Burke)
        C. make representation possible
        D. officials held accountable for decisions
        E. ties among officials in different branches and layers of government

    IV. American two-party system
        A. contrast with European multi-party systems
        B. Democrats and Whigs (1830s)
        C. modern Democrats and Republicans (GOP, or Grand Old Party)
            1. third parties discouraged by single-member district, simple-majority elections with one winner
            2. "umbrella" parties
            3. not ideological
            4. diverse in membership
            5. easy to join
            6. little party discipline (think back to party unity voting in Congress!)

  7. weak organizations
     a. no more party "machines"
     b. no more "bosses"

[The modern Democratic and Republican parties are weak in all the ways listed above. They were not always weak. The process of the parties' losing their strong role in American electoral politics is called *dealignment.* Professor Ladd is an expert on dealignment, its causes and its consequences. More is coming on dealignment in this chapter, but by knowing the concept now you will see how it acts as a unifying theme throughout the chapter.]

  8. attempts at reform, especially by the Democrats
     a. McGovern-Fraser Commission (early 1970s)
        1. presidential convention delegates to be chosen by the people in the party (rank-and-file) not by leaders in smoke filled rooms
        2. primaries and caucuses to select delegates
        3. proportional representation to allow more candidates a chance at the convention
        4. party officials not automatically delegates

[In other words, with the parties weakening in the early 1970s, the Democrats decided to act to strengthen their party by opening it up so that average people could have a say in the selection of the Democratic presidential candidate. But paradoxically, the reforms created the opposite of what they had intended. The Democratic Party became more open, true, but open to vocal activists with intense special interests instead of to average Americans. As admirable as it may have been to include more women, people with handicaps, African Americans, gays and lesbians, Hispanics, young people, elderly people, the poor in party affairs, the Democratic Party conventions did not nominate many winners in the November elections against the Republicans.]

     b. Hunt commission (early 1980s)
        1. less strict proportional representation
        2. party officials and office holders as superdelegates automatically selected to go to conventions

[The Hunt Commission and party groups that followed tried to strike a balance between proportional representation, which opens up the convention to many candidates, and superdelegates who emphasize the need for the party to nominate a candidate who can win against the Republicans in November. The 1992 Democratic ticket of Bill Clinton and Al Gore was a successful attempt to nominate candidates who could not only please the Democratic Party activists but could win the election.]

This discussion of party reform is an example of the excellent detail that Professor Ladd provides in chapter 12. Try to grasp the basic idea, but do not get bogged down learning every nuance. You can study party reform in depth in an advanced political science course on political parties.

Elections in the United States

Begin by reading pp. 346-52.

SINGLE-MEMBER DISTRICTS

Start with Professor Ladd's Votersland example. Do you see how different methods of electing officials can greatly influence who gets elected? In the outline above you have already seen that the United States uses primarily a single-member district, simple-majority, single-ballot system of elections. This can be quite a complicated subject to explore and to compare with plural-member, proportional representation systems. You will need to know more about electoral systems when you take a comparative government course. For now, think about most U.S. elections: two people run, one wins. The loser and the loser's party, no matter how close the election is (49.9 percent to 50.1 percent), win nothing.

PRIMARIES AND CAUCUSES

Also in the previous outline is mention of primaries, another form of American elections. Primaries choose the candidates who will run for each party, and they can occur at all levels, presidential elections to elections for seats in the state legislature. During what historical period were primaries introduced? What is their purpose? How important are primaries today? What degrees of commitment to a candidate are delegates who are selected in presidential primaries required to make? Primaries can be open (to independents) or closed (only for registered party members). Some states have caucuses (statewide party meetings) instead of primaries. Most famous in presidential years are the Iowa caucuses and the New Hampshire primary, the first real primary in the nation.

REAPPORTIONMENT

In chapter 2 you studied the ethnic and cultural make-up of the United States, called demographics. Is there socioeconomic mobility in America? Have the regions of the United States changed in their relative wealth? Individual and regional changes are both cause and effect of population changes, as people move from one area in the country to another to seek jobs, lower taxes, sun, or fun. Every ten years the census reveals the results of immigration, the numbers of children born to various groups, and the numbers of people who relocate. After the census congressional districts are redrawn (as are state legislative districts) and votes in the electoral college are refigured. Evening out district sizes is called *reapportionment*. In the early 1960s the Supreme Court said that "one person, one vote" must prevail. Be sure you know the two court cases which decided that districts had to be equal in population.

The way in which districts are reapportioned by state legislatures is even more interesting. *Gerrymandering* describes the process of drawing new district lines to benefit one party, the party that controls the legislature at the time of reapportionment. Gerrymandering can be done by people or by computers with various outcomes as a goal, such as making a safe Democratic seat competitive; protecting a safe Republican seat; electing a minority-group member to the legislature; even guarding an incumbent's job.

Study Figure 12.1 in the text. Be ready to note three specific population trends apparent from the 1990 census. How did they affect redistricting?

Democratic and Republican Strength in Recent Elections

Read pp. 352-65. There is a lot of material here. The main points to look for in the reading are:

> 1930s New Deal Democratic alignment
> changed party identification of certain groups in the 1980s
>
> 1992 party identification (Figure 12.2)
> the public's view of Democrats' versus Republicans' ability to insure
> prosperity (Figure 12.3)
>
> Democratic dominance of Congress
> Republican dominance of the presidency
> no majority party
> *Dealignment:* "A dealigned electorate is like an unanchored boat – it can
> be easily moved."
> ticket-splitting
> independents
> weakened party organizations
> stronger role for mass media
> ambivalence among voters

Democratic strength among older voters (Table 12.1)
Republican gains, especially among younger voters
increase in independents
one-third Democratic, one-third Republican, one-third Independent

black Americans – overwhelmingly Democratic (Chairman Brown,
    Mayor Dinkins, Governor Wilder, Reverend Jackson)
Hispanic Americans – party preference based on socioeconomic status
white Southerners – major shift to Republican Party from past Demo-
    cratic loyalty (once "Solid South")
women – some "gender gap" favoring Democrats
socioeconomic differences – more educated, higher income groups favor
    Republicans (Table 12.5)

In the section you have just completed Professor Ladd offers a wealth of demographic data on party loyalties in the past and in the present among American voters. You are not expected to memorize all these statistics. But try to be aware of the main trends noted in the list of key concepts above. This information is important for an understanding of what happened in the 1992 presidential election, as well as the outcomes of the 1994 off-year (congressional) and the 1996 presidential elections. You can also use the information you have just studied as a reference source for papers or in heated political arguments.

American Elections: Who Pays? Who Votes?

Finish reading chapter 12. Use the outline below as a guide. While there are some technical and statistical points you will have to learn from this section, much of this reading involves highly controversial topics. Review PACs (political action committees) from chapter 11. Get your facts assembled and then do not hesitate to join in the shouting match about money and voting in American elections.

    I. Campaigns are lengthy and costly.
        A. Federal Election Campaign Act (FECA) set up Federal Election
           Commission (FEC) to monitor money contributed to campaigns.
        B. Contribution limits exist for all national offices. (Table 12.6)
           1. An individual contributor can give each candidate $1,000 per
              election; can give a PAC $5,000 yearly; can give altogether
              $25,000 yearly.
           2. A PAC can give each candidate $5,000 per election; can give
              other PACs $5,000 yearly; no total yearly limit.
           3. Table 12.6 includes further FECA limits.

C. Spending limits exist for presidential candidates who take public funds for their campaigns.

   1. Public funding exists only for the presidential election, although Congress has considered public funding for congressional candidates.

   2. In the primary and caucus stage, presidential candidates who raise a certain amount of money get federal matching funds up to a set limit.

   3. After the party conventions select nominees, candidates get full federal funding to a limit of $45 million plus.

   4. A candidate who refuses public funds (as Ross Perot said he would in 1992) has no spending limit.

   5. A lot of non-FEC reported PAC money, called "soft money," finds its way into campaigns. Tighter limits on PAC contributions have been proposed in Congress but not passed. Surprised?

II. Too much money?

  A. Americans spend a lot of money on a lot of things. Should the nation economize on choosing public officials?

  B. Mass media dominates campaigns today, and media is expensive.

  C. Democratic candidates get more PAC money than Republicans because PAC money goes mostly to incumbents.

   1. For example, Table 12.7 shows that in 1989-90 corporate PACs gave $43.7 million to incumbents and only $4.9 million to challengers.

   2. This is a chicken-and-egg phenomenon.

   3. What does this tell you about the role of PAC money in politics?

  D. As a party the Republicans have been more successful at fundraising than Democrats. (Table 12.8)

  E. While proposals for reform have been suggested, interest-group money is probably here to stay in American politics. See the cartoon on p. 372.

  F. If nothing else, FEC reporting tells the public a lot about who contributes how much to whom. See the extremely interesting Table 12.9. Doctors, realtors, lawyers, teachers, public employees, union workers: Here is the place to remember the criticism that interest-group politics favors groups with a large cohesive membership, money, organization, and intensity. True?

Professor Ladd next goes on to examine the way American political campaigns are conducted. Both from the book and from your own experience, comment on:

political consultants
television
30-section sound bite
the press corps
C-SPAN
direct-mail
polling
"like selling soap?"
negative ads

The chapter on political parties and elections closes with one of the most important questions in political science today: Why is voter turnout so low? You need to know the turnout in the 1988 presidential election (53 percent) and in 1992 (see the special 1992 presidential election section in Appendix 4 of *The American Polity*). From Figure 12.4 in the text, what has happened to voter turnout since 1960? What was the turnout in the 1990 off-year congressional election? Organize the material on voter turnout and your own personal views on this problem around the following questions:

1. Is low voter turnout a result of legal barriers that prevent citizens from voting?
2. How do registration procedures affect voter turnout? What new measures are proposed to increase voter registration? If voter turnout were measured as a percentage of those registered, would turnout be more respectable?
3. How has dealignment increased the problem of low voter turnout?
4. Which demographic characteristics are the best predictors of who will vote? In other words, who votes in the highest percentages? What does having a stake in the system mean?
5. From Table 12.12, which age group votes in the least numbers? Which age groups votes in the highest numbers?
6. How do the many elections (national, state, local) that occur in the United States affect voter turnout?
7. What are two conflicting theories about the reason for low voter turnout? In what way could low turnout be a healthy sign for the American polity? By contrast, which people in the United States do not vote and what negative, even dangerous, attitudes may their opting out imply?

The debate about the reasons for low voter turnout is a loaded one because it gets at the question of how Americans feel about their role in the polity. Professor Ladd brings up the important question of voters' "efficacy," the sense that they matter in the political process. Could some voters lack a feeling of efficacy in the complicated, distant, inside-the-beltway world of postindustrial American politics? Recall the feelings of Ross Perot's supporters in 1992. As you go out into the real world and watch president after president be elected and take office, stay aware of voter turnout, of who votes and who does not. If you don't vote, ask yourself why.

For some colorful tidbits on parties and elections, spend a few minutes in the "Cases" section of the *Study Guide*. The chapter 12 excerpts begin with Gerald Gardner's single paragraph on 1950s presidential candidate Adlai Stevenson, then move to Christopher Matthews' brief account of two top campaigners from the 1980s. Celia Morris tells what worked and what did not for 1990 California gubernatorial (governor) candidate Dianne Feinstein. Former Senator Tim Wirth closes with his decision to leave the Senate in 1992.

Sample Test Questions

MULTIPLE CHOICE—SELECT THE *BEST* ANSWER

1. American political parties have all of the following characteristics *except*:
   a. They are informal.
   b. They are undisciplined.
   c. They are tightly organized.
   d. They are willing to accept a variety of views.
2. Which group is currently most solidly Democratic in its voting patterns?
   a. black Americans
   b. Hispanic Americans
   c. white Southerners
   d. women
3. The phrase that best describes the Supreme Court's view on reapportionment in *Baker v. Carr* (1962) and *Wesberry v. Sanders* (1963) is:
   a. "Ambition must be made to counteract ambition."
   b. "of the people, by the people, for the people."
   c. "the party's over."
   d. "one person, one vote."
4. The Democratic Party's 1972 McGovern-Fraser reforms:
   a. increased the number and importance of presidential primaries.
   b. added more superdelegates at the convention.
   c. were motivated by similar reforms already enacted by the Republican Party.
   d. made it easier for the party to choose a winning presidential candidate.
5. The single most important predictor of whether an American will vote or not is:
   a. income.
   b. race.
   c. education.
   d. occupation.

6. The gender gap means that:
   a. While black Americans usually vote Democratic, black women vote Republican.
   b. Men vote in much greater numbers than do women.
   c. Women vote for women candidates by overwhelming percentages.
   d. Women vote for Democratic candidates in higher percentages than do men with similar demographic characteristics.
7. Which of the following are provisions of the Federal Election Campaign Act?
   > I. Individuals can contribute $1,000 to each candidate at one election.
   > II. PACs can contribute $5,000 to each candidate at one election.
   > III. An individual has no limit on total yearly contributions.
   > IV. A PAC has no limit on total yearly contributions.
   a. I and II only
   b. I, III, and IV only
   c. I, II, and IV only
   d. I, II, III, and IV
8. The most dramatic change in a group's party loyalty during the 1980s came from:
   a. white Southerners' shift away from the Democrats and toward the Republicans.
   b. young people's shift away from the Republicans and toward the Democrats.
   c. Catholic voters' move toward the Democrats.
   d. wealthy Americans' new allegiance with the Republicans.
9. All of the following are characteristic of a time of dealigned political parties *except*:
   a. a large role for political consultants in campaigns.
   b. PAC financing for individual candidates.
   c. strong party bosses.
   d. campaigning dominated by mass media messages.
10. Which political thinker most favored the existence of strong political parties?
   a. Thomas Jefferson
   b. James Madison
   c. Edmund Burke
   d. Aristotle

TRUE/FALSE

11. Environmental PACs are the biggest contributors to campaigns in the United States.

12. The United States has among the most complicated voter registration laws of any democracy.
13. The Constitution contains a provision mandating the existence of two political parties to be named Democrats and Republicans, since the United States is both a democracy and a republic.
14. During the presidential primaries, candidates who receive a designated amount of contributions from the public receive federal funds that match their expenses up to a set limit.
15. Single-member district, simple-majority elections encourage a two-party system.

IDENTIFICATION—DESCRIBE BRIEFLY

16. "umbrella" parties
17. Hunt Commission
18. gerrymandering
19. incumbents
20. efficacy

ESSAYS

21. What does Professor Ladd mean when he says that "A dealigned electorate is like an unanchored boat. . . ."? Examine the concept of dealignment. What are some specific reasons for dealignment, and what are symptoms of it? How is party identification affected by dealignment? Form your own opinion about whether dealignment is a good or bad development in American electoral politics.
22. Describe the most dramatic changes that have taken place among voters as the 1930s New Deal Democratic alignment has given way to the current party system. Identify the group that has changed party identification significantly, as well as other key groups whose loyalties are important in the party system of the 1990s. Does one party dominate in elections today?
23. Chart the course of voter turnout in the United States over the past three decades. Cite some statistics to substantiate your point. Then explore fully the reasons advanced for low voter turnout in America. Be sure to include all the possible reasons even though some are contradictory. Could more than one explanation be correct? What are your views about why many Americans do not vote?

Answers

Multiple Choice

1. c pp. 342-44
2. a pp. 360-65
3. d pp. 350-51
4. a p. 345
5. c p. 382

6. d p. 364
7. c p. 367
8. a p. 362
9. c p. 344, 355-56
10. c pp. 339-40

True/False

11. f p. 371
12. t pp. 378-79
13. f p. 340
14. t p. 368
15. t pp. 347-49

Identification

16. Parties such as America's Democrats and Republicans are termed "umbrella" parties because they are not rigid in their ideologies. Each party contains a variety of political ideas underneath its wide banner, with compromise the method of achieving party unity. p. 342

17. The early 1980s Hunt Commission stepped back from the Democratic Party reforms of McGovern-Fraser a decade earlier by including more party officials at the nominating conventions as automatic superdelegates. The Hunt rules also reduced the splintering effect of proportional representation for candidates who had run in primaries and caucuses. Yet the Democratic convention remained more open to rank-and-file members than it had been before the 1970s, leading some insiders to feel that the party was actually weakening itself. pp. 345-46

18. As population shifts demand reapportionment every ten years after the census, state legislatures redraw district boundaries. Gerrymandering is an old American phenomenon that allows the majority party in the state legislature to redraw the lines in ways that will benefit the party, protect party incumbents, or insure a seat for a minority group member. Gerrymandering can be done by legislators or by computers, but its results are rarely unbiased politically. pp. 351-52

19. Incumbents are candidates who already hold office. In the past decade incumbents have been reelected by high percentages (95 percent plus) due to the availability of staff, the franking privilege, and media coverage. Most PAC dollars go to incumbents regardless of their party affiliation; Democrats get more PAC money because there are more Democratic incumbents. Because PAC contributions are so important in elections,

challengers have a difficult time raising campaign funds. Critics assert that PAC money is just a way for powerful interests to "buy" access to legislators. p. 369

20. Efficacy means a sense that your vote matters. One reason why half of the American electorate does not vote in presidential elections may be a sense of a lack of efficacy due to the size, scale, and impersonal nature of government in America today. p. 382

13 | The Media

Since discussion of the role of the mass media in American politics has been woven throughout the "Participation" section of *The American Polity*, it is a subject you already know a lot about. So it is not necessary to cover this chapter in depth. Instead, just read all of chapter 13 in one sitting. then confirm your grasp of the mass media with the sample test questions below. To make this short-cut successful, you must be attentive to the key ideas included in each question.

Sample Test Questions

MULTIPLE CHOICE—SELECT THE *BEST* ANSWER

1. News about international events such as the student uprising in China's Tiananmen Square in 1989, the 1989 American invasion of Panama, and the 1991 Persian Gulf War was brought into American homes most quickly and most fully by:
   a. Home Box Office (HBO).   c. college radio.
   b. Cable News Network (CNN).   d. the Voice of America.
2. Based on the information on television technologies in Figure 13.2, which of the following statements is true?
   a. Americans who purchase VCRs watch rented movies instead of network news shows.
   b. Almost all Americans have more than one TV set in their home.
   c. Color TV did not become available until 1975.
   d. Cable TV has become available to more U.S. homes each year since it began in 1970.

3. Most citizens gather information about politics today in all of the following ways *except*:
   a. first-hand experience.
   b. television.
   c. newspapers.
   d. news magazines.

4. Which national newspaper is most widely read?
   a. *New York Times*
   b. *Wall Street Journal*
   c. *Advocate*
   d. *Pentagon Papers*

5. Reporters for important national newspapers earn:
   a. very big bucks (over $200,000/year).
   b. big bucks (over $100,000/year).
   c. decent upper-middle class bucks (over $40,000/year).
   d. not very much, but the job is fulfilling (under $40,000/year).

6. Well-known TV news anchors earn:
   a. huge salaries.
   b. an average middle-class wage.
   c. only a percentage commission, based on how many scandals are uncovered.
   d. an amount equivalent to the official poverty level in the United States.

7. Who owns print and electronic media in the United States?
   a. political parties
   b. interest groups
   c. the government
   d. private individuals and corporations

8. Is there government regulation of media in the United States?
   a. some, but only of TV and radio stations
   b. some, but only of the printed press
   c. yes, of all forms of mass media
   d. no, not of any forms of mass media

9. The independent regulatory commission that licenses the use of the airwaves is the:
   a. FEC.
   b. FCC.
   c. CNN.
   d. CBO.

10. An independent regulatory commission is located in the _____ branch of government, and is subject to _____ amounts of political control.
    a. executive; minimal
    b. judicial; minimal
    c. legislative; moderate
    d. legislative; maximal

11. In the 1980s the regulatory commission identified in question 9 repealed the fairness doctrine, which had provided for:
    a. the fair treatment of female reporters.
    b. the same amount of time to be sold to opposing candidates.
    c. the broadcasting of an opposing viewpoint when a position on a much-debated issue was presented.
    d. fairness in court when libel cases were brought.

12. When is the equal-time provision administered by the commission identified in question 9 most important?
    a. during a revolution, so that the revolutionaries can run free ads
    b. during an election, so that opposition candidates can purchase campaign time
    c. during a session of Congress, so that citizens can be required to watch C-SPAN live twenty-four hours a day
    d. after an election, so that the news media can second-guess the decision of the American voters

13. The *Red Lion* case (1969) involved:
    a. the fairness doctrine.   c. the right-of-rebuttal.
    b. the equal-time provision.   d. libel law.

14. A libel case is difficult to win in court for all of the following reasons *except*:
    a. The Constitution prohibits a private citizen from suing the press.
    b. The accuser must prove that "actual malice" existed when the lie was written.
    c. People who are public figures can be written about negatively in a way that average people cannot be.
    d. The First Amendment gives the press a lot of latitude in what it writes.

15. An important publisher of the late 1800s who began the trend toward wide-circulation newspapers was:
    a. Walter Cronkite.   c. Joseph Pulitzer.
    b. Douglass Cater.   d. Brian Lamb.

16. An important turn-of-the-century publisher who encouraged newspaper sales through sensational "yellow journalism" was:
    a. William Randolph Hearst.   c. Robert McNeil.
    b. Patty Hearst.   d. Orson Welles.

17. For campaign and election news, approximately 86 percent of all Americans rely mostly on:
    a. newspapers.
    b. television.
    c. scholarly political science journals.
    d. door-to-door visits by party workers.

18. Polls show that the most trusted place for Americans to get their news today is:
    a. newspapers.   c. political science textbooks.
    b. television.   d. mailgrams from politicians.

19. The cartoon on p. 407 suggests that when members of the press act as "talent scouts" in promoting or sabotaging candidacies, they focus on:
    a. national issues.
    b. private vendettas.
    c. personal moral and character flaws.
    d. party positions.

20. The increased importance of the mass media in campaigns has con-
    tributed to:
    a. dealignment.   c. judicial activism.
    b. party cohesion.   d. the iron triangle.
21. The attitude of the contemporary press toward the president can best be
    described as:
    a. intense interest, usually hostile.
    b. little interest, thus indifferent.
    c. constant attention, often adversarial.
    d. much attention, always friendly.
22. The role that the mass media takes in checking the actions of government
    has led one journalist to describe the press as:
    a. "yellow-dog Democrats."
    b. "country-club Republicans."
    c. "first in the hearts of their countrymen."
    d. "the fourth branch of government."
23. Surveys have revealed that the personal political sentiment of a majority
    of journalists is:
    a. liberal.   c. fascist.
    b. conservative.   d. socialist.
24. Studies have revealed that significant political bias is found most often in
    the news coverage of:
    a. third-party candidates in presidential campaigns.
    b. military invasions and wars.
    c. Supreme Court decisions.
    d. public safety and consumer rights issues.
25. Overall, the attitude of the press in their political reporting can best be
    described as:
    a. disinterested.   c. nasty.
    b. cynical.   d. genteel.
26. The "neutral" or "liberal" approach to news coverage stresses:
    a. investigation and a willingness to take a position.
    b. impartial treatment of the facts.
    c. exposure of personal character flaws in public officials.
    d. the need to sell a lot of papers or achieve high TV ratings.
27. The "participant" or "partisan" approach to news coverage stresses:
    a. investigation and a willingness to take a position.
    b. impartial treatment of the facts.
    c. exposure of personal character flaws in public officials.
    d. the need to sell a lot of papers or achieve high TV ratings.

28. The FCC regulates radio and television by:
    a. monitoring all shows and looking for bias.
    b. conducting secret investigations to spot-check stations.
    c. checking compliance with rules when licenses come up for renewal.
    d. assigning X, R, PG, PG-13, or G ratings to all shows.
29. The constitutional provision protecting the right of the press to speak out is:
    a. the First Amendment's free exercise clause.
    b. the First Amendment's freedom of speech and freedom of the press clause.
    c. the Fourteenth Amendment's equal protection clause.
    d. the Fifth Amendment's noncompulsion to be a witness against oneself clause.
30. Live gavel-to-gavel coverage of the House of Representatives is available on cable TV on:
    a. CNN.
    b. the Playboy channel.
    c. C-SPAN.
    d. the shopping channel.

ESSAYS

31. Discuss the media's cynical attitude in its coverage of political campaigns and political news. First, offer several specific recent examples. Then, explore the historical origin of press cynicism. Is this negative attitude an inherent part of the media's role in American politics? Is it a good or a bad feature of the media?
32. What changes have occurred over time in the structure and influence of the press in the United States? Offer detail on the structure of the press today. How many Americans are reached, how are they reached, and how do they respond to mass media messages? Include in your answer as many specific pieces of evidence as you can.

For your perusal, the chapter 13 excerpts in the "Cases" section of the *Study Guide* highlight three reporters' stories. Choose between Russell Baker, a veteran newspaperman, and Helen Thomas, who recalls covering the White House during the Kennedy years. End by reading Gwenda Blair's tragic story of anchorwoman Jessica Savitch. This piece was not included in the *Study Guide* as sensational yellow journalism, but rather to illustrate what a talented, educated, energetic person (like you) should *not* do along the road to success.

THE MADISON TEST

Would Madison have praised or condemned the "fourth branch" as it operates to check governmental power today? Does the "fourth branch" balance or unbalance the power of the three branches of government?

Answers

Multiple Choice

1.	b	p. 389	16.	a	p. 402
2.	d	p. 391	17.	b	p. 403
3.	a	pp. 391-93	18.	b	p. 404
4.	b	p. 394	19.	c	p. 407
5.	c	p. 394	20.	a	pp. 406-7
6.	a	p. 394	21.	c	pp. 407-8
7.	d	pp. 395-96	22.	d	p. 408
8.	a	p. 396	23.	a	pp. 410-11
9.	b	p. 396	24.	d	p. 412
10.	a	p. 396	25.	b	pp. 412-13
11.	c	pp. 396-97	26.	b	pp. 413-14
12.	b	p. 397	27.	a	pp. 413-14
13.	c	p. 397	28.	c	p. 396
14.	a	pp. 398-99	29.	b	p. 399
15.	c	p. 401	30.	c	p. 400

14 | Civil Liberties and Civil Rights

In chapter 14, Professor Ladd opens his examination of public policy. Public policy involves applying the principles of American government to the world of real political problems and solutions. Actually, public policy has been considered throughout *The American Polity.* Here it becomes the primary focus.

Chapter 14, which examines civil liberties and civil rights in the United States is a natural extension of chapter 9 on the judiciary. (In fact, your professor may have coupled chapters 9 and 14 together in the course.) The chapter contains material on the Constitution; the civil rights movement; equal pay for women; the rights of persons accused of crimes; and freedom of speech. You will encounter many Supreme Court cases in this chapter, so refresh your memory of the judiciary material.

Just a note: Read chapter 14 both as an American government student and as an American citizen (or resident) for whom civil rights and civil liberties can be a lot more important than a chapter in a textbook, without warning, anytime.

Civil Liberties and Civil Rights

After reading pp. 421-23, you should be ready to elaborate on the following concepts to be used throughout the chapter.

Bill of Rights
Fourteenth Amendment

Civil liberties of individuals and those with minority beliefs
Civil rights of groups discriminated against by accident of birth

rights citizens are entitled to versus benefits given by political decisions
majority rule versus protection of the individual and minorities

If you can answer the questions that follow, you will be off to a good start.

1. What specific parts of the Constitution are involved in civil liberties and civil rights issues? State specific phrases from these constitutional provisions.
2. In what way do the phrases *civil liberties* and *civil rights* mean basically the same thing? How are they used differently when applied to specific situations?
3. How are civil liberties and civil rights different from political decisions that benefit or penalize certain citizens?
4. In what way is the tension between majority rule and minority rights – the essence of a polity! – exemplified by the issue of civil liberties and civil rights?

Flag Burning as a Symbolic Gesture

Read pp. 423-28. Do you see how your own strong feelings after reading these pages illustrate exactly what Professor Ladd writes about the importance of the issue in the United States?

TEXAS V. JOHNSON

After reading about *Texas v. Johnson* (1989), you should be able to explain:

1. what Gregory Lee Johnson had done, where he had done it, and why.
2. what state law Johnson had violated and what constitutional provision allegedly protected him.
3. what the majority of the Supreme Court decided about Johnson's act and why.
4. how the Court voted and what the dissenters argued.

UNITED STATES V. EICHMAN

After reading about *United States v. Eichman* (1990), you should be able to explain:

1. why the process for a constitutional amendment was not initially introduced.
2. how Congress responded.
3. how the Supreme Court responded to Congress's response.
4. what the Congress did next.
5. why the matter has ended for the present.

Summarize for yourself how the flag burning issue reveals the paradox of majority rule and minority rights.

The American Civil Rights Movement

As you read pp. 428-47, note that Professor Ladd is giving you not only the key legal decisions in recent civil rights cases but also a fine overview of the struggle for civil rights in the twentieth century. The many tables and figures provide up-to-date evidence on how racial (and gender) differences affect individuals' progress in American society. (Since issues of civil rights come up frequently in liberal arts courses, you should hold onto your copy of *The American Polity* so that you will have easy access to this kind of data. You can save yourself hours of research in the future by borrowing information from Professor Ladd – citing the source as explained in the *Study Guide*'s introduction, of course.)

To any student of history, government, sociology, or psychology, this material on the civil rights movement in America is extremely thought-provoking, whether or not you have studied it previously. Read the pages through first for pure interest and enjoyment, without worrying about each point you need to know. Then use the outline below to master the facts.

CIVIL RIGHTS FOR BLACK AMERICANS

   I. Historic discrimination
      A. southern states' "Jim Crow" laws
      B. *Plessy v. Ferguson* (1896) – "separate but equal"
      C. segregated facilities
      D. violence, even lynchings
      E. 5 percent black voter registration (1940)
      F. "A house divided against itself cannot stand." (President Lincoln, 1858)

   II. Demands for change
      A. movement of black citizens to the North (Figure 14.2)
         1. 90 percent in South – 1900
         2. 52 percent in South – 1975
         3. 54 percent in South – 1990
      B. movement of black citizens to the cities
      C. *Brown v. Board of Education of Topeka* (1954)
         1. NAACP
         2. overturned *Plessy*

    3. "Separate educational facilities are inherently unequal." (Chief Justice Warren)

    4. unanimous decision

  D. non-violent protest

    1. Rosa Parks (listen to the Neville Brothers' "Sister Rosa" on *Yellow Moon*)

    2. Reverend Martin Luther King, Jr.

    3. marches, sit-ins, protests

  E. federal laws

    1. Civil Rights Act of 1964

    2. Voting Rights Act of 1965

III. Successes and failures

  A. shifts in public opinion toward racial acceptance (National Opinion Research Center data and Figure 14.3)

  B. black voting

    1. similar percentage as whites (Figure 14.4)

    2. steady increase in black office holders (Figure 14.5)

  C. black educational achievements

    1. similar percentage as whites finishing high school (Figure 14.6, Table 14.2)

    2. some gap in college completion (Table 14.2)

  D. black unemployment twice that of whites (Figure 14.7)

  E. events such as Rodney King beating, trial, aftermath

  F. inner-city problems and poverty (chapter 15)

AFFIRMATIVE ACTION FOR MINORITY GROUPS

I. Programs to make up for past racial discrimination

  A. employment and education

  B. controversy among Americans and within black community

  C. *Sheet Metal Workers' International v. Equal Employment Opportunity Commission* (1986)

    1. union membership racially proportional to percentage of workforce

    2. 5-4 decision, with dissent denouncing quota

  D. *Wygant v. Jackson Board of Education* (1986)

    1. senior white teacher reinstated

    2. 5-4 decision, with dissent citing importance of more black teachers

  E. the classic *Regents of University of California v. Bakke* (1978)

    1. quotas for minority students at state medical school

    2. age, timing, qualifications, rejection of Allan Bakke

3. 4-4-1 decision, calling for Bakke's admittance but upholding some plans to correct past discrimination as valid
4. "both sides are right"

II. Comparable worth for jobs held by women
   A. women's pay is less than men's for a variety of reasons (Figure 14.8)
   B. congressional language of "equal work" instead of "comparable work"
   C. on-going debate on comparable worth and comparable pay for different jobs requiring similar abilities

Persons Accused of Crimes: The Bill of Rights and Selective Incorporation

Next Professor Ladd turns to one of the most important but, in all honesty, most difficult topics in the course: selective incorporation. As you read pp. 447-56, consider this topic both as a student of American government and as a citizen of the United States. The concept of selective incorporation must be understood on both levels.

As Professor Ladd relates, when the Bill of Rights (the first ten amendments) was passed, right after the Constitution was ratified, the American people were concerned about protecting the liberties of individuals against the newly strengthened national government. (Open to Appendix 2, pp. A13-A15, and scan the Bill of Rights to see what rights are protected; it is a familiar list.) What they had not foreseen were problems at the state level, where rights were included only if a state chose to include them in its constitution. There were problems particularly in the southern states, where, after the Civil War, black citizens were not given the same rights whites had. (Refer to the outline on civil rights earlier in this chapter to recall the term for the laws in southern states that discriminated against blacks.) To force the southern states to grant rights to African Americans, the Thirteenth, Fourteenth, and Fifteenth Amendments were ratified in 1865, 1868, and 1870. The Thirteenth Amendment – abolishing slavery – and the Fifteenth Amendment – extending the vote to black men – confer specific rights, but the Fourteenth Amendment is vague.

Read Section 1 of that amendment to pick out the two key phrases that apply to *state* governments: ". . . nor shall any State deprive any person of life, liberty, or property, without due process of law; nor deny to any person within its jurisdiction the equal protection of the laws." Since most people who run afoul of the law do so on the state level, the Supreme Court had a goal: to make the Bill of Rights apply to individuals on the state level where it was needed. Here is what the Supreme Court had to work with: a prohibition against *states*; a requirement for *due process*; a requirement for *equal protection*. By using these constitutional provisions the Supreme Court "incorporated," right by right and case by case, making the Bill of Rights apply to the states. The Supreme Court, in cases brought before it, determined that the due process clause of the Fourteenth Amendment required that specific rights in the Bill of Rights be guaranteed to individuals by states.

Selective incorporation is a fine example of judicial activism, which you learned about in chapter 9. Why is the process of selective (case by case) incorporation activist? Judicial activism creates precedent for actions that the Court believes are good for American society. When the Supreme Court decides a case not merely by reading and applying the exact words of the Constitution but by interpreting the Constitution's meaning, it sets precedent and extends the law. The Constitution does not actually say that the states cannot deny a individual freedom of speech, freedom of religion, freedom to assemble; the right to a speedy trial, to confront witnesses, to consult a lawyer, to be tried by a jury; protection from cruel and unusual punishments, self-incrimination, unreasonable search and seizure. But by interpreting the Constitution to *mean* that states must protect these rights, the Court sets precedent that becomes the law of the land.

Selective incorporation, by the way, not only revealed the activist nature of the Supreme Court (beginning earlier, but becoming particularly activist in the 1960s under Chief Justice Earl Warren), but also demonstrated the growth of the national government's power over the states in the era of the New Deal and beyond.

Supporters of selective incorporation believe that the Supreme Court interpreted the Constitution correctly by incorporating individual rights so that they apply to state governments. Why should a person be denied a right by a state when the right was protected from abuse by the national government? Opponents of incorporation feel that the Supreme Court went far beyond proper constitutional interpretation in creating restrictions on states that were not written into the Constitution. This debate has had an effect in many areas: in the areas of majority rule versus minority rights; national versus state authority; legislative versus judicial power.

In Table 14.3 Professor Ladd encapsulates the history of selective incorporation. Without memorizing every case, you should be able to answer the questions below:

> *Mapp v. Ohio* (1961)
> > What were the facts of the case?
> > What right was incorporated?
> > What is the exclusionary rule?
> > [You should also know how the exclusionary rule was modified as a result of *Brewer v. Williams*.]

Gideon v. Wainwright (1963)
> What were the facts of the case? [This is the best human story in all
> of political science.]
> What right was incorporated?
> [Read *Gideon's Trumpet* by Anthony Lewis when you have time; for
> now, rent the film starring Henry Fonda.]

Miranda v. Arizona (1966)
> What were the facts of the case?
> What are the Miranda Rules and your Miranda rights?
> How have the Miranda Rules been adjusted and changed in recent
> cases?

The Supreme Court must interpret individuals' rights according to the particular circumstances of the case in front of the Court. How has the Court dealt with unreasonable search and seizure protection in the case of drug and alcohol testing? Mention issues of public safety. What about random roadside checks for drunk drivers?

Professor Ladd concludes the section on rights protected by the Bill of Rights by returning to the paradox of a polity: majority rule vs. minority rights. Both are important, and finding the balance between them is difficult. The point of balance changes with the times. After reading this section, you should be able to answer the questions below.

1. Where was the emphasis during the 1960s when Earl Warren was Chief Justice of the Supreme Court: on the rights of the majority in society, or on the rights of individuals accused of crimes? Why was that the Court's emphasis then?
2. What problems arose from the Warren Court's decisions?
3. How did *Brewer v. Williams* (1977), the facts of which you should know because they are very dramatic, illustrate the Court's dilemma? Explain the Court's later "full and fair trial," "inevitable discovery," and "good faith exception" modifications to the exclusionary rule and the Miranda Rules.
4. How has the current Supreme Court further modified the exclusionary rule and Miranda rights? In what way does the Court's acceptance of a "coerced confession" as a "harmless error" in *Arizona v. Fulminante* (1991) reveal the changes in attitude of the Court from the 1960s to the 1990s?

Even after your American government course has ended, try to follow the Supreme Court's decisions as reported in the news. Decisions like *Mapp, Gideon, Miranda,* and *Arizona v. Fulminante* are not just items to be learned for a great grade on the final. They are cases that can affect any citizen unexpectedly on any day. It is easy to dismiss the rights of persons accused of crimes as unimportant because "they're all guilty anyway," until you are the person accused.

Free Speech

The final topic in chapter 14 is the First Amendment right to freedom of expression. Read and study pp. 456-60 on your own, keeping the following key concepts in mind:

> First Amendment
> *Schenck v. United States* (1919)
> Justice Oliver Wendell Holmes
> "falsely shouting fire in a theater"
>
> anti-Communist Smith Act
> *Dennis v. United States* (1951)
> "clear and present danger"
>
> *Brandenburg v. Ohio* (1969)
> "mere advocacy"
> "imminent lawless action"
>
> obscenity and pornography
> *Miller v. California* (1973)
> "contemporary community standards"
> "serious literary, artistic, political, or scientific value"

The "Cases" section for chapter 14 of the *Study Guide* will jog your memory about the 1990 controversy over 2 Live Crew's allegedly obscene lyrics. Edward de Grazia tells the story through the comments of those involved in *Girls Lean Back Everywhere.*

Sample Test Questions

MULTIPLE CHOICE—SELECT THE *BEST* ANSWER

1. In *Regents of University of California v. Bakke* (1978) the Supreme Court declared:
   a. all plans to admit minorities to medical school unconstitutional.
   b. all plans to admit minorities to medical school constitutional.
   c. some plans to admit minorities to medical school constitutional, but in this case Allan Bakke was entitled to admission despite the plan.
   d. Allan Bakke's plans to go to medical school unconstitutional because of his age and race.

2. The two most important pieces of legislation on civil rights were:
   a. the Civil Rights Act of 1964 and the Voting Rights Act of 1965.
   b. the Civil Rights Acts of 1957 and 1960.
   c. the Martin Luther King Act.
   d. the Smith Act.

3. *Texas v. Johnson* (1989) can only be effectively overturned by:
   a. a congressional law.
   b. a state law.
   c. an executive action.
   d. a constitutional amendment.

4. The Supreme Court's most long-standing test of free speech has been the doctrine of:
   a. "contemporary community standards."
   b. "imminent lawless action."
   c. "clear and present danger."
   d. "separate but equal."

5. *Comparable worth* means that:
   a. Jobs done by men and those done by women should be paid equally if they require the same skill.
   b. Men and women should be worth the same amount if Congress so deems.
   c. Men should be transferred to traditionally women's jobs and should be paid less to compensate for years of discrimination against women.
   d. No amount of effort needed to do a job well is worth it if the pay is not extremely high.

6. All of the following resulted from *Mapp v. Ohio* (1961) *except* that:
   a. Coerced confessions were no longer allowed.
   b. Evidence illegally obtained was excluded from the courtroom.
   c. Protection from an unreasonable search and seizure was granted on the state level.
   d. The Fourth Amendment's unreasonable search and seizure protection was incorporated into the Fourteenth Amendment.

7. The civil rights movement has brought progress to African Americans in all of the following ways *except*:
   a. rates of high-school graduation almost equivalent to white Americans.
   b. increasing numbers of African American office holders.
   c. lower unemployment rates than white Americans.
   d. rates of registration and voting almost the same as white Americans.
8. In the aftermath of *Brewer v. Williams* (1977) the Supreme Court modified the exclusionary rule by allowing illegally obtained evidence if:
   a. the evidence would have been found anyway.
   b. the accused was obviously guilty.
   c. the attorney for the accused had made the error.
   d. the police were unavoidably tired and irritable.
9. The best way to describe the nation's overall view of affirmative action is that:
   a. Quotas are favored over affirmative action.
   b. All black Americans favor affirmative action, while all white Americans oppose it.
   c. There are deep differences of opinion about affirmative action, with support present mostly where there is a clear history of past discrimination.
   d. Affirmative action is favored by all as an automatic solution to problems of racial imbalance.
10. Miranda Rules give all of the following protections *except*:
    a. the right to remain silent.
    b. the right to plea bargain.
    c. the right to consult an attorney.
    d. the right to have an attorney appointed if indigent.

TRUE/FALSE

11. In *Gideon v. Wainwright* (1963) the Supreme Court ordered the state to provide an attorney in state criminal court cases for people too poor to hire one for themselves.
12. The Supreme Court has been the most restrictive of free speech in pornography cases related to children.
13. *Arizona v. Fulminante* (1991) represents an interpretation of the exclusionary rule that gives more rights to the accused.
14. Once the Supreme Court embraced the incorporation theory, all the rights enumerated in the Bill of Rights were automatically incorporated into the Fourteenth Amendment and applied to states.
15. *Dennis v. United States* (1951) resulted in the conviction of Communists for advocating the violent overthrow of the U.S. government.
16. The main approach used by Martin Luther King, Jr., to achieve civil rights for black Americans in the 1960s was nonviolent protest.

17. Miranda rights can be superseded by considerations of public safety, the Supreme Court has said.
18. First Amendment rights are not subject to Supreme Court interpretation.
19. A constitutional amendment to prohibit flag burning is likely to be ratified soon.
20. *Brandenburg v. Ohio* (1969) continued the Supreme Court's willingness to stop free speech if it advocates violent behavior, even if no violent behavior is likely to occur.

IDENTIFICATION—DESCRIBE BRIEFLY

21. Rosa Parks
22. Clarence Earl Gideon
23. Oliver Wendell Holmes
24. Rodney King
25. Earl Warren

ESSAYS

26. Explain how the Fourteenth Amendment was used to incorporate the Bill of Rights' protections to apply to state governments. Cite at least three Supreme Court cases that show incorporation. Then assess in what way the process of selective incorporation represents judicial activism. Consider also the sense in which the Court's use of incorporation was not activist but rather based on the intent of the Constitution's authors.
27. Trace the major developments in the movement for civil rights for African Americans. Weigh the impact of the following factors: court cases, protests, legislation, individuals. Using some of the data available to you, evaluate the area of life in which the civil rights movement has been most successful and the area in which it has been most disappointing.
28. Using the example of either flag burning, affirmative action, or comparable worth, show the tension that exists in America between the power of the majority and the protection of the minority. Include specific references to Supreme Court cases in your answer.
29. Discuss the Supreme Court decisions that gave rights to those persons accused of crimes. In particular, touch on *Mapp, Gideon,* and *Miranda.* Conclude by pointing out the problems resulting from these rulings. How did later Supreme Court decisions modify the rights of the accused? Offer your view of the correct balance between protecting society and protecting individuals.

THE MADISON TEST

Are the American people always sympathetic to the importance of individual and minority rights? Did Madison expect them to be? Under what circumstances are people most likely to place value on civil liberties and civil rights? (This test may not be graded; still, it is an important one for U.S. citizens to ace.)

Answers

Multiple Choice

1.	c	pp. 442-44	6.	a	p. 449
2.	a	p. 433	7.	c	pp. 436-39
3.	d	pp. 425-27	8.	a	pp. 452-55
4.	c	p. 457	9.	c	pp. 439-40
5.	a	pp. 444-47	10.	b	pp. 449-51

True/False

11.	t	pp. 448-49	16.	t	p. 432
12.	t	p. 460	17.	t	p. 450
13.	f	pp. 455-56	18.	f	p. 456
14.	f	pp. 447-48	19.	f	p. 427
15.	t	pp. 457-58	20.	f	p. 458

Identification

21. Rosa Parks' unwillingness to sit at the back of the bus in Montgomery, Alabama, in 1955 led to the start of the nonviolent protests of the civil rights movement. p. 432

22. Clarence Earl Gideon, an alcoholic, was a poor Florida man who had been convicted of robbing a poolhall. He had no attorney at his trial because he could not afford one. Gideon asked the Supreme Court to hear his case by writing to them from prison in a penciled petition. As a result of *Gideon v. Wainwright* in 1963, Gideon was granted a new trial with an attorney to represent him. The lawyer easily proved that reasonable doubt existed about whether Gideon was the robber, and he was found not guilty. pp. 448-49

23. Oliver Wendell Holmes was a famous justice of the Supreme Court. A believer in judicial restraint ("I am not God"), Holmes authored in 1919 the classic limitation on free speech: "The most stringent protection of free speech would not protect a man in falsely shouting fire in a theater . . ." (*Schenck v. United States*). p. 456

24. In 1991 in Los Angeles, Rodney King, a black automobile driver, was stopped and beaten by police. A jury composed only of white citizens found the police not guilty of the serious charges; this decision led to days of rioting and looting in Los Angeles, which refocused the nation's attention on conditions in America's inner cities. p. 434

25. Chief Justice Earl Warren was appointed by President Eisenhower. Though thought initially to be a conservative, Warren led the Supreme Court in landmark civil rights and civil liberties decisions: *Brown v. Board of Education* (1954), *Mapp v. Ohio* (1961), *Gideon v. Wainwright* (1963), *Miranda v. Arizona* (1966), to mention only the most important. pp. 432-50

15 | The Economy and Public Welfare

Chapter 15 is of particular interest to those of you who enjoy economics and public administration. If you have taken introductory economics, you will breeze through the first part of the chapter. The second part of the chapter is an applied look at chapter 8, the "Executive Branch." Here you will study the many (and costly) programs administered by the executive agencies in charge of the public's welfare. As with all three public-policy chapter (14, 15, and 16), you need good recall of the material you have learned earlier in the course, so review, if necessary, as you go.

Economic Issues for the United States in the 1990s

Read pp. 462-65 for a general discussion of the key economic issues of the 1990s as they affect Americans. You will be familiar with most of these issues simply from living in the United States. Make sure you can comment on the following items:

1. The post-World War II economic order
   What was the world economy like from 1945 until the early 1970s?
   Does that economic situation still exist today?
   What changes have occurred and are occurring?
   Do these changes threaten American prosperity?

2. Growth of the economy
   How much did the GDP (gross domestic product: be sure to know
       what it measures) grow in the 1980s?
   How did the 1990s start off in terms of growth?

Where does the United States rank in per person GDP relative to
other nations?

Are Americans good savers?

Where do Americans rank relative to other nations in financing research and development?

3. Employment

Does the United States have a good record of creating new jobs?

How does job creation in the United States compare to job creation
in Europe? (See Figure 15.1.)

What impact did the recession of the early 1990s have on employment?

How did the American people react politically to the effects of the
recession on jobs?

4. Inflation

What does *inflation* mean? What Americans in particular are hurt by
it? Do other countries have problems with inflation?

When in the past decades was inflation a severe problem in the
United States?

Is inflation a problem so far in the 1990s?

Approximately what is the current rate of inflation?

The main issues in economic policy in the United States are matters not
only for the politicians and experts, but also for averge citizens. The people
who run corporations and banks, and the rest of the financial community in the
United States understand these problems well and can often insulate themselves in part from their effects – for example, from the effect of low interest
rates during a recession or very high rates during inflation. Average people,
such as the elderly living on Social Security and a small pension, feel the impact
of economic changes more directly.

An interesting point to note in the study of economic trends in the United
States is that each problem also provides a solution. During times of inflation,
the economy grows, with many new jobs created and much money being spent,
but prices are high too. Recessionary times mean jobs are lost, but prices are
low and goods more affordable for those who are working. Finding the right
balance within the "boom and bust" (cyclical) swings that seem to characterize
the American economy is not just a matter of letting things happen naturally or
of employing experts to make technical adjustments. Regulating the American
economy involves political policy decisions that are a matter of choice: the voters' choice. It is to the competing economic theories held by different groups of
Americans that Professor Ladd next turns.

Different Interpretations of Capitalism, and the
Role of the Federal Reserve Board

Read pp. 465-76. A little economic history is followed by an overview of those who make economic policy today. The outline below touches on the main points of this section. But remember – it is up to you to be able to fill in the details.

I. Possible approaches to managing a capitalist economy
   A. In a classically liberal laissez faire approach, the government keeps hands off the economy, except for printing money, enforcing legal contracts, and financing public works, such as roads. (Adam Smith's 1776 *Wealth of Nations* advocates this pure form of capitalism, "pure" because it contains the least amount of government management of the economy.)
   B. Keynesian economics
      1. John Maynard Keynes (British; Lord Keynes)
      2. Great Depression of the 1930s
      3. "priming the pump" by government
         a. reduce unemployment with government jobs
         b. promote consumption through government public-works projects
         c. inflate deflated prices
         d. government deficit okay in such times
      4. soon, revival of private industry
         a. reappearance of jobs in private sector
         b. consumption up
         c. investment recovery
      5. FDR in 1932, the New Deal, Democrats
         a. Keynesianism right for the times
         b. probably not enough government investment
         c. World War II's impact
      6. After the Depression and Keynes, big government remains
         a. increase in taxes (more on this coming in the next section)
         b. fiscal (taxing and spending – by Congress) and monetary (money supply – Federal Reserve Board) policy
         c. government regulation of the economy: how much?
   C. Monetarism
      1. Milton Friedman
      2. control only money supply and interest rates
      3. minimum control, with growth of the money supply equal to growth of GDP
      4. most conservative view

    D. Supply-side
      1. Reaganomics of the 1980s; "trickle-down"
      2. tax cuts (fiscal policy)
      3. more private investment, more growth, and, in theory, eventually more tax revenue
      4. very conservative view, controversial today
        a. who got tax breaks?
        b. taxes really cut for average person?
        c. huge deficit (in reality)
    E. Mainstream conservatism
      1. Michael Boskin, Martin Feldstein; influence on the Bush administration
      2. low government spending
      3. minimum inflation
      4. minimum deficit (in theory)
    F. Industrial policy
      1. Lester Thurow and Robert Reich; liberal; influence on Clinton/Gore
      2. government role in growth of economy
      3. competition with Japan
      4. encourage new industries; allow old to fail
    G. New Keynesianism
      1. demand-side
      2. large role for government through fiscal and monetary policy
      3. welfare-state programs: antipoverty, Social Security, Medicare – wherever needs arise
      4. Paul Samuelson, James Tobin; very liberal view, controversial today

II. Managing the economy: The Federal Reserve Board
    A. Federal Reserve – central bank, with twelve banks, twenty-five branches, many member banks
    B. Board of Governors
      1. independent executive agency, somewhat removed from direct presidential control
      2. seven members, fourteen-year, staggered terms
      3. chairman, chosen by president, with advice and consent of the Senate for four-year term
      4. Paul Volcker (1979-1987); Alan Greenspan (1987-   )
    C. extremely powerful
      1. reserve requirements affect available funds
      2. discount rate determines all interest rates
      3. money supply controlled by open-market committee

   D. political pressures on the Fed
      1. president and Fed
      2. president, Congress, Fed

Taxes

On pp. 476-83, Professor Ladd gives an in depth discussion of the hot political issue of taxation. From the time of "no taxation without representation" to
today's vocal protests about high taxes, government's claim on the earnings of
private citizens has been an issue in American society. The American belief in
individualism, freedom of choice, equality of opportunity but not of result, private property, and limited government are all tied to the issue of tax policy. In
the 1990s, questions about which segments in society are really carrying the
heaviest tax burden and how well tax money is being used to solve social problems have surfaced anew, sometimes with vehemence. You hardly have to read
to know about:

   high tax rates
   individual incentive

   tax burden on corporations and the wealthy versus tax burden on the
      middle class and poor

   $1.407 trillion federal budget (1991-92) = about 24 percent of GDP
      health and welfare (Social Security, Medicare, the needy)
      defense
      interest payments
   state and local budgets = 15 percent of GDP
   all government spending = 39 percent of GDP = big government!

   nation's debt = $15,750 per person in 1992
   nation's debt = 67.9 percent of GDP (or 51.1 percent calculated differ-
      ently)
   very large amount
   not so large as a percent of GDP compared to the past

   too much spending?
   too little taxation?

   spending increases at state and local level; on Social Security and Medi-
      care

public opinion on taxes
>   too high relative to services people want
>   much waste
>   tax at current level but reduce deficit
>   groups with higher socioeconomic status (SES) somewhat willing to
>   accept more taxes
>   groups with lower SES oppose new taxes
>   higher income taxes disliked by lower and middle (and lots of
>   higher) SES groups
>   sales tax more acceptable to lower SES groups
>   Social Security taxes okay because money comes back to taxpayers
>   someday
anti-tax public opinion expressed in election defeats

You have on hand in this section of chapter 15 much important data on the U.S. budget. Do not worry about memorizing all the numbers. By the time this edition of *The American Polity* hits the bookstores, the national debt will have grown to a new, higher amount anyway! But follow the trend, notice the problems, and be ready to take a personal stand on "taxation with representation."

The Welfare of the Public

Before you finish reading chapter 15, be aware that public welfare is about as controversial as any topic in American politics. As you proceed, think about weighing the facts you will learn from Professor Ladd about American health and welfare programs against your own personal biases (pro or con) about welfare. In the 1992 presidential election (and beyond) issues of welfare reform became prominent ones, as officials perceived the public's intense dissatisfaction with the status quo. *The American Polity*'s discussion of welfare aims at giving you information on who gets how much money for what. With this information you can make an informed judgment of what is fair and just.

Read pp. 483-506. As you proceed, remain alert to the actual meaning of *welfare* in the broad sense of the well-being of all Americans and the narrow meaning of welfare as a government hand-out. Begin by describing the support that each of the following groups receives from the government (state and federal). Do not be concerned about knowing the exact names of each program; instead, identify what kind of aid is available to each group.

farmers
low-income families who need housing
retired people
college students
disabled veterans

poor children
owners of run-down inner-city property
blind people
people who need job training
poor people who are ill
elderly people who are ill
people who have lost their jobs

Overall, who receives public welfare? Compare the reality of the groups that receive government support with the stereotype of the groups often thought to be the only recipients.

Now look at Table 15.3 to understand another facet of the controversy over welfare. What was the total cost of welfare programs on the federal level alone in 1992? Refer back to Table 15.1 to recall that programs related to health and welfare made up over 13 percent of the GDP. Out of a total federal budget in 1992 of $1.407 trillion, welfare programs cost almost $797 billion. Figure out what percentage of the budget that is. Which specific programs are the most costly, as listed in Table 15.3?

Do you see why the budget, taxes, and welfare reform are such hot political issues at every election? Also, do you recognize the complexities involved in trying to cut programs. Consider the ambivalence of the average American toward public welfare. Do you see how charges of waste, fraud, and abuse can be valid concerns, while at the same time, welfare programs are valued for protecting people who are unable, through no fault of their own, to help themselves?

Next Professor Ladd outlines the eight most important federal health and welfare programs. A couple of important points are worth noting. Many programs are funded by both the federal and state governments jointly. Some programs are funded federally but administered at the state level (remember federalism from chapter 5!). Certain programs are *means tested* – available only to people who qualify because of low income – while others are open to all people who fall into a certain demographic group. If you were a bureaucrat in an executive agency such as Health and Human Services (HHS), you would be aware of exactly how your particular program was run (remember the executive branch from chapter 8!).

Unless your professor asks you to learn about the details of the eight programs Professor Ladd highlights, you probably need only become an expert in one. From Table 15.4, select the program that interests you most, and learn:

1. What it is called.
2. How much it costs (using 1992 stats.).
3. When Congress enacted it.
4. Who pays for it.
5. Whether it is federally funded or state funded.

6. Whether it is federally administered or state administered.
7. Whom it serves and how.

While you may not need to know every detail of every major public health and welfare program, it is important for you at least to be able to recognize the goal of each one of the eight that Professor Ladd has selected. So give a one or two phrase description of each of the following programs:

1. Old Age, Survivors', and Disability Insurance (OASDI or Social Security)
2. Supplemental Social Security Income (SSI)
3. Medicare
4. Medicaid
5. Aid to Families with Dependent Children (AFDC)
6. Food Stamps
7. Unemployment Compensation
8. Veterans' Benefits

(Table 15.4 contains a wealth of information that may be useful to you in the future. *The American Polity* can serve as a ready reference for this kind of information.)

Next, review your knowledge of the executive agencies by stating for yourself the basic role each of the following agencies plays in administering the nation's health and welfare programs.

Health and Human Services (HHS)
Department of Agriculture (USDA)
Department of Housing and Urban Development (HUD)
Department of Education
Department of Veterans Affairs (VA)

Again, do not worry about every detail of every program. Try instead to summarize what kinds of programs each agency handles.

Now see if you can answer these questions:

1. By which agency is the food-stamp program run?
2. Which agency gives out Pell grants?
3. In which agency do most of the health and welfare programs exist?
4. Which agency provides medical services for people disabled in war?
5. Under what agency is the Social Security Administration?
6. Public housing for low income Americans is administered by which agency?
7. By what agency is Medicare run?
8. From what agency can middle-income students receive loans for college?

9. The Public Health Service is part of what agency?
10. Through what agency can poor women, infants, and children receive additional nutritional foods beyond food stamps?

Professor Ladd closes chapter 15 with some thoughts on the controversy over welfare in America in the 1990s. You have been asked to think about this controversy as you learned the details of the chapter. Concern over this topic is shared by most Americans. The 1992 Republican and Democratic presidential candidates George Bush and Bill Clinton dealt extensively in their campaigns with their plans to change priorities and make cuts in the nation's health and welfare budget. Why is this topic so important and so controversial? You can follow along with Professor Ladd's discussion by noting these key points:

1. The United States is a nation that is built on individualism and, therefore, rejects a full-scale "welfare state" where everyone is taken care of equally by government. However, the United States also rejects social Darwinism (survival of the fittest), which would let people in trouble starve in the streets or at least fall hopelessly to the bottom with no help available. As is often true, Americans are ambivalent about welfare; they also make complex distinctions between different kinds of help.

2. Americans support welfare for those who need it to join the mainstream of the nation's competitive society. Americans do not support welfare for those who rely on it in place of making personal efforts to take care of themselves. For example, Americans favor job-training programs, grants for education, benefits for those temporarily out of a job. Americans criticize programs that give cash payments to people for an unlimited period, with no real expectation that the recipients will eventually become self-sufficient.

3. *Workfare,* requiring welfare recipients to take jobs, perhaps even government-created jobs, is a popular political goal in the 1990s. Many politicians and citizens believe workfare would train people for eventual employment in private companies and break the cycle of dependency on welfare that has arisen for some recipients. There are many practical problems with implementing a large-scale workfare program, and, at first, it would probably cost more than it would save.

4. Public schools and state universities are a kind of welfare often not thought of as such – welfare for the middle class. But Americans justify the vast sums spent on education as an investment in the future.

5. The largest welfare program in America, Social Security, is also the most popular. For the most part, Social Security benefits the middle class. Begun by President Roosevelt as part of the New Deal in the 1930s, Social Security assists the elderly in living the end of their lives with adequate income to meet basic needs. It includes Medicare – health coverage for those who have retired. Social Security is not thought of as welfare for

two reasons. First, everyone gets it; it is not means-tested. Second, Americans pay into it during all their working years through payroll taxes, and, thus, people feel that they are getting back their own money. Look at the Figure 15.7 data on the public's support for Social Security and their willingness to pay into it! If you were a politician, would you be able to cut Social Security benefits easily?

Social Security is a potential target for political officials in the 1990s who need to cut government spending because (1) programs within Social Security make up a big chunk of federal spending, (2) their costs are increasing rapidly, and (3) not all recipients are poor and in need of benefits. Social Security is a difficult target for cuts because (1) Americans pay into it all their lives with the expectation that they will receive benefits, and (2) it is considered an "entitlement" – a sacred, unbreakable promise made to citizens by government beyond the power of current political decision making to alter.

6. The cost of health care, both in government programs like Medicare (for the elderly) and Medicaid (for the poor) and in private health insurance, is increasing alarmingly. The lack of health insurance for some Americans, especially the working poor, was an important issue in the 1992 presidential campaign and remains a central political topic, with some calling for a system of national health insurance for all citizens.

7. Although AFDC is not the most costly among America's welfare programs, it has become a symbol of the controversy over welfare and the ambivalence Americans feel about it. From modest beginnings in the 1930s, AFDC has come to represent much that has gone wrong with American welfare. The debate over AFDC incorporates the most abstract of discussions, over the meaning of America's classical liberal ideology, and the most concrete of concerns involving race, rights, and taxes (as discussed in Thomas Edsall and Mary Edsall's 1991 *Chain Reaction*).

Professor Ladd began chapter 15 by offering you an overview of economic theory. He closes with a bit of sociology. Figure 15.9 reveals that, despite many government programs, poverty levels have not changed much in the United States in the past decades. Figure 15.10 (and a great deal of research that has been done by all sorts of policy groups in the past decade) shows mostly where poverty lies: in households headed by young, relatively uneducated, unemployed single mothers with several children. Much of the focus on "family values" by both the Bush and Clinton campaigns in 1992 was aimed at opening up for discussion this phenomenon in American society. The "post-marital" family, which has been analyzed extensively by Senator Daniel Patrick Moynihan (Democrat-New York) demands attention by sociologists, economists, political scientists, and average citizens. The eventual success or failure of the Family Support Act of 1988, designed to educate, train, and employ AFDC recipients, and new legislation that goes even further in reforming the welfare system, will have a great impact on the lives of all Americans, including poor children, their parents, and taxpayers.

Whatever your position on health and welfare spending in the United States, remember to consider public policy from sociological, economic, and political points of view. To give you a taste of the sociology of poverty, end your study of the political economy with two readings from the "Cases" section of the *Study Guide*. Chapter 15 presents Kevin Phillips, once known as a strong supporter of Republican conservatism, exposing the Reagan years as a time when, contrary to administration claims, the rich got richer and the poor got poorer. Journalist Mort Rosenblum hangs out in New York City with the homeless, people who seem to be even one rung lower than those aided by government programs. Though without homes, they do not lack character.

Sample Test Questions

MULTIPLE CHOICE—SELECT THE *BEST* ANSWER

1. Which of the following economic approaches advocates the *least* amount of government intervention?
   a. Keynesianism   c. supply-side
   b. industrial policy   d. monetarism
2. The largest percentage of the federal budget goes to:
   a. interest on the debt.   c. defense.
   b. health and welfare programs.   d. foreign aid.
3. All of the following are health and welfare programs for the poor *except*:
   a. Medicaid.   c. AFDC.
   b. Medicare.   d. food stamps.
4. Public opinion surveys regarding taxes reveal that most Americans believe that:
   a. Good services cost a lot, and they are willing to pay for the best through high taxes.
   b. A massive tax cut is needed, despite its effect on Social Security and all other programs.
   c. A massive tax increase is needed to wipe out the deficit, no matter how much it hurts individual taxpayers.
   d. Taxes are too high, especially in light of the amount of revenue that is wasted.

5. When Keynesian economics was introduced by FDR in the 1930s during the Depression, the American economy was suffering from all of the following *except*:
   a. high unemployment.
   b. deflation (very low prices).
   c. underconsumption (not enough buying).
   d. inflation (very high prices).

6. Senator Daniel Patrick Moynihan, a Democrat from New York, identifies the main factor in poverty for Americans now as:
   a. the movement of jobs to the Third World.
   b. families headed by single mothers.
   c. crop failures in the midwest.
   d. women returning to the labor market.

7. The 1992 federal budget was approximately:
   a. $1,407.   c. $1.407 trillion.
   b. $1.407 million.   d. $1.407 zillion.

8. All of the following are responsibilities of the Federal Reserve Board *except*:
   a. lending money to government employees to buy vacation homes.
   b. influencing interest rates by setting the discount rate.
   c. controlling the money supply.
   d. lending money to member banks.

9. Which of the following health and welfare programs is *not* means tested?
   a. food stamps   c. Social Security
   b. Medicaid   d. AFDC

10. Supply-side economics places greatest emphasis on:
    a. tax cuts to stimulate investment.
    b. supplying guaranteed government jobs.
    c. government involvement only in controlling the money supply.
    d. capital supplied by government to start up new high-tech industries.

TRUE/FALSE

11. Job creation has been steadily declining in the United States since the end of World War II.

12. Health and welfare programs are often funded and administered jointly by the federal and state governments.

13. Medicaid is national health insurance that pays for the health care of any American not covered privately or by Medicare.

14. The U.S. government has borrowed from surpluses in the Social Security trust fund so that it would not be necessary to borrow as much on the open market, through selling treasury obligations.

15. The U.S. Constitution contains a balanced-budget amendment.

16. The American people accept a high income tax but dislike high Social Security payroll taxes.
17. The largest percentage of the federal budget is spent by the Department of Health and Human Services.
18. Fiscal and monetary policy are both determined by the Federal Reserve Board.
19. Veterans receive benefits only if they have dependent children or are elderly.
20. The federal debt could be paid off if each person in the country kicked in an extra $15,750 plus beyond regular taxes.

MATCHING*

Economic policies and presidents/economists:

21.	Milton Friedman	_____	a. Keynesian
22.	Robert Reich	_____	b. monetarist
23.	Michael Boskin	_____	c. mainstream conservative
24.	Lord Keynes	_____	d. industrial policy advocate
25.	George Bush	_____	e. supply-sider
26.	James Tobin	_____	f. New Keynesian
27.	Lester Thurow	_____	
28.	Martin Feldstein	_____	
29.	Ronald Reagan	_____	
30.	Paul Samuelson	_____	
31.	FDR	_____	
32.	Bill Clinton	_____	

Health and welfare programs and federal government agencies:

33.	unemployment compensation	_____	a. USDA
			b. HHS
34.	Special Supplemental Food Program for Women, Infants, and Children (WIC)	_____	c. HUD
			d. VA
			e. Educ. Dept.
35.	disabled veterans	_____	f. Labor Dept.
36.	Pell grants	_____	
37.	public housing	_____	
38.	Medicaid	_____	
39.	National School Lunch Program	_____	

---

*These questions ask for very specific information that you are only expected to know if your professor has indicated such.

40. Aid to Families with
    Dependent Children
    (AFDC)   _____
41. Social Security (OASDI)   _____
42. enterprise zones in
    cities   _____
43. food stamps   _____

ESSAYS

44. Contrast the basic premise of Keynesian economics with that of supply-side economics. For what conditions are each approach designed? What problems does each try to solve? From your own knowledge of twentieth-century history, assess the success of Keynesianism in the 1930s and supply-side economics in the 1980s. You can include your own view on the two approaches, but be sure to support opinion with information.

45. Give a brief profile of the federal budget in the 1990s, borrowing some of Professor Ladd's statistics to substantiate how much money goes to what programs. Identify what you believe to be the most crucial area of government spending. Mention where you feel cuts could be made. Analyze the impact that your proposed changes would have on the whole economy. Also, speculate on the reaction of various groups in the population to your proposals.

46. In what ways is American public opinion ambivalent about taxation? Cite surveys that show ambivalence. What taxes do people support? How do they favor their tax money being spent? Where do they oppose spending? Have recent political decisions about the make-up of the U.S. budget reflected public preferences?

47. Outline the debate in the 1990s about the cost and success of health and welfare programs run by the federal and state governments. Name some of the programs, offering the main criticisms that have been made of each. What proposals exist to reform the welfare system? Conclude your essay by evaluating how well health and welfare programs fit with the American tradition of classical liberalism.

Answers

Multiple Choice

1.	d	pp. 466-73		6.	b	pp. 503-6
2.	b	p. 477		7.	c	p. 477
3.	b	pp. 484-85		8.	a	pp. 473-76
4.	d	pp. 480-83		9.	c	pp. 484-85
5.	d	pp. 466-69		10.	a	pp. 470-71

True/False

11.	f	pp. 464-65
12.	t	pp. 485-88
13.	f	pp. 485-86
14.	t	p. 478
15.	f	pp. 476-83

16.	f	p. 482
17.	t	p. 488
18.	f	pp. 469, 475
19.	f	p. 491
20.	t	p. 478

Matching

21.	b	p. 470
22.	d	pp. 471-72
23.	c	p. 471
24.	a	pp. 466-69
25.	c	p. 471
26.	f	pp. 472-73
27.	d	pp. 471-72
28.	c	p. 471
29.	e	pp. 470-71
30.	f	pp. 472-73
31.	a	pp. 466-69
32.	d	

33.	f	pp. 485, 487
34.	a	p. 490
35.	d	pp. 484, 487, 491
36.	e	pp. 484, 491
37.	c	pp. 490-91
38.	b	pp. 485-86
39.	a	p. 490
40.	b	pp. 485-86
41.	b	pp. 486, 488-90
42.	c	pp. 484, 490-91
43.	a	pp. 487, 90

16 | America in the World

"The revolutionary shifts have come so rapidly that the conditions obtaining just four years ago now seem like ancient history," remarks Professor Ladd, opening his discussion of America in the world. By the time you read this, you may have to add to the foreign policy chapter several new sections that were "written" after *The American Polity* went to press. For you, as American government students at the very end of the course, chapter 16 provides a solid introduction for the next political science course you may take – an international relations class. If you do take a course in international relations, you should review chapter 16 to get a grounding in U.S. foreign policy in the early 1990s. Chapter 16 also underscores the importance of a good history background for anyone who wishes to pursue international relations. In past policy chapters, you have seen how some knowledge of economics and sociology fit into the study of American government. An understanding of history is just as important. If this material on foreign policy intrigues you, sign up for a twentieth-century world history course as you pursue related political science courses.

Recent Events in America's Relations with the World

Reading pp. 509-14 may well be a review of the newspaper and TV news of the past years for those of you who stay abreast of world events. Here are the events, people, and nations that you should be able to identify from block-buster developments in 1989-91:

Soviet Union
Communist Party of the Soviet Union
Eastern European Communist nations
Mikhail Gorbachev's *glasnost*
Boris Yeltsin
Russian Republic
Commonwealth of Independent States (CIS)

Poland
Solidarity
Lech Walesa

East Germany
opening of the Berlin Wall
unification of East and West Germany

Czechoslovakia
Vaclav Havel

Romania
execution of Nicolae Ceausescu

Persian Gulf War

ethnic violence among Yugoslavian states

Any one of these events is worthy of detailed study and analysis. Indeed, advanced international relations classes deal with such specialities. Professor Ladd chooses to focus on the events that led to the fall of the Soviet Union as a unified Communist nation, since these events are undoubtedly the most dramatic and significant of recent developments. As a result, you should be able to comment on the following:

1. Did the fall of the Soviet Union occur "overnight," rapidly and unexpectedly?
2. Before the 1980s, how well regarded was the Soviet Union economically, militarily, and politically, by the rest of the world? By small developing nations?
3. Were the Soviet crises of the late 1980s solely economic?
4. How did sociologist Tatyana Zaslavskaya assess the underlying social, cultural, and psychological problems in the Soviet Union in her 1990 analysis of poll and interview data? Give one specific example of her findings.
5. What role did the mass media play in the spreading of revolutionary hopes throughout Eastern Europe and the Soviet Union?
6. How did Mikhail Gorbachev contribute to the changes in the Communist world?

At the end of chapter 16 Professor Ladd will consider America's relationship with the new Commonwealth of Independent States, especially Russia. By the time you read this you may have to add even more to the discussion based on events in the mid-1990s. U.S. foreign policy after the cold war contains challenges very different from those of the cold war period when Soviet-American hostility explained much of international politics. Still, you should learn something of the history that led up to the challenges of the 1990s.

Historical Background

Read pp. 514-24. You can read the boxed material also, but the *Study Guide* will take you through Boxes 16.1, 16.2, 16.4, 16.5, and 16.6 separately in the next section. The outline below highlights recent directions in U.S. foreign policy. If you are familiar with many of these events, congratulate yourself on being well-informed about world politics. If you do not know much about these references, you will not be able to attain a full understanding from these short accounts, but at least you now know where in your twentieth-century history you need to fill in gaps.

RECENT U.S. FOREIGN POLICY

I. Pre-World War II
   A. isolationist
   B. actually, unilateralist
      1. United States on its own
      2. support Britain's balance-of-power doctrine

II. Post-World War II
   A. containment of Communism
      1. George Kennan's statement of the theory
      2. Truman Doctrine (1947)
      3. aid to Greece and Turkey
      4. Marshall Plan to rebuild Europe (1947)
      5. NATO (1949) as a response to the Soviet military threat (Box 16.3)
   B. applications of containment
      1. John Foster Dulles's idea of reversing Communism
      2. Eisenhower and the Korean War
      3. continued Soviet aggression in Eastern Europe
      4. Kennedy and the Cuban Missile Crisis (Box 16.1)
      5. Vietnam
         a. Johnson's troop commitment
         b. enormous cost in lives and money
         c. containment possible by military force?
         d. protests at home
         e. "misapplication" of containment

III. Aftermath of Vietnam
    A. lag in U.S. defense spending
    B. Soviet invasion of Afghanistan
    C. U.S. hostages in Iran
    D. Carter Doctrine to protect flow of oil
    E. renewal of containment in Reagan years
       1. large defense increases
       2. CIA activities
       3. support of anti-Communist forces in Central America, Africa, Afghanistan
       4. Grenada intervention (Box 16.1)
    F. Bush's use of troops in Panama and the Persian Gulf (Box 16.1)

Makers of American Foreign Policy

The next section will review the boxed material, which focuses on the individuals and specialized groups in American government involved in making and carrying out foreign policy.

To begin, read the material in Boxes 16.1, 16.2, 16.4, 16.5, and 16.6. All of these individuals and groups are familiar to you from chapters 7 and 8–"The Presidency" and "The Executive Branch." Now you will meet them once more in their roles as shapers of America's place in the world. Use the list below to make sure you have absorbed the information in these boxes.

THE PRESIDENT (BOX 16.1)

       commander in chief
       crises and treaties
       the national interest

       agency and congressional input, but presidential leadership

DEPARTMENT OF STATE (BOX 16.2)

       international organizations
       negotiations
       foreign aid
       policy expertise

       embassies
       consulates

Arms Control and Disarmament Agency
United States Information Agency (USIA)
International Development Cooperation Agency and Agency for International Development (AID)

NATIONAL SECURITY COUNCIL (NSC) (BOX 16.4)

president, vice president, secretary of state, secretary of defense
director of the CIA, chairman of the Joint Chiefs of Staff

influential in advising the president

can circumvent State Department

INTELLIGENCE SERVICES (BOX 16.5)

Department of Defense (DOD), especially Air Force Intelligence and
National Security Agency (NSA)
Central Intelligence Agency (CIA)

debate over CIA's secret activities and accuracy of information gathered
on the Soviet Union

congressional desire for inclusion in secret activities of CIA

DEPARTMENT OF DEFENSE (DOD) (BOX 16.6)

largest employer in the United States: 2 million military personnel, 1
million civilian personnel

Joint Chiefs of Staff from army, air force, navy, marines

traditionally strong ties among DOD, Joint Chiefs, and civilian foreign-
policy makers

Before you move to the concluding part of chapter 16, take a few minutes to
look at the "Cases" section of the *Study Guide*. The chapter 16 reading by
Loch Johnson suggests a new role for the CIA in the post-cold war era.

Contemporary Foreign Policy Issues

This last section of the chapter will bring American foreign policy up to date
by looking at some of the challenges in the post-Soviet, post-cold war, *unipolar*
(as described by some experts) world of the 1990s.

Finish up chapter 16 by reading pp. 525-33. From this overview of contemporary foreign-policy issues, you can see the kind of topics that are explored in depth in international relations courses. Certain topics Professor Ladd touches on may pique your interest more than others. Nevertheless, be sure to know the basics and be able to answer the following questions:

1. What problems do less-developed nations face that advanced industrial countries do not have to contend with? Approximately how much American foreign aid goes to help less-developed nations, based on statistics that can be compiled from Table 16.1? Is that amount a lot relative to the need? Is it a lot relative to the U.S. budget?

   In the aftermath of the 1992 presidential election and the tremendous public pressure to reduce the deficit, try to stay alert to proposed cuts in foreign-aid spending. Why does the American public often target foreign aid in its demands for cuts? Which two nations receive the greatest share of U.S. military aid? Is there frequently much political debate over these allocations? How did Americans react to the deployment of troops and the cost of humanitarian aid to Somalia in 1992-93?

2. What is a global marketplace and an interdependent world economy? What is GATT? What is the North American Free Trade Agreement (NAFTA)? Briefly, what are the pros and cons of the NAFTA for the United States? Has the NAFTA been agreed upon by the time you are reading this chapter?

3. How did the United Nations Security Council resolution against Iraqi actions in 1990, before the Persian Gulf War, demonstrate the post-cold war cooperation between the United States and the Soviet Union (now, the Commonwealth of Independent States)?

4. What does the photograph on p. 528 suggest about the prospects for overall world peace in the post-cold war era? Have you studied earlier conflicts among the people of Serbia, Croatia, and Bosnia-Herzegovina – before the 1990s – in European history class? Could the dissolution of the Soviet Union have actually contributed to the violence in the former Yugoslav nation?

5. What impact will the diminution of the NATO-Warsaw Pact competition eventually have on America's NATO troop levels in Europe?

6. What impact will cooperation between the United States and Russia eventually have on the number of these nations' nuclear weapons by the year 2003? (See Figure 16.1.)

7. Does the end of American-Soviet hostilities mean that the United States will be able to cut all its defense spending in coming years? What are realistic levels of defense cuts projected for the near future? Identify several ways to cut military expenditures; include the political considerations that will undoubtedly influence the decisions on cuts in the 1990s.

8. What is your home state? Are you aware of any major proposals for cuts in defense spending that would affect your state significantly? Why are senators and members of Congress so cross-pressured about voting for specific defense cuts?

Why has Professor Ladd decided to close his book on American government by featuring the ideas of a long-dead Frenchman? The reason, as you will remember from chapter 1 of *The American Polity,* is that Alexis de Tocqueville knew the United States well and made many brilliant observations about American government that have held up remarkably over time. Tocqueville was also a great predictor: He saw that democratic ideas would eventually sweep the whole world. In America, he believed, other nations could see what the future might be like. Though it did not look like Tocqueville was on target for much of the twentieth century, by the 1990s Tocqueville's prophesy was beginning to look pretty remarkable.

However, Alexis de Tocqueville did not think that American democracy was wonderful in every way. He gave many warnings in *Democracy in America.* In your own lifetime, in the early 1990s, you have witnessed the strong appeal of American ideology for the rest of the world. In the pages of *The American Polity* you have studied in depth the system that Tocqueville saw as so alluring. You have also studied the flaws – real and potential – of American democracy. You have taken your first, not your last, step in doing your part to keep the American polity headed where you want it to go.

Sample Test Questions

MULTIPLE CHOICE—SELECT THE *BEST* ANSWER

1. The dominant American foreign policy goal after World War II was to:
   a. conquer the Soviet Union with military force.
   b. contain Soviet expansion by confronting Communist aggression in certain situations.
   c. accept the inevitability of Communist dominance.
   d. join with the Soviet Union in confronting Fascism worldwide.

2. Who was elected president of Russia in 1991?
   a. Mikhail Gorbachev.   c. Lech Walesa.
   b. Nicolae Ceausescu.   d. Boris Yeltsin.

3. Since World War II, American presidents have relied increasingly for foreign policy advice on:
   a. the National Security Council (NSC)
   b. the Department of Health and Human Services (HHS)
   c. the State Department
   d. the North Atlantic Treaty Organization (NATO)

4. Out of a total yearly (1992) budget of $1.407 trillion, foreign aid takes up:
   a. $13,900
   b. $13.9 million
   c. $13.9 billion
   d. $13.9 trillion

5. In the early and mid 1990s, the amount the United States spends on defense relative to the entire GDP has:
   a. risen steadily due to the need to keep defense workers employed.
   b. declined dramatically as defense has become a low priority.
   c. stayed the same as since the Vietnam years.
   d. declined to the lowest percentage since before the Korean War.

6. All of the following groups involved in intelligence gathering are part of the Defense Department *except*:
   a. the Central Intelligence Agency (CIA).
   b. the National Security Agency (NSA).
   c. the National Reconnaissance Office.
   d. Air Force Intelligence.

7. The person responsible for authoring the Containment Doctrine in 1947 was:
   a. George Bush.
   b. George Kennan.
   c. William Casey.
   d. Joseph Stalin.

8. After the dissolution of the Soviet Union, in the 1990s, the republics of the former Soviet Union were called:
   a. the Commonwealth of Independent States.
   b. the Russian Commonwealth.
   c. the GATT Commonwealth.
   d. the Commonwealth of Former Communists.

9. The attitude expressed by the American and Russian leaders toward nuclear weapons in the 1990s is that:
   a. Vast reductions can be made by each nation.
   b. Weapons should be maintained at 1980s levels to protect the world from terrorism.
   c. It is unrealistic to cut the number of nuclear weapons now, since Soviet-American hostility could resurface, necessitating a build-up.
   d. Russia should cut its weapons drastically because it has no money to maintain them, but the United States can keep building, since it has plenty of funds.

10. Members of the National Security Council include all of the following *except*:
   a. the Secretary of Defense.
   b. the Secretary of State.
   c. the Speaker of the House of Representatives.
   d. the vice president.

IDENTIFICATION—DESCRIBE BRIEFLY

11. North American Free Trade Agreement (NAFTA)
12. Central Intelligence Agency (CIA)
13. Agency for International Development (AID)
14. National Security Agency (NSA)
15. North Atlantic Treaty Organization (NATO)

ESSAYS

16. Describe the changes that have taken place in the former Soviet Union and in the Eastern European countries in the past few years. Include in your discussion some of the specific problems that plagued these nations, the individuals who were instrumental in bringing about change, and the American response to developments in the formerly Communist world. Conclude your essay by expressing your opinion on whether the United States should aid these nations today, and if so, in what form the aid should come.
17. What foreign-policy doctrines were responsible for America's becoming involved in the Vietnam War? Were they valid theories? More specifically, did the premises seem valid at the time? Do they seem valid today, in retrospect?
18. Discuss the new challenges facing the United States in the post-cold war world. Include political, social, military, humanitarian, and economic concerns. As you deal with each facet of contemporary foreign policy, illustrate it with a specific example and mention a strategy that the United States is employing to solve it.

Answers

Multiple Choice

1.	b	pp. 515-19	6.	a	pp. 524-25
2.	d	p. 510	7.	b	p. 517
3.	a	p. 523	8.	a	p. 511
4.	c	p. 526	9.	a	pp. 529-32
5.	d	p. 531	10.	c	p. 523

Identification

11. The NAFTA calls for the removal of all tariffs on items moving between the United States and Canada and the United States and Mexico. The Canadian agreement became effective in 1989, but the controversial Mexican agreement was still being debated in the United States in 1992.

Loss of U.S. jobs due to cheaper labor in Mexico is a key fear of the opponents of the NAFTA. p. 526

12. The CIA, an executive agency whose head is appointed by the president, is the best-known intelligence-gathering group in the American government. Although the CIA is responsible for only a small part of all intelligence activities, it is the center of secret operations. Several examples of apparent CIA miscalculations, including inaccurate estimates of Soviet military strength in the 1980s, led to questions about the CIA's effectiveness and reliability. Today, the CIA faces new challenges as it forges a role in post-cold war American foreign policy. pp. 524-25

13. The AID is an agency tied to the State Department. It is responsible for handing out and managing most of the foreign aid that the U.S. Congress votes to appropriate for countries abroad. p. 517

14. The NSA lies within the Department of Defense. Its role is to make and break codes for other government agencies who need such specialized technical services. p. 524

15. NATO was created in 1949, after World War II and the start of the cold war, to provide a military alliance of American and Western European democratic nations as a counterweight to the threat of the Soviet-backed Warsaw Pact. The breakup of the Soviet Union into the Commonwealth of Independent States means that the functions and membership of NATO will change greatly in the 1990s. p. 519

Credits and
Copyright Notices